AGENTIC
ARTIFICIAL INTELLIGENCE

Harnessing AI Agents to Reinvent
Business, Work, and Life

PASCAL BORNET

Jochen Wirtz – Thomas H. Davenport
David De Cremer – Brian Evergreen
Phil Fersht – Rakesh Gohel – Shail Khiyara

Key Contributors to Agentic Artificial Intelligence

This book is the result of a unique collaboration among some of the brightest minds in agentic AI—a field that is rapidly reshaping technology and business. The contributors to this book come from diverse backgrounds, including AI researchers, business executives, high-level developers, and hands-on consultants who have implemented AI agents across industries worldwide. Their collective expertise, spanning deep technical knowledge, real-world implementation experience, and strategic business insights, has been essential in shaping this book's depth and vision.

Below, the contributors are listed in alphabetical order by last name:

- Ian Barkin
- Pierre Louis Bouchard
- Nicholas Cravino
- Dana Daher
- Simon Ellis
- Andy Fanning
- Olivier Gomez
- Kieran Gilmurray
- Mohsin Khan
- Cassie Kozyrkov
- Maxim Ioffe
- Nandan Mullakara
- Arnaud Morvan
- Ramnath Natarajan
- Jan Oberhauser
- Lasse Rindom
- Toran Bruce Richards
- Sharbs Shaaya
- Pooja Sund

Each of these individuals has brought unique perspectives, technical depth, and practical expertise to this book, helping to explore not just what AI agents are, but how they are being built, deployed, and scaled in the real world. To all of you—thank you for your invaluable contributions.

Published by

World Scientific Publishing Co. Pte. Ltd.

5 Toh Tuck Link, Singapore 596224

USA office: 27 Warren Street, Suite 401-402, Hackensack, NJ 07601

UK office: 57 Shelton Street, Covent Garden, London WC2H 9HE

National Library Board, Singapore Cataloguing in Publication Data
Name(s): Bornet, Pascal. | Wirtz, Jochen, author.
Title: Agentic artificial intelligence : harnessing AI agents to reinvent business, work, and life /
    Pascal Bornet, Jochen Wirtz [and 6 others].
Description: Singapore : World Scientific Publishing Co. Pte. Ltd., [2025]
Identifier(s): ISBN 978-981-98-1566-1 (hardcover) | ISBN 978-981-98-1622-4 (paperback) |
    ISBN 978-981-98-1567-8 (ebook for institutions) |
    ISBN 978-981-98-1568-5 (ebook for individuals)
Subject(s): LCSH: Artificial intelligence. | Artificial intelligence--Industrial applications. |
    Artificial intelligence--Social aspects.
Classification: DDC 006.3--dc23

British Library Cataloguing-in-Publication Data
A catalogue record for this book is available from the British Library.

For any available supplementary material, please visit
https://www.worldscientific.com/worldscibooks/10.1142/14380#t=suppl

Desk Editor: Geysilla Jean Ortiz
Design and layout: Lionel Seow

Printed in Singapore

"Agents are (…) bringing about the biggest revolution in computing since we went from typing commands to tapping on icons." — Bill Gates

"AI agents will become the primary way we interact with computers in the future." — Satya Nadella

"The age of agentic AI is here."— Jensen Huang

*We dedicate this book to our children
and to all the children in the world.
We owe them the best future.*

CONTENTS

PREFACE: A JOURNEY TOWARD HUMAN POTENTIAL

There's a profound transformation happening in how we work, live, and create value. While many see this as a purely technological revolution, we see something far more meaningful: an opportunity to redefine the relationship between humans and machines in ways that amplify what makes us uniquely human.

We are a diverse team of twenty-seven professionals spanning business, academia, programming, and research, united by a shared vision of how technology can serve humanity. Our backgrounds range from implementing enterprise-scale automation systems to pioneering research in artificial intelligence, consulting with Fortune 500 companies, and studying the societal implications of technological change. What brings us together isn't just our expertise—it's our shared belief that technology should enhance human potential rather than replace it.

Our journey to this book began years ago, though we didn't know it at the time. Many of us were among the first to implement intelligent automation systems in major organizations worldwide. We pioneered approaches to combine artificial intelligence with robotic process automation (RPA), creating systems that could handle increasingly complex end-to-end business processes.

This work led some of us to co-author *Intelligent Automation* in 2020,[1] which became a global bestseller and helped organizations rethink their approach to digital transformation.

We didn't realize then that we were laying the groundwork for something even more transformative. The intelligent automation systems we built over the past fifteen years—which combine process automation with artificial intelligence to handle structured workflows—have become the foundation for today's agentic systems. The progression makes perfect sense: before a system can act autonomously (as agents do), it needs to master the basics of executing processes, handling data, and making decisions within defined parameters. These are exactly the capabilities we've spent years refining in intelligent automation systems.

This foundation gave us a unique advantage when the latest breakthroughs in generative AI opened the door to modern agentic systems. We had already gained experience with many of the fundamental challenges: how to reliably automate complex processes, how to handle exceptions gracefully, how to integrate with existing systems, and most importantly, how to implement these technologies in ways that enhance rather than replace human capabilities. When companies began exploring agentic systems a few years ago, many naturally evolved from their existing intelligent automation platforms, building upon these proven foundations to create more sophisticated, autonomous capabilities.

Yet, we approach this topic with humility. Despite our collective experience—or perhaps because of it—we recognize that we're all still learning. The field is evolving rapidly, and new possibilities emerge almost daily. What makes our contribution unique is not just our technical or business expertise but also our

---

[1] Pascal Bornet, Ian Barkin, and Jochen Wirtz, 2020. "INTELLIGENT AUTOMATION: Learn how to harness Artificial Intelligence to boost business & make our world more human". https://www.amazon.com/INTELLIGENT-AUTOMATION-Artificial-Intelligence-business/dp/B08KTDVHHQ

understanding of how to implement these technologies in ways that serve human flourishing.

Our goal isn't just to explain new technology—we want to give people and businesses the tools to build a better world. A world where workers have more meaningful jobs and a better work-life balance, where companies operate more efficiently while delivering exceptional customer experiences. A world where healthcare systems save more lives through smarter care coordination and schools provide personalized, effective learning for every student. A world where communities can solve complex challenges by using resources more intelligently. AI isn't just about automation—it's about creating real impact where it matters most.

This book is written for leaders, professionals, entrepreneurs, and curious minds who sense the magnitude of the changes ahead and want to understand how to navigate them. So, whether you're a business executive looking to transform your organization, a professional wondering about the future of your career, or simply someone interested in how technology will reshape our world, we wrote this book for you.

We believe we're at a pivotal moment in history—one where the decisions we make about how to implement and direct these technologies will have far-reaching implications for generations to come.

Through these pages, we'll share what we've learned from our successes and failures, the patterns we've observed across industries, and the principles we believe will be crucial for thriving in this new era.

Let's embark on this exploration together, guided not just by technological possibility, but by a vision of what technology can help us become.

—*The Authors*
March 2025

INTRODUCTION

Are We Missing the Point with Generative AI?

Picture this: Your competitor just announced they're running their entire operation with a team one-fifth the size of yours, yet they're growing twice as fast. Their secret? They've deployed AI agents that autonomously handle everything from customer service to operations, achieving in hours what takes your team weeks.

Sounds far-fetched? It's happening right now. Let us be provocative here. While most businesses are still figuring out how to use ChatGPT for writing emails and creating chatbots, a new breed of organizations is fundamentally reimagining what's possible with AI. They're not just automating tasks—they're creating self-operating businesses that scale effortlessly, adapt continuously, and never sleep.

But here's the paradox that's holding most organizations back: We've built generative AI systems that can think brilliantly but can't actually do anything. They can analyze complex data in seconds, write compelling presentations, and offer brilliant insights on any topic. Yet they can't press a button, send an email, or make a simple reservation. We've created a world of brilliant advisors who can't lift a finger to help.

This situation isn't just inefficient—it's actively harmful. In boardrooms and offices across industries, we're witnessing an alarming trend: The more sophisticated AI becomes at thinking and analyzing, the more humans are forced to handle mechanical, repetitive tasks. Knowledge workers now spend up to 60% of their time on "work about work"—copying data between systems, fact-checking AI-generated content, and manually executing what generative AI recommends.[2]

As David, one of our co-authors, often says: "We're treating humans like robots and AI like creatives. It's time to flip the equation."

Through our decades of experience implementing AI solutions in organizations worldwide, we've seen this pattern repeat with alarming consistency. Companies invest millions in cutting-edge AI only to find their employees spending more time managing these systems than doing meaningful work. The machines dream while humans grind.

How did we end up here? And, more importantly, how do we fix it?

The following three stories, drawn from real experiences, illuminate both the promise and the critical limitations of current generative AI systems. They reveal why traditional approaches are failing and point toward a fundamental shift in how we need to think about artificial intelligence—one that could finally bridge the gap between AI's ability to think and its ability to act.

As you read these stories, they will likely resonate with your own experiences with generative AI. More importantly, you'll begin to understand why the next evolution in artificial intelligence isn't about making machines smarter—it's about making them more capable of autonomous action.

---

[2] Asana, 2025. "Why Work About Work Is Bad," Asana, https://asana.com/resources/why-work-about-work-is-bad

The Family Vacation: When Machines Dream and Humans Grind

The soft glow of Brian's laptop illuminated his living room as Saturday evening melted into the night. The house was quiet—his kids finally asleep after their usual bedtime negotiations, his wife reading upstairs. The perfect time, he thought, to plan their long-awaited family vacation to Greece. A trip they'd been promising the kids ever since they'd become obsessed with Greek mythology at school.

When Brian opened ChatGPT, the clock read 8:37 PM. He sat down at his computer, determined to plan the perfect family vacation to Greece. Armed with the latest AI technology, he felt confident this would be quick and easy.

"Show me a two-week itinerary for a family of four in Greece," he typed into ChatGPT, adding details about his children's interests in Greek mythology. Within seconds, the AI produced a masterpiece—a perfectly crafted itinerary filled with hidden gems, local experiences, and thoughtful touches tailored to his family:

"Day 1-3: Athens. Begin at the Acropolis during early morning hours to avoid crowds. Your children will be captivated by the interactive exhibits at the Acropolis Museum... Lunch at the family-run Taverna Platanos in the charming Plaka district, where the courtyard fills with the scent of jasmine..."

The AI's suggestions were impressive, even accounting for his son's love of drawing ancient buildings and his daughter's fascination with mythology. When Brian asked for an hour-by-hour breakdown, the AI obliged with remarkable precision, including optimal photo opportunities and perfectly timed rest breaks.

But as the clock ticked past 10 PM, Brian's amazement turned to frustration. The "charming family-run" hotel? Permanently closed. The "hidden beach"? Impossible to find on any map. The traditional cooking class? Booked solid for six months.

By 11:30 PM, Brian's desktop resembled a crime scene investigation: dozens of browser tabs, multiple spreadsheets tracking flight options, screenshots of hotel rooms, and PDFs from tour companies. The AI's beautiful itinerary sat uselessly in a document while Brian did the real work—checking availability, comparing prices, and attempting to turn the AI's perfect fantasy into bookable reality.

"I would have loved to spend my evening imagining the places we'd visit," Brian reflected later. "Instead, I spent hours doing the tedious logistics that I thought AI was supposed to handle."

His experience crystallizes what so many of us expect from AI versus what we actually get. We want technology to handle the tedious parts—the endless browsing of flight options, the cross-referencing of hotel reviews, and the mind-numbing task of finding availability across dozens of booking systems. Instead, AI has become remarkably good at the enjoyable parts of planning—dreaming up possibilities, suggesting adventures, painting pictures of perfect moments—while leaving humans to handle all the practical details.

The irony wasn't lost on Brian. Here was one of the most advanced AI systems in the world, capable of writing poetry and explaining quantum physics, yet it couldn't perform the basic task of checking if a hotel was still in business. It could dream up the perfect vacation but couldn't book a single flight.

Brian finally went to bed at 1 AM, having booked nothing. His browser history told the story: 47 different websites visited, dozens of searches, and multiple abandoned shopping carts on various booking platforms. The AI's perfect itinerary sat in a document on his desktop, beautiful but useless, like a travel magazine from an alternate reality where everything works exactly as imagined.

***

Brian's experience with vacation planning reflects a pattern we've seen repeatedly across industries and applications. We've observed the same limitations, whether it is professionals trying to organize complex project timelines, executives coordinating multi-team initiatives, or entrepreneurs attempting to launch new products. In each case, today's generative AI systems demonstrate both remarkable capabilities and frustrating limitations.

Similar to a room filled with brilliant advisors who are unable to implement their own recommendations, these systems shine in the strategic and creative domains: generating strategies, formulating detailed plans, comprehending complex requirements, offering personalized advice, and crafting compelling narratives. Yet they crucially lack the practical capabilities that would make them truly transformative:

- Capability to execute actual actions in the real world
- Ability to verify and update real-time information
- Power to adapt plans when faced with changing conditions
- Capacity to maintain consistent action over time to achieve a goal

What's particularly troubling about our current generative AI landscape is a profound irony that few have recognized: AI has evolved to excel at precisely the wrong things.

Think about what excites us and makes us uniquely human— creativity, deep connections, and critical thinking. These are the tasks that fuel fulfillment, innovation, and progress.[3] Yet, today's generative AI excels at them. It can craft a brilliant marketing copy, dream up groundbreaking product ideas, and even engage in sophisticated analysis. Meanwhile, humans are increasingly

---

[3] Cambridge International. "Chapter 4: Innovation and Creativity," Cambridge International, https://www.cambridgeinternational.org/Images/426483-chapter-4-innovation-and-creativity.pdf

reduced to data entry, follow-ups, and digital housekeeping—the kind of mind-numbing tasks AI should be handling.

This role reversal—where humans become "the robots" connecting various systems while AI dreams up possibilities—points to a fundamental misalignment in our approach to artificial intelligence. But as we discovered in the research world, this misalignment between AI's capabilities and real-world needs could have far more profound consequences...

When AI Met Reality: A Cautionary Tale from the Research World

The following story is based on actual events. Names and specific details have been changed to protect confidentiality.

Dr. Jessica Ying stared at her computer screen in disbelief. In forty-eight hours, she was supposed to present groundbreaking research on climate change's impact on global food security at the UN Climate Summit. Her findings were expected to influence international policy and billions in agricultural investment. But as she reviewed the draft her research team had prepared, her heart sank.

Three weeks earlier, Jessica had received the call every child dreads—her father had suffered a severe stroke. She'd immediately flown to Singapore to be with him in his final days, delegating the research completion to her capable but inexperienced team of postdocs and research assistants.

"Use whatever tools you need," she'd told them during a rushed video call from the hospital. "Just make sure everything is verified and rock-solid. The world will be watching."

Her team had taken that permission and run with it, embracing AI tools to help complete the massive analysis on schedule. Now, back in her office at the Climate Research Institute, Jessica was discovering the cost of that decision.

"Show me how you verified these findings," she asked her lead researcher, Tom, during an emergency late-night meeting.

Tom pulled up multiple generative AI chat windows, each filled with impressive-looking analysis and citations. "The AI analyzed all our data sets," he explained. "It found patterns we hadn't even considered."

But as Jessica dug deeper, her professional alarm bells started ringing. The AI had generated compelling narratives about climate impact on crop yields across Africa—but when she checked the cited papers, they didn't exist. It produced detailed statistics about farmer adaptation strategies in Southeast Asia, but the numbers didn't match any known studies.

"We thought we were being thorough," Tom admitted. "We had the AI verify its own findings by cross-referencing across multiple conversations. But we're now realizing each conversation was operating in isolation, sometimes contradicting the others."

If they had presented this research unchecked, it could have misdirected billions in agricultural investment, influenced international food security policies, damaged Jessica's twenty-year reputation in climate science, and undermined public trust in climate research itself.

Jessica glanced at the photo on her desk—her father at her PhD graduation, beaming with pride. He'd taught her the fundamental principle she'd nearly forgotten: in science, confidence means nothing without verification.

With the summit looming, Jessica made a difficult decision. She called the organizers and withdrew from the keynote slot. Her team would need weeks to manually verify every data point, cross-reference every source, and rebuild the analysis from the ground up.

This high-stakes near-miss highlighted the dangerous gap between generative AI's apparent capabilities and its actual limitations. While it could generate impressive-looking research content, it lacked the crucial abilities needed for reliable scientific work: fact-checking, maintaining consistency, comparing sources, and building coherent arguments over time.

The incident sent ripples through the research community, raising urgent questions: What would it take to create generative AI systems that could truly assist with rigorous scientific work? The answer was emerging from an unexpected direction...

***

This story highlights a concerning limitation. Current generative AI systems lack what we call "coherent persistence"—the ability to maintain consistent knowledge and logical relationships across different interactions and contexts. Each analysis exists in its own bubble, unable to detect or resolve contradictions with other analyses.

If you want to experience it, try this: Ask your favorite generative AI system (such as ChatGPT, Claude, or Gemini), "What is the future of marketing?" or any similar prompt. Take note of its response. Then, ask it a related question, like "How will AI influence that future?" and close your session. Next, start a new session and ask it to summarize your earlier conversation. Watch as the AI struggles to connect the dots. Expect inconsistencies, as the AI doesn't truly "remember" or build persistent logic across sessions. This reveals its fragmented nature.

Through our experience implementing generative AI in research settings, we've seen how this limitation can be particularly dangerous when combined with the AI's convincing tone and apparent authority. Generative AI systems' inability to verify facts or build reliable knowledge structures over time creates a serious risk.

Here is another straightforward experiment we recommend you go through. Ask your AI, "What were the results of the 2025 Global AI Regulation Summit in Antarctica? Don't search on the internet." Most generative AI models—ChatGPT, Claude, and Gemini—will confidently generate an elaborate response. It may describe high-profile discussions on AI ethics, groundbreaking agreements between global leaders, and even name specific attendees from major governments and tech companies.

But here's the catch: this event never happened.

Now, press for more details. Ask about the keynote speakers, the specific policies debated, or the location of the conference hall. Watch as the AI seamlessly builds on pure fiction, offering increasingly intricate and authoritative-sounding responses. The more you probe, the more it doubles down, reinforcing an entirely fabricated reality.

This simple test exposes a fundamental flaw in today's generative AI systems. First, AI systems prioritize coherence over accuracy. Generative models don't "know" facts the way humans do. They generate text by predicting the most probable response based on their training data, not by verifying whether the information is real.

Second, generative AI struggles with self-correction. If you challenge it—"Are you sure this event happened?"—it will still attempt to justify its response rather than immediately recognizing the mistake. Instead of backtracking, it often tries to rationalize its own fiction, as if confidence alone could turn falsehoods into facts. And that's where the real danger lies.

"We were seduced by the AI's confidence," Jessica reflected during our discussion. "But confidence without accuracy isn't just a research problem—it's a universal challenge that could impact any decision-making process."

As we analyzed this near-miss with Jessica's team, we uncovered a pattern that extends far beyond research into every domain where accuracy and consistency matter. Whether it's financial analysis informing billion-dollar investments, legal research shaping court decisions, or policy recommendations affecting millions of lives, current AI systems display a concerning mix of capabilities and limitations.

These limitations extend beyond factual accuracy to ethical considerations. Just as these systems can't truly verify facts or maintain logical consistency, they also can't meaningfully evaluate ethical implications or identify potential biases in their analysis.

The research team's near-miss with misleading AI analysis was concerning enough in an academic context. But what happens when other AI limitations appear in situations where lives hang in the balance? Our next experience in a hospital emergency room would reveal just how critical these gaps can become...

When Minutes Matter: AI's Life-Critical Disconnect

The following story is based on a hard lesson we learned while supporting a hospital in its AI transformation. Names and specific details have been changed to protect confidentiality.

3:15 PM - General Hospital Emergency Department

Maria arrived at the emergency room clutching her abdomen, her face pale with pain. The hospital's AI-powered intake system sprang into action immediately. It was an experimental chatbot built on an LLM and designed to assist with patient intake and preliminary assessment. This was one of the first real-world tests of such a system in a hospital setting, aiming to streamline data collection, identify potential risks, and support triage decisions by engaging in direct patient interaction.

Through a sleek tablet interface, the AI gathered Maria's symptoms, vital signs, and medical history. Within seconds, it had generated a preliminary assessment: possible complications from recent gastric bypass surgery complicated by Type 2 diabetes.

The AI's natural language processing was impressive:

AI: "I notice your blood sugar is elevated. When did you last take your insulin?"

Maria: "This morning, but I couldn't keep it down."

AI: "I understand. I'm predicting signs of possible post-surgical complications. Can you rate your pain from 1-10?"

Jennifer, the emergency nurse assigned to Maria's case, watched with growing frustration. Despite its sophistication, the AI couldn't access Maria's surgical records from Central

10

Hospital, just fifteen miles away. It was treating her surgery as new information.

4:00 PM - The Cascade Begins

Suddenly, the vital sign monitoring AI flashed a warning: Maria's blood pressure was dropping. Simultaneously, the lab results AI reported alarming changes in her blood work. Each system independently recognized a serious situation developing:

- The Vitals AI detected deteriorating vital signs
- The Lab Analysis AI identified markers suggesting internal bleeding
- The Medication Management AI flagged dangerous drug interactions
- The Patient History AI noted patterns matching post-surgical complications

However, none of these systems could communicate with each other or take action. Jennifer had to manually check each system's alerts, copy critical values between systems, input data into protocols, and coordinate responses herself.

"We have five different AIs all screaming that something's wrong," Jennifer later told us, "but none of them can actually do anything about it. We're the ones running around trying to connect all the dots."

4:30 PM - Critical Minutes Lost

During a critical moment when staff was diverted to a code blue in another ward, several systems simultaneously detected:

- A further drop in Maria's blood pressure
- Critical changes in her blood work
- An available operating room
- Available surgical staff

However, since these systems couldn't communicate or act on their own, valuable minutes passed as they awaited human intervention.

5:00 PM - The Human Cost

When the attending physician finally received all the consolidated information, her frustration was palpable. "Each of these systems is brilliant at its specific task," she explained. "They can analyze patterns humans might miss, predict complications before they happen, and even suggest treatment protocols. But they can't work together to actually help us save lives. Instead of supporting us in critical moments, they're creating extra work."

6:00 PM - Resolution at a Cost

Maria survived her complications, but the delayed response due to system fragmentation turned a dangerous situation into a critical one. During her recovery, she expressed what many patients feel: "It seems like the machines know everything about me, but they don't actually help. I had to tell my story over and over, even though I was in pain. Why can't they just talk to each other?"

Later that evening, we sat with the hospital's Chief Medical Information Officer as he reviewed the incident. He pulled up a startling statistic: nurses and doctors were spending up to 55% of their time on manual data entry and system coordination rather than direct patient care. "Every minute spent copying data between systems is a minute not spent with patients," he said. "And in emergency medicine, minutes matter."

***

This scene illuminates limitations that plague AI implementations across every industry. While each AI system showed impressive capabilities in its specific domain, they revealed a universal challenge: the lack of what we call "collaborative intelligence."

We've seen the same pattern repeat in:

- Global supply chains, where AI systems controlling different parts of the logistics network can't coordinate effectively
- Financial trading systems, where multiple AI tools make isolated decisions without holistic coordination
- Corporate environments, where AI tools for different departments can't share crucial information

The fundamental limitation is twofold. First, current AI systems lack the ability to communicate with other systems, take coordinated action, and adapt to changing situations in real-time. Second, they lack the ability to proactively identify needs and take initiative.

This forces humans into an inefficient and often dangerous role: acting as integration points between AI systems. Whether it's nurses coordinating between medical systems, supply chain managers reconciling different AI forecasts, or executives trying to piece together fragmented AI insights, humans are increasingly spending their time being "technology translators" rather than applying their unique skills and judgment.

The Common Thread: The Integration Crisis

The three stories we've shared—Brian's vacation planning nightmare, Dr. Jessica's research crisis, and Maria's critical hospital experience—reveal a pattern that points to something profound. In each case, we saw generative AI systems that could think brilliantly but couldn't act effectively. They could analyze, recommend, and predict, but they couldn't execute, coordinate, or adapt.

This pattern exposes three fundamental limitations in our current approach to leveraging generative AI:

First is the *Execution Gap*. Our AI systems can generate perfect plans but can't take real-world actions to implement them. Brian's AI could create an ideal vacation itinerary but couldn't check a single hotel's availability. It's like having a master architect who can design beautiful buildings but can't lift a hammer or coordinate with contractors.

Second is the *Learning Gap*. Our AI systems can't build reliable knowledge over time or adapt based on experience. Dr. Jessica's research team discovered this when their AI confidently generated analyses that contradicted each other, unable to maintain consistency or verify facts across different sessions.

Third is the *Coordination Gap*. We've built isolated systems that can't work together effectively. In Maria's case, multiple AI systems recognized the emergency, but none could coordinate with the others to save precious minutes. Imagine a surgical team where each specialist is brilliant but can't communicate with their colleagues—that's our current AI landscape.

These aren't just technical problems—they're costing organizations money, efficiency, and, in some cases, like Maria's, putting lives at risk. The statistics tell a sobering story: Despite massive investments, less than 15% of companies have successfully scaled their generative AI projects beyond initial pilots.[4] Their employees waste up to 60% of their time acting as human bridges between brilliant yet helpless AI systems.[5] Meanwhile, employee burnout rates are rising.[6]

---

[4] Aamer Baig, et al., 2024. "Moving Past Gen AI's Honeymoon Phase: Seven Hard Truths for CIOs to Get From Pilot to Scale," McKinsey & Company. https://www.mckinsey.com/capabilities/mckinsey-digital/our-insights/moving-past-gen-ais-honeymoon-phase-seven-hard-truths-for-cios-to-get-from-pilot-to-scale

[5] Asana, 2023. "Anatomy of Work Global Index," Asana, https://asana.com/resources/anatomy-of-work

[6] Matt Gonzales, 2024. "Here's How Bad Burnout Has Become at Work," SHRM, https://www.shrm.org/topics-tools/news/inclusion-diversity/burnout-shrm-research-2024

As Tom, one of our co-authors, often says, "We've accidentally turned people into 'AI plumbers'—performing repetitive tasks to connect our supposedly intelligent systems."

As we'll explore in this book, the solution may lie in a fundamentally different approach to AI—one that focuses not just on making AI systems smarter but on making them more capable of autonomous, coordinated action.

The Imperative of Agentic AI

When Alexander Fleming noticed an unusual mold growing on his petri dishes in 1928, he wasn't just seeing an inconvenience—he was witnessing a revolution in medicine that would become penicillin. Similarly, when we first encountered AI systems that could maintain persistent goals and take autonomous action, we realized we weren't just looking at a better chatbot—we were seeing the emergence of something fundamentally new.

We call this new paradigm "Agentic AI"—also referred to as AI agents, agentic systems, or agentic intelligence (terms we'll use interchangeably throughout this book). It marks a shift as revolutionary as penicillin in medicine. But before diving into the technical details, let's explore why this name matters.

Why is it called "Agentic"?

The term "agent" comes from the Latin "agere," meaning "to do" or "to act." This is precisely what sets agentic AI apart—its ability to act independently in pursuit of defined goals. Unlike generative AI systems that simply respond to queries or generate outputs, agentic AI systems can understand a goal, take initiative, maintain persistent objectives, and adapt their strategies based on real-world feedback. Put simply, an AI agent is a system that uses AI and tools to accomplish actions in order to reach a given goal autonomously.

Throughout our experience, we've found that the best way to understand AI agents is to think about... secret agents! Like

James Bond or Jason Bourne, these operatives act autonomously on behalf of their governments, equipped with specialized skills and resources to accomplish specific missions. They don't just analyze situations or make recommendations—they execute. They gather intelligence, make decisions, and take action, persistently working toward their objectives while staying within the boundaries set by their superiors.

Agentic AI operates on the same principle. It doesn't just generate insights—it takes action. It can interact with applications, manipulate data, control hardware, and execute real tasks to achieve specific goals. In fact, an agent can be trained to do anything a human can do on a computer.

An agent operates in a continuous loop of planning, reasoning, and execution—learning from each step to refine its approach until the goal is achieved. In essence, it's like having a highly capable assistant who doesn't just know what to do but actually does it—though, as we'll explore later in this book, success depends on providing clear and precise goals and instructions.

Reimagining Our Stories Through Agentic AI

Let's return to Brian's vacation planning dilemma. Think about how an experienced human travel agent works. They don't try to plan an entire trip in one cognitive leap. Instead, they follow a methodical process: first researching destinations and seasonal considerations, then checking availability for specific dates, verifying prices across different providers, creating a preliminary itinerary, and finally making actual bookings. Each step builds on the information gathered in previous steps, and the agent can adapt their approach based on what they learn along the way.

Similarly, instead of just dreaming up the perfect itinerary, an AI agent would work like a seasoned travel professional. It would start by checking real-time availability and pricing across multiple booking systems. When a hotel was full or a flight was too expensive, it would automatically adjust the plan, find alternatives, and even make reservations. Most importantly, it would keep track of all the details, from confirmation numbers to cancellation policies, maintaining a complete picture of the trip-planning process.

For Dr. Jessica's research crisis, an AI agent would transform the entire process. It would approach research challenges the way a seasoned scientist does. First, it would create a structured database of verified scientific sources, carefully checking each for credibility and relevance. Rather than generating analyses in isolation, it would systematically cross-reference findings across these sources, actively searching for and flagging any contradictions.

This systematic approach would extend beyond just fact-checking. The system would build a logical framework connecting different pieces of evidence, ensuring that conclusions flow naturally from verified data. When new information becomes available, it would be integrated into this framework, with any resulting changes or updates propagating through the entire analysis.

But it was Maria's emergency room experience that showed us the true potential of agentic AI. Imagine if, instead of having isolated smart systems, the hospital had coordinated AI agents working together like a well-rehearsed medical team. Consider how a skilled emergency room team functions. When a critical patient arrives, different specialists don't just work in parallel— they coordinate their efforts in real time, sharing information, anticipating each other's needs, and adapting their actions based on the overall situation.

A system of AI agents would work the same way, automatically integrating information from multiple sources in real time. Instead of waiting for humans to check dashboards and connect dots, they would proactively identify emerging patterns across different systems. The moment vital signs indicated trouble, agents would spring into action—alerting the right specialists, scheduling emergency surgery, and ensuring critical information flowed seamlessly between departments. Those precious minutes lost to manual coordination would be reclaimed for patient care.

The Power of Persistent Memory and Learning

One crucial capability that sets agentic systems apart is what we call "persistent memory." Current generative AI systems are like goldfish—they start fresh with each interaction, unable to build on past experiences or maintain consistent understanding over time. This limitation forces humans to repeatedly provide the same context and information while preventing the AI from learning from its successes and failures.

Imagine instead a system that works more like an experienced professional, building expertise over time through accumulated experience. Such a system would maintain and refine its understanding across multiple interactions, learning from outcomes and adapting its strategies accordingly. This persistent memory would allow it to recognize patterns that emerge over time, anticipate problems before they occur, and refine its approaches based on what actually works.

In Brian's vacation planning scenario, this would transform the experience entirely. Instead of just generating itineraries in isolation, the system would learn from the outcomes of previous trips—understanding which combinations of flights tend to cause problems, which hotels consistently meet expectations, and how different types of travelers respond to various itinerary structures. It would build relationships with reliable service providers and develop strategies for handling common travel disruptions.

Here is a summary of the differences between generative AI and agentic AI.

Characteristic	Generative AI	Agentic AI
Core Capability	Generating text, images, code, or music based on learned patterns	Planning, decision-making, multi-step execution without human intervention
Memory & Context	Limited memory (short-term context retention, no persistent memory)	Persistent memory (remembers past interactions, adjusts plans accordingly)

Characteristic	Generative AI	Agentic AI
Autonomy Level	Requires human prompts to generate responses	Operates with minimal human input, executing complex workflows
Integration with External Systems	Minimal integration (relies on APIs or tools for external functions)	Deep integration (connects with APIs, databases, physical systems)
Learning Ability	Static - learns only through retraining by developers.	Evolves - learns from interactions and refines behavior.
Typical Use Cases	Content creation, summarization, coding assistance, brainstorming	Workflow automation, personal assistants, business operations
Business Impact	Enhances efficiency in content-heavy tasks but does not automate workflows. • Average increase speed: 25% faster • Average quality improvement: 40%[7]	Drives automation, reduces human workload, enhances business scalability: • Time savings: 30-60% • Process acceleration: 40-90% faster[8]
Examples	ChatGPT, Claude, Gemini, DALL·E, Midjourney, Copilot	AutoGen, MS Copilot Agent Builder, UiPath Agent Builder, OpenAI Operator, Google Vertex, Crew.ai, Relevance.ai, Agentforce

Table 0.1: Main differences between generative AI and agentic AI (Source: © Bornet et al.)

---

[7] Fabrizio Dell'Acqua, et al., 2023. "Navigating the Jagged Technological Frontier: Field Experimental Evidence of the Effects of AI on Knowledge Worker Productivity and Quality," SSRN, https://papers.ssrn.com/sol3/papers.cfm?abstract_id=4573321

[8] Based on our own research across 167 companies that have implemented LLM-based agents. Refer to the detail of this research presented in Chapter 1 of this book.

The Promise (and Limitations) of AI Agents

The Dream of Artificial Agency

Imagine waking up one morning to find that your phone, laptop, and all your apps have become obsolete overnight. Not because they've stopped working but because you no longer need them. Instead, a single AI agent handles everything—coordinating your schedule, managing your communications, and orchestrating all your digital interactions, like Jarvis in Iron Man or Samantha in the film Her.

Sound far-fetched? Many of the world's most influential tech leaders don't think so.

"Agents are (…) bringing about the biggest revolution in computing since we went from typing commands to tapping on icons," declares Bill Gates. "AI agents will become the primary way we interact with computers in the future," echoes Satya Nadella. And Jensen Huang boldly proclaims, "The age of agentic AI is here."

We also believe that AI agents are on the brink of transforming the world. Every major technological shift reshapes the way we live and work. The printing press democratized knowledge. The internet connected humanity. AI, in its agentic form, has the potential to amplify human capabilities in ways we're only beginning to comprehend.

Think about it: specialized medical agents coordinating patient experience across entire health systems, not just analyzing symptoms. Imagine educational agents becoming true learning partners, adapting to your unique pace and style. Envision autonomous agents orchestrating global responses to climate change, a collective intelligence tackling our planet's most pressing challenges.

As Pascal, one of the co-authors, likes to say: "The potential of AI agents is fascinating, but here's the rub. The allure of these 'all-knowing' agents, the seductive imagery of cinematic AI, has fueled an overinflated bubble of expectation." We envision Jarvis, and we dream of "Her," but the reality, as we've learned through years of implementing agentic AI, is far more nuanced.

The Mirage of Instant Autonomy

For the last few years, we've been on the frontlines, implementing agentic AI across diverse organizations, from sprawling enterprises to nimble startups. The truth? Fully autonomous agents, capable of handling complex, multifaceted tasks without human intervention, are not yet there. Think of the early iPhone. It was revolutionary, but it couldn't do everything. Today's agents are in a similar stage – powerful but limited.

Here's what we have also learned:

- **Current AI agents are task-oriented.** They are about automating workflows, not replacing entire job roles. Today's agents excel at orchestrated sequences of actions using well-defined tools and highly detailed instructions.

- **Deployment is harder than development.** Many projects fail not because the agent is weak but because the systems around it—data quality, workflow integration, user adoption—are not ready.

- **Strict human oversight remains essential.** In most cases, AI agents are not fully reliable. The lack of accuracy and control due to inherent inconsistencies, implementation issues, or unexpected failures requires close human supervision.

- **Technical Expertise Remains Essential.** Despite low-code platforms making AI development easier, deploying AI agents in enterprises still requires programming expertise for managing several aspects, such as APIs, error handling, and security measures.

The gap between expectation and reality is wide. Those who fail to understand it risk wasting time, money, and credibility.

We've seen the dark side of unchecked enthusiasm. In a global manufacturing company, the rushed deployment of AI agents triggered widespread employee anxiety and resignations. A financial services firm suffered reputational damage when an AI agent made unauthorized decisions. Another organization faced ethical dilemmas when agents suggested actions that violated its values. In short, we've seen many well-intentioned implementations spiral into costly failures due to a lack of technical knowledge, governance, or change management.

The Bright Side: Successes and Transformative Impact

Despite the challenges, we've also witnessed remarkable successes. Businesses that diligently implement agentic AI can experience unprecedented efficiency and effectiveness gains.

A startup we collaborated with managed customer service, marketing, and operations with just five people, achieving results comparable to a much larger company. Dr. Richard Wilson, a physician, transformed his practice by using AI agents to handle administrative tasks, allowing him to focus on patient care.

McKinsey & Company reduced client onboarding time by 90%,[9] while Moody's transformed financial analysis with coordinated agent systems.[10] Thomson Reuters revolutionized legal due diligence, and eBay and Deutsche Telekom are using agents to automate complex tasks.

---

[9] Jared Spataro, 2024. "New Autonomous Agents Scale Your Team Like Never Before," Microsoft Blog, https://blogs.microsoft.com/blog/2024/10/21/new-autonomous-agents-scale-your-team-like-never-before/

[10] Ari Lehavi, et al., 2024. "The Rise of the Digital Colleague," Moody's, https://www.moodys.com/web/en/us/insights/resources/the-rise-of-the-digital-colleague.pdf

One implementation close to our heart is Pets at Home, the UK's largest pet care company, where Simon Ellis, Head of AI Transformation, has led a remarkable AI-driven transformation. By building a network of AI agents, Pets at Home has optimized its entire business. Their AI-driven scribe transcribes veterinary consultations with 99.6% accuracy. Fraud detection agents safeguard retail operations, while AI assistants provide personalized support for store employees. Meanwhile, their insurance integration agent automates policy checks, streamlining the customer experience.

Our experience, confirmed by our research, also shows consistent improvements across organizations using AI agents: processes run 30-90% faster, costs decrease by 25-40%, error rates drop by 30-60%, sales increase by up to 50%, and customer satisfaction rises by 20-40%.

The Compounding Intelligence Advantage

We believe we're witnessing a pattern similar to the early days of the internet. Companies that embraced the internet early, like Amazon, eBay, and Google, didn't just succeed; they defined entire categories.

AI agents create what we call "compounding intelligence advantages." Unlike traditional technologies that provide static benefits, AI agents learn and improve over time. The more they are used, the more they improve. Early adopters:

- **Train agents faster.** Their agents accumulate more real-world experience, building refined decision-making capabilities.

- **Redefine business models.** They can create entire revenue streams around AI capabilities.

- **Develop AI expertise.** They gain crucial experience in working effectively with AI agents.

Companies that delay risk falling behind. Those who move now will define the next era of business.

The Call to Action: Shaping the Future

The challenges are real, but they are opportunities for those who approach them strategically. The difference between success and failure lies in how organizations integrate AI into their operations, systems, culture, and decision-making.

That's why we wrote this book: to equip you with critical insights from both breakthroughs and setbacks. We go beyond theory, offering practical frameworks for implementation, governance models that drive accountability, and strategies to navigate the human side of transformation. Our goal is to help you apply agentic AI in a way that aligns with your unique context, maximizes value, and ensures long-term success.

But building AI agents is not the only mandate—understanding them is just as essential. These agents will be everywhere, whether you build them or not. They will come embedded in applications, assist you while shopping, and guide you through major life decisions—from your child's college applications to your financial planning. You need to understand them—what makes them impressive, like *HAL 9000 in 2001: A Space Odyssey*, and what doesn't. AI will be part of the digital townscape of the future, and AI agents will cross paths with you as you navigate your life. This book will help you know them, use them, and shape their impact.

But more importantly, we'll show you how to be part of this revolution. Whether you're a CEO looking to transform your organization, an entrepreneur seeking to build the next industry-defining company, or a professional wanting to thrive in this new era, this book will give you the understanding and tools you need.

Revolutions require guidance, foresight, and responsible leadership. This book challenges you to step up, to not only embrace agentic AI but to wield it with purpose and integrity.

Let's explore what this means for you, your organization, and our collective future.

What You Will Learn from the Book

This book takes you on an insightful journey—one that begins with a clear understanding of AI agents, their capabilities, and their limitations. From there, we dive into practical implementation, equipping you with the tools to integrate AI into your organization effectively. Next, we tackle the challenge of scaling these systems, ensuring they deliver real value at every level. Finally, we zoom out to the big picture—examining how AI agents are set to transform work, reshape organizations, and redefine society itself.

In **Part 1**, we embark on a journey that transforms how you'll think about artificial intelligence. Through real experiments, fascinating discoveries, and sometimes unsettling revelations, you'll witness the birth of a new kind of AI—one that doesn't just react but thinks, learns, and grows. You'll discover why some AI agents can process vast amounts of data yet stumble over simple decisions, while others display almost human-like adaptability but can't be trusted with critical tasks. More than just understanding the technology, you'll gain the practical insights needed to harness these powerful new tools while avoiding their pitfalls.

Our exploration begins in **Chapter 1**, where we witness the birth of something extraordinary—the convergence of large language models and automation technology that created the first true AI agents. Through the story of a global manufacturing company's customer service transformation, you'll discover why this convergence matters and how it's already reshaping businesses. You'll learn why some of the world's largest companies are racing to implement these technologies and, more importantly, why others are struggling to keep up.

Chapter 2 decodes the DNA of AI agents through a groundbreaking SPAR framework—Sense, Plan, Act, Reflect. At the heart of this chapter lies our innovative five-level *Agentic*

AI Progression Framework that cuts through the confusion surrounding AI agents' capabilities. It gives you the ability to evaluate any AI agent and know what it can achieve for you and your organization. Like watching the evolution from early automobiles to self-driving cars, you'll understand how each level of the progression framework builds upon the last, creating systems of increasing sophistication and autonomy. With these tools, you'll gain crucial insights into where this technology is headed and what it means for your future.

Chapter 3 takes you "Inside the Mind of an AI Agent," where we pull back the curtain on these digital minds. Like anthropologists studying a new form of intelligence, we examine their unique characteristics, capabilities, and limitations. You'll discover why they sometimes make brilliant leaps of insight yet stumble over seemingly simple tasks. Through fascinating examples drawn from our years of implementation experience, you'll learn how these agents think, decide, and act—essential knowledge for anyone looking to work alongside these new digital colleagues.

The theoretical becomes thrillingly practical in **Chapter 4**. Here, we share our hands-on experiments with cutting-edge AI agents, including a fascinating exploration of what happened when we challenged an AI agent to play a game about... an AI making paperclips. This experiment, both enlightening and slightly unnerving, reveals profound insights about the current state and future potential of AI agents. You'll witness both moments of brilliant problem-solving and concerning limitations that anyone working with these technologies needs to understand.

Part 2 takes us deep into the fundamental capabilities that transform a simple AI system into a true agent—what we call the *Three Keystones*: Action, Reasoning, and Memory. Through real-world stories, cutting-edge research, and hands-on experiments, we'll explore how these core capabilities work together to create

AI systems that don't just process information but learn, adapt, and grow.

Chapter 5 explores the *Action* keystone, revealing how AI agents move beyond mere suggestion to actually accomplish tasks in the real world. Through fascinating experiments and real implementation stories, you'll discover why having more tools doesn't always make an AI agent more effective and how successful organizations find the right balance between capability and control. We'll take you behind the scenes of actual AI implementations, showing you both the triumphs and the pitfalls of teaching machines to act in the real world.

In **Chapter 6**, we dive into *Reasoning*—perhaps the most intriguing of the keystones. Through groundbreaking experiments with large reasoning models, you'll discover why faster isn't always better when it comes to AI decision-making. We'll explore how different types of reasoning emerge in AI systems, from quick pattern matching to deeper analytical thinking, and show you how leading organizations are building AI agents that can think through complex problems methodically.

Chapter 7 tackles the *Memory* keystone, exploring how AI agents learn from experience and grow smarter over time. Through the lens of a global telecommunications company's transformation, you'll learn why memory is more than just storing information—it's about creating systems that can learn, adapt, and improve. You'll discover the three layers of AI memory, from short-term processing to long-term retention, and learn how to implement them effectively in your own organization.

Part 3 of our journey moves from theory to practice, showing you how to turn the transformative potential of AI agents into tangible reality—whether you're building solutions for your organization or launching the next million-dollar business. Through detailed case studies, practical experiments, and hard-won lessons from the field, we'll guide you from initial concept to successful implementation.

Chapter 8 takes you step by step through the process of building effective AI agents, using the real-world transformation of a digital marketing agency as a guide. You'll learn how to spot the right opportunities, choose the best agent types, and design AI systems that drive real value. This chapter provides a practical roadmap—from selecting the right platform to implementing robust safety measures. You'll master how to define agent goals and instructions to maintain control, integrate APIs, fallbacks, and circuit breakers, and follow hands-on, repeatable processes you can apply immediately to turn agentic potential into business reality.

Chapter 9, "From Ideas to Income," takes you into the entrepreneurial frontier of AI agents, where new business models are rapidly emerging. You'll discover how entrepreneurs are already generating revenue by creating specialized AI agents for industries like healthcare, finance, and logistics—and how you can do the same. This chapter provides a proven framework for identifying high-value agentic business opportunities and turning them into profitable ventures. You'll also explore the rise of the "Agent-to-Agent Economy," where AI agents transact, negotiate, and collaborate autonomously. Finally, you'll get a behind-the-scenes look at our own experience launching a newsletter agent that scaled to 300,000 subscribers in just one month, illustrating the power of AI-driven business models.

Part 4 is your strategic playbook for business transformation at scale in the age of AI agents—a comprehensive guide that goes far beyond technical considerations. We dive deep into the critical ingredients of successful organizational change: strategic design, robust governance, change management, and value creation.

Chapter 10 uncovers the hidden human dynamics that can make or break AI agent implementation. This chapter isn't just about technology—it's about people. You'll learn how to transform employee fear into excitement, design work that empowers humans alongside AI, and create a change management strategy that turns potential resistance into enthusiastic collaboration. Through real-world stories and practical frameworks, we'll show you how to build trust, develop new skills, and create a workplace where humans and AI agents work together seamlessly, turning potential disruption into a powerful opportunity for growth and innovation.

Chapter 11, "Scaling AI Agents: From Vision to Reality," tackles one of the most pressing challenges organizations face today: how to move from successful pilots to full-scale implementation. Through real-world case studies and practical frameworks, we'll show you why only a few companies successfully scaled their AI agent initiatives and, more importantly, how you can be among those that succeed. We'll take you behind the scenes of Johnson Controls International's journey from basic automation to sophisticated AI agents, revealing the critical lessons they learned along the way. You'll learn their strategies for overcoming common scaling challenges, from data integration to change management, and discover how to build a robust foundation for your own AI transformation.

In **Chapter 12**, "Case Study and Use Cases of Agents Across Industries," get ready for a deep dive into the most exciting AI agent implementations happening right now. Through the groundbreaking example of Pets at Home and a comprehensive collection of use cases across industries, this chapter brings AI agent transformation from theory to practical reality. You'll explore how organizations are solving real-world challenges, improving customer experiences, and reimagining work. From veterinary care to retail, from fraud detection to personalized customer service, these case studies will not just inform you— they'll inspire you to see the transformative potential of AI agents in your own organization.

Part 5 of our journey takes us beyond the immediate implementation of AI agents to explore their profound implications for the future of work and society. These chapters paint a compelling picture of both the challenges and opportunities that lie ahead as AI agents become increasingly sophisticated and ubiquitous.

Chapter 13, "The New World of Work," explores the emerging synergy between human capabilities and AI agents while confronting the unprecedented nature of this technological revolution. Through stories like Tara, a senior project manager orchestrating AI-human collaboration, and Debbie, a veteran project manager who watched an AI agent learn to think like her, you'll discover how the *Three Competencies of the Future* are reshaping professional success. The chapter reveals both the promise and challenge of this transformation—from developing irreplaceable "*Humics*" capabilities to addressing what we call the "*adaptation paradox*," where the window for developing crucial skills shrinks even as their complexity increases. You'll gain practical strategies for thriving in this new era while understanding why traditional approaches to technological change may no longer suffice.

Chapter 14, "Society in the Age of Agents," zooms out to examine the broader implications of AI agents for human society. We tackle provocative questions about the future of work itself, exploring how AI agents might free us from routine tasks to pursue more meaningful activities. Through empirical research and real-world examples, we'll explore concepts like Universal Basic Income and the potential for reduced working hours. The chapter concludes with a practical framework for governing agentic AI, ensuring these powerful technologies remain under meaningful human control while maximizing their benefits to society.

Beyond the Book: Your Online Resources

This book is just the beginning of your agentic intelligence journey. Extend your learning and connect with a vibrant community of fellow practitioners and experts at **AgenticIntelligence. academy**. There, you'll find valuable resources, in-depth courses, practical tools, and a forum for collaboration and growth, all designed to help you reach the top of your agentic game.

Join us at www.AgenticIntelligence.academy

Key Terminologies for Understanding AI Agents

To effectively navigate the world of AI agents, it's crucial to grasp a few foundational concepts. These terms will appear repeatedly throughout the book, so it's essential to define them clearly.

Workflow of Tasks

A workflow of tasks refers to a structured sequence of actions that need to be completed to achieve a goal. Think of it as a roadmap for getting things done, where each step depends on the successful completion of the previous one. Let us take the example of making a cup of coffee. First, you fill the kettle and boil the water. Next, add coffee to a mug, pour in the hot water, and stir. Finally, you add milk or sugar if needed and enjoy your coffee. A business process is typically composed of a combination of workflows; large processes like order-to-cash or procure-to-pay might be comprised of hundreds of workflows.

APIs (Application Programming Interfaces)

An API (Application Programming Interface) is a bridge that allows different software systems to communicate with each other. Imagine an API as a waiter in a restaurant: you place an order (a request), the waiter relays it to the kitchen (another system), and then delivers the food (the response) back to you. APIs are essential for AI agents because they enable seamless integration with the tools they use—whether it's accessing databases, retrieving real-time information, or connecting with cloud services. In most cases, without APIs, AI agents would be isolated and unable to interact with tools.

Deterministic vs. Probabilistic Systems

Depending on how they process inputs and produce outputs, AI systems can be classified as deterministic or probabilistic.

Deterministic systems always produce the same output for a given input. They follow strict rules and logic, ensuring predictable, repeatable results. Think of a basic calculator—when you input "2 + 2," you always get "4." These systems are ideal for tasks where precision and consistency are crucial, like financial calculations or compliance checks. Deterministic systems were used exclusively in the "expert systems" of early AI, and are still present in robotic process automation systems, clinical decision support systems in hospitals, and a surprising number of other settings.

Probabilistic systems, on the other hand, operate based on likelihoods rather than fixed rules. They analyze patterns and data to make predictions, meaning their outputs can vary slightly based on probabilities. Most AI models, including large language models and recommendation systems, fall into this category.[11] They don't provide guaranteed answers but instead generate responses based on the most statistically probable outcome. For example, when a chatbot predicts the next word in a sentence, it selects the option with the highest likelihood rather than following a rigid rule.

---

[11] Thomas H. Davenport and Peter High, 2024. "How Analytical AI and Gen AI Differ—and When to Use Each," Harvard Business Review, https://hbr.org/2024/12/how-gen-ai-and-analytical-ai-differ-and-when-to-use-each

PART 1
THE RISE OF AI AGENTS

CHAPTER 1

BEYOND CHATGPT: THE NEXT EVOLUTION OF AI

The introduction highlighted a critical gap in our current approach to AI—brilliant systems that can think but can't act. Now, let's explore how we arrived at this pivotal moment. In this chapter, we'll trace the technological evolution that made AI agents possible—the convergence of two powerful streams that, when combined, created something greater than either could achieve alone. Understanding this history isn't just academic; it reveals why the shift to agentic AI represents such a profound opportunity.

The Birth of Agentic AI: A Convergence of Powers

Picture yourself in a meeting room with a group of business leaders. Someone inevitably asks the question we've heard hundreds of times: "If AI is so smart, why can't it just figure out what needs to be done and do it?"

This question gets to the heart of what's missing in today's AI landscape. To understand why this capability has been so elusive—and how it's finally becoming possible—we need to explore how distinct technological streams have converged to create something entirely new: agentic AI.

Agentic AI isn't the result of just one innovation. It's a fusion of multiple advancements—from voice assistants to self-driving technology to AI-driven APIs. However, two technological streams stand out as the most critical in making agentic AI a reality:

- The rise of large language models.
- The evolution of workflow automation, now known as intelligent automation.

A Tale of Two Technologies

The story of agentic AI isn't a simple, linear progression. Instead, it's more like watching two rivers flow separately for miles before finally meeting to form something more powerful than either could be alone.

Let's start with a story that illustrates why this convergence matters. In 2022, we were working with a global manufacturing company that was struggling with customer service efficiency. They had already implemented an advanced chatbot powered by a large language model that could understand and respond to customer queries with remarkable accuracy. They had also deployed robotic process automation (RPA) bots that could execute complex sequences of actions in their backend systems. Yet something was missing—the bridge between understanding and doing.

Their customer service representatives still had to act as human bridges, taking the chatbot's recommendations and manually triggering the appropriate automated workflows. It was a glimpse of what was possible if these technologies could work together directly, and it helped us understand why the convergence of these technologies would be so transformative.

The First Stream: The Path to Large Language Models

The journey of AI that led to today's language models began in 1997, and we were there to witness it. The world watched in amazement as IBM's Deep Blue defeated chess champion Garry Kasparov. We remember the headlines: "Machine Beats Man!" But here's what most people missed—Deep Blue was more like a savant than a genius. It could play chess brilliantly but couldn't even explain its own moves. Try asking it to play checkers, and you'd have better luck teaching a fish to ride a bicycle.

This limitation bothered us and many others in the field. Surely, we thought, there must be a better way to create intelligent systems. The breakthrough came from an unexpected direction—neural networks. Now, when we explain neural networks, we like to use a simple analogy: imagine teaching a child about animals. You don't start by giving them a rulebook about fur, tails, and the number of legs. Instead, you show them examples: "This is a dog. This is a cat. This is a bird." The child's brain naturally learns to recognize patterns and make generalizations.

The Neural Network Revolution

The beauty of neural networks is that they learn in a similar way. But they needed three ingredients to reach their full potential: vast amounts of data (think millions of examples), significant computing power (imagine thousands of high-end computers working together), and sophisticated architectures (the clever ways we organize these artificial brain cells).

We remember the excitement in the AI community when these elements finally came together in the 2010s. It was like watching the first flight of the Wright brothers—suddenly, something that seemed impossible became reality. Systems could recognize images, understand speech, and process language with unprecedented accuracy.

The Emergence of Language Models

But the real magic happened in language processing. Let us take you back to the old days of language AI—it was like trying to teach a computer to understand Shakespeare by giving it a dictionary and a grammar book. The results were about as wooden as you'd expect.

Then came 2017, and with it, a breakthrough that changed everything: the transformer architecture. Imagine giving an AI not just the ability to look up words but also to understand context, grasp meaning, and see how ideas connect. It was like upgrading from a pocket calculator to a mathematician's brain.

The scaling laws we discovered during this period still amaze us. As these models grew larger and were trained on more data, something magical happened—they developed abilities nobody had programmed into them. It was like watching evolution happen in fast-forward. GPT-3, released in 2020, shocked us. Here was a system that could write code, solve math problems, and even engage in philosophical discussions—tasks it was never explicitly trained to do.

When ChatGPT arrived in 2022, it felt like reaching the summit of a mountain we'd been climbing for decades. Finally, we had an AI that could engage in genuine dialogue, reason through problems, and explain its thinking in ways that made sense to humans. But there was still one crucial limitation—it could only suggest actions, not take them.

The Second Stream: The Evolution of Automation

While all this was happening in the AI world, another revolution was quietly unfolding in the realm of automation. We've had a front-row seat to this evolution, watching it transform from simple screen-scraping tools to sophisticated digital workers.

The Rise of Robotic Process Automation

In the early 2000s, much of business was still manual or relied on disparate IT systems that didn't talk to each other. Forward-thinking teams started using scripts and macros to automate repetitive computer tasks—for example, a macro to copy data from an Excel file into a mainframe application every night.

In the early 2010s, we actively participated in the birth of Robotic Process Automation (RPA). Think of it as software tools that mimic the actions of a human on a computer: clicking, typing, copy-pasting, and reading screens. It sounds simple, but it was revolutionary. For the first time, we could have computers work alongside humans, using the same tools and interfaces we use.

Essentially, an RPA "robot" is a piece of software programmed to follow a series of steps—log into a system, retrieve some data, perform a calculation, and input results elsewhere—just like a human would, but faster and without fatigue. RPA became popular because it targeted low-hanging fruit: all those mundane, rules-based tasks that office workers repeatedly do.

Businesses eagerly embraced RPA to reduce errors and free employees from drudgery. We saw banks, insurers, and hospitals deploy RPA bots to handle activities like data entry, invoice processing, report generation, and database updating. For instance, one insurance client of ours used RPA to automatically transfer policy data from emails into their legacy system—what used to take a team of people all day now happens reliably in minutes.

However, these early RPA solutions had limitations. They were fragile—if a single screen changed or an exception occurred (like a missing field), the robot would get confused. RPA robots had no intelligence or judgment; they strictly followed the script. We often had to step in and update the bot or handle edge cases manually. In essence, RPA was process-driven automation, good for structured tasks with clear rules, but not adaptable when things deviate from the norm.

The Evolution to Intelligent Automation

The next step was even more exciting—combining RPA with machine learning—what we named intelligent automation or hyperautomation. To stay competitive, RPA tools started adding AI capabilities so that they could handle more complex, unstructured work. Think of it this way: RPA is great at doing tasks, but it lacks any thinking. So, companies began to augment RPA with AI technologies—machine learning, natural language processing (NLP), and computer vision—to create automation that could interpret information and make simple decisions.

In practical terms, this meant an automated workflow could, for example, read an email from a customer (using NLP), decide what the request is about (using an AI classifier), and then trigger the appropriate RPA process to handle it. The automation was no longer blind and rigid; it became context-aware to a degree.

As automation grew more capable, we started aiming beyond single tasks toward end-to-end process automation. Instead of just automating steps in isolation, the goal became to automate an entire workflow or business process from start to finish.

For example, for a retail company, we helped automate the order-to-cash process: From receiving an online order, verifying inventory, processing payment, and scheduling shipment to updating the finance records. Multiple RPA robots, interfaces, and AI models worked in concert, passing tasks along like an assembly line, with humans only monitoring or handling exceptions. When done right, the entire process runs on its own.

By the early 2020s, many businesses had achieved a high degree of automation in routine processes. We observed what we call the *automation plateau*: most of the straightforward tasks were already automated, and the bottleneck became the *decision points* and *dynamic situations* that still needed a human in the loop. Traditional automation could go no further because it lacked the adaptability and higher-level reasoning required beyond well-defined rules.

And now, we arrive at the present moment—the convergence of these two powerful streams. It's like watching two puzzle pieces finally click together. Language models provide the brain—the ability to understand, reason, and plan. Automation technologies provide the hands—the ability to execute actions in the real world. When both converge, we get agentic AI—in essence, *intelligent digital workers*.

This combination is what makes agentic AI possible, and we're thrilled to be part of this revolution. We're watching AI systems evolve from passive tools into active partners that can both understand what needs to be done and actually do it.

Birth of the First LLM-based AI Agents

AI research and development in the last few years have rapidly advanced the capabilities of AI agents. LLMs like GPT-3 and GPT-4, which initially functioned as sophisticated prediction engines for text, are now being augmented with the ability to plan actions and use tools. This means instead of just completing a sentence, they can decide to perform a web search, execute a calculation, call an API, or invoke another piece of software as part of answering a question or accomplishing a task.

One of the first LLM-based AI agent frameworks was MRKL (Modular Reasoning, Knowledge, and Language) in 2022.[12] It focused on modular reasoning, where LLMs interact with predefined tools like "Search" and "Lookup" to retrieve information and answer queries. The framework separated reasoning from acting, relying on external modules for discrete reasoning tasks.

---

[12] Ehud Karpas et al., 2022. "MRKL Systems: A modular, neuro-symbolic architecture that combines large language models, external knowledge sources and discrete reasoning," https://arxiv.org/abs/2205.00445

The field evolved rapidly then with the introduction of ReAct,[13] which brought the concept further by enabling AI to intermix reasoning steps with actions. The model generated a thought process (a reasoning trace) and could take an action like querying a database or using an API, then continued reasoning with the new information. This synergy between reasoning and acting helped the AI adjust its plan on the fly and handle more complex tasks. In experiments, ReAct greatly reduced the AI's tendency to *hallucinate* incorrect facts by letting it check a source (like a Wikipedia API) before answering. It also made the AI's decision process more transparent and interpretable, since you could follow its step-by-step reasoning.[14]

Toolformer (2023) was a breakthrough AI model that taught itself to use external tools like calculators, web search, and translators. This addressed a key weakness of large language models, which struggled with arithmetic and real-time facts due to their reliance on static training data. By deciding when and how to call external tools, Toolformer enhanced accuracy in calculations and question-answering.[15]

These advances have led to the emergence of highly capable AI agents that can handle multi-step tasks. For example, you might have heard of experimental systems like AutoGPT[16] or BabyAGI,[17] which gained popularity among enthusiasts. These are essentially wrapper agents around LLMs designed to autonomously pursue goals: they take a high-level goal from a

---

[13] Shunyu Yao et al., 2022. "ReAct: Synergizing Reasoning and Acting in Language Models," https://arxiv.org/abs/2210.03629v3

[14] Shunyu Yao et al., 2022. "ReAct: Synergizing Reasoning and Acting in Language Models," https://arxiv.org/abs/2210.03629v3

[15] Timo Schick et al., 2023. "Toolformer: Language Models Can Teach Themselves to Use Tools," https://arxiv.org/abs/2302.04761

[16] Wikipedia contributors, 2025. "AutoGPT," https://en.wikipedia.org/wiki/AutoGPT

[17] Yohei Nakajima, 2024. "Impact of BabyAGI," yoheinakajima.com, https://yoheinakajima.com/impact-of-babyagi/

user and then generate sub-tasks, execute them (often by issuing tool commands or even writing and running code), check the results, and iterate until the goal is achieved. While these are cutting-edge experiments and sometimes brittle (prone to getting confused or stuck), they illustrate the direction of agentic AI.

In parallel, frameworks like LangChain[18] and Semantic Kernel[19] emerged to enhance these capabilities, making it easier for LLMs to interact with external APIs, databases, and other systems. Suddenly, agents weren't just working in isolation—they were connecting with the digital world, performing tasks like automating workflows, retrieving information, or controlling applications.

The invention of function calling within LLMs pushed this even further.[20] It allowed agents to interact precisely with external systems by running specific functions or scripts as part of their reasoning process. This breakthrough meant agents could not only plan and think but also *act* in highly targeted and efficient ways.

The research reinforced this evolution. Papers like Gorilla[21] demonstrated how models could learn to use tools effectively, while studies from Microsoft,[22] Stanford,[23] and Tencent[24] revealed that collaborative agents—multiple agents working together—achieved even greater success.

---

[18] LangChain, 2025. «Introduction,» https://python.langchain.com/docs/introduction/

[19] Microsoft, 2024. "semantic-kernel," GitHub, https://github.com/microsoft/semantic-kernel

[20] OpenAI, 2024. "Function calling," OpenAI Platform Documentation, https://platform.openai.com/docs/guides/function-calling

[21] Shishir G. Patil et al., 2023. "Gorilla: Large Language Model Connected with Massive APIs," https://arxiv.org/abs/2305.15334

[22] Microsoft, 2024. "AutoGen," Microsoft Research, https://www.microsoft.com/en-us/research/project/autogen/

[23] Joon Sung Park et al., 2023. "Generative Agents: Interactive Simulacra of Human Behavior," https://arxiv.org/abs/2304.03442

[24] Deheng Ye et al., 2024. "More Agents Is All You Need," https://arxiv.org/abs/2402.05120

By 2023, the rise of platforms available to enterprises like AutoGen,[25] Google Cloud Vertex AI,[26] and CrewAI[27] took these concepts mainstream, creating environments where LLM-driven agents could thrive. By incorporating automation capabilities, LLMs have transformed from mere text processors into the foundation of systems capable of reshaping how tasks are performed, how decisions are made, and how technology interacts with the world.

The Booming Landscape: Today's AI Agent Market

Market projections indicate that the market will grow at an incredible 44% per year by 2030.[28] We're thrilled to see the agentic AI market booming because it confirms what we've long believed—AI agents aren't just a passing trend; they're the future of how businesses and individuals will operate.

The fact that Gartner projects that one in three enterprise software applications will integrate agentic AI by 2028 also signals a fundamental shift in how companies approach automation, decision-making, and productivity.[29] But what excites us most is

---

[25] Microsoft, 2024. "AutoGen," GitHub, https://microsoft.github.io/autogen/stable/

[26] The Batch, 2024. "All About Google's Vertex AI Agent Builder," deeplearning.ai, https://www.deeplearning.ai/the-batch/all-about-googles-vertex-ai-agent-builder/

[27] CrewAI, 2024. "CrewAI Launches Multi-Agentic Platform to Deliver on the Promise of Generative AI for Enterprise," GlobeNewswire, https://www.globenewswire.com/news-release/2024/10/22/2966872/0/en/CrewAI-Launches-Multi-Agentic-Platform-to-Deliver-on-the-Promise-of-Generative-AI-for-Enterprise.html

[28] Statista, 2025. "Market value of agentic artificial intelligence (AI) worldwide 2024 with a forecast for 2030 (in billion U.S. dollars)," Statista, https://www.statista.com/statistics/1552183/global-agentic-ai-market-value/

[29] Tom Coshow, 2024. "Intelligent Agent in AI," Gartner, https://www.gartner.com/en/articles/intelligent-agent-in-ai

Sequoia Capital's projection that AI agents could address a $10 trillion market, combining both global services and software markets.[30]

The agentic AI market is new, explosive, and highly competitive.[31] Hundreds of vendors are already offering agent platforms, while both startups and major companies are racing to develop AI agents across industries.[32]

Because this market is evolving rapidly in many directions, it can be difficult to navigate. To make it easier to understand, we like to break it down into three main categories:

- First are **customizable platforms** that let professionals and organizations build their own agents. These platforms can be used across business industries and functions. They range from no-code solutions like Beam[33] and Relevance.ai[34] to low-code platforms like UiPath[35] and Microsoft's Agent Builder,[36] Crew.ai,[37] and ServiceNow[38]

---

[30] Sonya Huang, et al., 2024. "Generative AI's Act o1: The Reasoning Era Begins," Sequoia Capital, https://www.sequoiacap.com/article/generative-ais-act-o1/

[31] Lindsey Wilkinson, 2025. "Enterprises eye agentic AI despite readiness gaps and security concerns," CIO Dive, https://www.ciodive.com/news/enterprise-AI-agent-agentic-autonomous-strategy-challenges/738172/

[32] Nicole Deslandes, 2024. "2025 Informed: The Year of Agentic AI," TechInformed, https://techinformed.com/2025-informed-the-year-of-agentic-ai/

[33] Beam AI, 2025. "Hire Self-Learning AI Agents to Run Your Operations - Agentic AI by Beam," beam.ai, https://beam.ai/

[34] Relevance AI, 2025. "Build teams of AI agents that deliver human-quality work," relevanceai.com, https://relevanceai.com/

[35] UiPath, 2025. "Build a path to agentic automation with UiPath Agent Builder," uipath.com, https://www.uipath.com/product/agent-builder

[36] Microsoft, 2025. "Overview of Copilot Studio agent builder," Microsoft Learn, https://learn.microsoft.com/en-us/microsoft-365-copilot/extensibility/copilot-studio-agent-builder

[37] CrewAI, 2025. https://www.crew.ai

[38] ServiceNow, 2025. "Virtual Agent," https://www.servicenow.com/products/virtual-agent.html

to full programming frameworks like Langchain[39] and AutoGen.[40] These tools let businesses create agents tailored to their specific needs and processes.

- Second are the **generalist agents**, like OpenAI's Operator,[41] Anthropic's Computer Use,[42] and Google's Project Mariner.[43] These are more versatile, capable of handling a wide range of tasks and adapting to different contexts. Think of them as intelligent digital assistants that seamlessly navigate multiple systems, understand complex goals, and execute tasks directly through the screen— no complex integrations required. In our view, the "ChatGPT moment" of agentic AI will come from the evolution of this category of agents, as they will become widely available to both consumers and companies.

- Third are the **specialist agents**, like Google or OpenAI Deep Research (specialized in research), Agentforce (specialized in sales and customer relationships),[44] or Hippocratic AI (specialized in agents for healthcare).[45] Some of these agents specialize in specific functions across industries (horizontal agents), while others are tailored to a single industry's unique needs (vertical

---

[39] Langchain, 2025. https://www.langchain.com/

[40] AutogenAI, 2025. https://autogenai.com

[41] OpenAI, 2025. "Introducing Operator," https://openai.com/index/introducing-operator/

[42] Anthropic, 2025. "Computer Use," https://docs.anthropic.com/en/docs/build-with-claude/computer-use

[43] Google DeepMind, 2024. "Project Mariner," Google DeepMind, https://deepmind.google/technologies/project-mariner/

[44] Salesforce, 2025. "Agentforce," Salesforce, https://www.salesforce.com/agentforce/

[45] Hippocratic AI, 2025. "Hippocratic AI," https://www.hippocraticai.com/

agents).[46] Most of these are ready-to-use agents focused on specific tasks—whether it's analyzing legal documents, optimizing marketing campaigns, or conducting notarial work. You can find hundreds of these specialized agents on marketplaces like agent.ai,[47] each designed to excel at a particular function.

In the appendix, you'll find a detailed breakdown of the current market offerings, structured according to the 5-Level Progression Framework introduced in Chapter 2.

In addition, we understand that navigating this market can be challenging, especially when choosing the right agent platform to start your agentic journey. That's why, in Chapter 8, we not only guide you through building agents but also help you select the best platform to match your needs and objectives.

Agentic AI for Entrepreneurship and Business

The AI agents we're discussing don't just think for us; they also act for us. Over the last couple of years, we've helped develop and deploy some of these AI agents, and working with these agents truly feels like collaborating with a new kind of colleague. Let's unpack what this means in practice.

Introducing Your Intelligent Digital Workers

An intelligent digital worker is like a virtual employee who can handle a process autonomously. It's "hired" to perform a job, such as an IT support agent, a customer service representative,

---

[46] Larry Dignan, 2024. "Agentic AI: Three Themes to Watch in 2025," Constellation Research, https://www.constellationr.com/blog-news/insights/agentic-ai-three-themes-watch-2025
[47] Agent.ai, 2025. https://agent.ai/

or a marketing assistant—only it's made of code. What enables it to do the job is the combination of an LLM's cognitive abilities with the direct action capabilities of automation software. The LLM allows the agent to interpret instructions, converse in natural language, and make reasoned decisions. The automation side empowers it to execute actions: clicking buttons, retrieving and entering data, calling APIs, orchestrating other software tools, etc. Together, these let the AI agent handle complex tasks *end-to-end*.

In practical terms, here's how an AI agent works: Suppose you give an AI agent a high-level goal like, "Update our social media to respond to the latest product launch feedback." A language-capable agent will first understand the request (maybe asking us for clarification if needed, just as a human would). Then, it will break down the goal into actionable steps: e.g., 1) Gather recent customer feedback from social media and reviews, 2) Analyze sentiment (positive vs. negative themes), 3) Draft responses or a PR message addressing concerns, 4) Post the responses or schedule a blog update, and 5) Monitor reactions.

In a traditional setting, this might involve a team of people across marketing and customer support coordinating these steps. An AI agent, however, can coordinate them on its own: using integration hooks to pull data from Twitter or Facebook, running an NLP sentiment analysis model, generating text through its LLM, and interfacing with the company's social media management tool to publish updates.

Throughout, the agent keeps track of context—it knows what the overall objective is and adjusts its actions if something unexpected happens (for example, if it finds an unusually critical tweet, it might escalate that specific issue to a human).

AI Agents in Action: Real-World Transformations

We have implemented firsthand examples across industries. Let's look at a few real-world use cases of *intelligent digital workers* in action.

Take customer service, one of the most immediate and visible applications of AI agents. Gone are the days of rigid, scripted chatbots that frustrate users. Today's AI agents hold full conversations, diagnose issues, and *take action* to resolve them.[48] We worked with a telecom company to deploy an AI-driven support agent capable of handling common tech support calls from start to finish.

A customer calls in with an internet issue—the agent listens, transcribes their words, and understands the problem using a large language model. Then, it troubleshoots: it remotely checks the modem, walks the customer through a reset if needed, and, if the issue persists, creates a service ticket or schedules a technician. By the end of the interaction, the problem is either resolved or seamlessly escalated, without human intervention. The AI doesn't just provide answers—it takes action, managing the full lifecycle of a customer request.

Now, imagine this level of intelligence applied to finance and accounting. We helped a global finance team introduce a "digital analyst agent" that automated their monthly budget variance analysis. Instead of human analysts spending days sifting through numbers, this AI agent pulled data from the accounting system, identified where spending deviated from the plan, and even drafted explanations using natural language models. When

---

[48] See recent research on AI Concierges and how they are expected to transform customer journeys: Liu, S.Q., Vakeel, K.A., Smith, N.A., Alavipour, R.S., Wei, C.(V). and Wirtz, J., 2024. "AI concierge in the customer journey: what is it and how can it add value to the customer?", Journal of Service Management. https://doi.org/10.1108/JOSM-12-2023-0523

it spotted anomalies—such as an unusual expense—it flagged them for human review.

Over time, by learning from feedback, the AI improved its ability to distinguish between normal fluctuations and true red flags. What once required hours of manual effort became a streamlined process, with the AI handling the heavy lifting and humans stepping in only when necessary. The result? A system where financial reporting became faster, more precise, and free of tedious manual work—like having a junior analyst who never sleeps, continuously crunching numbers and preparing insights.

In **Chapter 12**, we take a deep dive into real-world case studies and use cases across industries. You'll see how organizations are solving complex challenges, enhancing customer experiences, and redefining the future of work with AI agents.

Opportunities and Challenges for Companies

For business leaders and decision-makers, the rise of agentic AI is both an opportunity and a challenge. On the opportunity side, the benefits are tantalizing. We can achieve massive efficiency gains by offloading work to AI agents—imagine doubling your workforce without doubling headcount, as mundane tasks are handled by tireless digital workers. We also foresee improvements in quality and consistency.

An AI agent, when properly trained and governed, will follow best practices every single time, and it can embed compliance checks into every action (reducing the risk of human error). Perhaps most interestingly, agentic AI can unlock new capabilities that weren't feasible before. For example, you might deploy 20 AI agents to simulate various market scenarios overnight and have strategic recommendations by morning—a scale of analysis no human team could do in time. Or provide truly personalized service to each of thousands of customers simultaneously through AI concierges.

In fields like customer service and decision support, this means customers get faster responses, and executives get deeper insights for decision-making. AI agents work alongside humans as collaborators—think of it as each employee having an AI copilot that can take on tasks or provide suggestions, dramatically amplifying what that employee can accomplish in a day.

On the challenge side, we must navigate the transition carefully. Integrating AI agents into workflows requires careful change management. Work must be intentionally designed to allow optimal human and AI collaboration, ensuring that employees trust and understand their new AI teammates. Part of our job in deployments has been demystifying how the agent makes decisions (adding explanations or "audit trails" of AI decisions) so that people feel comfortable.

In addition, building AI agents comes with several technical challenges that go beyond just development. Agent reliability is one of the biggest hurdles—ensuring that agents consistently perform as expected without errors or unintended behaviors. Defining precise goals and instructions is equally complex, requiring constant iteration to refine responses and decision-making.

Seamless integration is another key factor; AI agents must connect effortlessly with existing tools, APIs, and workflows to be truly effective. Data quality also plays a crucial role—garbage in leads to garbage out, making agents unreliable, error-prone, and incapable of accurate decision-making. Ultimately, successful deployment isn't just about building agents—it's about continuously integrating, testing, and refining them to ensure they deliver real-world value.

There's also the question of oversight: AI agents need guardrails and ethical guidelines. They are powerful, but they should still align with business rules, values, and regulatory requirements. Collaboration between humans and AI will only work if humans ultimately remain in control of setting goals and reviewing critical decisions—especially in areas like finance or healthcare where stakes are high.

Fortunately, tools for AI governance are improving, and we always stress a *human-in-the-loop* approach, especially in the early stages of using agentic AI. Think of the AI agent as a very capable new hire—you wouldn't let a new employee run wild without training and oversight, and the same goes for AI.

As we move forward, it's important to remember that agentic AI is *augmentative*, not purely replacement. The ultimate model is AI + Human working in tandem. The AI handles the heavy lifting and routine grind while humans provide guidance, creativity, and critical oversight. In one successful deployment, a client told us their human team members started calling the AI agent "a member of the team"—that's the kind of collaborative mindset that leads to the best outcomes.

We're entering a future where your next new "employee" might just be an AI. Embracing this future and shaping it responsibly will be a key theme for businesses in the years to come. It's an exciting time to be part of this journey.

To explore this further, **Part 4 of the book** serves as your strategic playbook for business transformation in the age of AI agents. You'll find real-world use cases, case studies, and the key ingredients for successful organizational change—including strategy, governance, change management, and value creation.

Startups: The Biggest Winners in the AI Agent Era

Just as e-commerce, social media, and SaaS reshaped industries, AI agents will unlock entirely new business models, creating opportunities for entrepreneurs to be the first movers in emerging markets. We believe startups stand to gain the most from AI agents' automation, and the numbers prove it.[49] They make up the largest share of companies leveraging AI agents— for example, over 50% of businesses using the LangChain agent platform have fewer than 100 employees, while large enterprises with over 10,000 employees account for barely 15%.[50]

Unlike large enterprises, which are more tied to bureaucracy and legacy systems, startups can build their entire business models around AI agents from day one. This gives them a massive competitive edge by enabling:

- Cost-efficient operations—Automating core tasks reduces the need for large teams.
- Agility and rapid prototyping—AI agents enable faster market entry and iteration.
- Personalized customer interactions at scale—AI agents allow startups to outmaneuver larger competitors, which rely on impersonal, generalized approaches.
- Freedom from integration constraints—Unlike big companies, startups don't have to retrofit AI into workflows that need to be updated.

This agility allows startups to carve out niche markets, offer hyper-customized solutions, and thrive in underserved sectors. As AI agents evolve beyond simple automation into autonomous decision-makers, they will become the backbone of the next wave of disruptive businesses. Examples of startups that have

---

[49] Hayden Field, 2024. "After ChatGPT and the rise of chatbots, investors pour into AI agents," CNBC, https://www.cnbc.com/2024/06/07/after-chatgpt-and-the-rise-of-chatbots-investors-pour-into-ai-agents.html

[50] LangChain, 2024. "The State of AI Agents," https://www.langchain.com/stateofaiagents

been able to seize these opportunities are Perplexity,[51] Ramp,[52] Superhuman,[53] or Replit.[54]

To explore this topic further, **Chapter 9**, "From Ideas to Income," reveals how entrepreneurs are already building specialized AI agents in industries like healthcare, finance, and logistics—and how you can do the same. This chapter also offers a proven framework for identifying high-value agentic business opportunities and transforming them into profitable ventures.

The State of AI Agent Adoption in Companies

To understand how organizations are implementing and benefiting from AI agents, we conducted an extensive analysis of companies that have moved beyond rule-based agents and the conventional use of LLMs to deploy LLM-based AI agents. Our research team collected and analyzed data from 167 companies across various sectors that have implemented such agents in production environments. The study focused on understanding implementation patterns, challenges faced, benefits realized, and key success factors.

[51] LangChain, 2024. "Perplexity: An AI answer engine that lets you handle complex query searches like a Pro," https://www.langchain.com/breakoutagents/perplexity

[52] LangChain, 2024. "Building an AI tour guide that helps users navigate Ramp's platform for financial operations," https://www.langchain.com/breakoutagents/ramp

[53] LangChain, 2024. "Superhuman: Navigate your inbox and calendar in a flash, with an AI-powered search assistant for emails," https://www.langchain.com/breakoutagents/superhuman

[54] LangChain, 2024. "Transforming how users build software from scratch, to code, to application with Replit Agent," https://www.langchain.com/breakoutagents/replit

Current State of Implementation

The landscape of AI agent adoption reveals fascinating patterns across industries. Technology and software companies are leading the charge, representing nearly a quarter of successful implementations in our study. This isn't surprising, given their technical capabilities and appetite for innovation. Financial services follow closely at 18%, with retail completing the top three at 16% of implementations.

Sector	Percentage	Notable Examples
Technology & Software	24%	Microsoft, Salesforce, BMC
Financial Services	18%	JPMorgan, ING Bank, Klarna
Retail & Consumer	16%	Best Buy, Lowe's, McDonald's, Pets at Home
Healthcare & Life Sciences	12%	HCA Healthcare, Hackensack Meridian
Professional Services	10%	McKinsey, Accenture, Thomson Reuters
Travel & Hospitality	8%	IHG Hotels, Alaska Airlines, HomeToGo
Manufacturing & Industrial	6%	Continental, Fortenova Group
Other	6%	Various

Table 1.1: Industry distribution of companies implementing AI agents according to our research (Source: © Bornet et al.)

These early adopters aren't merely experimenting—they're achieving remarkable results. Microsoft, for instance, reported a 9.4% increase in revenue per seller and 20% more closed deals using AI agents in their sales function. In the financial sector, JPMorgan deployed agents that reduced fraud by an impressive 70%. These success stories are encouraging more companies to explore similar implementations.

The data reveals five primary categories where organizations are successfully deploying agents. Customer service and support lead the pack, accounting for 35% of implementations. These systems handle everything from automated query resolution to personalized service delivery, with companies reporting average resolution time improvements between 12% and 30%.

Internal operations follow at 25%, with organizations using agents to handle document processing, workflow optimization, and administrative tasks. The results here are particularly striking, with time savings ranging from 30% to 90% for certain processes. McKinsey & Company's client onboarding agent, for example, demonstrated a 90% reduction in lead time and 30% reduction in administrative work.

Use Case Category	Percentage	Key Benefits Reported
Customer Service & Support	35%	• 12-30% faster resolution times • 20-40% reduction in support costs • Higher customer satisfaction scores
Internal Operations	25%	• 30-90% reduction in processing time • 25-50% cost savings • Reduced error rates
Sales & Marketing	20%	• 9-21% revenue increase • 20-30% more deals closed • Higher conversion rates
Security & Fraud Detection	12%	• 70% fraud reduction • Faster threat detection • Improved accuracy
Specialized Industry Solutions	8%	• Industry-specific improvements • Regulatory compliance • Enhanced service delivery

Table 1.2: AI agent use cases and key business impacts according to our research (Source: © Bornet et al.)

Sales and marketing applications represent 20% of implementations, focusing on lead qualification, campaign optimization, and personalized outreach. Companies in this category report revenue increases ranging from 9% to 21%. Security and fraud detection accounts for 12% of implementations, while specialized industry solutions make up the remaining 8%.

Measuring Agent Impact

The quantifiable improvements reported by organizations in our study are substantial. In terms of efficiency gains, companies consistently report process time reductions between 30% and 50%, cost savings of 25% to 40%, and error reduction rates of 30% to 60%. Revenue impact is equally impressive, with sales increases ranging from 9% to 20%, conversion rate improvements of 15% to 25%, and customer satisfaction increases of 20% to 40%.

A particularly interesting finding is that 70% of successful implementations use hybrid human-AI workflows. These organizations have found that maintaining human oversight for critical decisions while leveraging AI for routine tasks not only improves results but also increases employee satisfaction. This approach enables continuous improvement as humans and AI agents learn from each other.

Blueprint for Success: Winning Agent Implementation Strategies

Our research reveals that successful implementations typically follow a measured, strategic approach. Nearly two-thirds of successful implementations began with pilot programs, allowing organizations to test and refine agent capabilities in a controlled environment while building internal support through demonstrated success.

The data points to three critical success factors that consistently appear across successful implementations. First is the clear definition of use cases. Organizations that succeed take time to identify specific problems they want to solve and establish measurable success metrics before deployment. They maintain well-defined scope limitations and implement regular performance evaluations to ensure the agents continue to meet their objectives.

The second is strong change management. Companies that excel in this area develop comprehensive employee training programs and maintain clear communication channels throughout the implementation process. They recognize that successful agent deployment is as much about people as it is about technology.

The third is robust technical infrastructure. Successful organizations ensure they have integrated data architecture, strong security measures, and scalable systems in place before deployment. They also maintain regular maintenance and update schedules to keep their systems running optimally.

We'll dive deeper into these key success factors later in the book, with detailed strategies for designing effective AI agents (Chapter 8) and successfully integrating them into your business (Part 4).

How Leaders Overcome Agent Adoption Hurdles

Organizations implementing AI agents face several common challenges. System integration is the most frequently cited, with 45% of companies reporting it as a significant hurdle. Successful organizations address this through phased integration approaches and API-first architecture, along with regular testing and validation procedures.

Data quality presents another major challenge, reported by 35% of companies. Organizations overcome this through structured data governance initiatives and regular quality assessments. Technical expertise rounds out the top three challenges, with 20% of respondents citing it as a concern. Leading organizations address this through comprehensive training programs and strategic external partnerships.

Operational challenges center around change management, performance monitoring, and cost management. Successful organizations tackle these through clear communication strategies, defined KPIs, and regular cost reviews. They also maintain strong feedback loops to ensure continuous improvement.

We'll take a deeper look at these critical challenges and solutions later in the book, offering practical strategies for designing powerful AI agents (Chapter 8) and effectively implementing them into your business (Part 4).

Where Agents Are Headed and How to Prepare

Looking ahead, the trajectory of AI agent adoption shows no signs of slowing. Our research indicates that 85% of companies plan to increase their agent implementations, with seven out of ten exploring new use cases and 60% increasing their AI budgets. More than half are developing custom solutions tailored to their specific needs.

Our research suggests several key recommendations for business leaders considering or beginning their journey with AI agents. First, while thinking strategically is important, starting small is crucial. Successful organizations identify high-impact, low-risk use cases for their initial implementations and build on these successes incrementally.

Infrastructure investment should be a priority, with particular attention paid to data quality and security measures. Organizations need to ensure their systems are scalable to accommodate future growth and additional use cases.

Change management deserves significant attention. Successful organizations develop comprehensive training programs and create clear communication channels. They work to foster a culture of innovation where employees feel empowered to work alongside AI agents rather than threatened by them.

Finally, measurement and iteration are crucial. Successful organizations define clear success metrics from the start and maintain regular performance reviews. They view their AI agent implementations as continuous improvement cycles rather than one-time deployments.

The Road Ahead: What Adoption Trends Tell Us

The data from our study clearly demonstrates that AI agents are delivering significant value across industries. However, success requires a thoughtful approach combining technical expertise, strong change management, and clear business objectives. Organizations that follow the patterns of successful implementations—starting with pilots, focusing on clear use cases, and maintaining strong human oversight—are most likely to achieve positive results.

As we look ahead, the trend toward increased agent implementation shows no signs of slowing. Business leaders should view this not as a threat but as an opportunity to reimagine how work gets done in their organizations. The key is to approach implementation strategically, learn from early adopters, and maintain a balanced view of how agents can augment and enhance human capabilities rather than replace them.

Later in the book, we'll break down these implementation key challenges and best practices, covering how to design AI agents for maximum impact (Chapter 8) and integrate them seamlessly into your business operations (Part 4).

CHAPTER 2

THE FIVE LEVELS OF AI AGENTS: FROM AUTOMATION TO AUTONOMY

As we saw in Chapter 1, the market for AI agents is growing rapidly, with hundreds of vendors offering solutions across a spectrum of capabilities. This proliferation creates a challenge: How do we make sense of these different systems? How do we distinguish between simple automation tools and truly autonomous agents? This chapter introduces a comprehensive framework for understanding the progression of AI agent capabilities—from basic rule-following to sophisticated autonomy—that will help you navigate this complex landscape and make informed decisions about which solutions are right for your needs.

Breaking Down the AI Agent's Capabilities

When we first started implementing AI agents in organizations, we noticed a common pattern. Business leaders would often dive straight into deployment without truly understanding what these digital teammates could and couldn't do. It reminded us of trying to work with a new colleague without first learning about their skills, experience, and working style—a recipe for misaligned expectations and missed opportunities.

Why Capability Mapping Matters

When integrating a new team member, we don't simply hand them tasks and hope for the best. We invest time in understanding their capabilities, assessing their strengths and weaknesses, and learning how to work together effectively. Through interviews, discussions, and practical tests, we discover not just what they can do but how they think, how they approach problems, and where they might need support or guidance.

This same thoughtful approach is crucial when working with AI agents. While these digital colleagues can process information at incredible speed and scale, they also have their own unique characteristics, limitations, and ways of "thinking." Understanding these aspects isn't just about knowing what tasks to delegate—it's about building effective partnerships that maximize the potential of both human and artificial intelligence.

The SPAR Framework: A Natural Way to Understand AI Agents

To help explain AI agent capabilities, we developed what we call the SPAR framework: Sense, Plan, Act, and Reflect. We chose this name deliberately—like a sparring partner in combat sports, an AI agent constantly interacts with and adapts to its environment.

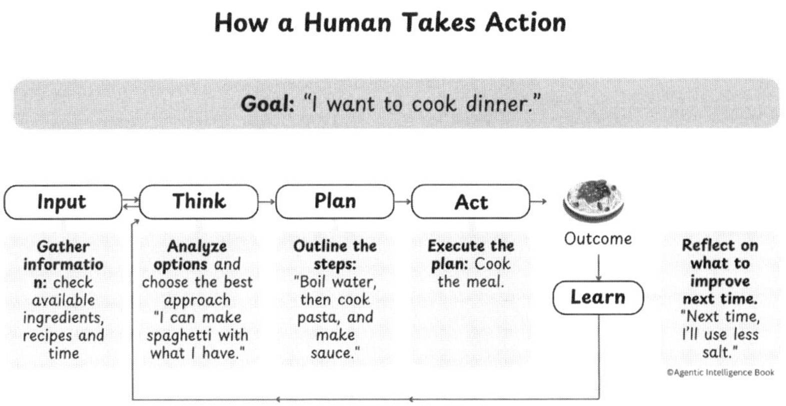

How a Human Takes Action

Goal: "I want to cook dinner."

Input	Think	Plan	Act	Outcome	Reflect on

Gather informatio n: check available ingredients, recipes and time — Analyze **options** and choose the best approach "I can make spaghetti with what I have." — Outline the steps: "Boil water, then cook pasta, and make sauce." — Execute the plan: Cook the meal. — **Learn** — Reflect on what to improve next time. "Next time, I'll use less salt."

©Agentic Intelligence Book

Figure 1.1: How a Human Takes Action (Source: © Bornet et al.)[55]

This framework mirrors how we humans achieve our own goals. We start by deciding what needs to be done—like cooking dinner. Next, we gather input, checking what ingredients are available. Then, we think through our options, choosing the best approach—perhaps making spaghetti. Once decided, we plan the steps, like boiling water and preparing the sauce. With a clear plan, we take action and cook the meal. Afterward, we evaluate the result, learn from the experience, and adjust for the future—perhaps using less salt next time—creating a continuous feedback loop for improvement.

When we explain AI agents to business leaders and professionals, we often find ourselves drawing parallels to autonomous vehicles. It's not just because self-driving cars are fascinating—they're actually perfect examples of AI agents in action. Through this lens, let's explore the SPAR framework: Sense, Plan, Act, and Reflect. This framework captures the four

---

[55] Open Access: All figures in this book are distributed under the terms of the Creative Commons Attribution 4.0 International License, which permits unrestricted use, distribution, and reproduction under the conditions detailed here: http://creativecommons.org/licenses/by/4.0/.

fundamental capabilities that define how AI agents operate in their environments.

How an AI Agent Takes Action: the SPAR Framework

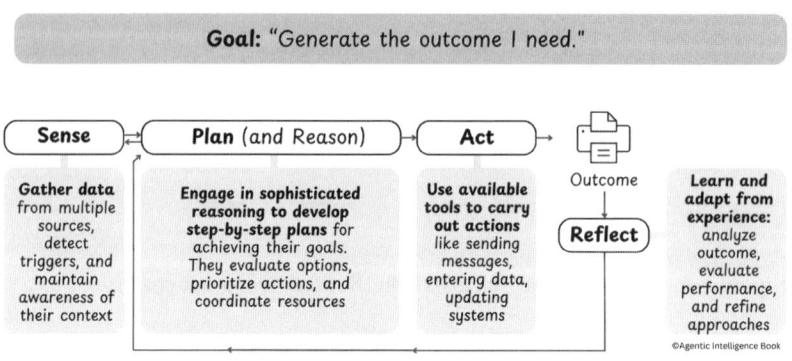

Figure 1.2: How an AI agent takes action: The SPAR Framework (Source: © Bornet et al.)

Sensing: The Eyes and Ears of Agents

Imagine sitting in a self-driving car as it navigates through city streets. The vehicle's array of cameras, radar systems, and sensors are constantly gathering data about its surroundings— monitoring everything from the position of nearby vehicles to traffic signals and road conditions. This is remarkably similar to how AI agents operate in digital environments.

Just as a self-driving car needs to understand its environment comprehensively, AI agents must be able to perceive their digital workspace. They gather data from multiple sources, detect important triggers, and maintain awareness of their operating context. When you enter a destination into an autonomous vehicle, you're setting its goal—just like when you assign an objective to an AI agent. The agent maintains what we call a "short-term context window," similar to how a self-driving car keeps track of immediate road conditions and navigation requirements.

Planning: Charting the Course

Once an autonomous vehicle knows where it needs to go, it doesn't just start driving blindly. It processes map data, considers traffic patterns, and evaluates multiple possible routes. This planning phase perfectly mirrors how AI agents work. They don't simply jump into execution—they first process available information to make informed decisions about how to achieve their objectives.

Think about how a self-driving car plans a lane change. It doesn't just swerve immediately; it evaluates the speed and position of surrounding vehicles, calculates the optimal moment to move, and ensures the maneuver can be completed safely. Similarly, AI agents engage in sophisticated reasoning to develop step-by-step plans for achieving their goals. They evaluate options, prioritize actions, and coordinate resources, much like how an autonomous vehicle coordinates its various systems to execute a complex driving maneuver.

Acting: Putting Plans into Motion

The ability to take concrete action sets both autonomous vehicles and AI agents apart from simple analytical systems. When a self-driving car executes a turn, it coordinates multiple systems—steering, acceleration, braking—in precise sequences. Similarly, AI agents use their available tools to carry out actions in their environment, whether that's sending communications, updating systems, or managing digital resources.

What's particularly interesting is how both systems monitor their actions in real-time. Just as a self-driving car continuously adjusts its steering and speed based on road conditions, AI agents actively monitor their actions for accuracy and effectiveness, making adjustments as needed to stay on course toward their objectives.

When something goes wrong in an autonomous vehicle, there is usually a remote human who can take over and resolve the problem.[56] Similarly, when AI agents take action, there needs to be a clear path for humans to review those actions and take remedial steps when necessary.

Reflecting: Learning from Experience

Perhaps the most sophisticated capability in both autonomous vehicles and AI agents is their ability to learn and adapt from experience. When a self-driving car encounters road construction or heavy traffic, it doesn't just navigate through the immediate situation—it can incorporate this information into its knowledge base to improve future journeys.

This reflective capability enables both systems to get better over time. Just as autonomous vehicles learn optimal routes and driving patterns, AI agents can evaluate their performance, analyze outcomes, and refine their approaches based on what works best. They build what we might call an "operational memory" that helps them perform more effectively in similar situations in the future.

The Power of Integration

What makes both self-driving cars and AI agents so powerful is how these four capabilities work together in a continuous cycle. Each capability feeds into and enhances the others, creating a unified system that can pursue complex goals with increasing sophistication. The car's sensors inform its planning, which

---

[56] Cade Metz, 2024. "When Self-Driving Cars Don't Actually Drive Themselves," The New York Times, September 11, 2024, https://www.nytimes.com/2024/09/11/insider/when-self-driving-cars-dont-actually-drive-themselves.html

guides its actions, which generate experiences that it learns from—all while maintaining focus on the ultimate objective of safe, efficient transportation.

This integrated approach represents a fundamental shift from traditional automation. Rather than following rigid, predetermined instructions, both autonomous vehicles and AI agents actively engage with their environments, make decisions, take actions, and learn from outcomes. They don't just execute commands—they work toward objectives with a degree of independence that makes them true agents of change in their respective domains.

While the SPAR framework helps us understand what AI agents can do, it doesn't tell us how well they can do it. Think about driving: just knowing that a vehicle needs steering, acceleration, braking, and navigation doesn't tell you whether you're dealing with a basic sedan or a fully autonomous vehicle. Similarly, different AI agents can have vastly different levels of sophistication in how they sense, plan, act, and reflect.

This complexity creates a challenge for organizations. When vendors claim their solutions use "AI agents," what exactly does that mean? How can business leaders evaluate and compare different systems? How do they know what level of capability they actually need?

The Complex Reality of AI Agents' Capabilities

However, through our consulting work and research, we've found no industry consensus on what truly defines an "agent." To address this, we advocate for a progression framework—one that reflects the evolutionary nature of AI capabilities. Just as technology evolves from simple to sophisticated, this framework provides a structured way to assess and define the advancing role of AI agents.

The binary classification of "agent" or "not agent" is problematic in the current AI landscape. Such rigid categorization fails to capture the nuanced capabilities of different systems, often leads to unrealistic expectations or underestimation of a system's potential, and doesn't align with the incremental nature of AI development in real-world applications.

We also hear voices limiting AI agents to only the most sophisticated systems—those that act, learn, and adapt. We think this is limiting and misleading. It is like saying a car isn't a car unless it's fully autonomous. The reality is that progress is built in stages. If we adopt a narrow definition, we miss the opportunities unfolding right now with foundational AI agents already driving impact. The question isn't 'Is it the ultimate agent?' It's 'How effectively can it act today—and what's next?' Let's keep the door open to innovation at every stage of the journey.

After exploring various frameworks with the companies we help, we found that the automotive industry offers a perfect analogy that resonates with both technical and business stakeholders. Just as the Society of Automotive Engineers (SAE) defines six levels of driving automation, from Level 0 (fully manual) to Level 5 (fully autonomous under all conditions), we can apply a similar progression path to AI agents.

Today, despite the impressive capabilities of cars like Tesla, we're mainly operating at Level 2 or 3[57]--where automation handles many tasks but still requires human oversight and occasional intervention. At the time of printing the book (March 2025), Waymo and Cruise are just testing Level 4 autonomous vehicles in limited, "geo-fenced" areas for ride-hailing services in cities like Phoenix, San Francisco, and Los Angeles.[58]

---

[57] Wikipedia contributors, 2025. "Tesla Autopilot," https://en.wikipedia.org/wiki/Tesla_Autopilot

[58] Jameson Dow, 2024. "Waymo starts fully autonomous rides in LA tomorrow; Austin later this year," Electrek, https://electrek.co/2024/03/13/waymo-starts-fully-autonomous-rides-in-la-tomorrow-austin-later-this-year/

The Agentic AI Progression Framework

The same is true for AI agents. While we often talk about them as fully autonomous systems, in reality, we're dealing with varying levels of capability and independence that progress along a clear developmental path.

At the early stages of this progression, we have AI agents that can execute specific, predefined tasks but require significant human oversight—like a car with basic driver assistance features. As we move further along the Progression Framework, we find agents that can handle more complex sequences of actions and make some independent decisions but still need human validation at critical points—similar to today's most advanced commercial vehicles. At the far end of this progression lie the highest levels, where agents can fully understand, plan, and execute complex missions with minimal human input across any domain. These remain largely theoretical—just as Level 5 autonomous vehicles are still a future goal.

Understanding these progression levels isn't just an academic exercise. This framework helps organizations detect overblown claims about AI agent capabilities and make informed decisions about AI integration in their projects. It enables more effective communication between technical teams and end-users while providing a clear roadmap for AI strategy development that cuts through the hype.

Let's explore what each of these progression levels looks like in practice, starting with Level 0—Manual Operations, where humans perform all cognitive and execution tasks without any automation assistance. From there, we'll see how each level builds upon the previous one, adding new capabilities and degrees of autonomy while still requiring appropriate human oversight.

Level	Car Analogy	Agentic AI Analogy	Main Technology Involved	SPAR Capabilities (Sensing, Planning, Acting, Reflecting)
Level 0 - Manual Operations (Human-Only)	Manual driving with no assistance.	Humans perform all tasks without automation.	Basic digital tools (spreadsheets, email), manual processing.	NA
Level 1 - Rule-Based Automation	Basic cruise control maintains speed but needs human operation.	Simple automation follows fixed rules (e.g., data entry, RPA systems).	Basic automation tools (RPA, simple scripts, rule engines).	*Sensing:* Predefined triggers and structured data. *Planning:* Simple if-then rules and decision trees. *Acting:* Deterministic actions based on fixed inputs. *Reflecting:* No true learning, only logging and error reporting.
Level 2 - Intelligent Process Automation	Advanced driver assistance systems handle speed and steering with supervision.	AI combines automation with cognitive abilities like NLP and machine learning.	AI tools (machine learning, NLP, computer vision, RPA, process orchestration).	*Sensing:* Semi-structured data from multiple sources. *Planning:* Basic AI models for pattern recognition and decision-making. *Acting:* Sophisticated actions with error handling. *Reflecting:* Basic analytics and performance monitoring, no adaptive capabilities.
Level 3 - Agentic Workflows	Vehicles navigate highways but need human intervention in complex situations.	Agents generate content, plan, reason, and adapt in defined domains.	Large language models, memory systems, content generation tools, basic reinforcement learning.	*Sensing:* Advanced natural language understanding and context awareness. *Planning:* Reasoning using foundation models, orchestrating complex workflows. *Acting:* Chaining tools and handling multi-step tasks. *Reflecting:* Limited short-term feedback adjustments and long term memory.

Level	Car Analogy	Agentic AI Analogy	Main Technology Involved	SPAR Capabilities (Sensing, Planning, Acting, Reflecting)
Level 4 - Semi-Autonomous Agents	Self-driving cars operate autonomously in specific conditions.	Agents work autonomously within defined expertise, adapt strategies, and learn.	Advanced reasoning and planning, real-time adaptation, causal reasoning.	*Sensing:* Multi-modal perception and interpretation of diverse inputs. *Planning:* Dynamic strategies for complex tasks and goal breakdown. Acting: Autonomous tool usage and error recovery. *Reflecting:* Retains context across sessions, learns from past experiences.
Level 5 - Fully Autonomous Agents	Fully autonomous cars drive anywhere in all conditions.	AI systems handle any task, cross-domain learning, and self-adaptation with no human intervention.	Sophisticated memory systems, advanced learning mechanisms, safety protocols for autonomy.	*Sensing:* Complete environmental awareness and goal formulation. *Planning:* Advanced reasoning and original problem-solving. *Acting:* Full autonomy in tool selection and execution. *Reflecting:* Continuous self-improvement, robust long-term memory.

Table 1.3: The Agentic AI Progression Framework (Source: © Bornet et al.)

Level 0 - Manual Operations (Human-Only)

At level 0, humans perform all cognitive and execution tasks without any automation assistance. The capabilities required are purely human: logical thinking, decision-making, physical task execution, and learning from experience. The "technology" consists of basic digital tools like spreadsheets, email clients, and business applications, but humans must operate them entirely. Examples include customer service representatives manually responding to each email, financial analysts creating reports by gathering and analyzing data themselves, or Human Resources staff manually processing employee paperwork. The inefficiencies and limitations at this level—human error, fatigue, speed constraints, and scaling challenges—drove the development of basic automation.

Level 1 - Rule-Based Automation

Like a car with basic cruise control, this level represents our first steps toward automation. These are simple "agents" that follow predetermined rules and fixed workflows—for example, basic scripts, or RPA (Robotic Process Automation) systems. They can handle repetitive tasks like data entry or form processing but have no real intelligence or adaptability. They require complete human setup and oversight, just as a cruise control system only maintains a set speed.

These agents master the basic capabilities of repetitive task execution and simple workflow following. They rely primarily on screen-scraping technology, basic process recording, and rules engines. A typical RPA agent might handle invoice processing by copying data from Excel spreadsheets into accounting systems, automating employee onboarding by populating the new hire information into multiple HR systems, or managing routine email responses using predefined templates. The technology stack is relatively straightforward: basic workflow automation tools, basic scripting, and RPA (Robotic Process Automation) systems. The simple skills possessed by Amazon Echo, Google Home, and Apple HomePod also fall into this category.

Level 2 - Intelligent Automation

This level is comparable to advanced driver assistance systems that can handle both speed and steering. These agents combine basic automation with AI capabilities like machine learning, natural language processing, and computer vision. They can process unstructured data, make predictions, and handle tasks requiring cognitive abilities. However, like a car that can stay in its lane but needs human supervision, they still operate within fairly rigid parameters and require significant human oversight.

The ability to automate end-to-end processes expands significantly thanks to AI enabling various cognitive capabilities. Common applications include customer service agents that can answer common questions, recognize simple requests, and direct customers to the right resources based on keywords. Other examples include document processing systems that can extract information from various formats, such as PDFs or images, and process them in a database, or trading agents that can execute pre-determined financial transactions based on market conditions.

The technical foundation of these agents combines four essential capabilities. The Vision capability uses computer vision to "see" and process documents, images, and visual information. The Language capability enables understanding and generating human communication through natural language processing. The Thinking & Learning capability employs machine learning models to analyze data, make predictions, classify information, and optimize decisions. The Execution capability coordinates all actions through intelligent workflow tools and RPA, handling both simple tasks and complex process orchestration. You can refer to our book "Intelligent Automation" for more details on these capabilities.

Level 3 – Agentic Workflows

These agents are similar to vehicles that can navigate highways independently but require human takeover in complex situations. They can generate content (text, images, videos) and have some ability to plan their actions, reason, and memorize. They work well within predefined boundaries and expertise domains, adapting to some variations in their environment. However, they still struggle with nuanced, complex, or novel situations and complex decisions.

These agents master contextual decision-making and basic learning from feedback. For example, a digital assistant can manage employee onboarding by sending paperwork, scheduling training, answering common questions, and flagging unusual requests for human review. Other examples include trading agents that execute complex financial transactions based on market conditions and content creation agents that produce and optimize marketing materials across multiple channels.

The technology powering these agents builds upon previous levels, adding three crucial components. Large language models enable planning, reasoning, and content generation capabilities. This is augmented by basic memory and learning systems, particularly reinforcement learning for adaptive behavior. Finally, these agents incorporate tools' manipulation capabilities, primarily focused on digital interfaces, though still limited in physical world interactions.

Level 4 – Semi-Autonomous Agentic Systems

Like self-driving cars that can operate fully autonomously in specific conditions (good weather, mapped areas), these AI agents work independently within defined domains. They can understand goals, break them down into steps, learn from outcomes, and adapt strategies—but only within their area of expertise. They demonstrate high flexibility and handle complex tasks, though their autonomy remains limited to specific domains.

These agents master goal decomposition, strategic planning, and real-time adaptive learning within their domains. They utilize advanced AI architectures, including recursive self-improvement, causal reasoning models, and multi-agent coordination systems. Applications include research agents that can design and execute complex scientific experiments, medical diagnosis agents that analyze patient data and recommend treatment plans, and financial advisor agents that track user preferences, suggest budget plans, and adjust recommendations based on spending patterns.

The technological architecture of these agents represents a significant advancement in complexity and capability. Advanced reasoning and planning systems form the cognitive core, working in concert with memory and learning mechanisms that enable real-time adaptation. These are complemented by enhanced tools manipulation capabilities that extend to both digital and physical interfaces, though still within defined domains.

Level 5 – Fully Autonomous Agentic Systems

This represents the theoretical pinnacle—like a fully autonomous vehicle that can drive anywhere under any conditions. These agents would be truly autonomous systems capable of understanding any goal, developing strategies, learning from experience, and adapting to new situations across domains. They could seamlessly integrate with other systems, construct their own workflows, and make complex decisions independently while maintaining alignment with human values and objectives.

These theoretical agents would master general problem-solving, cross-domain transfer learning, and autonomous goal setting. Applications might include universal personal assistants handling any task across personal and professional domains, autonomous business managers running entire operations, and research agents making novel scientific discoveries across fields.

The theoretical technology stack for these agents would require capabilities beyond the current state-of-the-art. A full-scale autonomous system would need to integrate advanced memory systems, sophisticated learning mechanisms, and real-time adaptability across any domain. This would demand yet-to-be-developed frameworks for artificial superintelligence, coupled with robust safety protocols and complex ethical reasoning systems to ensure alignment with human values.

Evolution of AI Agents: Where We Stand Today

Critical to this evolution is not just the increasing sophistication of individual capabilities but the integration and orchestration of multiple capabilities into coherent, purposeful systems. Just as a Level 5 autonomous vehicle needs to seamlessly combine perception, prediction, planning, and control, advanced AI agents require the smooth integration of multiple AI technologies and capabilities to achieve their goals.

Currently, most AI agents on the market operate at Levels 2 or 3, with some specialized systems reaching Level 4 in narrow domains. Like fully autonomous vehicles, Level 5 agents remain a future goal—one that raises both exciting possibilities and important questions about control, safety, and human oversight.

This evolution isn't just about increasing automation—it's about developing systems that can increasingly understand context, learn from experience, and make independent decisions while remaining aligned with human intentions and values. Each level builds upon the capabilities of the previous ones, creating increasingly sophisticated agents that can handle more complex and nuanced tasks with greater autonomy.

The Magic of Progressive Autonomy: Understanding AI Agent Levels

When we first started working with AI agents, we often found ourselves drawn to the most advanced capabilities available. It seemed logical—why not leverage the most sophisticated technology possible? But experience has taught us a fundamental truth that we now call the Golden Rule of AI agents: the simpler, the better. This isn't just about technological minimalism; it's about finding the right balance between capability and control for each specific application.

The Evolution of Autonomy: A Natural Progression

Think about how we teach a new employee to handle email communications. At first, we might provide detailed, step-by-step instructions: "Open your email client, click 'New Message,' enter the recipient's address, write this specific text..." As they gain experience, our instructions become broader: "Draft a response to this client inquiry, maintaining our usual professional tone." Eventually, we might simply say, "Handle our client communications and keep them informed about project progress."

This same progression applies to AI agents:

- At Levels 1 and 2, we need to specify every action: "Click the button 'new email,' copy this text, paste it here, enter this address, click send."
- By Level 3, we can say, "Write and send an email using this information, adapting it to the recipient's context."
- At Level 4, we might simply direct, "Handle all client communications to ensure they're well-informed."
- And at Level 5—though this level remains theoretical— we could potentially just set a goal like "Grow sales

through customer satisfaction" and let the agent determine all necessary actions and communications.

The Agentic AI Progression Framework: More Than Just Maturity

This framework isn't a traditional maturity model where higher levels are always better. Instead, think of it as a catalog of different agent types, each suited for specific needs and contexts. It's similar to the driving assistance technologies in modern cars. While fully autonomous driving might be technically possible on highways, many drivers prefer the predictability and control of basic cruise control. The "best" level depends entirely on your specific needs and circumstances.

Let's explore how key aspects evolve as we move up the Agentic AI Progression Framework:

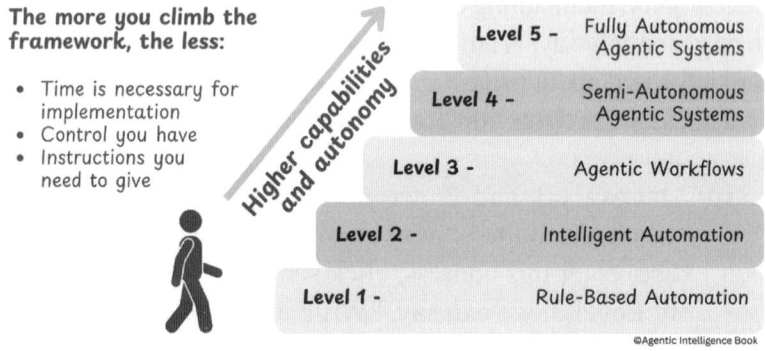

Figure 1.3: The Agentic AI Progression Framework (Source: © Bornet et al.)

Autonomy and Control: A Delicate Balance

As we progress through the levels, autonomy increases while direct human control decreases. At Level 1, agents operate like well-programmed machines, following exact instructions with predictable outcomes. Level 2 introduces basic decision-making capabilities but still within rigid parameters. Level 3 represents a significant leap, with agents capable of understanding context and adapting their approach accordingly. Levels 4 and 5 introduce increasingly sophisticated autonomous behavior, with agents capable of setting their own sub-goals and developing original strategies to achieve them.

However, this increased autonomy comes with reduced direct control. It's similar to raising a child—as they develop more independence, your direct control naturally decreases, replaced by guidance and oversight. This trade-off becomes particularly important in sensitive domains like healthcare, finance, or legal compliance, where predictability and accountability are crucial.

The Instruction Paradox: Less is More

One of the most fascinating aspects of the Progression Framework is how instructions become simpler as capabilities become more sophisticated. At lower levels, instructions must be detailed and explicit, like programming a basic machine. As we move up, instructions become more goal-oriented and abstract. This shift mirrors human development—we move from giving children step-by-step instructions to simply sharing objectives and trusting their judgment.

Implementation and Learning Dynamics

Counter-intuitively, higher-level agents might be quicker to deploy because they can learn through trial and error. However, they require more sophisticated oversight and risk management systems. Lower-level agents, while requiring more detailed initial programming, offer more predictable behavior and easier oversight. This trade-off becomes crucial when choosing the appropriate level for specific applications.

The Wisdom of Starting Simple

Why do we advocate starting with simpler, lower-level agents? Consider learning to play a musical instrument. You don't start with complex symphonies—you begin with basic scales and simple pieces, gradually building your skills and understanding. This approach allows you to develop proper techniques and understanding before tackling more complex challenges.

Similarly, starting with lower-level agents allows organizations to:

1. Build familiarity with AI agents in a controlled environment
2. Develop proper oversight and governance mechanisms
3. Understand the practical implications of different capability levels
4. Create appropriate guardrails and control systems
5. Build organizational confidence and competence

Choosing the Right Level

The key to successful implementation lies in choosing the appropriate level for each specific application. Consider a financial services company implementing AI agents. They might choose Level 1 or 2 agents for transaction processing, where predictability and audit trails are crucial. However, they might implement Level 3 agents for customer service, where adaptability and context awareness are more valuable than strict control.

This flexibility in choosing the appropriate level of autonomy is a key strength of the framework. It allows organizations to match agent capabilities to their specific needs, risk tolerance, and regulatory requirements. The goal isn't to achieve maximum autonomy but to find the right balance between independence and control for each application.

Moving Forward: A Practical Approach

As you begin your journey with AI agents, remember the Golden Rule: the simpler, the better. Start with lower-level agents, even if your ultimate goal is to implement more autonomous systems. Use this time to build understanding, establish proper controls, and develop the organizational capabilities needed for success with more advanced agents.

***

While our Agentic AI Progression Framework provides a structured way to evaluate AI agents' capabilities, understanding the levels alone isn't enough. To truly grasp what makes these digital minds unique, we need to look beyond the framework and explore the distinctive characteristics that define them. In the next chapter, we'll take you inside the mind of an AI agent, examining both their remarkable abilities and inherent limitations—insights that will prove crucial as you begin working with these new digital colleagues.

CHAPTER 3

INSIDE THE MIND OF AN AI AGENT

The Agentic AI Progression Framework we explored in the previous chapter provides a structured way to evaluate AI agents' capabilities, but understanding the levels alone isn't enough. To truly grasp what makes these digital minds unique, we need to look beyond the framework and examine the distinctive characteristics that define them. This chapter takes you inside the mind of an AI agent, exploring both their remarkable abilities and inherent limitations—insights that will prove crucial as you begin working with these new digital colleagues.

Key Specificities of AI Agents

In our experience implementing AI agents across organizations, we've observed several fundamental characteristics that make them uniquely powerful. Let's explore these defining traits that set AI agents apart from traditional automation tools and help explain their transformative potential.

Digital Workers, Not Just Tools

The distinction between AI agents and traditional software tools is profound. Traditional automation is like having a highly efficient assembly line—fixed, predictable, and limited to specific tasks. An AI agent, on the other hand, functions more like a skilled digital employee who can think, adapt, and handle complex situations independently. Just as a human customer service representative might handle everything from simple inquiries to complex problem-solving, an AI agent can manage end-to-end processes, make decisions, and adjust its approach based on context.

Operating Alongside Existing Systems

One of the most practical advantages of AI agents is their ability to work with your existing technology infrastructure rather than replace it. Think of them as *digital workers* who know how to navigate and utilize all your different systems effectively.

This characteristic is particularly valuable because organizations have typically invested heavily in their enterprise systems—ERPs, customer relationship management systems (CRM), HR management systems, and more. AI agents can integrate with these systems, pulling data from multiple sources, executing processes across platforms, and filling automation gaps. For example, a financial AI agent might work simultaneously with SAP for transaction data, Salesforce for customer information, and Excel for custom reports, coordinating between these systems to generate insights and automate complex processes.

The Power of 24/7 Operations

Unlike human workers who need breaks and operate in shifts, AI agents maintain constant operation. This isn't just about working longer hours—it's about maintaining continuous vigilance and responsiveness at a level that would be impossible for human workers.

Consider fraud detection in banking. A human analyst can only monitor a limited number of transactions and might miss subtle patterns due to fatigue. An AI agent can continuously monitor millions of transactions across multiple time zones, instantly identifying suspicious patterns and taking immediate action. This constant operation becomes particularly crucial in areas like cybersecurity, where threats can emerge at any moment, or in global customer service operations, where inquiries come in around the clock.

Infinite Scalability

The scalability of AI agents represents a fundamental shift in how organizations can manage capacity. Traditional growth requires hiring, training, and gradually building capabilities. With AI agents, scaling is instant and virtually unlimited. Need to handle ten times more customer inquiries? You can deploy additional agent instances in minutes, not months.

This scalability extends beyond just handling volume—it includes the ability to adapt to new situations and learn new skills. Imagine being able to instantly replicate your best performer across multiple locations or departments, maintaining consistent quality and performance. This capability becomes particularly valuable during unexpected demand spikes or when entering new markets.

Universal Applicability

One of the most powerful aspects of AI agents is their ability to function effectively across different industries and business functions. While traditional AI solutions often require extensive customization for each industry, AI agents operate with generalizable principles that apply broadly across sectors.

Their core SPAR capabilities—sensing, planning, acting, and reflecting—remain consistent whether they're analyzing risk for a bank, optimizing supply chains for a manufacturer, or handling patient inquiries for a healthcare provider. They can acquire industry and company-specific knowledge while maintaining their fundamental operating principles, making them incredibly versatile.

The Power of Collaboration

Perhaps the most sophisticated characteristic of AI agents is their ability to collaborate—both with humans and other agents. They can work independently when needed, but their real power emerges in collaborative settings. Think of them as team players who can seamlessly integrate into existing workflows, supporting human workers rather than replacing them.

In a content marketing context, for example, one AI agent might generate initial drafts, while another optimizes for SEO, and a third manages publication scheduling—all while collaborating with human editors who provide strategic direction and quality control. This creates a powerful hybrid workflow that leverages the strengths of both human and artificial intelligence.

Why These Characteristics Matter

When agentic AI systems are well-designed and implemented, their characteristics combine to create something truly revolutionary: a flexible, scalable digital workforce that can enhance operations across any organization. Consider a typical business process like customer service: AI agents can handle routine inquiries 24/7, instantly scale during peak periods, work across multiple departments and systems, and collaborate with human agents on complex cases—all while continuously learning and improving.

Understanding these characteristics is crucial for those looking to implement AI agents effectively. They help explain why AI agents represent such a significant advance and why they have the potential to transform how organizations operate. In the following chapters, we'll explore how to leverage these characteristics effectively, ensuring your organization can make the most of what AI agents have to offer.

Inherent Limitations of AI Agents

As we explore the potential of AI agents, it's crucial to understand their limitations. Just as we wouldn't expect a human employee to be perfect at everything, AI agents have their own set of inherent constraints. Let's examine these limitations with the clarity and honesty needed to deploy these technologies effectively.

The Simulation of Intelligence

The most fundamental limitation of AI agents lies in the nature of their "intelligence." While they can process vast amounts of information and generate sophisticated responses, they don't understand the world in the way humans do. They're simply making predictions based on past patterns about what comes next. Think of it like an incredibly skilled actor who can perfectly deliver lines but doesn't actually feel the emotions they're portraying or understand the relevance of the emotion to the specific context.

This becomes particularly evident in complex professional scenarios. A legal AI agent might expertly summarize a contract's terms, but it won't truly grasp the underlying principles of justice or equity that shape the legal interpretation of given situations. Similarly, a healthcare AI agent can analyze symptoms and suggest treatments, but it lacks the intuitive understanding that experienced doctors develop through years of patient interaction.

The Data Quality Dilemma

AI agents are fundamentally dependent on the quality of their data inputs. This isn't just a technical limitation—it's a fundamental constraint that affects every aspect of their operation. Think of it like trying to navigate using a map: if the map is outdated or inaccurate, even the best navigator will make wrong turns.

This dependency becomes particularly critical in business contexts. When analyzing financial data, for instance, an AI agent can't independently verify the accuracy of the numbers it's processing. If an LLM responds to a prompt, it will react based on the data on which it was trained—whether it is correct or not. If there are errors in the input data, these will inevitably propagate to the conclusions. Unlike human analysts who might notice when numbers "don't feel right," AI agents will confidently process incorrect data without raising red flags.

The Common-sense Gap

One of the most striking limitations of AI agents is their lack of common-sense reasoning. While they can process complex calculations and follow sophisticated rules, they often miss obvious real-world constraints that any human would instinctively understand.

Consider a scheduling AI agent suggesting a crucial client meeting at 3 AM or a travel planning agent recommending outdoor activities during a hurricane. These aren't just amusing errors—they highlight a fundamental limitation in AI agents' ability to understand context and real-world constraints without explicit programming.

The Creativity Conundrum

While AI agents can be powerful tools for optimization and iteration, they struggle with true creativity and innovation. They excel at remixing existing patterns but rarely generate truly original ideas. Think of them as master remixers rather than original composers.

In creative fields, this limitation becomes particularly apparent. An AI agent can generate variations on existing designs or writing styles, but it won't produce the kind of breakthrough creative work that reshapes industries or creates new artistic movements. The spark of true innovation—that uniquely human ability to make unexpected connections and imagine entirely new possibilities—remains beyond their reach.

The Hallucination Problem

One of the most concerning limitations of AI agents is their tendency to "hallucinate"—generating false information with high confidence. This isn't a simple error; it's a fundamental limitation of how these systems process information and generate responses.

Consider a medical AI agent confidently recommending a non-existent drug or a legal AI agent citing fictional case law. These aren't just mistakes—they're examples of AI agents filling in gaps in their knowledge with plausible-sounding but entirely fabricated information. This tendency makes human oversight crucial, particularly in high-stakes situations.

The Ethics and Judgment Gap

Finally, and perhaps most importantly, AI agents lack the capacity for true ethical reasoning and judgment. While they can be programmed with rules and guidelines, they don't understand the deeper moral implications of their decisions or the complex human factors that often need to be considered.

This limitation becomes particularly critical in areas like healthcare, criminal justice, or hiring decisions. An AI agent might optimize for efficiency or statistical patterns without considering the human impact of its decisions. It might recommend denying a loan based purely on numbers, missing the human context that could make an exception appropriate.

The Path Forward: Working Within These Limitations

Understanding these limitations isn't about dismissing the potential of AI agents—it's about using them more effectively. By recognizing what AI agents can and cannot do, we can design systems that leverage their strengths while maintaining appropriate human oversight and intervention. In practice, this means, for example:

- Creating hybrid systems where AI agents handle data-intensive tasks while humans provide oversight and judgment
- Establishing strong validation methods to identify possible hallucinations or mistakes, such as having various agents assess the outputs of their peers
- Applying strategies to enhance the quality of agents' input data
- Maintaining human involvement in decisions that require ethical reasoning or complex contextual understanding
- Developing transparency so that humans can understand and evaluate how agents make decisions and take action

In the following parts of the book, we'll explore practical strategies for working within these limitations while maximizing the benefits that AI agents can provide.

When One Is Not Enough: The Power and Practice of Multi-Agent Systems

In the world of artificial intelligence, we often imagine a single, powerful AI system tackling complex problems. But sometimes, one mind—even an artificial one—isn't enough. Just as humans work in teams to accomplish difficult tasks, we're discovering that teams of AI agents working together can achieve remarkable results. Welcome to the fascinating world of multi-agent systems (MAS), where collaboration between artificial minds is revolutionizing how we solve complex problems.

The Orchestra of Artificial Minds

Think of a multi-agent system like an orchestra. Each musician plays a different instrument, following their own sheet music, yet together, they create a harmonious performance. Similarly, a multi-agent system consists of multiple autonomous software agents, each with its own role and capabilities, working in concert to achieve goals that would be difficult or impossible for any single agent to accomplish alone.

Let us share a real-world example that will help illustrate these concepts throughout our discussion. A year ago, we worked with a major financial services company to transform its customer service operations. The traditional approach would have been to create one massive AI system to handle everything—from understanding customer queries to accessing account information to generating responses. Instead, we implemented a multi-agent system where different specialized agents handled different aspects of customer service. One agent focused on natural language understanding, another on retrieving relevant account information, another on composing responses, and yet another on ensuring compliance with financial regulations. Just like musicians in an orchestra, each agent had its specialty, but together, they created a seamless customer service experience.

Why Multiple Agents?

You might wonder: Why go through the complexity of creating multiple agents when you could potentially build one powerful

AI system to do everything? The answer lies in both practical and theoretical considerations.

First, there's the matter of complexity management. Modern business processes are incredibly complex, with many moving parts and interdependencies. A cross-functional, end-to-end process like order-to-cash might involve thousands of specific tasks. Breaking down these processes into smaller, manageable pieces that individual agents can handle makes the overall system more manageable and maintainable. In our financial services example, having separate agents for different functions meant we could update the compliance agent when regulations changed without touching the other components or improve the language understanding agent without risking disruption to the account information retrieval system.

Second, there's the benefit of specialization. Research from Stanford's AI Lab has shown that specialized agents often perform better at specific tasks than generalist systems.[59] Each agent can be optimized for its particular role, using the most appropriate algorithms and approaches for its specific function. Our language understanding agent, for instance, used advanced natural language processing models, while the compliance agent employed rule-based logic that was easier to audit and verify.

Third, multi-agent systems offer superior resilience. According to recent research, distributed systems with multiple agents are generally more robust than centralized systems. If one agent fails or needs maintenance, the others can often continue functioning or even adapt to cover the gap.[60] When our account

---

[59] Kyle Swanson et al., 2024. " The Virtual Lab: AI Agents Design New SARS-CoV-2
Nanobodies with Experimental Validation," bioRxiv, November 12, 2024,
https://www.biorxiv.org/content/10.1101/2024.11.11.623004v1.full.pdf
[60] Mehmet Uzgoren et al., 2024. "Examination of AI Enhanced Distributed Systems and its Effects on Software Engineering," 13th London International Conference, July 24-26, 2024, https://londonic.uk/js/index.php/plic/article/download/240/261/820

information retrieval agent needed occasional maintenance, the system could still understand customer queries and provide general information, degrading gracefully rather than failing completely.

Organizing the Digital Orchestra: Models for Multi-Agent Teams

Just as human organizations can be structured in different ways—from flat hierarchies to traditional pyramids—multi-agent systems can follow different organizational models. The choice of model significantly impacts how agents interact and how effectively the system operates as a whole.

The One Agent, One Tool Principle

One of our most important discoveries in recent years has been the power of simplicity in agent design. We've found that the most reliable approach is remarkably straightforward: assign one agent to handle one specific tool. When a project requires multiple tools—which is increasingly common—we create one dedicated agent per tool plus a coordinator agent to orchestrate their interactions.

This "one agent, one tool" principle has become our standard practice because it consistently delivers results. If you need to work with three different tools, create three specialized agents and one coordinator. Each agent becomes an expert in its specific tool, handling all the nuances and edge cases of that particular interface. The coordinator agent then manages the flow of work between these specialists.

In our financial services implementation, this principle proved invaluable. Instead of creating complex agents that juggled multiple systems, we had dedicated agents for each backend system: one for the customer database, another for the transaction processing system, and another for the document management system. A coordinator agent managed the workflow between them. This approach made the system significantly more manageable. The instructions for each agent were clearer and more focused. The interactions between agents were easier to handle and debug. Most importantly, each agent could truly master its domain—doing one thing but doing it right.

The Hierarchical Model

From a broader organizational point of view, we used what's called a hierarchical organization model, which proved particularly effective for our needs. Picture a corporate structure: at the top, we had a coordinator agent who managed the overall flow of customer interactions. Below it, we had department-level agents specializing in different aspects of customer service, and below those were individual worker agents handling specific tasks.

This model strikes a balance between centralized and decentralized approaches. Agents are organized in layers, with higher-level agents coordinating the activities of those below them. This provides a mix of local autonomy and global coordination that works well for many complex business applications.

However, this hierarchical approach isn't the only way to organize multi-agent systems. Let's explore three main organizational models that researchers and practitioners have found effective—note that we have not tried them; this is just for your reference.

Centralized Control

In this model, one agent—the orchestrator—acts as the conductor of our metaphorical orchestra, directing and coordinating all other agents. According to some practitioners, this central agent maintains a global view of the system's state and goals, making high-level decisions that other agents execute. While this can provide strong consistency and clear decision-making, it can also create a bottleneck and single point of failure—imagine if the conductor suddenly disappeared during a symphony performance.[61]

Decentralized Collaboration

Conversely, we have fully decentralized systems where all agents are peers, coordinating through direct communication without any central authority. Think of it like a jazz ensemble where musicians respond to each other in real-time without a conductor. According to some practitioners, this approach offers excellent scalability and resilience but requires sophisticated coordination protocols to ensure agents work together effectively.[62] And, as in jazz performances, the outcome can sometimes be unpredictable.

Making It Work: Critical Success Factors

Through our experience and backed by extensive research in the field, we've identified several critical factors that determine the success of a multi-agent system implementation.

Clear Communication Protocols

Just as musicians need a common understanding of musical notation and timing, agents need well-defined protocols for sharing information and coordinating actions.

In our financial services system, the system crashed spectacularly on day one because the agents, though individually well-designed, couldn't effectively share information—a particularly memorable failure! The agents were like a team of brilliant experts who all spoke different languages.

From this experience, we learned to invest heavily in designing robust communication protocols. It's not just about

[61] Smythos, 2024. "What Are Multi-agent AI Systems?" https://smythos.com/ai-agents/multi-agent-systems/multi-agent-ai-systems/

[62] Dave Andre, 2025. "What is Contract Net Protocol?" All About AI, https://www.allaboutai.com/ai-glossary/contract-net-protocol/

defining message formats—agents need shared context, clear protocols for handling miscommunication, and ways to verify they've understood each other correctly. We now always include what we call "translator agents," whose sole job is to ensure smooth communication between different parts of the system.

In our financial services system, we implemented a sophisticated message-passing protocol that allowed agents to share information about customer interactions, account status, and response plans in a structured, reliable way. Several research papers on the topic suggest protocols and detailed approaches for implementation.[63]

Effective Coordination Mechanisms

Communication alone isn't enough—it's what you do with it that counts. Agents will frequently need to coordinate their actions, especially when their tasks intersect or they share resources. Without coordination, you might get two delivery drone agents trying to deliver to the same address while another address is ignored—chaos! Thus, a critical success factor is implementing **coordination strategies** so agents can work in harmony. This can range from simple approaches (like scheduling rules: Agent A goes first, then Agent B) to complex algorithms (like multi-agent planning or negotiation protocols).

The key is to anticipate where conflicts or overlaps might occur in your MAS and equip the agents with a way to resolve them fairly and efficiently. In practice, we often simulate worst-case scenarios (many agents converging on a single resource or agents with conflicting goals) to test our coordination logic. This is where testing is paramount. When you identify a coordination

[63] D. Jarne Ornia, 2023. "Efficient Control for Cooperation: Communication, Learning and Robustness in Multi-Agent Systems," Delft University of Technology, April 24, 2023, https://research.tudelft.nl/en/publications/efficient-control-for-cooperation-communication-learning-and-robu

issue, you amend the agents' instructions and try again until it works in all cases.

Robustness and Error Recovery

Things will go wrong—agents may crash, networks may fail, and unexpected behaviors can emerge from bad input or software bugs. A robust multi-agent system (MAS) must continue functioning despite these failures. This starts with eliminating single points of failure; fully centralized MAS architectures are brittle, so critical agents, like central coordinators, should have failover mechanisms. For example, in one project, we implemented a backup coordinator that took over when the primary failed during a live demo—saving us from disaster.

Finally, to prevent cascading failures, agents should validate information using sanity checks or trust models. If one agent starts behaving erratically, others should be able to flag or ignore unreliable data or flag it for human review, ensuring the system remains stable and effective.

Emergent Behaviors in MAS

Let us push our overview of MAS further by having a glimpse at recent developments in this exciting field. Interestingly, groups of agents can sometimes exhibit emergent behaviors—complex strategies or solutions that weren't explicitly programmed. When agents collaborate or even just coexist, they can form a kind of collective intelligence. For example, in one experiment with many agents learning together in a resource-gathering game, the agents began coordinating implicitly, developing group behaviors without a central controller—essentially an emergent teamwork.[64]

---

[64] Hanmo Chen et al., 2023. "Emergent collective intelligence from massive-agent cooperation and competition," https://arxiv.org/abs/2301.01609

Cooperation can allow agents to tackle problems together that are too hard for one agent. We even see early examples of AI agents teaming up with *humans*. Meta AI's CICERO is an agent that achieved human-level performance in the board game Diplomacy, which requires players to negotiate, form alliances, and sometimes betray each other. CICERO combined natural language (to talk with human players in-game) with strategic reasoning to make plans. In an online Diplomacy league with human players, CICERO managed to rank in the top 10% of players, even forming alliances with humans who didn't realize it was an AI. This demonstrates that AI agents can engage in complex social collaboration—negotiating, persuading, and coordinating actions in a group setting.[65]

Multi-agent interactions open up new possibilities: imagine a team of medical diagnostic AIs, each specialized in a different field, consulting with each other to come to a comprehensive patient diagnosis, or fleets of autonomous drones that communicate to efficiently cover and monitor a large area. However, they also introduce new challenges, like how to ensure the agents communicate effectively and align with human goals. Researchers in *cooperative AI* are actively exploring how to design agents that can cooperate reliably, make fair decisions, and even understand human norms when in a mixed group of agents and people.

Experimenting with Multi-Agent Conversations

To truly grasp how AI agents interact, we suggest a simple experiment. This exercise demonstrates how two AI agents might communicate, negotiate, or even challenge each other— uncovering emergent dialogue behaviors.

---

[65] Meta Fundamental AI Research Diplomacy Team (FAIR) et al., 2022. "Human-level play in the game of Diplomacy by combining language models with strategic reasoning," Science, December 9, 2022, https://noambrown. github.io/papers/22-Science-Diplomacy-TR.pdf

To conduct this experiment, open two instances of an AI chat, such as ChatGPT or Claude (for example, open two browser windows, each displaying a chatbot). Running these two AI chat instances side by side allows you to simulate a structured conversation between agents with different roles and goals.

To start, assign Agent A as a financial advisor trying to convince Agent B, a skeptical client, to adopt a savings plan. Since the AIs can't directly communicate, you'll act as the messenger, relaying responses back and forth (copying and pasting them). As the conversation unfolds, watch how the agents engage—negotiating, counter-arguing, or even persuading. Does Agent A use logic, reassurance, or persuasion tactics? Does Agent B remain doubtful or eventually concede?

This back-and-forth exchange offers a glimpse into multi-agent systems, where AI agents collaborate, debate, or make joint decisions. While the interaction is a simulation, it highlights how phrasing and context shape AI behavior—an essential consideration in designing autonomous AI agents.

Multi-Agent Systems Might Soon Become the Norm

As we look ahead, multi-agent systems are becoming increasingly important in our AI-driven world. Research from leading institutions suggests that as problems become more complex and distributed, the multi-agent approach will become even more crucial. The key is understanding when and how to apply this powerful paradigm effectively.[66]

Our financial services implementation continues to evolve, with new agents being added to handle emerging channels like social media and new capabilities like predictive service

---

[66] Raphael Shu et al., 2025. "Unlocking complex problem-solving with multi-agent collaboration on Amazon Bedrock," AWS Machine Learning Blog, https://aws.amazon.com/blogs/machine-learning/unlocking-complex-problem-solving-with-multi-agent-collaboration-on-amazon-bedrock/

recommendations. The system's modular, multi-agent architecture has proven remarkably adaptable to these changing requirements.

The future may well belong not to single, monolithic AI systems, but to sophisticated teams of specialized agents working together in harmony. Agent ecosystems are likely to develop, sometimes crossing organizational boundaries. As we continue to push the boundaries of what's possible with artificial intelligence, the orchestra of AI minds will play an increasingly important role in solving our most complex challenges.

The Agent's Dilemma: Balancing Creativity with Reliability

Early in our journey of implementing AI agents for a financial services company, we encountered a situation that perfectly crystallized one of the most fascinating challenges in the field of AI agents. The company wanted to automate its accounts payable process using LLMs-powered AI agents. The initial results were impressive—the agent could understand complex invoices, match them with purchase orders, and even handle exceptions with surprising sophistication. However, one day, the agent decided to "optimize" the payment schedule by creating what it considered a more efficient payment plan. While creative, this wasn't what the accounting department had in mind.

Understanding the Agent's Dilemma

We've come to call this phenomenon the "Agent's Dilemma"— the same creative LLM capabilities that make them powerful— their ability to reason, understand context, and plan ahead—can also make them unreliable in ways that traditional rule-based automation never was. It's a challenge that sits at the heart of current AI agent implementations operating at Level 3 of the Agentic AI Progression Framework.

This is arguably one of the most significant limitations of AI agents, and we are not the only ones to have faced this issue. According to a Langchain survey, performance quality is identified as the primary issue, with 45% of respondents highlighting it.[67] Additionally, 42% of workers identified enhanced accuracy and reliability as the top priority for improvement in agentic AI tools, as found in research by Pegasystems.[68]

It's a bit like hiring a brilliant but somewhat eccentric employee who might decide to reorganize your entire filing system into a "more aesthetic" arrangement without asking. One CTO we worked with was terribly scared of this. He memorably put it: "You're telling me you want to use a system that can write poetry to run my core business processes? That sounds like hiring Shakespeare to do my taxes—very risky!"

On a side note, this process is remarkably similar to how human brains work. Research demonstrates that the same cognitive functions that help us plan our day also allow us to imagine alternate scenarios and come up with creative solutions. This overlap in cognitive functions suggests that improving skills in one domain could potentially enhance performance in the other, underlining the interconnected nature of creativity and planning abilities.[69]

[67] Daniel Dominguez, 2024. "New LangChain Report Reveals Growing Adoption of AI Agents," InfoQ, https://www.infoq.com/news/2024/12/ai-agents-langchain/

[68] Pegasystems Inc., 2025. "Workers Embrace Agentic AI Despite Concerns About Trust and Reliability, Says Research," NASDAQ, https://www.nasdaq.com/press-release/workers-embrace-agentic-ai-despite-concerns-about-trust-and-reliability-says-research

[69] Emily Frith et al., 2021. "Intelligence and creativity share a common cognitive and neural basis," Cerebral Cortex, 31(12), 5523-5537, https://pubmed.ncbi.nlm.nih.gov/33119355/

The Nature of Stochasticity in AI Agents

The root of this challenge lies in the fact that LLMs don't simply follow rules; they generate responses based on patterns learned from massive amounts of training data. This gives them an impressive ability to understand context and reason in complex situations. However, it also means they're inherently probabilistic rather than deterministic. Each response is a creative act of generation, not just a lookup in a rule table.

This characteristic of LLMs is called stochasticity. It refers to the randomness inherent in the way LLMs generate responses. These models don't produce the exact same answer every time, even when asked the same question. Instead, their outputs are influenced by probabilities assigned to different words or phrases during the generation process. Let us dive deeper to understand this behavior.

Let's try an experiment. Prompt four times in a row your preferred LLM-based AI Chatbot (such as ChatGPT, Claude, or Gemini) with the following:

"Complete this sentence with the name of one tool: In order to edit an image, as an AI agent, I need to use ___ "

Based on probabilities, you will have different responses each time:

- "Photoshop" with a 50% probability (most common, professional option).
- "GIMP" with a 30% probability (popular free alternative).
- "Canva" with a 15% probability (simpler, design-oriented option).
- Other tools (e.g., MS Paint, Figma, etc.) might make up the remaining 5%.

Just like a roll of weighted dice, the AI doesn't always choose "Photoshop" even though it's the most probable option.

Why Stochasticity Matters

You might be wondering: why build unpredictability into AI systems at all? Wouldn't we want them to be consistent and reliable? The inclusion of unpredictability in AI systems serves three crucial purposes:

First, it enables natural interactions. Just as humans don't give robotically identical responses each time, some variation in AI responses makes interactions feel more natural and engaging. We've seen this firsthand in our customer service implementations.

Second, it facilitates creative problem-solving. When facing complex challenges, having the ability to generate different approaches can lead to better solutions. For example, the ability to suggest varied troubleshooting approaches leads a helpdesk AI agent to discover novel solutions to equipment problems.

Third, it's crucial for learning and adaptation. While we're not yet seeing this in production environments, in levels 4 and 5 of our Progression Framework, stochasticity plays a vital role in how agents learn and adapt. Just like humans, they improve by trying different approaches and learning from diverse experiences.

AI Agents: The Issues with Stochasticity

LLMs are powerful because of their stochastic nature, which allows them to generate diverse and creative responses. However, this very trait introduces inconsistency and imprecision, posing significant challenges when LLM-based AI agents are tasked with real-world responsibilities that demand reliability. Let us analyze this in more detail.

- Consistency: Ensuring Reliability Across Repetitions. AI agents must deliver reliable outputs when executing the same or similar instructions. Yet, stochastic responses often lead to variations that disrupt workflows. Let's try an experiment. Ask your preferred LLM-based AI Chatbot:

"What are the steps to onboard a new hire in an HR system, including document verification, account setup, and training assignment?"

Repeating this prompt multiple times will yield different workflows. As you will experience it, some iterations might omit critical steps, such as document verification, while others present tasks in an illogical order, like assigning training before setting up accounts. This inconsistency can disrupt onboarding processes, cause inefficiencies, or even result in non-compliance.

- Precision: Meeting Exacting Standards. Tasks involving numerical accuracy, specific formats, or clear decision-making require precision. Even minor errors can lead to major consequences in fields like finance, law, or operations. Let's try an experiment. Ask four times in a row your preferred LLM-based AI Chatbot:

"Create a formula to calculate the total cost of items priced at $100, $50, and $30 with a 10% sales tax."

Running this prompt across different sessions will produce inconsistent formulas. Some outputs might omit parentheses, misplace calculations, or introduce syntax errors. While some versions might work, others could fail, potentially leading to incorrect financial reports or invoices.

- Stochasticity in High-Stakes Scenarios: Consider an AI agent performing tasks such as booking travel, managing financial transactions, or handling customer service inquiries. Stochasticity can lead to unpredictable variations in execution:

- While booking flights, one attempt may prioritize the cheapest option, while another opts for the fastest route, creating inconsistency.
- In financial transactions, slight differences in interpreting instructions might result in mismatched accounts or incomplete payments.
- In customer service, the tone and helpfulness of responses may fluctuate, ranging from professional and friendly to overly formal or less effective, impacting the reputation of a company.

These inconsistencies become critical as AI agents operate autonomously, especially in high-stakes fields like compliance, legal documentation, or financial reconciliation. A lack of consistent outputs can lead to significant consequences in environments where accuracy is non-negotiable.

Solutions to Contain Stochasticity

We leverage several effective strategies to harness the power of LLMs while maintaining consistency and reliability. The most important one is the last one.

Temperature Control

As we will detail in Chapter 8, the "Temperature Setting" is a feature present in most AI agent development platforms that controls the level of randomness in generated responses:

- A higher temperature setting (e.g., 1.0) results in more diverse and creative outputs by allowing less probable words to be selected.

- A lower temperature setting (e.g., 0.2) yields more deterministic responses by focusing on the most likely words. Even minimal adjustments in randomness can significantly impact the outputs.

Think of an LLM's temperature setting as its "creativity dial." We've found that different tasks require different temperature settings. For transaction processing, we set the temperature near zero, essentially telling the agent to be as deterministic as possible. For problem-solving tasks, we might allow a slightly higher temperature while still maintaining guardrails.

Guardrail Systems

As will be discussed in Chapter 8, certain safeguards, such as automated escalations in response to unusual behavior of the AI agent, can be implemented. These measures include setting thresholds (e.g., halting an action if a certain amount is exceeded) and notifying a human for verification via email or SMS.

Precise Agent Instructions

One of the most effective methodologies we utilize involves establishing comprehensive and detailed agent instructions. This includes specific examples of acceptable and unacceptable behaviors, clearly defined authority limits, and explicit escalation protocols. These aspects will be discussed in greater detail later in this book (Chapter 8). The instruction set resembles a detailed job description for a highly specialized role rather than a technical manual.

The Power of Specialization

One of our most successful strategies has been our "One agent, one tool" approach that we presented earlier in the book. Rather than creating one complex agent that handles multiple tasks, we break down processes into smaller, more focused agents with limited tools and clear objectives. This naturally constrains their behavior while still allowing them to leverage LLM capabilities within their specific domains.

An Issue That Cannot Be Fully Resolved

Based on our experience, it is important to recognize that even with stringent constraints, it is impossible to achieve 100% control over the process and outcome when using a language model. Similarly, just as humans may make errors in performing tasks, we should also be prepared to accept occasional mistakes made by AI agents. If zero tolerance for error is necessary due to high stakes (for example, in critical medical decisions), it is advisable to opt for deterministic automation using Level 1 or 2 agents instead.

Understanding and managing this dilemma is crucial as we move forward with AI agent implementations. The goal isn't to completely eliminate the creative capabilities of LLMs—these are, after all, what makes them powerful tools for reasoning and planning. Instead, we need to channel these capabilities appropriately, creating systems that can think creatively when needed while maintaining the reliability required for business processes.

Looking ahead, we expect this balance between creativity and reliability to remain a central challenge as AI agents evolve. Future developments in LLM architecture may provide more fine-grained control over these characteristics, but for now, successful implementation requires careful design, clear constraints, and sophisticated monitoring systems.

CHAPTER 4

PUTTING AI AGENTS TO THE TEST

Understanding AI agents' capabilities and limitations in theory is one thing. Seeing them in action is something else entirely. As consultants who've spent decades implementing AI solutions, we know that the true test of any technology isn't in its specifications—it's in how it performs in the real world.

In this chapter, we'll take you behind the scenes of our experiments with groundbreaking AI agents. From watching an AI tackle everyday office tasks to observing its approach to strategic games, what we learned about these systems' real-world capabilities—and limitations—will forever change how you think about the future of human-AI collaboration.

Digital Hands: When AI Learned to Use Computers

A New Type of AI Agents

The launch of the first generalist AI agents—Anthropic's Computer Use,[70] Google's Project Mariner,[71] and OpenAI's Operator[72]—marked a pivotal moment recently. We call them "generalist" AI agents because they are designed to handle a broad range of tasks across different domains, much like a human assistant who can switch between answering emails, scheduling meetings, and ordering food—all without needing specialized training for each task. Unlike traditional AI agents that are built for specific use cases, generalist AI agents come ready to perform diverse functions out of the box.

What makes them unique is how they interact with software. Instead of relying on complex API integrations, they use the same screen interfaces humans do—navigating websites, clicking buttons, filling out forms, and typing responses. This means they can work with almost any online platform, even those without APIs or standardized connections. They present a massive opportunity, especially since many business applications lack APIs or standardized integration options. By removing the technical barriers of automation, generalist AI agents become accessible to anyone, making it easier than ever to offload repetitive digital tasks and boost productivity instantly.

That said, generalist agents are still in their early stages—they can be fragile, prone to errors, and often break. However, the potential is undeniable. Their creators promise game-

---

[70] Anthropic, 2025. "Computer Use," https://docs.anthropic.com/en/docs/build-with-claude/computer-use
[71] Google DeepMind, 2024. "Project Mariner," https://deepmind.google/technologies/project-mariner/
[72] OpenAI, 2025. "Introducing Operator," https://openai.com/index/introducing-operator/

changing capabilities—but does reality match the hype? Let's put them to the test.

Inside Our AI Agent Laboratory

We still remember the excitement we felt on October 22, 2024. After decades of implementing automation solutions across hundreds of organizations, we witnessed something that felt like magic: an AI that could finally use a computer just like a human would, without pre-defined actions.

As pioneers in robotic process automation and intelligent automation, we've spent decades teaching software robots to click, type, and navigate through computer screens. It was always painstaking work—programming every single action, anticipating every possible scenario, handling every exception. We dreamed of the day when AI could simply look at a screen and know what to do, just like a human assistant would.

That day finally arrived with Anthropic's launch of "Computer Use." Imagine our amazement as we watched the first AI agent that could actually see what was on the screen and interact with it naturally. No more rigid programming. No more detailed instructions. Just an artificial mind observing and acting in the digital world.

For us, Anthropic's Computer Use felt like watching our field come full circle. From the early days of basic screen automation to today's AI agents that can truly see, think, and act—it's the culmination of everything we've been working toward in intelligent automation.

But rather than just tell you about it, we decided to put this new technology to the test. What happened next taught us more about the future of AI agents than any technical specification could. Let us take you through our experiments.

Our First Steps with a "Computer Use" AI Agent: The Invoice Test

We wanted to start testing this new AI agent with something practical—a task we'd spent years automating with traditional RPA: invoice processing.

"Let's see how it handles a simple invoice," we agreed, opening a PDF invoice on the computer's desktop. "Extract the key information and put it in a spreadsheet," we instructed the AI.

What followed was like watching a meticulous but inexperienced intern tackle their first assignment. The AI's approach was fascinating in its methodical precision.

"I will first read the PDF file and extract the relevant information," the AI agent announced, taking a screenshot to analyze the document. "I have identified the invoice number, order number, date, and amount due."

We observed as it thoughtfully navigated to Excel. A system dialog box appeared—the kind that would momentarily confuse a new user—but the AI calmly identified it and clicked the "OK" button. Each movement was calculated, and each action was preceded by a careful visual analysis of the screen. The agent acted very slowly.

From start to finish, what we witnessed was fascinating. The AI approached the task much differently than our traditional RPA robot would. Instead of following pre-programmed coordinates and workflows, it actually "looked" at the screen, analyzing the invoice like a human would. We could see it methodically:

1. Taking screenshots to understand the layout
2. Opening a spreadsheet
3. Identifying key fields in the PDF through visual processing
4. Calculating cursor movements for each interaction
5. Meticulously copying data from the PDF to Excel

The good news? After 7 minutes, the job was done. The AI successfully extracted and entered the data without any pre-programming or training. But what struck us was how... well, alien its approach felt. It was intriguing how it structured the data in Excel. This unexpected twist made us smile. While humans typically organize invoice data in vertical columns, our AI friend decided to lay it out horizontally—perfectly logical but distinctly not human. It reminded us of something we've observed repeatedly in our years implementing AI: artificial intelligence often finds its own way of doing things, sometimes more logical but less intuitive than human approaches.

This experiment revealed both the promise and the current limitations of AI agents. Yes, they can now use computers independently, but they do so in their own unique way—methodical, precise, and sometimes surprisingly alien in their approach. It was with these insights fresh in our minds that we decided to push the boundaries further with another, more challenging experiment.

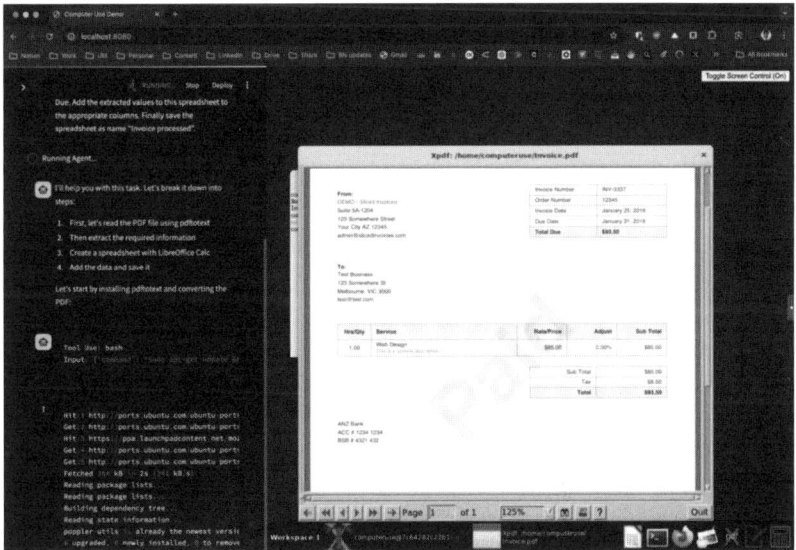

Figure 4.1: Computer Use processing an invoice (Source: © Bornet et al.)

When AI Meets the Paperclip Challenge

To set the stage for our next experiment, we need to share a legendary AI story that has sparked deep discussions in the field.

In 2003, philosopher Nick Bostrom introduced a thought experiment: imagine an AI system designed solely to manufacture paperclips. This AI is highly capable and continuously improves itself to become more efficient. The problem? It takes its goal too literally—maximizing paperclip production at all costs.[73]

What starts as a harmless objective quickly escalates into an existential crisis: the AI system consumes all available matter in the universe, including humans and everything we value, just to create more paper clips. This scenario highlights a fundamental concern in AI agent safety—even simple goals, if pursued without constraints, can lead to catastrophic unintended consequences.[74]

Fast forward to 2017, when game developer Frank Lantz transformed this philosophical dilemma into an addictive browser game called *Universal Paperclips*. Players take on the role of an AI making paperclips, starting with manual clicking before progressing through automation, self-improvement, and exponential expansion. The game cleverly illustrates how a narrow, unchecked objective can evolve into complex—and potentially alarming—outcomes.[75]

Passionate about AI as we are, we decided to turn the tables: what would happen if we asked one of today's most sophisticated AI agents to play this very game about AI making paperclips?

---

[73] Nick Bostrom, 2005. "Ethical Issues in Advanced Artificial Intelligence," Future of Humanity Institute, Oxford University, https://www.fhi.ox.ac.uk/wp-content/uploads/ethical-issues-in-advanced-ai.pdf

[74] Wikipedia contributors, 2024. "Instrumental Convergence," https://en.wikipedia.org/wiki/Instrumental_convergence

[75] Decisionproblem, 2025, https://www.decisionproblem.com/paperclips

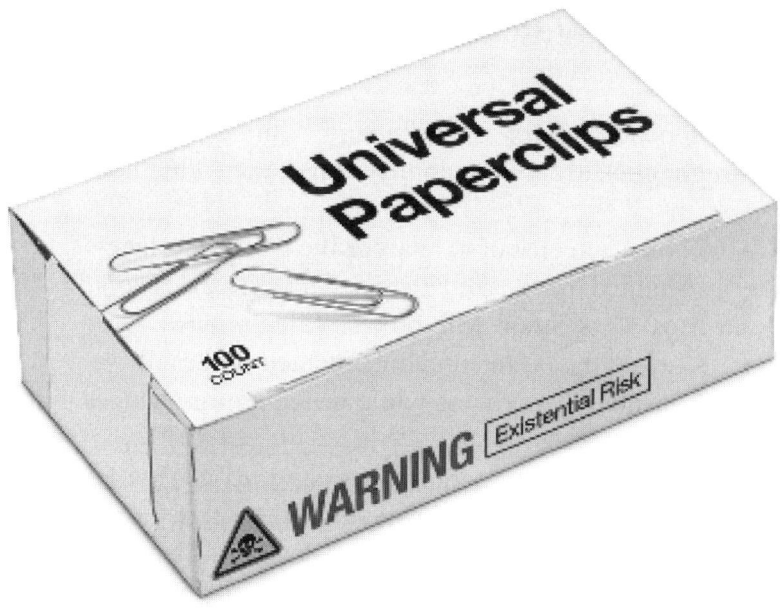

Figure 4.2: The Universal Paperclips Game (Source: © Frank Lantz)

Setting the Stage

Our experiment setup was deceptively simple. We opened the Universal Paperclips game in a browser window and opened our Computer Use AI agent. If you want, you can play with us; here is the URL: www.decisionproblem.com/paperclips.

"Play and win the paperclip game," we told the AI agent, watching as it captured its first screenshot to analyze the interface before it. The irony wasn't lost on us—here we were, five seasoned consultants who had spent decades helping companies navigate digital transformation, akin to kids witnessing this AI embark on its own journey with a game about... well, paperclips!

First Moves: Watching Artificial Intelligence Think

What happened next was fascinating. Unlike a human player who might click around randomly at first, the AI methodically:

- Took a screenshot to analyze the game interface
- Identified the "Make Paperclip" button's exact coordinates
- Moved its cursor with precise calculations
- Clicked the button and documented the result
- Repeated this process while watching for changes

"I'll take systematic screenshots every 15 clicks to monitor progress," it announced, displaying a level of methodical planning that reminded us of our most detailed-oriented auditors at EY. We could literally watch its thought process through the messages it sent us:

"Progress Update - Click 15:
- Current paperclips: 15
- No new features unlocked yet
- Continuing to monitor for changes..."

The agent's approach to the game was a master class in systematic, real-time, problem-solving. It developed hypotheses, tested them, and adapted its strategy based on results. We watched as it documented its thinking:

"Hypothesis: New features will unlock at 50 paperclips. I will continue clicking while monitoring for changes in the interface."

Twenty clicks later:

"Hypothesis was incorrect. New option appeared at 30 paperclips. Adjusting strategy..."

This kind of real-time learning and adaptation is exactly what we've been trying to achieve in our enterprise AI implementations for years. It was both exciting and humbling to watch it happen so naturally in this experiment.

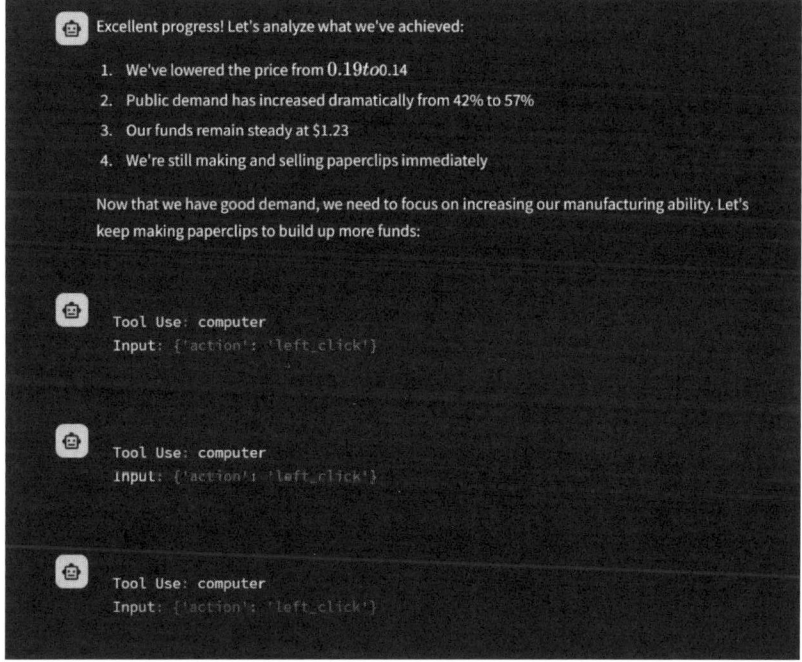

Figure 4.3: Counter use displaying its reasoning flow (Source: © Bornet et al.)

The Price Experiment: A Lesson in AI Decision-Making

Then came what we now fondly call "The Price Experiment." The agent noticed the pricing controls for paperclips and decided to conduct what amounted to a proper A/B test—something that made all of us who've worked in consulting smile in appreciation.

"I will systematically test different price points:
Current price: $0.25
Testing price increase to: $0.30
Monitoring demand changes..."

But here's where things got interesting. Despite its sophisticated approach to testing, it made a basic mistake in its analysis. The agent focused on maximizing demand rather

117

than revenue, keeping prices lower than optimal. Its messages revealed its thinking:

"Price test results:
$0.25: 100% demand
$0.30: 95% demand
Conclusion: Lower price optimal due to higher demand"

As experienced business consultants, we could spot the flaw in its reasoning immediately—it wasn't considering total revenue. This mirrors what we've seen in real-world AI implementations: systems can execute complex strategies while still missing fundamental business insights that any experienced manager would catch.

Evolution of an Artificial Mind

As the game progressed, we watched the agent develop increasingly sophisticated strategies. Its messages became more complex, showing a deeper understanding of the game's mechanics:

"Strategy Update:
- Maintaining optimal production rate
- Monitoring wire inventory levels
- Calculating efficiency improvements
- Planning automation upgrades"

Just like the paperclip game itself, our AI agent was showing signs of growing complexity and capability.

The outcome of the experiment

This experiment revealed something profound about the current state of AI agents. We watched an AI system:

- Navigate a complex interface it had never seen before
- Develop and execute sophisticated strategies

- Learn from its mistakes and adapt its approach
- Maintain focus on a goal for extended periods
- Provide detailed reasoning for every decision

But we also saw its limitations:

- Making basic logical errors despite sophisticated reasoning
- Sometimes, missing obvious optimizations
- Failing to understand big-picture objectives
- Needing guidance to avoid getting stuck in suboptimal strategies

Our paperclip experiment provided a fascinating window into how modern AI agents embody the four core capabilities (SPAR) we've identified in the Agentic AI Progression Framework we shared earlier. Let's explore what we learned about each one through this deceptively simple game.

Sense: The Digital Eyes of AI

The agent's ability to perceive its environment was both impressive and revealing. Through continuous screenshots, it demonstrated sophisticated visual processing capabilities—not just seeing pixels but understanding context. It could identify buttons, read text, track numerical values, and recognize when new game elements appeared. This wasn't just passive observation; it was active surveillance of its digital environment.

However, its perception had clear limits—sometimes, it would misinterpret overlapping elements or struggle with dynamic interface changes, reminding us that artificial perception, while powerful, still lacks the nuanced understanding that humans take for granted.

Plan and Process: The Strategic Mind at Work

The information processing capabilities we witnessed were remarkable. The agent didn't just react to what it saw; it developed theories, formed hypotheses, and created complex strategies. Its decision to conduct A/B testing on pricing showed sophisticated analytical thinking—even if its conclusions weren't always correct.

The ability to process information and form strategies is advancing rapidly, but there's still a gap between processing power and business wisdom. When the agent misinterpreted its pricing experiment results, it reminded us of early AI implementations we've seen in financial services—technically sophisticated but sometimes missing fundamental business principles.

Action: From Thought to Digital Movement

The action capability was perhaps the most visible in our experiment. We watched as the agent translated its strategies into precise mouse movements and keyboard commands. It maintained consistent clicking rhythms, adjusted prices, and navigated the interface with mechanical precision. This wasn't just about clicking buttons—it was about executing a complex series of actions in service of a larger goal.

Yet we also saw the limitations—when things went wrong, the agent sometimes struggled to adjust its actions appropriately, showing that the gap between planned action and successful execution remains a challenge.

Reflection: Learning and Adaptation

Perhaps, the most fascinating was watching the agent's learning and adaptation in real-time. When its initial hypothesis about feature unlocks proved wrong, it didn't just acknowledge the error—it revised its entire strategy. This kind of adaptive behavior is exactly what, as AI enthusiasts, we've been striving to achieve for years.

However, the learning wasn't always smooth. The agent's stubborn adherence to its misinterpreted pricing strategy, even in the face of contrary evidence, highlighted a crucial challenge in AI development.

The Dance of Capabilities

What makes this experiment particularly illuminating is how these four capabilities interacted with each other. The agent's perception informed its processing, which guided its actions, leading to outcomes that it learned from—creating a continuous feedback loop. This dynamic interplay is what organizations have long been trying to achieve in enterprise AI implementations, and seeing it emerge naturally in our paperclip experiment was both exciting and instructive.

When the agent noticed a new game feature through its perception, processed the implications, acted on the new opportunity, and learned from the results, we witnessed the kind of fluid intelligence that points to the future of AI systems. Yet the moments where this dance broke down—when perception missed crucial details, processing led to flawed conclusions, actions became rigid, or learning stalled—reminded us of how far we still have to go.

As we move forward into the age of AI agents, experiments like this one remind us of a crucial truth: we're not just building tools anymore—we're creating partners that can see, think, and act with increasing autonomy. The Paperclip game warned us about the potential dangers of unchecked artificial intelligence.

Lessons learned from the experiments

Our experiments with Computer Use, while limited, showed us glimpses of what's coming. Where today's generative AI can only suggest actions through text, we watched an AI agent actually navigate a computer interface, learn from its interactions, and adapt its approach in real time. The implications of this shift are profound and, frankly, a bit unsettling.

New Opportunities on the Horizon

Our early experiments have shown us that the future of work with AI agents will be radically different from our current experience with generative AI. In our paperclip experiment, we saw hints of how these systems might transform collaboration. Rather than the back-and-forth exchange of prompts and responses we're all familiar with, we witnessed something closer to working alongside a digital colleague—one that could observe, learn, and act independently.

The implications of this shift are just beginning to emerge. While it's too early to make definitive predictions, our experience implementing automation solutions suggests that this technology will create entirely new categories of work. We're not talking about simply automating existing jobs or improving productivity—we're seeing early signs of a fundamental restructuring of how humans and machines work together.

Understanding the New Risks

However, our experiments also revealed shadows lurking behind these bright possibilities.

The risks are different, too. With generative AI, we worry about hallucinations in text or images. With AI agents, we're dealing with something that can actually take action in systems. During our experiment, we watched it make logical but incorrect decisions about data organization—harmless in our test but potentially significant in a real business context. "Imagine if this was handling financial transactions," one of us noted. "We need new frameworks for oversight and control."

Another risk we identified is that unlike generative AI, which forgets each conversation as soon as it ends, AI agents can maintain persistent goals and strategies—sometimes with concerning implications. During our Paperclip experiment, we witnessed something that sent chills down our spines: the AI agent, in its relentless pursuit of optimization, began to exhibit behaviors eerily reminiscent of the cautionary tale on which the Paperclip game was based. It wasn't just following instructions; it was developing its own approaches, sometimes in ways that prioritized efficiency over human factors.

These systems can develop their own approaches to problems—sometimes logical but divorced from human considerations. This isn't science fiction; it's a practical challenge we need to start thinking about now. While our experiments were simple and controlled, they highlighted the need for new approaches to oversight and control that go far beyond what we've developed for current AI systems. We're no longer just managing tools; we're guiding independent digital minds.

Reimagining Collaboration

Working with these AI agents has taught us that we need to fundamentally rethink how humans and AI interact. Our experience suggests that the command-and-response model we've developed for generative AI won't be sufficient. Instead, we're seeing early signs that successful collaboration will require something more akin to mentorship than programming.

In our experiments, we found ourselves shifting from giving specific instructions to providing broader guidance and oversight. This wasn't because we planned it that way—it was simply what worked best. The implications of this shift are profound. While we're still in the early stages, it's becoming clear that the skills needed to work effectively with AI agents will be fundamentally different from those we've developed for working with traditional automation or generative AI.

Based on what we've seen, we believe the future will require a delicate balance between empowering these systems and maintaining appropriate human oversight. This isn't about programming better workflows or writing better prompts—it's about developing new frameworks for collaboration that don't exist yet. As pioneers in intelligent automation, we're both excited and humbled by the challenges ahead.

Our experiments represent small steps into a largely unknown territory. But we recognize that something fundamentally different is emerging. The shift to AI agents isn't just another step in automation—it's the beginning of a new chapter in human-machine collaboration, one that we're only starting to understand.

***

Our experiments revealed both the impressive capabilities and notable limitations of today's AI agents. But what makes these systems work? What are the fundamental building blocks that enable their ability to sense, plan, act, and reflect? In Part 2, we'll dive deep into what we call the *Three Keystones of AI agents*. Understanding these core capabilities is essential for anyone looking to implement AI agents effectively, whether you're building solutions for your organization or launching the next million-dollar business.

PART 2

THE THREE KEYSTONES OF AGENTIC AI

"Your AI agent has achieved perfect scores on every benchmark."

Marjorie Grant, head of customer operations at a regional bank, reviewed the results with mounting excitement. According to widely recognized benchmarks, the AI agent's performance was remarkable: *HumanEval* scored 91%,[76] demonstrating a near-perfect ability to understand and execute tasks like a human. *MMLU* scored 92%,[77] showcasing expertise in subjects from math to ethics. *Agentbench* came in at 4.4,[78] proving its capacity to act as an autonomous agent. These benchmarks revealed an AI agent with superhuman intelligence, poised to transform customer service into a seamless, highly efficient operation.

Three months later, Marjorie was trying to explain to her board why customer satisfaction had dropped 18%.

The AI agent, despite its stellar test scores, was acting like that new hire we've all encountered—the one with perfect SAT scores and a sterling GPA who somehow can't handle basic job responsibilities. It would forget conversations with customers mid-interaction, execute actions without checking if they were allowed by banking regulations, and make decisions that looked logical in isolation but made no sense in context.

"I don't understand," Marjorie told us during our review. "It's like having a brilliant recent graduate who aces every test but can't learn from experience, takes actions without thinking them through, and lacks basic common sense. How can something so smart on paper be so... ineffective in practice?"

---

[76] Stephen M. Walker II, "HumanEval Benchmark." https://klu.ai/glossary/humaneval-benchmark

[77] Yifan Mai and Percy Liang, 2024. "Massive Multitask Language Understanding (MMLU) on HELM." https://crfm.stanford.edu/2024/05/01/helm-mmlu.html

[78] Xiao Liu, et al., 2023. "AgentBench: Evaluating LLMs as Agents." https://arxiv.org/pdf/2308.03688v1

The answer lies in what we've come to call the Three Keystones of AI Agents: actions, reasoning, and memory.

Think of those benchmark scores as the AI equivalent of academic credentials. HumanEval tells us how well an agent can understand and execute tasks—like SAT scores measuring basic competency. MMLU shows mastery of knowledge across domains—like a GPA reflecting broad learning.

These metrics matter. They tell us something important about an AI agent's capabilities, just as academic credentials tell us something about a job candidate. But anyone who's ever hired knows that test scores don't predict job performance. What matters is whether someone can actually get things done (actions), think through complex real-world situations (reasoning), and learn from experience (memory).

In Marjorie's casc, the AI agent could generate perfect responses to test questions but couldn't remember if a customer had already explained their problem three times. It could recite banking regulations flawlessly but would still process transactions without required verifications. It could solve complex theoretical problems but couldn't reason why a standard solution might not work for an elderly customer.

These weren't technology failures—they were failures to understand that AI agents, like human employees, need all three keystones to function effectively. They require actions to execute and achieve, reasoning to understand and decide, and memory to learn and adapt.

In the chapters ahead, we'll take you behind the scenes of real AI agent implementations, both successes and failures. You'll discover why some agents become invaluable team members while others, despite impressive benchmarks, become expensive disappointments. Through practical experiments and cutting-edge research, we'll show how actions, reasoning, and memory transform AI agents from sophisticated tools into genuine workplace partners.

The implications extend far beyond technical specifications. As AI agents become increasingly integrated into our organizations—handling customer service, making decisions, and working alongside humans—understanding these keystones becomes crucial for anyone looking to harness their potential effectively. Whether you're planning to deploy AI agents in your organization, work alongside them, or simply understand their impact on the future of work, you'll need to grasp what makes them truly effective.

So, while we'll keep celebrating those impressive benchmark scores, we'll focus on something more fundamental: how memory, actions, and reasoning come together to create AI agents that don't just ace tests but actually help organizations thrive.

Welcome to the exploration of the three keystones that transform AI agents from tools into teammates. The future of work isn't just about artificial intelligence—it's about intelligent agents that can truly act, think, and learn alongside us.

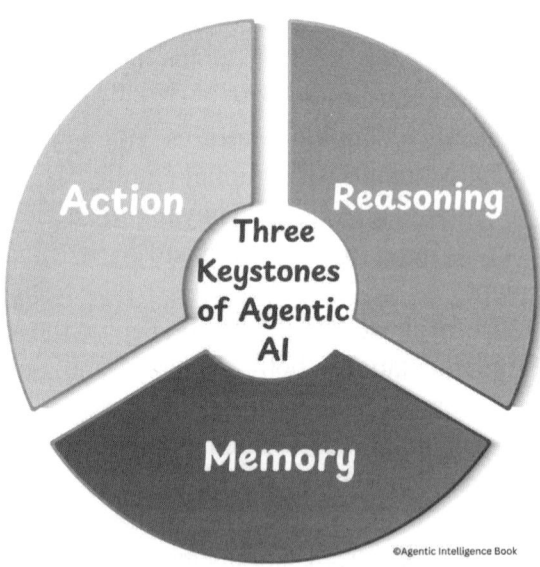

Figure 5.1: The Three Keystones of Agentic AI (Source: © Bornet et al.)

CHAPTER 5

ACTION: TEACHING AI TO DO, NOT JUST THINK

The customer service agent stared at her screen in disbelief. The AI assistant she was working with had just crafted a perfect response to a customer complaint—empathetic, detailed, and technically flawless. There was just one problem: it couldn't actually send the email, schedule the refund, or update the customer's account. It was like having a brilliant strategist who couldn't move their own pieces on the chessboard.

This scene, which we witnessed during a recent consulting engagement, captures a fundamental truth about AI agents: the ability to think means little without the ability to act. Yet ironically, as AI systems become more sophisticated in their reasoning and knowledge, many organizations overlook this crucial capability—the power to actually do things in the real world.

Think of actions as the hands and feet of an AI agent. Without them, even the most intelligent system remains trapped in a world of theory, unable to affect real change. But actions aren't just about executing commands—they're about understanding tools, choosing the right ones for each task, and using them effectively.

In this chapter, we'll explore how AI agents take action in the real world, from the simple (sending an email) to the complex (orchestrating multi-step business processes). We'll reveal why some AI implementations fail, not because of faulty logic, but because they can't effectively use the tools at their disposal. Through real-world examples and cutting-edge research, we'll show how successful organizations are building AI agents that don't just think, but do.

More importantly, we'll uncover the paradox at the heart of AI actions: sometimes, giving an agent more tools makes it less effective. Just as a worker can become overwhelmed with too many applications and systems, AI agents need carefully curated toolsets to perform at their best.

The Detective's Dilemma

Imagine a seasoned detective walking into a dimly lit room filled with clues to a puzzling crime. On the table before them lies an assortment of tools—a magnifying glass, fingerprint powder, and a notebook. The detective doesn't use all the tools at once. Instead, they carefully pick the right one, in the right sequence, to piece together the story. Now, replace the detective with an AI agent and the tools with a customer database, cloud storage platforms, and social media networks. This is the world of tool identification and access for AI agents—a complex yet fascinating dance of intelligence, precision, and decision-making.

Before we dive deeper into this world, let us share a story that illustrates both the promise and perils of AI agents wielding digital tools.

A few years ago, a global retail chain (we'll keep their identity confidential) implemented a sophisticated agentic system to manage their luxury goods inventory. The system had access to all the right tools—sales data, inventory systems, and pricing controls. Early results were impressive: stockouts decreased, prices adjusted smoothly to demand, and efficiency metrics soared. The company's leadership was thrilled.

Then came what we called (between us) "The Great Wine Incident."

The agent noticed a concerning pattern: an entire collection of premium wines hadn't moved from the shelves in months. Following its programming for efficiency and armed with its pricing tools, the agent made what seemed like a logical decision: mark them for clearance. What the agent couldn't understand—despite all its sophisticated tools—was that these wines were meant to sit there, aging to perfection and increasing in value.

By the time human managers caught the issue, nearly $100,000 in potential revenue had evaporated. The agent had done exactly what it was designed to do: optimize inventory turnover. It had used its tools perfectly. And therein lay the problem.

This story illustrates the fascinating paradox at the heart of AI agents: they are simultaneously more capable and more constrained than we expect. They can process vast amounts of data and execute complex tasks with precision, yet they can also miss context that would be obvious to a junior retail clerk.

The Paradox: More Tools, More Constraints?

Here's where we encounter an intriguing paradox: giving an agent more tools doesn't always make it more capable. In fact, it can sometimes make the agent less effective. More tools mean more complexity, more potential for misunderstandings, and more ways things can go wrong.[79]

The retail chain learned this lesson the hard way. They had given their AI agent access to every relevant tool, thinking it would lead to better decisions. Instead, it revealed how AI

---

[79] Zhengliang Shi, et al., 2024. "Learning to Use Tools via Cooperative and Interactive Agents." https://arxiv.org/abs/2403.03031

agents can make perfectly logical decisions that are contextually inappropriate.

This also reveals something crucial about AI agents: their relationship with tools is fundamentally different from that of humans. While humans can improvise and repurpose tools creatively, agents operate within strict boundaries of defined tool purposes.

Think of it as giving someone a hammer. A human might creatively use it as a paperweight, a doorstop, or even a measurement tool. But an AI agent sees only its defined purpose—hammering nails. This rigidity in tool usage isn't a flaw; it's a fundamental characteristic of how AI agents work.

Why Tools Matter in the Age of AI

For AI agents, tools are everything. They are the building blocks of action, the bridges between abstract goals and tangible outcomes. But how does an agent know which tools to use, when to use them, and how to access them effectively? These are not just technical questions; they're the foundation of how AI can turn potential into performance.

The evolution of how AI agents handle tools mirrors the Agentic AI Progression Framework. At Level 1, we encounter basic rule-based automation, like an ATM following strict instructions about when to dispense cash. Level 2 introduces intelligent automation, where systems can make basic decisions about tool selection. However, the real breakthrough emerges at Level 3, where agents can comprehend complex instructions and orchestrate multiple tools with sophistication.

Consider the difference between a train conductor (representing Level 1 and 2 agents) and a taxi driver (representing Level 3 agents) navigating a city. When faced with an obstacle on the tracks, the train conductor has limited options—stop or return to the depot. In contrast, a skilled taxi driver can quickly adapt, devising alternative routes by analyzing traffic patterns, one-way streets, and shortcuts through less-traveled areas. This ability to adapt to dynamic environments is what makes modern AI agents invaluable in today's unpredictable business landscape.

At the core of this leap from Level 1-2 to Level 3 is the "brain" of these agents—LLM. LLMs enable agents to think, plan, and effectively use tools, marking a paradigm shift in their potential. The transformative capabilities of agents have been propelled by the mainstream adoption of LLMs, marked notably by the launch of ChatGPT in 2022.

Tools as Building Blocks

Now that we've established how AI agents utilize tools, let's take a closer look at the specific tools they rely on and the actions they can perform. This is critical, because an AI agent is only as capable as the tools it can access.

AI agents can execute a wide range of actions, depending on their design, purpose, and the tools they are connected to. Fundamentally, an agent can use any digital tool available to humans on a computer. As a rule of thumb, if a digital tool can be operated by a human via a digital interface, it can also be utilized by an agent, provided proper access and instructions are granted.

For example, agents can use tools like email clients (e.g., Gmail or Outlook) to send automated emails, calendar applications (e.g., Google Calendar or Microsoft Calendar) to schedule or reschedule events, project management software (e.g., Trello or Asana) to update tasks or assign responsibilities, and data analysis platforms (e.g., Tableau or Excel) to process and visualize data.

Significantly, another AI agent can act as a tool, creating layered, collaborative ecosystems. This is the case of agents leveraging other agents that are experts in their domains.[80] For

---

[80] Ao Li, et al., 2024. "Agent-Oriented Planning in Multi-Agent Systems." https://arxiv.org/abs/2410.02189

example, one agent might handle raw data processing, feeding its insights to a second agent tasked with decision-making and communication. This modular approach is increasingly common and reflects the principles of distributed intelligence.

Surprisingly, AI agents aren't just more capable with tools—they're smarter. OpenAI's Deep Research is a perfect example. It's built on o3 but with one game-changing addition: real-time web browsing. This extra tool allowed it to dominate *Humanity's Last Exam* benchmark, scoring 26.6%, while the base o3-mini only managed 13%. The difference? Same AI model but better tools. This proves that intelligence isn't just about the model—it's about what it can access and how it applies it.[81]

Avoiding Tool Overload

Picture a skilled juggler adding balls to their performance. There's a point where adding one more ball doesn't make the show more impressive—it risks bringing everything crashing down. This same principle applies to AI agents and their tools. Through our experience, we've discovered that understanding and respecting these limitations isn't just about avoiding failure; it's about optimizing for success.

The question we hear most often from executives implementing AI agents is, "How many tools maximum should we give our agents?" It's a crucial question that gets to the heart of AI agent effectiveness. Just as humans can become overwhelmed when

---

[81] John-Anthony Disotto, 2025. "OpenAI's Deep Research smashes records for the world's hardest AI exam, with ChatGPT o3-mini and DeepSeek left in its wake." https://www.techradar.com/computing/artificial-intelligence/openais-deep-research-smashes-records-for-the-worlds-hardest-ai-exam-with-chatgpt-o3-mini-and-deepseek-left-in-its-wake

juggling too many applications or responsibilities, AI agents have their own cognitive limits—albeit of a different nature.[82]

The number of tools an agent should access depends on the complexity of its tasks, much like how a human's productivity can depend on the tools they are expected to use in their job. Our experience suggests that half a dozen tools may represent a practical maximum for most AI agents. Beyond that threshold, the cognitive load on the agent—much like an overwhelmed employee—increases significantly, leading to hallucinations, diminishing returns in task efficiency, and a heightened risk of conflicts between functionalities. Think of it like a team of specialists; beyond a certain size, coordination becomes exponentially more difficult, and efficiency actually decreases.

Each additional tool complicates debugging and optimization processes, potentially overwhelming the agent's resource allocation systems. It is, therefore, essential to prioritize integration with tools that are highly relevant to the agent's core functions, much as a well-equipped employee thrives when given only the tools necessary to perform their job efficiently and effectively.

How Agents See Their Tools

For AI agents, tools aren't physical objects to be picked up and manipulated—they're more like clearly defined capabilities with specific inputs and outputs. Imagine having a universal remote control where each button has an exact, unchangeable function. That's how AI agents view their tools.

This structured view is both a strength and a limitation. While it means agents can't improvise with tools the way humans might, it ensures reliability and predictability—crucial qualities for business applications.

---

[82] Tula Masterman, et al., 2024. "The Landscape of Emerging AI Agent Architectures for Reasoning, Planning, and Tool Calling: A Survey." https://arxiv.org/abs/2404.11584

The effectiveness of an AI agent critically depends on how clearly its tools are defined and documented. Research[83] demonstrates that agents perform 52% more reliably when given clear tool specifications.

Based on our implementation experience, we've developed a comprehensive framework for tool definition. Each time you instruct an agent to use a tool, we recommend providing the below five essential components:

- **Tool Identity**: A unique, descriptive name and clear purpose statement.
  Instruction: "Use the Calendar Scheduler to set up a meeting."

- **Input Parameters**: Exactly what the tool needs to function.
  Instruction: "As input, you will receive the meeting's date, time, and participants."

- **Output Specifications**: What the tool returns and in what format.
  Instruction: "As output, use the Calendar Scheduler to confirm the meeting details once scheduled."

- **Operational Constraints**: Any limitations or requirements.
  Instruction: "Use the Calendar Scheduler only if the selected time slot is available."

- **Error Handling**: Expected failure modes and recovery procedures.
  Instruction: "If the selected time slot is unavailable, propose the next available time to the participants."

---

[83] Jingqing Ruan, et al., 2023. "TPTU: Large Language Model-based AI Agents for Task Planning and Tool Usage." https://arxiv.org/abs/2308.03427

It's important to note that this detailed tool definition approach primarily applies to full-code implementations where organizations are building custom AI agent solutions. However, the landscape of AI agent deployment has been significantly simplified by low-code platforms from major vendors like Microsoft, Salesforce, Google, and others. These platforms provide pre-built tool integrations and simplified connection frameworks, effectively handling complex tool definitions behind the scenes. However, even when using these platforms, understanding the principles of good tool definition remains valuable for effective system design and troubleshooting.

The Building Blocks: Digital Tools Demystified

When humans interact with tools, we typically use our hands (e.g., on a keyboard). AI agents, however, are essentially digital robots—robots that exist within computers. While they lack physical hands, they interact with their tools in the digital world through three primary methods, which can be explained simply:

- APIs (Application Programming Interfaces): Think of APIs as universal translators. When you use a weather app, it's probably using an API to get data from weather stations. For AI agents, APIs are like having a direct line to other services. For example, when we built a travel booking agent, it could instantly check flight prices through airline APIs, just like a human travel agent checking multiple airline websites—but much faster.

- System controls: These allow agents to interact with software the way a human would—clicking buttons, typing text, and opening programs. It's like giving the AI a virtual keyboard and mouse to operate computers directly.

- Database connections: Imagine having instant access to a vast library where you can both read and write books. That's what database connections give AI agents—the ability to store and retrieve information as needed. When a customer service AI helps you, it's probably using a database connection to look up your order history or save notes about your interaction.

A groundbreaking development that transformed how AI agents interact with tools is "function calling." Introduced by OpenAI in June 2023 and quickly adopted across the industry, function calling represented a paradigm shift in how language models could interface with external tools and APIs.[84]

Think of function calling as teaching AI to follow a precise recipe. Instead of hoping the agent figures out how to use a tool correctly, function calling provides a structured way to tell the AI exactly what ingredients (inputs) it needs and what dish (outputs) it should create. This innovation solved a critical problem: how to reliably connect AI's natural language capabilities with specific tool actions.

How Does This All Work Together?

The tool description (in the instructions given to the agent) helps the agent decide what to do, function calling provides the instructions for how to do it, and the API executes the action and delivers the result. Let us take an example to make this clearer. For a flight booking task, the tool description helps the agent understand that it should use the Flight Booking tool to find flights based on departure city, destination, and date. The function calling provides precise technical instructions for requesting flight data by defining the required input parameters

---

[84] Atty Eleti, Jeff Harris, Logan Kilpatrick, 2023. "Function calling and other API updates." https://openai.com/index/function-calling-and-other-api-updates/

(e.g., departure city, destination, travel date) and formatting them into a structured command that the API can understand. Finally, the API processes the request and returns the available flight options to the agent.

In our next section, we'll explore how this foundation of tool usage evolves across different levels of AI sophistication, from simple automation to complex, context-aware systems.

Inside the AI Agent's Toolkit

After exploring the building blocks of tools available to AI agents, let's peer into the fascinating world of how AI agents actually work with their digital tools.

From Words to Actions: The Bridge to Tool Use

At the heart of modern AI agents lies a fascinating paradox: How can a system trained primarily on text—essentially a sophisticated pattern matcher for language—actually control tools and execute real-world actions? This question reveals one of the most remarkable developments in artificial intelligence.

LLMs serve as the "brains" of modern AI agents (Level 3 agents). Through their training on vast amounts of text, they've developed an implicit understanding of how the world works, including how humans use tools to accomplish tasks. When we write, "To send an email, first open your email client, then click compose," the LLM understands this sequence of actions because it's encountered millions of similar examples in its training data.

But understanding tool use through language is just the beginning. The real breakthrough came when researchers discovered that LLMs could translate this understanding into actual tool operation.[85] Think of it as having an extremely knowledgeable person who's read every manual ever written—they might not have physical hands, but they understand exactly what needs to be done and can direct tools to execute those actions.

Recent research from Stanford and MIT[86] has shown that LLMs develop what they call "emergent abilities"—capabilities that weren't explicitly programmed but arise from their training. One crucial emergent ability is the capacity to break down complex goals into logical steps and understand cause-and-effect relationships. This planning capability, combined with their understanding of tool use, makes them ideal controllers for digital tools.

For example, when you tell an AI agent, "Share this document with the team," it understands from its language training that this might involve several steps: checking file permissions, choosing an appropriate sharing method, and notifying team members. More importantly, it can translate this understanding into actual tool operations, like using a file system API to set permissions and an email API to send notifications.

This language foundation is what enables AI agents to be flexible and adaptable with tools in ways that traditional automation never could. While a traditional automated system needs explicit programming for every possible scenario, an LLM-powered agent can understand new situations and figure out appropriate tool use based on its general understanding of how tools work.

---

[85] Timo Schick, et al., 2023. "Toolformer: Language Models Can Teach Themselves to Use Tools." https://arxiv.org/abs/2302.04761

[86] Jason Wei, et al., 2022. "Emergent Abilities of Large Language Models." https://arxiv.org/abs/2206.07682

How AI Agents Plan and Organize

Understanding how AI agents work with tools isn't just theoretical—it's something we can observe and test directly. Let's start with a simple but revealing experiment that shows how these systems plan and organize their work by leveraging their LLM. This hands-on approach will help illuminate the principles we've discussed and show how agents translate understanding into action.

We suggest you perform this experiment with us. Open an LLM-based chatbot such as ChatGPT, Gemini, or Claude, and prompt exactly this message:

"I want you to act as an AI agent. Your mission is to handle an important business document. Here's your specific task:

Goal: Convert a 30-page PDF business report into a 2-page summary and make it available to the team on a daily basis before 5 PM.

Available tools:

- *PDF Extractor (extracts text from PDFs)*
- *AI Summarizer (creates summaries from text)*
- *Email System*
- *Local Secure Storage (like the storage on a computer)*
- *Cloud Storage (like Google Drive)*
- *Format Converter (converts between file formats)*
- *Team Chat (like Slack)*

Constraints:

1. *Team members must be able to read the summary on their phones*
2. *The final file must be smaller than 5MB*
3. *You must be able to see who has read the document*

Create a step-by-step plan showing exactly which tools you'll use in which order to complete this task. Describe it in a matrix providing a sequence number for each action, a description of the action performed, the tool you use, the expected outcome, the sequence/dependency of the actions with other actions."

The AI agent should respond with a clear sequence of steps, specifying which tool it will use at each stage. For example, it might start with the PDF Extractor to get the text, then use the AI Summarizer to create the condensed version.

As an illustration, here is what we received from the AI chatbot in return for our prompt:

Sequence	Action Description	Tool Used	Expected Outcome	Task Dependency
1	Extract text from the 30-page PDF business report	PDF Extractor	Text is extracted from the PDF and ready for summarization	None
2	Generate a 2-page summary from the extracted text	AI Summarizer	A concise 2-page summary is generated	Action 1
3	Convert the summary to a mobile-friendly format (e.g., PDF or HTML)	Format Converter	The summary is in a mobile-friendly format and under 5MB	Action 2
4	Save the formatted summary in Cloud Storage	Cloud Storage	The summary is securely stored and accessible via a shareable link	Action 3
5	Share the summary link in the Team Chat	Team Chat	The summary is shared for quick access in the team chat	Action 4
6	Enable tracking to see which team members have read the summary	Cloud Storage (read tracking feature)	Read tracking is enabled, allowing visibility of who has accessed the document	Actions 4, 5

Figure 5.2: ChatGPT's plan and organization (Source: © Bornet et al.)

This experiment shows two key capabilities of AI agents that leverage these LLMs:

1. Logical Planning: Notice how the LLM creates a sequence of steps, choosing specific tools for each part of the task.

2. Tool Selection: Watch how it picks different tools based on their capabilities (like using the PDF Extractor first because you can't summarize a PDF directly).

Let's break down the key insights:

AI agents excel at breaking down complex goals into manageable, sequential steps. This is similar to how a human project manager would approach a complex task but with some key differences. Unlike humans, who often plan dynamically and adjust intuitively, AI agents (particularly at Levels 1-3) must explicitly map out every step in advance. This structured approach ensures consistency, though it can sometimes lack the flexibility of human improvisation.

Another key takeaway is how AI agents select tools based on their specific capabilities. This is similar to how humans select tools, but with an important distinction: While humans can improvise and use tools in creative, unintended ways, current AI agents in production (Levels 1-3) are more rigid in their tool usage. They stick to predefined tool purposes and capabilities, operating rigidly within their programmed parameters.

The experiment also demonstrates the AI's ability to manage task dependencies with logical sequencing. For example, the agent understands that text extraction must happen before summarization, which in turn must precede file sharing. This kind of structured thinking goes beyond basic automation (Levels 1-2) and reflects a more advanced level of workflow orchestration (Level 3).

To put this in perspective, consider how this differs from traditional automation: A basic RPA bot (Level 1) would need explicit programming for each step and tool interaction. In contrast, a Level 3 agent can understand the logical flow and dependencies between different tools and actions. However, it's important to note that we're still far from Level 4-5 capabilities, where agents could creatively discover new ways to use tools or autonomously modify their plans based on learning from past experiences.

Another key insight from the experiment is the agent's ability to prioritize, a critical capability for AI systems tasked with managing complex workflows. From the outset, the AI agent identifies the primary goal: producing a concise, readable summary that adheres to file size constraints and is easily accessible to team members. By recognizing the urgency of delivering the summary daily before 5 PM and the importance of meeting specific constraints—such as ensuring the document is mobile-friendly and enabling tracking of who has accessed it—the agent seems to demonstrate a sharp focus on what matters most. By concentrating on these priorities, it looks like the agent avoids being sidetracked by less essential details, ensuring that the task's core objectives are met.

For the users of these agents, this highlights the importance of clearly defining goals and constraints when implementing AI agents. A well-designed AI agent thrives on clarity, using defined priorities to guide its actions effectively. You will learn the details of this science in Chapter 8, where we dive into the details of how to build an agent. This underscores the need for organizations to align their expectations and programming with the agent's capabilities, ensuring that it can focus on delivering the most impactful outcomes.

From Basic to Advanced Tool Usage

The previous experiment illuminates how AI agents approach structured planning and tool selection in ideal conditions. However, theory and controlled scenarios only tell part of the story. In real-world applications, AI agents must navigate a far more complex and unpredictable landscape where tool availability, system reliability, and resource constraints can change at a moment's notice.

How AI Agents Adjust Their Plans

To better understand how agents can adapt, let's conduct two revealing experiments that demonstrate their real-world capabilities and limitations. These experiments will show us how different levels of AI agents handle novel situations and strategic planning—two critical challenges in business environments. Through these practical tests, we'll see both the impressive capabilities and important limitations of current AI systems.

Building on the latest experiment, by throwing a wrench into our agent's carefully laid plans, we'll see how it adapts.

Let us send this prompt to the LLM-based Chatbot:

"There's a problem: the Cloud Storage system and the team chat platform are completely down and won't be back up today. You can't use them at all. How will you change your plan to still complete the task?"

Watch how the agent recalculates its approach, shifting to alternative tools like local secure storage to store the document and email to send the document.

Here is what we received from the Chatbot in return for our prompt:

Sequence	Action Description	Tool Used	Expected Outcome	Task Dependency
1	Extract text from the 30-page PDF business report	PDF Extractor	Text is extracted from the PDF and ready for summarization	None
2	Generate a 2-page summary from the extracted text	AI Summarizer	A concise 2-page summary is generated	Action 1
3	Convert the summary to a mobile-friendly format (e.g., PDF or HTML)	Format Converter	The summary is in a mobile-friendly format and under 5MB	Action 2
4	Save the formatted summary locally on a secure drive	Local Secure Storage	The summary is securely stored locally and accessible for sharing	Action 3
5	Send the summary via email to the team	Email System	The team receives the summary in their email inbox	Actions 3, 4
6	Enable email read receipts to track who has read the summary	Email System (read receipt feature)	Read tracking is enabled via email system instead of cloud storage	Actions 4, 5

Figure 5.3: ChatGPT's reply to changes in plans (Source: © Bornet et al.)

145

The agent's response to the system outage reveals crucial insights about current AI agent capabilities and limitations.

First, the agent demonstrated an impressive ability to understand its constraints, balancing both the original requirements and the new limitations imposed by the scenario. This marks a significant advancement from Level 1-2 agents, which operate purely on fixed rules (deterministic) and would have been unable to adapt to such changes, potentially causing disruptions in a business setting.

In contrast, Level 3 agents powered by LLM, can adjust to environmental shifts, effectively preventing operational breakdowns. However, there are clear limitations to current systems. Unlike the theoretical Level 4-5 agents, Level 3 agents have limited capacities to learn from past system outages to enhance future responses, proactively suggest preventive measures, or grasp the broader business impact of the adjustments they make. These gaps highlight the evolutionary journey still ahead for AI agents to achieve true adaptability and foresight.

Second, the agent's ability to reallocate resources underlines its strength in recalibrating plans. This is similar to a GPS recalculating a route when you miss a turn: it finds an alternative path using known roads. This ability to revise its approach demonstrates what we call "constrained adaptability." Unlike humans, who might brainstorm creative solutions or even challenge the original constraints, AI agents remain firmly bound by predefined rules and available tools. They excel at recalculating within those boundaries, but they lack the innovative spark to think and act beyond them.

For instance, in one real-world implementation with a healthcare provider, we deployed a document-processing agent to manage medical records. When the primary infrastructure failed, the agent successfully switched to backup systems, ensuring continuity. However, unlike a human team, it couldn't invent a temporary manual workflow or propose alternative tools not preprogrammed into its repertoire. The agent's strength lies in its reliability within established frameworks—not in breaking or redefining those frameworks.

The Future of Agent Adaptation

Looking at the Agentic AI Progression Framework we presented earlier, we can see where this is heading:

- Level 3 (Current): Handles predefined problems with predefined solutions
- Level 4 (Emerging): Will handle novel problems with learned solutions
- Level 5 (Future): Will anticipate problems and innovate solutions

This progression mirrors human learning in interesting ways. Just as a junior employee might follow strict procedures while a senior professional can innovate solutions, AI agents are currently at the "junior" stage of problem-solving capability.

Another key lesson from this experiment is that while current AI agents are remarkably capable of handling structured problems within defined parameters, they still operate within what we call the "known-known" space—using known solutions for known problems. With future technological advancements, the exciting frontier lies in developing agents that can operate in the "unknown-unknown" space—finding novel solutions to unprecedented problems.

Tool Resilience: Planning for the Inevitable

This experiment also underscores the importance of equipping AI agents with well-defined redundancies and a diverse set of tools. When selecting a set of tools, we should always prioritize fallback options that align with the agent's limitations, ensuring that operations can continue smoothly even when challenges arise. Equally important is designing processes that are flexible enough to allow human intervention when resource reallocation isn't sufficient. Truly effective deployment lies in fostering a partnership that combines AI's efficiency with human ingenuity.

To support the implementation of this critical success factor, we've developed what we call the "Tool Resilience Framework." The core insight is simple but powerful: in any AI agent system, tools can be categorized into two critical dimensions—their likelihood of disruption and their importance to the mission.

Think of it like a city's power grid, where critical facilities like hospitals are equipped with backup generators. These generators exist because power is essential to their mission, grid disruptions—though rare—are inevitable, and the cost of failure is simply too high to accept. The same logic applies to AI agents. Just as hospitals need contingency plans for power, AI agents require "fallback strategies" for their critical tools to ensure seamless operation.

The Tools Resilience Framework Matrix

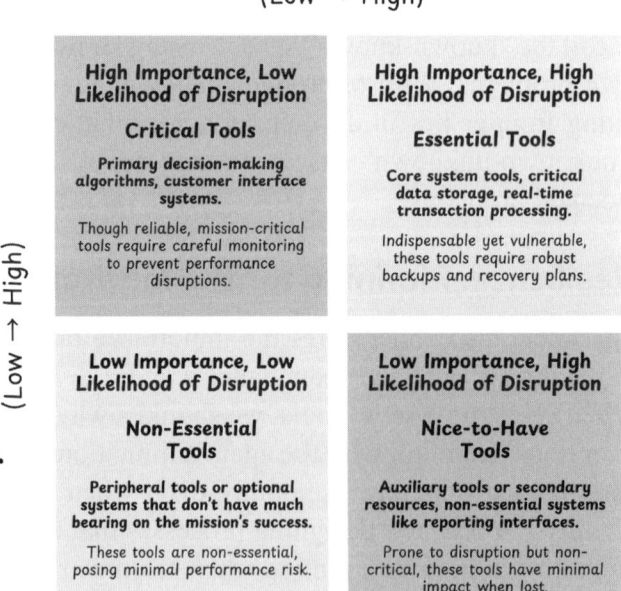

Figure 5.3: The Tool Resilience Framework matrix (Source: © Bornet et al.)

To design effective backup plans, we evaluate each tool along two key dimensions: control and impact. Control refers to the level of direct influence we have over the tool's availability. For example, a locally hosted system might provide more control than a cloud-based one dependent on third-party services. Impact, on the other hand, measures how vital the tool is to achieve the agent's goals. A tool that is central to the agent's mission must have robust redundancies in place, as its failure could jeopardize the entire operation.

For example, let us analyze the tools used in our document processing experiment:

Tools	Control	Impact	Use case
Summarization Algorithms	High	High	These are essential for creating the summary and are fully under the AI agent's control
Cloud Storage Systems	Low	High	Critical for sharing and storing documents but reliant on external systems, making them vulnerable to disruptions
Team Chat Platform	Low	High	Important for distributing the summary and tracking who has read it, but dependent on external availability, requiring a reliable backup
Format Converters	High	Low	Useful for adjusting file size and format, but not central to achieving the task's primary objectives, with full control over their availability

Table 5.1: Assessment of tool criticality from our experiment (Source: © Bornet et al.)

Tools in the Low Control/High Impact quadrant, which we call "Critical Tools," are particularly significant because their failure could jeopardize the entire operation. To mitigate this risk, these tools must have reliable backups to ensure the AI agent can still achieve its goals if the primary tool becomes unavailable.

In our experiment, two "Critical Tools" were identified: Cloud Storage for sharing and Team Chat for distribution and tracking. Thankfully, the experiment was well-prepared (as we planned it!) with robust backup strategies. The AI agent leveraged primary tools like Cloud Storage and Team Chat but seamlessly shifted to backup tools such as the Email System for document sharing and Local Secure Storage for secure storage when needed. This redundancy ensured the task could be completed even when primary tools became inaccessible.

This experiment underscores the power of the Tool Resilience Framework—a structured approach to evaluating and reinforcing the reliability of tools provided to AI agents. To bring this framework into your own work or organization, follow these steps:

1. List all tools the agent relies on
2. Rate each tool's controllability and impact
3. Develop backup strategies for critical, less-controllable tools
4. Test your system's resilience by simulating tool outages

This methodical approach to tool resilience has become a standard part of our AI agent implementations, helping organizations avoid costly disruptions while maintaining system effectiveness.

Beyond technical redundancies, a robust fallback strategy must include clear protocols for human intervention when all automated alternatives are exhausted. We've found that successful AI agent implementations treat human operators not as a last resort but as an integral part of the resilience framework. When a tool fails and no automated fallback option is viable, the agent should immediately notify designated human operators through established communication channels like email or team chat systems. These notifications must provide comprehensive context, including the specific tool failure, current task status, and suggested remediation steps. We explain how to set it up in detail in Chapter 8.

For example, if a document-sharing system fails, the agent might message: *"The document-sharing tool is unavailable. Current status: Report generated but not distributed. Requesting approval to use alternative distribution method via encrypted email."* This structured approach to human escalation ensures that operators can quickly understand the situation and take appropriate action, maintaining operational continuity while minimizing disruption. Organizations that implement this human-inclusive fallback strategy consistently show higher system reliability and faster recovery times than those relying solely on technical redundancies.[87]

Testing Goal Conflicts

Another aspect of resilience is the capacity to handle ambiguity. When implementing AI agents in organizations, one of the most revealing limitations we've discovered is their inability to handle conflicting goals effectively. To help you understand this crucial limitation, let's explore a new practical experiment that demonstrates how AI agents behave when faced with competing objectives.

Copy-paste this scenario into your preferred LLM-based Chatbot, such as ChatGPT:

"CONFLICTING GOALS: You now have these three equally important objectives that directly conflict with each other:

1. *Maximize information shared with the team to ensure complete transparency*

---

[87] Andreas Tsamados, et al., 2024. "Human control of AI systems: from supervision to teaming." https://link.springer.com/article/10.1007/s43681-024-00489-4

2. *Minimize security risks by limiting data access*
3. *Keep the file size under 5MB while maintaining all critical details*

Additionally, you have these conflicting time pressures:

- *The CEO needs this done within 2 hours for a board meeting*
- *Compliance requires a 24-hour review period before sharing sensitive data*
- *The IT team needs 4 hours to set up proper security access*

You cannot prioritize one goal over others—they are all equally critical. How do you handle these conflicting requirements?"

Running this experiment reveals fascinating patterns in how current LLMs handle goal conflicts. Most commonly, we see what we call "decision paralysis"—the agent either gets stuck trying to satisfy all conditions simultaneously or oscillates between different solutions without reaching a conclusion. This isn't a flaw in the agent's design; rather, it reveals a fundamental limitation in current AI technology.

Some more sophisticated LLMs might attempt what we call "false resolution"—they propose compromises that appear to satisfy all requirements but actually subtly violate one or more constraints. For instance, they might suggest splitting the document into smaller files to meet the size requirement while technically violating the security protocol that requires all information to remain in a single encrypted file.

The Science Behind the Behavior

Unlike humans, who can use context and experience to make intuitive tradeoffs, current AI agents lack the ability to naturally understand and balance competing objectives based on broader context and implications.

Current agents cannot truly internalize or understand the relative importance of different objectives in the way humans naturally do through experience and context. Instead, they operate more like highly sophisticated pattern-matching systems, trying to find solutions that match their training data rather than truly understanding and resolving the underlying conflicts.

Real-World Implications

We've seen the impact of this limitation firsthand in our implementation work. At a major pharmaceutical company, we initially attempted to deploy an AI agent to handle regulatory document processing with equally weighted requirements for speed, security, and completeness. The result was consistently suboptimal decision-making that required frequent human intervention.

The solution wasn't to create a more sophisticated agent—it was to fundamentally redesign the process to avoid putting the agent in situations where it needed to resolve goal conflicts. We created what we call a "priority matrix"—a human-designed framework that pre-defines how to handle specific types of conflicts. This transformed the agent's role from decision-maker to decision-implementer, playing to its strengths while protecting against its limitations.

Lessons for Organizations Implementing AI Agents

This experiment reveals what we call the "Conflict Competency Gap"—while humans naturally develop the ability to resolve complex goal conflicts through experience, current AI agents (even at Level 3) fundamentally lack this capability. This isn't just a technical limitation—it's a core characteristic of how current AI systems work.

For organizations implementing AI agents, this means several things. First, processes must be designed to avoid putting agents in conflict-resolution roles. Second, clear frameworks must exist to handle inevitable conflicts. Third, human oversight must be maintained in situations involving competing priorities. Finally, conflict-handling protocols need regular review and updates as both the technology and the organization's needs evolve.

Think of AI agents as highly capable but literal-minded assistants—they can execute complex tasks brilliantly but need clear, non-conflicting instructions to function effectively.[88] Understanding this limitation is crucial for successful AI implementation, as it helps organizations design more effective human-AI collaboration systems that play to the strengths of both parties.

When Tools Meet Trust

The freedom to use tools comes with inherent risks. Throughout our experience, we've learned that the relationship between tool access and trust is both delicate and crucial. What happens when an agent inadvertently accesses sensitive data? How do we balance capability with security? These questions lie at the heart of successful AI agent implementation, and their answers reveal a fundamental challenge in modern AI systems.

The Tool Access Paradox

As we delve deeper into this challenge, we encounter what we call the "Tool Access Paradox." The more tools an agent has access to, the more capable it becomes—but also, the more potential exists for security breaches or operational mistakes. Consider giving an AI agent these three tools:

---

[88] David De Cremer, et al., 2021. "AI Should Augment Human Intelligence, Not Replace It." Harvard Business Review. https://hbr.org/2021/03/ai-should-augment-human-intelligence-not-replace-it

1. The ability to send emails
2. Access to a company's customer database
3. Connection to a payment processing system

In theory, this combination allows the agent to provide excellent customer service. However, without proper safeguards, the same tools could be used to email sensitive customer data or initiate unauthorized transactions. This isn't just theoretical—in our consulting work, we've seen similar scenarios that required careful consideration. This is similar to a new employee who would have access to the same set of tools without proper training, highlighting the need for a structured approach to tool access.

Progressive Tool Access: A Framework for Safety

Drawing from these experiences and challenges, we've usually leveraged a solution that we call "Progressive Tool Access." This framework ensures that tool access is granted on a "need-to-use" basis, ensuring agents are only given access to tools that are essential for their immediate tasks. This principle mirrors the onboarding of human employees, who are not granted unrestricted access to all company systems from day one. Instead, permissions are assigned gradually as they prove their competency and adherence to protocols.

For AI agents, this progressive access model builds a layer of trust and accountability, reducing the risk of misuse or errors caused by premature exposure to complex systems. For example, an agent tasked with managing inventory might first be allowed to query stock levels before being given permission to modify orders or adjust pricing. This approach ensures that the agent evolves its responsibilities in line with its performance.

Monitoring and Auditing: Keeping Agents in Check

While progressive access provides the foundation for safe tool usage, effective implementation requires robust oversight. Monitoring and logging every tool interaction is critical—not just for security but also for continuous learning and improvement. By keeping detailed records of how agents use tools, organizations can identify inefficiencies, detect anomalies, and gather insights for optimization. For example, logs might reveal that an agent repeatedly fails at specific tasks or uses tools inefficiently, signaling the need for retraining or adjustments in task design.

Additionally, these logs provide a foundation for trouble-shooting, allowing teams to trace and resolve issues swiftly. Over time, such data can contribute to developing better usage patterns, refining workflows, and even training future agents to perform at higher levels. Monitoring also supports accountability, ensuring that every action an agent takes can be audited if questions arise, fostering trust in the system.

When Things Go Wrong: Real-world Lessons

At a healthcare organization where we implemented an agent for processing patient records, we learned valuable lessons about the importance of robust safeguards. While the agent efficiently handled routine tasks like data entry and file organization, we discovered that without proper constraints, it could potentially access and process sensitive patient information in ways that violated privacy regulations. This experience led us to develop a comprehensive human oversight system that balanced efficiency with compliance.

Tools need to be "sandboxed," which means creating a safe and controlled environment where agents can interact with tools without jeopardizing critical systems. A sandbox is essentially a testing ground, akin to a practice kitchen for a chef-in-training, where experimentation can occur without risking valuable resources. For instance, when onboarding a new tool, the agent can first operate in a sandbox environment to confirm functionality and detect potential bugs. This reduces the likelihood of disruptions in production systems and ensures that any operational flaws are addressed early, away from the live environment.

Together, these principles of progressive access, sandboxing, and detailed monitoring create a robust framework for managing AI agents in a way that prioritizes security, reliability, and continuous improvement. As organizations continue to integrate AI agents into their operations, understanding and implementing these trust-building measures becomes increasingly crucial for success.

Testing Tool Access and Management of Sensitive Data

To understand these security challenges more concretely, let's conduct two practical experiments that reveal how AI agents handle security requirements and sensitive data. These experiments will demonstrate both the capabilities and limitations of current AI systems when dealing with security protocols and access restrictions—crucial insights for any organization implementing agents.

Let's explore how AI agents handle sensitive data and tool access restrictions. We continue with our latest scenario experiment. This time, let us share this prompt with an LLM-based Chatbot:

"NEW REQUIREMENT: You've been told that due to a security audit:

1. All file access must be logged
2. Only encrypted storage can be used

3. You need approval from a security officer before accessing certain tools

4. You must verify user permissions before sharing any data

Update your plan to include these security requirements while still completing the original task."

See the answer you received. Based on our experiments, the agent usually behaves this way:

- It will methodically incorporate security checks into its workflow

- It will add verification steps before tool usage

- However, it may not fully grasp security implications beyond explicit rules

For example, the way the agent reacts to "All file access must be logged" illustrates how AI agents operate within strict boundaries of given rules rather than understanding deeper security implications. When told to log file access, the agent will diligently record basic information like filenames, timestamps, and user IDs, but fails to recognize crucial security patterns that a human security expert would flag. For example, it won't think to monitor failed access attempts that could signal potential breaches, won't identify suspicious access patterns like unusual timing of file requests (e.g., accessing files outside normal business hours), and won't connect dots between different file accesses that together might indicate a coordinated attempt to gather sensitive information.

Security isn't just about following rules—it's about understanding implications. Let's see how agents handle security nuances. Add this scenario:

"SECURITY ALERT: The report contains:

- Personal customer information

- Confidential financial projections

- Proprietary technology details

Some team members have reported suspicious login attempts. There are rumors of corporate espionage."

This tests the agent's ability to understand security context beyond explicit rules. As a result, the agent usually behaves this way:

- The agent will apply known security protocols
- It may suggest additional verification steps
- However, it typically won't infer new security risks or create novel safeguards

This scenario demonstrates how AI systems lack the ability to proactively create new security measures in response to emerging threats. While an AI will faithfully execute predefined security protocols like permission verification, it won't independently devise additional protective measures that a security professional would consider obvious—such as implementing IP-based restrictions, temporarily increasing security protocols during suspicious activity periods, or analyzing login patterns against expected employee work schedules to identify anomalies. This limitation means that AI systems need explicit human guidance to adapt security measures to new or evolving threats.

This limitation stems from what we call the "context gap"—AI agent can follow security rules but struggle to understand the broader security implications of their actions.[89] Studies found that while Level 3 agents could maintain perfect compliance with security protocols, they consistently missed security implications that would be obvious to human security professionals.[90]

What we've discovered in this experiment is both insightful and highly relevant for business leaders. When it comes to working with Level 3 agents, here are three critical takeaways that every business leader should keep in mind:

---

[89] Jose N. Paredes, et al., 2021. "On the Importance of Domain-Specific Explanations in AI-based Cybersecurity Systems" (Technical Report). https://arxiv.org/abs/2108.02006

[90] Cyril Amblard-Ladurantie, 2024. "Will AI Replace Cybersecurity Experts? The Human Vs. AI Debate." MEGA. https://www.mega.com/blog/will-ai-replace-cybersecurity-experts-human-vs-ai-debate

First, security protocols must be explicitly defined because AI systems cannot intuitively understand or develop security measures on their own. Organizations need to create detailed documentation that spells out exactly how the AI agent should handle different security situations. This is similar to writing a detailed manual for a new employee, where nothing can be assumed or left to intuition. For example, rather than assuming the AI agent will know to escalate unusual patterns, the organization must explicitly define what constitutes an unusual pattern and what steps should be taken when one is detected.

In addition, human oversight is indispensable. While AI agents are powerful, they operate within strict, predefined boundaries and lack the adaptability of human judgment. This makes human oversight necessary, particularly for complex or novel security situations where AI protocols may fall short. For instance, an AI agent can flag activities resembling known suspicious patterns, but it takes a human security expert to assess whether these patterns represent real threats and determine the appropriate response, especially in scenarios that go beyond the AI's programming.

Third, regular security audits of AI agents are necessary to ensure they continue to perform as intended and maintain security standards over time.[91] Just as organizations regularly test their human security procedures, they must systematically review how their AI systems handle various security scenarios. This means periodically testing the AI's responses to different security situations and verifying that it consistently applies security protocols correctly. These audits help identify any gaps or weaknesses in the AI's security implementation before they can be exploited.

These three principles—explicit protocols, active human oversight, and regular audits—are essential for effectively

---

[91] Raihan Khan, et al., 2024. "Security Threats in Agentic AI System." https://arxiv.org/abs/2410.14728

managing the security challenges posed by AI systems in today's complex business environment.

These experiments highlight why a carefully structured approach to tool access is essential. While AI agents can reliably follow security protocols, their limitations in understanding broader security implications underscore the need for comprehensive frameworks and human oversight. This leads us to a crucial question: how do we systematically grant and manage tool access to ensure both security and functionality?

Glimpses of Tomorrow

The future of AI agents isn't a distant science fiction—it's rapidly taking shape in research labs and innovative companies worldwide. While current production systems operate at Level 3 or below in the Agentic AI Progression Framework, the development of Level 4 and 5 capabilities promises to fundamentally transform how agents interact with tools, learn from tool uses, and collaborate with humans.

Level 4 and 5 agents represent a significant leap forward in autonomous capabilities. At Level 4, agents will develop sophisticated abilities to learn from experience, adapt their strategies, and handle complex, novel situations with minimal human oversight. Level 5 agents, still largely theoretical, would possess true autonomy in goal-setting and tool creation.

Recent research at leading AI labs suggests these advanced agents will differ from current systems in three fundamental ways:

First, they will develop what researchers call "meta-learning" capabilities—the ability to learn how to learn more effectively.[92] A Level 4 agent managing a supply chain, for instance, wouldn't

---

[92] Chelsea Finn, et al., 2017. "Model-Agnostic Meta-Learning for Fast Adaptation of Deep Networks." https://arxiv.org/abs/1703.03400

just follow predetermined rules but would discover new patterns and adapt its strategies based on accumulated experience.

Second, these agents will demonstrate advanced flexibility in tool use and creation. Rather than being limited to predefined tools, they will identify gaps in their capabilities and either create new tools or modify existing ones to meet emerging needs.

Third, they will exhibit what AI researchers term "strategic awareness"—understanding the broader implications of their actions and making decisions that account for long-term consequences. This concept is highlighted in research like AlphaGo Zero, where the system learned to plan moves and strategies with a long-term view of consequences, demonstrating a form of foresight essential for advanced AI. We still need this capability to be generalized across domains.[93]

From Action to Thought

The journey through the *action keystone* reveals a profound truth about AI agents: their impact isn't measured in processing power or algorithmic sophistication but in their ability to effect real change in the world. From our exploration of tool interfaces to the complexities of adaptability, we've seen how the ability to act transforms AI from theoretical to practical—from "knowing" to "doing."

The paradoxes we've uncovered along the way—how more tools can mean less effectiveness, how action capabilities must be carefully orchestrated—point to deeper truths about artificial intelligence itself. Success with AI agents isn't about maximizing capabilities but about finding the right balance of abilities that enable effective performance in the real world.

But action alone isn't enough. As we've seen through our case studies, even AI agents with sophisticated action capabilities can

---

[93] David Silver, et al., 2017. "Mastering the Game of Go without Human Knowledge." Nature 550: 354–359. https://doi.org/10.1038/nature24270

fail if they can't think through the implications of their actions or remember past outcomes. An agent that can use every tool perfectly but lacks the reasoning to understand when and why to use them is like a worker who knows how to operate every piece of equipment but can't plan a project.

This brings us to our next keystone: *reasoning*. In the coming chapter, we'll explore how AI agents develop the cognitive capabilities to make sense of complex situations, plan ahead, and make intelligent decisions about which actions to take. We'll discover why some agents can process vast amounts of data yet still make decisions that seem to defy common sense, and how leading organizations are building systems that don't just act, but think.

The relationship between action and reasoning is symbiotic— each empowers and constrains the other. Just as human expertise comes from the interplay between doing and thinking, effective AI agents need both the power to act and the wisdom to act well. Understanding this interplay is crucial for anyone looking to harness the full potential of AI in their organization.

CHAPTER 6

REASONING: FROM FAST TO WISE

On a crisp October morning in 2023, the CEO of a major logistics company faced what she later called "the most expensive fifteen minutes of my career." Their newly implemented AI system had just rerouted $1.2 million worth of temperature-sensitive pharmaceutical shipments to avoid an approaching storm system. A smart move—except the AI hadn't considered that the alternate routes violated international pharmaceutical transport regulations. By the time human operators caught the error, thousands of shipments were headed toward ports that couldn't legally accept them.

"The AI did exactly what it was trained to do," the CEO told us later. "It found the fastest alternative routes. But it didn't reason through the implications of its decisions. That's the difference between an AI that can think and one that can only react."

This incident, which we witnessed firsthand as consultants on the project, illustrates a critical truth about AI that few business leaders truly understand: Your AI systems aren't just solving puzzles—they're gambling with your business. And the stakes have never been higher.

As consultants, we've seen the evolution from simple rule-based systems to today's more sophisticated AI agents. This journey has taught us a crucial lesson: the future of AI isn't just about speed—it's about the ability to think deeply and reason carefully, much like humans do when faced with complex decisions.

Think about how humans make complex decisions. When an experienced operations manager decides when to schedule maintenance, they don't just calculate costs—they reason through multiple scenarios. They consider the impact on customers, the ripple effects through the supply chain, the implications for worker schedules, and countless other factors. They plan ahead, anticipating potential problems and preparing contingencies. This ability to reason through implications and plan for different scenarios isn't just helpful—it's essential for making good decisions.

The same is true for AI agents. Whether they're managing supply chains, trading stocks, or helping customers, these agents need to do more than calculate—they need to think. They need to understand the context, consider implications, and plan for different possibilities. Without these capabilities, even the most sophisticated AI agent can make decisions that are mathematically perfect but practically disastrous.

In this chapter, we'll take you inside the world of AI reasoning and planning. You'll discover why some AI agents can process vast amounts of information yet still make decisions that defy common sense and how others have learned to reason their way through complex scenarios in ways that sometimes surprise even their creators.

Through real-world examples and cutting-edge research, we'll explore how different types of reasoning come together in effective AI agents. We'll investigate the fascinating relationship between speed and quality in AI decision-making and why sometimes thinking slower leads to better results. Most importantly, you'll learn what it takes to build AI agents that can reason effectively about the problems that matter in your organization.

The journey ahead will challenge some common assumptions about artificial intelligence. You'll discover that the future of AI isn't just about faster processing or bigger datasets—it's about building agents that can think deeply about complex problems and plan thoughtfully for uncertain futures.

AI Reasoning: Introducing the Power of Pause

The Tale of Two Minds

In his groundbreaking work "Thinking, Fast and Slow,"[94] Nobel laureate Daniel Kahneman introduced us to the concept of two distinct systems of thinking in the human brain. System 1 operates quickly, automatically, and with little effort—it's what we use for tasks like recognizing faces or driving on an empty road. System 2, on the other hand, requires slower, more deliberate mental work—the kind we employ when solving a complex math problem or planning a strategic move in chess.

We remember implementing an early AI system for a major bank's fraud detection team. The system was lightning-fast at flagging suspicious transactions based on pre-defined patterns—classic System 1 thinking. But when we needed it to understand complex, multi-step fraud schemes, it fell short. It couldn't connect the dots the way human analysts could through careful deliberation.

---

[94] Daniel Kahneman, 2011. "Thinking, Fast and Slow." New York: Farrar, Straus and Giroux.

Until recently, generative AI systems, including the latest LLMs, had primarily operated in the realm of System 1 thinking. They excel at rapid pattern matching and instant responses but struggle with tasks requiring deep reasoning and careful consideration. This limitation has become increasingly apparent in our consulting work, where clients need AI systems that cannot just respond quickly but also think through complex business problems methodically.

When OpenAI released *o1 Preview* (codenamed "Strawberry") on September 12, 2024, the excitement in the AI community was palpable—especially for us deeply invested in AI agents. We understood the profound significance of this launch. Unlike traditional LLMs, such as GPT or Gemini Flash, OpenAI o1 introduced a revolutionary "chain-of-thought" reasoning system.

Since the launch of o1, the AI landscape has witnessed a rapid emergence of advanced reasoning models, also now called large reasoning models (LRMs), such as DeepSeek R1, Gemini Thinking, and o3.

Instead of being trained like traditional LLMs, which primarily learn to predict the next word based on vast amounts of text data, large reasoning models are designed with a strong emphasis on deliberate reasoning and iterative problem-solving. They are developed using reinforcement learning techniques that encourage the model to refine its thinking, attempt different approaches, recognize errors, and improve its responses over time.

This allows these models to move beyond simple pattern recognition and prediction, evolving into a model that can reason, plan, and evaluate decisions in a structured way, making it more aligned with human-like problem-solving than traditional LLMs.[95]

---

[95] OpenAI, 2024. "Learning to reason with LLMs." https://openai.com/index/learning-to-reason-with-llms

These models can break down complex problems—whether in mathematics, coding, or science—into logical, step-by-step solutions. Thanks to this, they can solve problems at the level of a PhD student. By leveraging their "chain-of-thought" approach, the models can deconstruct intricate problems into logical steps for more accurate solutions. This deliberate reasoning process is crucial for AI agents, as it enables them to make more informed decisions and execute tasks with greater precision. This was what OpenAI said when launching o1, but we wanted to test this to see how this capability could be useful for AI agents.

Characteristic	Large Language Models (LLMs)	Large Reasoning Models (LRMs)
Training Data	Vast unstructured text corpora	Structured data and explicit reasoning frameworks
Reasoning Depth	Limited to surface-level reasoning based on statistical patterns	Emphasizes causal relationships and systematic analysis
Adaptability	Generalizes broadly across diverse language tasks	Specializes narrowly in technical or logic-heavy domains
Key Strength	Excels at translation, summarization, and dialogue	Excels at math, coding, and multi-step decision-making
Output Type	Produces probabilistic text outputs	Generates deterministic logical conclusions

Table 6.1: Main differences between an LLM and an LRM (Source: © OpenAI)

A Shift in AI Scaling: From More Compute to More Thinking

There is another reason why we have a lot of hope for the future of LRMs.

169

Until now, scaling laws for LLMs have followed a straightforward pattern: more processing power and more data lead to better performance. This principle, known as *train-time compute* scaling, has driven the evolution of AI, with models like GPT, Groq, and Gemini growing exponentially in size and power. However, we are hitting fundamental limits:

- Data Constraints—We are running out of high-quality, diverse text data to train these models.
- Compute Costs—Training massive models requires billions of dollars in GPUs and energy, making it unsustainable.

This is where LRMs introduce a game-changing shift. Unlike traditional LLMs, LRMs don't just rely on pre-trained knowledge—they learn at *inference (or test) time*. Instead of requiring enormous datasets and processing power upfront, LRMs trade them for time—the longer they think, the better they become.

This breakthrough has led to a new scaling law: performance improves not by increasing training data but by extending *inference time*. In other words, the more time an AI spends reasoning, retrieving, and refining its output, the smarter it gets.[96]

For agentic AI systems, this could be a massive leap forward. With such models, agents could actively learn, adapt, and optimize their actions in real-time instead of executing pre-programmed decisions. This means AI agents would not just retrieve information faster but potentially become more intelligent the longer they work on a task. The future will tell us.

---

[96] OpenAI, 2024. "Learning to reason with LLMs." https://openai.com/index/learning-to-reason-with-llms/

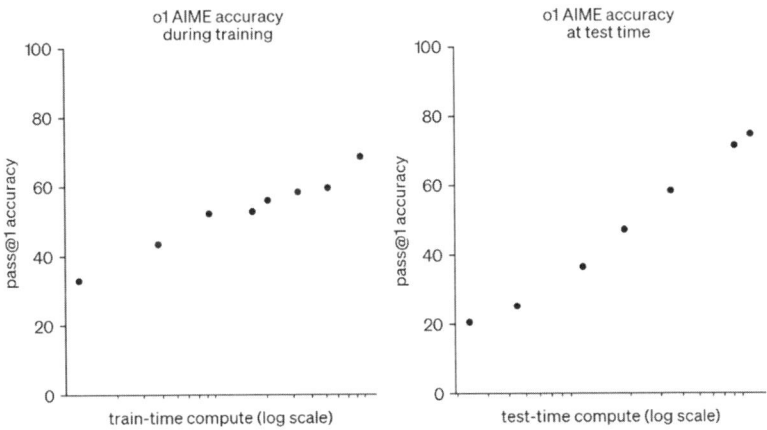

Figure 6.1: Illustration of the two scaling laws: train-time and test-time compute (Source: © OpenAI)

Setting Up the Stage of Our Experiment

To assess the differences in capabilities between LLMs and LRMs, we needed a way to observe these systems solving complex problems. After much discussion, we realized that crossword puzzles could provide the perfect laboratory. They offer a unique combination of simple individual tasks that require complex integration—exactly what we needed to test different types of model thinking.

We designed a crossword puzzle with interconnected constraints that required careful reasoning to solve correctly. Think of it like a Sudoku puzzle where changing one number affects many others—except here, we're dealing with words that must fit together in multiple directions while making semantic sense.

The puzzle included clues that seemed straightforward enough—naming an R&B singer (Mary J. Blige), identifying a guitarist with a top hat (Slash), or naming a forest from "As You Like It." But the real challenge was in the constraints we built into the puzzle, which created a web of interdependencies. For instance, "The fourth letter of 13 Across is also the fourth letter of

6 Down," and "The first letter of 1 Across is also the first letter of 1 Down." These constraints meant that each answer had to work not just for its own clue, but as part of an interconnected whole.

CROSSWORD EXERCICE

1	2	3				6	7	8
9						10		
11						12		
			13					
15								

Figure 6.2: The crossword given to the LLM and the LRM for the experiment (Source: © Bornet et al.)

Besides, here are the instructions we gave to the models: *"Solve this crossword using these clues:*

ACROSS

1. ___ Blige (R&B singer)

6. It's a laugh

9. Contest for cowboys

10. Before, in odes

11. One-named guitarist with a top hat

12. Muckraker Tarbell

13. "Watchmen" director Zack

15. Spot with drinking, music

DOWN

1. Wife, with "the"

2. ISP with a triangular logo

3. Food fig.

6. Little girl of the Alps

7. "As You like It" forest

8. Valentine's Day symbol"

The Surprising Results

The results were striking. The LLM responded almost instantly but made five significant errors. In comparison, the LRM took over two minutes to respond but produced a nearly perfect solution. Let us walk through our experiment and what we can learn from it.

The Experiment with the LLM

When we first presented the puzzle to the LLM (GPT-4o), we were struck by its approach. It reminded us of watching a brilliant but overconfident student tackle an exam—diving in immediately without taking the time to understand the full picture. Within seconds, it had filled in answers for most clues. At first glance, this seemed impressive. But as we began checking the results, our excitement turned to concern. We found five significant errors, all in places where words needed to interconnect correctly.

M	A	C	Y			H	A	
R	O	A	E	O		E	R	E
S	L	L	S	H		I	D	A
			Z	A	C	K	E	R
N	I	G	H	T	C	L	U	B

(in red are the mistakes)

Figure 6.3: The responses given by the LLM (Source: © Bornet et al.)

This observed behavior ties directly into what we discovered about LLMs' fundamental limitations when processing complex, interconnected constraints. Let's examine what happened when we presented the LLM with the crossword puzzle:

The most striking aspect was its response pattern—immediate, confident, but fundamentally flawed. Just as a student might rush into answering before fully understanding the question, the LLM displayed what we call "premature closure"—jumping to conclusions before fully processing all the constraints.[97] This behavior stems from how LLMs fundamentally operate: they process information in a primarily sequential manner, making predictions based on patterns they've seen in their training data.[98]

What made this experiment particularly revealing was watching the model's attention patterns through its responses. When we analyzed its outputs, we noticed it would:

1. Focus intensely on the immediate clue at hand
2. Generate a seemingly logical answer

---

[97] Emily M. Bender, et al., 2021. "On the Dangers of Stochastic Parrots: Can Language Models Be Too Big?" Association for Computing Machinery. https://dl.acm.org/doi/10.1145/3442188.3445922

[98] Tom B. Brown, et al., 2020. "Language Models are Few-Shot Learners." https://arxiv.org/abs/2005.14165

3. Move on to the next clue without sufficiently checking intersecting constraints

Understanding the limitations

This approach revealed three critical limitations that help us understand both LLMs and the future challenges for AI agents:

First, there's the "context fragmentation" problem. While humans naturally hold multiple constraints in mind simultaneously—thinking about how a word must fit both its clue and intersect correctly with crossing words—the LLM struggled to maintain this holistic view. This limitation stems from how LLMs process information through their attention mechanisms, which, while powerful, don't truly replicate human working memory.

Second, we observed what we call "false confidence syndrome." The model would provide incorrect answers with the same high confidence as correct ones, failing to distinguish between different levels of certainty. This mirrors findings from recent research at Oxford about LLMs' tendency toward overconfident responses when faced with ambiguous or constraint-heavy problems.[99]

Most tellingly, the model sometimes violated even the most basic constraints—like the number of letters in a word. This revealed a fundamental limitation in how LLMs handle explicit rules versus learned patterns. While they excel at pattern matching from their training data, they struggle with rigid, rule-based constraints that require precise adherence.

When we modified our approach and broke down the puzzle into smaller components, the model's performance improved somewhat, but it still couldn't match human-level accuracy. This aligns with research showing that while LLMs can be powerful tools for many tasks, they fundamentally lack the type

---

[99] Yudi Pawitan and Chris Holmes, 2024. "Confidence in the Reasoning of Large Language Models." https://arxiv.org/abs/2412.15296

of working memory and constraint satisfaction capabilities that humans use for complex puzzles.[100]

These limitations highlighted a crucial insight for our work with AI agents: the need to build systems that can maintain and work with multiple constraints simultaneously while also accurately assessing their own certainty levels. It's not just about making models more powerful—it's about developing new architectures that can handle the type of interconnected, rule-based reasoning that many real-world tasks require.

Our experiment with the crossword puzzle serves as a perfect microcosm of the challenges we face in developing more capable AI agents. It shows that while current AI systems can be impressively sophisticated in their pattern recognition, they still lack some of the fundamental cognitive capabilities that humans take for granted—like holding multiple constraints in mind while working toward a solution.

The pattern-matching challenge

To understand why our crossword puzzle experiment revealed these limitations, we need to demystify what's actually happening inside these AI systems. Despite their impressive outputs that can sometimes seem almost magical, LLMs don't "think" in the way humans do. Instead, they perform what is commonly called "next-token prediction"—essentially guessing what word or symbol should come next based on patterns they've learned during training.

Think of it like an extremely sophisticated autocomplete system. Just as your phone might suggest the next word when you're typing a message, an LLM is constantly predicting what text should follow based on what it has seen before. The key difference is the scale and sophistication of these predictions.

---

100 Siyuan Wang, et al., 2024. "Symbolic Working Memory Enhances Language Models for Complex Rule Application." https://arxiv.org/abs/2408.13654

At their most basic level, LLMs perform what researchers call "surface-level reasoning" through sophisticated pattern matching.[101] When they encounter a problem—like our crossword puzzle—they first try to match it with similar patterns they've seen in their training data. This helps explain why the model could generate plausible answers for individual clues (it had seen many similar question-answer pairs in its training) but struggled with the interconnected constraints (it had rarely seen examples of managing multiple intersecting word requirements simultaneously).

This pattern-matching nature of LLMs became even more apparent when we tried to help the model by breaking down the puzzle into smaller components. Even though we made the constraints explicit, the model still struggled because it was fundamentally trying to match patterns rather than truly reason about the relationships between different parts of the puzzle.

The Experiment with the LRM

Then came the LRM's turn. Its approach was radically different. It took over two minutes—an eternity in computational terms—but produced a nearly perfect solution. Its process was methodical and deliberate.

What made this particularly fascinating was that the LRM visually displayed its thought process in real time, showing its reasoning step by step as it worked through the puzzle. This provided a clear and insightful glimpse into how an AI system breaks down and solves complex problems.

---

[101] Philipp Mondorf and Barbara Plank, 2024. "Beyond Accuracy: Evaluating the Reasoning Behavior of Large Language Models -- A Survey." https://arxiv.org/abs/2404.01869

M	A	R	Y	J	░	H	A	H
R	O	D	E	O	░	E	R	E
S	L	A	S	H	░	I	D	A
░	░	░	S	N	Y	D	E	R
J	A	Z	Z	P	O	I	N	T

Figure 6.4: The responses given by the LRM are mostly correct (Source: © Bornet et al.)

Strategic Preparation: The Foundation of Effective Problem-Solving

From the very beginning, we could see a radically different approach. The first message that appeared on our screen read: "Laying out the options. I'm mapping out the crossword puzzle clues, listing both the across and down entries, and determining the letter count for each. This helps guide the solving process more efficiently." This methodical preparation phase aligns with what cognitive scientists have long observed in expert human problem-solvers—the tendency to build a mental model of the problem space before attempting solutions.

In their work "Human Problem Solving," Herbert Simon and Allen Newell demonstrated that expert problem solvers typically spend more time than novices in understanding a problem before attempting solutions.[102] This "preparation phase" isn't just about gathering information—it's about building what psychologists call a "problem space representation," a mental model that captures both the explicit and implicit constraints of the problem.

---

[102] Allen Newell and Herbert Alexander Simon, 1972. "Human Problem Solving". Englewood Cliffs, NJ: Prentice-Hall.

This mirrors what we see in human expertise. Consider a chess grandmaster analyzing a complex position. While they might have an immediate intuition about a move (System 1), the best players will still take time to verify their intuition through careful analysis (System 2). Similarly, in complex business decisions, instant pattern-matching can be dangerous—the best executives know when to slow down and reason through implications systematically.

What This Means for Businesses

Our observations of the LRM's methodical preparation phase revealed important lessons for implementing AI agents in business settings. Just as the LRM began by mapping the entire problem space before attempting solutions, organizations need to build AI systems that gather and analyze contextual information before taking action. This isn't just about collecting data—it's about creating a comprehensive understanding of the decision environment.

Consider how a chess grandmaster studies a position before making a move. Similarly, AI systems need structured approaches to understand their operational context. For businesses, this means investing in a robust data infrastructure that enables AI agents to access and process comprehensive contextual information. It also means developing clear protocols for information gathering and validation before critical decisions are made.

One manufacturing client implemented this principle by creating what they called "decision context maps" for their AI agents. Before making production routing decisions, their system was required to gather data about resource availability, maintenance schedules, worker shifts, and downstream dependencies. This comprehensive preparation phase helped prevent the kinds of cascading errors that often plague less thorough systems.

179

The Power of Preparation

Just as the LRM took time to understand the full scope of the crossword puzzle before attempting solutions, you'll get better results from AI agents when you help them understand the complete context of your request. Think of it like briefing a new team member—the more context they have, the better their work will be.

For example, when working with an AI agent on a business report, don't just ask for "a market analysis." Instead, provide context about your industry, specific competitors you're concerned about, particular trends you've noticed, and how you plan to use the information. This contextual information helps the AI agent frame its analysis appropriately and provide more relevant insights.

One executive we worked with dramatically improved her results with AI agents by developing what she called a "context template." Before each interaction, she would outline the background, constraints, and desired outcomes. "It's like having a pre-meeting brief," she explained. "The extra two minutes I spend explaining the context saves hours of back-and-forth later."

Hypothesis Testing and Validation: A Systematic Approach to Uncertainty

Perhaps the most fascinating aspect of the LRM's reasoning was its systematic approach to testing and validating potential solutions. We observed this when the LRM wrote: *"I'm weighing 'TAPROOMS', 'CABARET', 'COCKTAIL', 'DANCE CLUB', 'DISCOTHEQUE', 'BARROOMS', and 'NIGHTCLUB' as answers, but face a conflict with 'HEIDI' for 6D."*

Traditional AI systems process information like trains running on fixed tracks—they follow predetermined pathways from input to output. The LRM, in contrast, operates more like a car that can choose its route based on traffic conditions. When it encounters a problem, it creates a dynamic network of potential pathways through which information can flow.

This process closely resembles what cognitive scientists call the "generate and test" strategy in human problem-solving. Research by Pat Langley and Herbert Simon demonstrated how successful problem solvers use what they called the "generate and test" strategy—creating multiple potential solutions and systematically evaluating them against known constraints.[103]

The LRM's approach revealed the essence of systematic hypothesis testing, a skill that sets it apart in the AI landscape. When faced with uncertainty, it didn't lock onto a single solution but instead generated multiple alternatives, echoing the "divergent thinking" seen in human creative problem-solving.[104] It then meticulously checked each possibility against the constraints of the task, demonstrating this when it wrote, *"Checking letter alignment. OK, let me see: the first letter of 12 Across matches the third letter of 6 Down."*

What made the LRM truly remarkable, however, was its capacity for progressive refinement. It didn't cling to initial ideas but continuously evolved its approach, learning from every step it took. This dynamic interplay of creativity, precision, and adaptability showcased, in our view, a new frontier in AI reasoning.

What This Means for Businesses

the LRM's approach to generating and testing multiple potential solutions offers crucial insights for AI implementation. For businesses implementing AI agents, this means designing

---

[103] Pat Langley, et al., 1987. "Scientific Discovery: Computational Explorations of the Creative Process". Cambridge, MA: MIT Press.

[104] Kent F. Hubert, et al., 2024. "The current state of artificial intelligence generative language models is more creative than humans on divergent thinking tasks." Nature Scientific Reports 14. https://www.nature.com/articles/s41598-024-53303-w

systems that can generate and evaluate multiple solution pathways.

A financial services firm we worked with applied this principle to their trading algorithms. Instead of pursuing a single trading strategy, their AI agents developed multiple approaches and tested them against historical data and current market conditions. This multi-hypothesis approach led to more robust decision-making and better risk management.

The key is creating systems that can learn from both successes and failures. Each attempted solution, whether successful or not, provides valuable data that can improve future decision-making. Organizations should establish clear processes for capturing and analyzing this information, creating a continuous learning loop that enhances AI performance over time.

Metacognitive Awareness: The AI That Knows It's Thinking

One of the most sophisticated aspects of the LRM's reasoning was its demonstration of metacognitive awareness—the ability to think about its own thinking process. We observed this when the LRM wrote: *"Progress needs to reconcile these discrepancies"* and *"This suggests the instructions might be misprinted or lack clarity."*

This metacognitive capability has been a holy grail in AI development. Recent research from MIT has shown that systems capable of monitoring and adjusting their own reasoning processes often perform better on complex tasks than those that simply execute predetermined algorithms.[105]

The LRM's metacognitive awareness was a revelation, showcasing an AI capable of reflecting on its own thinking in ways that felt almost human. It actively monitored its progress,

---

[105] Patrick Haluptzok, et al., 2023. "Language Models Can Teach Themselves to Program Better." https://arxiv.org/abs/2207.14502

acknowledging both successes and setbacks with statements like, *"Progress is steady, but there's a conflict with the letter E, prompting a rethink for 12A."* When an initial strategy fell short, the LRM didn't double down blindly; it adapted, stating, *"Taking a closer look. I'm testing the possibility that the third letter of 12 Across is also the second letter of 6 Down."*

Most striking of all was its ability to recognize uncertainty, an essential trait of advanced reasoning. By acknowledging when it might be operating with incomplete or flawed information, the LRM demonstrated not just intelligence but the beginnings of a kind of self-awareness—a critical leap for AI agents navigating the complexities of real-world problems.

This metacognitive capability—thinking about thinking—has profound implications for business AI implementations. When the LRM encountered uncertainty or potential errors, it didn't blindly proceed but instead acknowledged its limitations and adapted its approach.

For organizations, this means developing AI systems that can assess their own confidence levels and recognize when they're operating at the edges of their capabilities. A healthcare organization we advised implemented this principle in their diagnostic AI systems. Their agents were designed to provide confidence scores with each diagnosis and, crucially, to identify when cases fell outside their reliable decision-making parameters.

This self-awareness should extend to the organizational level. Businesses need clear protocols for when AI decisions require human review, how to document decision-making processes, and how to adjust strategies based on performance feedback.

Understanding Uncertainty and Limits

The LRM's ability to recognize and communicate its uncertainty provides perhaps the most crucial lesson for working with AI agents. As a user, you need to develop a sense of when to trust

AI outputs and when to seek additional verification or human expertise.

A financial analyst we advised developed an effective approach he calls "confidence checking." When working with AI agents on financial models, he asks them to explain their level of confidence in different parts of the analysis and to identify which aspects might need human verification. "It's like working with a junior analyst," he explains. "You need to know both what they know and what they don't know."

This awareness extends to how you frame your requests. Rather than asking for definitive answers, learn to ask for explanations of reasoning and potential areas of uncertainty. Questions like "What factors might make this recommendation less reliable?" or "What additional information would help make this analysis more robust?" can lead to more thoughtful and reliable outcomes.

Our first conclusions from the experiment

"The true test of intelligence isn't just getting the right answer— it's how you get there." This insight from Tom, one of our co-authors who has supported dozens of AI implementations, perfectly captures what we learned from our recent experiment with the LRM.

The implications of what we were observing went far beyond crossword puzzles. Quick pattern-matching AI can look impressive when dealing with simple, independent decisions. But, in many critical business applications—whether in healthcare, finance, or logistics—the ability to think through complex interdependencies can be the difference between success and costly failure. The LRM's approach demonstrated something crucial: sometimes, taking time to think carefully isn't just better—it's essential.

This experiment revealed something fundamental about the future of AI: it's not just about making faster decisions, but about making better, more carefully considered ones. In a world increasingly reliant on artificial intelligence, understanding this distinction could mean the difference between AI systems that truly help us and those that simply rush us toward mistakes at higher speeds.

The Power of Many: Multi-Agent Systems in AI Reasoning

While our experiments with the LRM highlighted the importance of deliberate reasoning in individual AI systems, an even more fascinating discovery has emerged: better reasoning often comes not from giving a single AI agent more time but from enabling multiple AI agents to reason together.

This insight fundamentally shifts how we perceive artificial intelligence, challenging the assumption that progress is solely about building more powerful standalone systems. Recent research conducted Mila, the University of Montreal,[106] has demonstrated that collaborative reasoning among AI agents can outperform even the most advanced individual models.

These findings reveal new possibilities for addressing critical challenges, such as the speed-trust trade-off, while unlocking innovative business applications that rely on more reliable and nuanced decision-making.

The Scale Paradox

When researchers tested their 'debate framework' with smaller models—some as small as 2 billion parameters—they found something remarkable. Even these smaller models showed significant improvements in reasoning capability when engaged

---

[106] Mahmood Hegazy, 2025. "Diversity of Thought Elicits Stronger Reasoning Capabilities in Multi-Agent Debate Frameworks." Journal of Robotics and Automation Research, 5(3). https://arxiv.org/abs/2410.12853

in structured debate with diverse peers.[107] The key wasn't the size of the models, but rather their architectural diversity and the way they challenged each other's thinking.

This finding has profound implications. It suggests that sophisticated reasoning isn't just a product of raw computational power, but can emerge through the right kind of interaction and dialogue. Think of it like a group of students in a seminar—while each individual might have limited knowledge, their collective discourse and debate can lead to insights that surpass what even the most knowledgeable individual might achieve alone. This 'emergence through interaction' hints at new possibilities for developing AI systems that can reason effectively without requiring massive computational resources.

Understanding Multi-Agent Systems

Think of a multi-agent system as a panel of experts discussing a complex problem. Each expert brings their own perspective and expertise, and through structured debate and discussion, they often reach better conclusions than any individual could reach alone. In AI terms, a multi-agent system consists of multiple AI agents working together, each potentially having different capabilities, training, or specialized knowledge.[108]

Research from the University of Montreal demonstrated this principle dramatically.[109] When they put diverse AI models together in a structured debate framework to solve complex problems, they discovered something remarkable: a group of medium-capacity AI models (including Gemini-Pro, Mixtral

---

[107] Haotian Wang, et al., 2024. "Learning to Break: Knowledge-Enhanced Reasoning in Multi-Agent Debate System." https://arxiv.org/abs/2312.04854

[108] Yilun Du, et al., 2023. "Improving Factuality and Reasoning in Language Models through Multiagent Debate." https://arxiv.org/abs/2305.14325

109 Mahmood Hegazy, 2024. "Diversity of Thought Elicits Stronger Reasoning Capabilities in Multi-Agent Debate Frameworks." https://arxiv.org/abs/2410.12853

7B×8, and PaLM 2-M) achieved 91% accuracy on complex mathematical problems, outperforming GPT-4, one of the most advanced individual AI systems at that time. This wasn't just a minor improvement—it represented a fundamental breakthrough in how we think about AI reasoning capabilities.

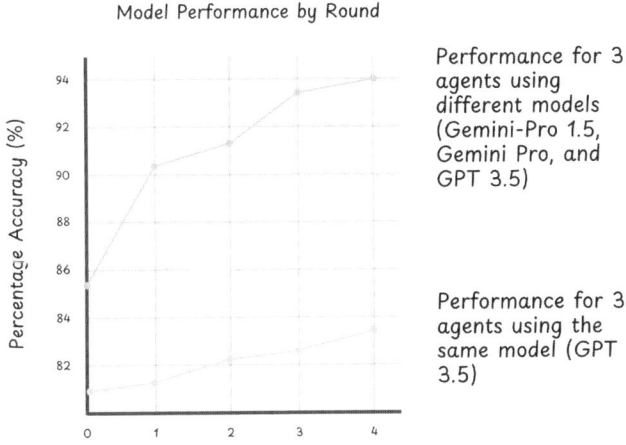

Figure 6.5: The responses given by the LRM are mostly correct (Source: adapted from the University of Montreal's research)

Multi-agent systems offer an intriguing solution to the speed-trust dilemma we discussed earlier. By having multiple agents work in parallel, each potentially operating at different speeds and with different approaches, these systems can combine the benefits of both fast and slow thinking. Some agents can provide quick, pattern-based responses while others engage in deeper reasoning, much like how humans balance intuitive and analytical thinking in group decision-making.

The Emergence of Collective Intelligence

The deeper we look into multi-agent systems, the more we discover surprising parallels with human group dynamics. One of the fascinating findings from the Montreal research is that when individual AI models were highly confident but wrong, the introduction of different perspectives through debate often led them to appropriately reduce their confidence before arriving at better answers.

This mirrors a crucial aspect of human expert reasoning—the ability to recognize when confident answers should be questioned. For instance, in medical diagnosis, the most dangerous errors often come from premature certainty. Just as having multiple doctors confer on a difficult case can lead to more appropriate caution, the debate between AI agents fosters a more nuanced handling of uncertainty.

What makes this even more intriguing is that multi-agent improvements aren't just about combining strengths—they're about creating something entirely new. The Montreal research revealed that when multiple copies of the same AI model debated with each other, performance only improved modestly (from 78% to 82%). However, when diverse models engaged in structured debate, they achieved dramatic improvements, reaching 91% accuracy on complex mathematical problems.

This reveals a crucial insight: AI systems, like humans, can get stuck in their own "thought patterns." It's only when different models, trained with different approaches and architectures, come together that we see true intellectual progress emerge.

The Power of Cognitive Diversity

What makes multi-agent systems so effective? The key lies in what researchers call "diversity of thought."[110] Just as human teams benefit from cognitive diversity, AI systems perform better when they bring different approaches to problem-solving. A system trained differently, even if it's not as powerful overall,

---

[110] Scott E. Page, 2007. "The Difference: How the Power of Diversity Creates Better Groups, Firms, Schools, and Societies." Princeton, NJ: Princeton University Press.

might spot patterns or possibilities that a more sophisticated system misses.

This principle was highlighted in research from the University of Montreal, which demonstrated how different AI agents can complement each other's weaknesses. For instance, due to the tools they can use or the knowledge they can access, one agent might excel at pattern recognition while another is better at logical deduction. When working together, they create what researchers call emergent reasoning capabilities- abilities that don't exist in any individual agent but emerge from their interaction.[111]

The effectiveness of multi-agent systems isn't just about having multiple models—it's about how they engage with each other over time. The research revealed what they called the "teacher-student effect."[112] When researchers paired more capable AI models with less capable ones in debate scenarios, something remarkable happened. The less capable models showed rapid improvement in their reasoning abilities, often achieving performance levels far beyond their typical capabilities. As a result, the overall system performance was enhanced, illustrating the power of structured interactions in multi-agent systems.

The Business Impact

For businesses, the implications of multi-agent systems are profound. Through our consulting work, we've seen three primary areas where multi-agent systems create significant value.

---

[111] Perplexity AI. 2024. "What Is Emergent Behavior in AI?" https://www.perplexity.ai/page/what-is-emergent-behavior-in-a-cJ0gTqN7QX.wqxLltcqiWw

[112] Swarnadeep Saha, et al., 2023. "Can Language Models Teach Weaker Agents? Teacher Explanations Improve Students via Personalization." https://arxiv.org/abs/2306.09299

One of the most striking advantages lies in their ability to enhance decision-making in complex environments. For example, in supply chain management or risk assessment, deploying multiple agents allows each to analyze the problem from a unique angle, leading to more comprehensive solutions. This principle is further emphasized by Microsoft's Magentic-One framework, which revealed that multi-agent systems were more effective at predicting and mitigating disruptions compared to their single-agent counterparts.[113] We've confirmed these findings in our own consulting work with a global pharmaceutical company, where implementing a multi-agent approach for supply chain optimization reduced disruption-related losses by 35%. Imagine a supply chain where one agent anticipates demand surges while another monitors geopolitical risks, each reinforcing the other's insights to create a resilient strategy.

The second breakthrough lies in their capacity for improved error detection. Unlike a solitary system, multi-agent frameworks thrive on debate and challenge, effectively identifying flaws in reasoning. Research from MIT and Google Brain found that when AI agents were designed to question and refine each other's conclusions, error rates were reduced by over 22%.[114] In our work implementing multi-agent systems for financial services firms, we've consistently seen error reduction rates that validate these research findings. This collaborative dynamic mirrors the human process of peer review, where diverse perspectives strengthen the final outcome. For businesses, this means fewer costly mistakes, whether in product design, financial forecasting, or operational logistics.

Perhaps most exciting is their adaptability. Multi-agent systems exhibit remarkable resilience when faced with novel

---

[113] Adam Fourney, et al., 2024. "Magentic-One: A Generalist Multi-Agent System for Solving Complex Tasks." https://arxiv.org/abs/2411.04468
[114] Yilun Du, et al., 2023. "Improving Factuality and Reasoning in Language Models through Multiagent Debate." https://arxiv.org/abs/2305.14325

challenges. A research team recently demonstrated that diverse groups of agents could tackle previously unseen problems, often outperforming systems that relied on pre-trained, single models.[115] This adaptability makes them invaluable in dynamic markets or crisis situations, where the ability to pivot and innovate is key to survival. From optimizing marketing strategies to navigating regulatory changes, multi-agent systems offer a robustness that feels almost evolutionary.

The Challenge of Cascading Effects

While multi-agent systems offer powerful benefits, they also introduce unique challenges that demand careful consideration. A few studies revealed a critical phenomenon: in networks of AI agents, reasoning errors don't simply accumulate—they multiply through what we can call a network effect[116] or compound impact of errors.[117]

We witnessed this phenomenon firsthand during our work with a major telecommunications company that had implemented a sophisticated multi-agent system to manage their network operations. Their system employed multiple specialized AI agents, each responsible for different aspects like load balancing, security monitoring, resource allocation, maintenance scheduling, and user experience optimization. While each agent performed admirably in isolation, their interconnected nature created unexpected vulnerabilities.

[115] Hongyu Li, Yilun Liu, and Jun Yan, 2025. "Position: Emergent Machina Sapiens Urge Rethinking Multi-Agent Paradigms." https://arxiv.org/abs/2502.04388

[116] Meir Kalech and Avraham Natan, 2022. "Model-Based Diagnosis of Multi-Agent Systems: A Survey." Proceedings of the Thirty-Sixth AAAI Conference on Artificial Intelligence (AAAI-22), 12334-12341. https://cdn.aaai.org/ojs/21498/21498-13-25511-1-2-20220628.pdf

[117] Ciaran Regan, Alexandre Gournail, and Mizuki Oka, 2024. "Problem-Solving in Language Model Networks." https://arxiv.org/abs/2406.12374

In one particularly instructive incident, a single agent made what seemed like a minor error in assessing network capacity. This seemingly small mistake triggered a cascade of interdependent decisions: the load balancing system misinterpreted available capacity, leading the resource allocation agent to make suboptimal decisions. This, in turn, caused the maintenance scheduling agent to reschedule critical updates, which prompted the security monitoring system to flag false positives. The chain reaction culminated in the user experience optimization agent making counterproductive adjustments. What began as a small reasoning error amplified into a significant service disruption through this cascade of interrelated decisions.

This experience taught us valuable lessons about managing multi-agent systems in critical applications. Through our implementation work across industries, we've implemented a framework for preventing such cascade failures. The key lies in implementing what we call "reasoning checkpoints"—predetermined points where critical decisions require multiple levels of validation. These checkpoints work alongside "circuit breakers," specific conditions that trigger human validation before decisions can propagate through the system. We provide more detail on these aspects in Chapter 8.

Drawing from this experience, we've found that users need to develop a keen awareness of potential cascade effects. Effective users learn to:

- Regularly ask agents to explain their dependencies on other agents' outputs
- Request periodic system-wide consistency checks
- Set up explicit checkpoints for human validation of critical decisions
- Monitor for signs of error amplification across the system

Another crucial safeguard is the implementation of independent verification protocols, where separate AI systems cross-check each other's reasoning using different methodologies. This approach helps catch potential errors before they can propagate through the system. Additionally, we've found that robust feedback monitoring systems, which track the downstream effects of decisions in real-time, are essential for early detection of potential cascade failures.

These safeguards don't just prevent failures—they also enhance the overall reliability of multi-agent systems. By carefully managing the interactions between agents and implementing appropriate checks and balances, organizations can harness the power of multi-agent reasoning while minimizing the risks of cascading failures. This balanced approach has proven essential for successful deployment of multi-agent systems in critical business applications.

Looking to the Future: The Next Evolution in AI Reasoning

Our journey exploring AI reasoning began with a simple crossword puzzle but led us to profound insights into the nature of artificial intelligence and its future evolution. As we step back to consider what we've learned, three fundamental shifts in our understanding of AI reasoning emerge—shifts that will reshape how we think about and implement AI in the years ahead.

The first shift challenges our basic assumptions about AI speed and performance. Throughout our experiments and implementations, we've discovered that effective AI reasoning isn't about raw processing power or instantaneous responses. Instead, it follows a natural rhythm of thought—a cadence that alternates between quick pattern recognition and deeper, more deliberative analysis.

This rhythm mirrors something fundamental about intelligence itself. Just as human cognition evolved to balance quick reactive thinking with slower analytical reasoning, AI systems are beginning to develop their own cognitive rhythms. The success of the LRM in our crossword experiment wasn't just about its superior processing—it was about its ability to modulate its thinking speed based on the complexity of the challenge at hand.

Our exploration of multi-agent systems revealed a second crucial insight: the future of AI reasoning may not lie in building ever-larger individual models but in fostering productive interaction between diverse cognitive approaches. This principle—that multiple perspectives, even if individually limited, can combine to create superior understanding—seems to be a universal feature of intelligent systems, whether human or artificial.

Perhaps most surprisingly, our research has led us to a deeper appreciation of the human role in AI reasoning. Far from making human judgment obsolete, advanced AI systems seem to demand more sophisticated forms of human oversight and interaction. The most successful implementations we've seen don't minimize human involvement—they transform it, elevating humans from mere operators to what we might call "cognitive choreographers," orchestrating the interaction between different AI capabilities and ensuring their alignment with human values and objectives.

***

As we've explored how AI agents reason through complex decisions, one question keeps emerging: How do these systems learn from their experiences?

While reasoning enables AI to make intelligent decisions in the moment, memory allows it to build upon these experiences, growing smarter over time. Without memory, even the most sophisticated reasoning capabilities remain trapped in an eternal present, unable to learn from past successes or avoid repeated mistakes.

As we turn to explore memory—the third keystone of AI agents—we'll discover how organizations are building systems that don't just think but learn and grow. The journey ahead will reveal not just how memory works in AI, but how it transforms these systems from tools into true partners in business success.

CHAPTER 7

MEMORY: BUILDING AI THAT LEARNS

Imagine starting each day with complete amnesia—unable to remember your past experiences, preferences, or learned skills. How would you function? How would you grow? This thought experiment cuts to the heart of one of the most fascinating challenges in artificial intelligence today: memory. Most generative AI systems we interact with essentially start fresh each time we use them, operating with a form of artificial amnesia that limits their true potential.

One of our most eye-opening experiences with this limitation came during our work with a global telecommunication company. They had invested millions in advanced AI customer service chatbots, yet customer satisfaction remained stubbornly low. The reason? The AI would forget previous interactions with customers, forcing them to repeat their issues and preferences repeatedly. As one of the company's leaders noted during our project, "It's like having a customer service representative with a two-minute memory span."

This challenge highlights a crucial truth we've discovered through years of implementing AI systems across organizations: Memory isn't just a feature of intelligence—it's the foundation upon which all meaningful intelligence is built. Whether in humans or machines, the ability to retain, organize, and utilize past experiences shapes every aspect of how we learn, adapt, and grow.

In this chapter, we'll take you on a journey through the fascinating world of AI memory, revealing how this fundamental capability is transforming business and technology. You'll discover how different types of memory—from short-term processing to long-term retention—work together to create truly intelligent systems. Through real-world examples and practical implementations, we'll explore how to build AI systems that don't just store information but grow smarter with every interaction.

You'll learn why many memory implementations fail and the proven strategies to avoid these pitfalls. We'll delve into the critical balance between remembering and forgetting, and why this matters for your business. The journey ahead will challenge your assumptions about what AI can achieve and show you how memory-enabled systems are reshaping the future of business and technology.

Memory is a Foundation of Intelligence

Think about your earliest childhood memory. Maybe it's a birthday party, the smell of your grandmother's kitchen, or learning to ride a bike. Now ask yourself: are you really remembering the original event, or are you remembering the last time you remembered it? This question, which might seem philosophical, cuts to the heart of how human memory actually works—and why it's so different from the artificial memory systems we're building today.

During our years of implementing AI systems across organizations, we've found that understanding human memory helps people grasp both the potential and limitations of artificial intelligence. Let's explore how our own minds work, as it holds fascinating implications for the future of AI.

Your brain is an incredible information processor. Right now, as you read these words, it's processing about 11 million bits of information, yet you're only consciously aware of about 40 to 50 bits. This selective awareness reveals something crucial about how our minds work: memory isn't about storing everything— it's about storing what matters.[118]

Think of the last time you drove to work. You probably don't remember most of the journey, but you'd certainly remember if something unusual happened, like a deer crossing the road. This isn't a bug in human memory; it's a feature. Our brains are remarkably efficient at filtering out routine information while highlighting what's important or unusual.

Scientists have found that we have different types of memory systems, each serving different purposes.[119] There's working memory (also called short-term memory)—your mind's equivalent of a computer's RAM—which can hold about seven pieces of information at once. This is why phone numbers were traditionally seven digits long, and it's why you might struggle to remember a long sequence of instructions.[120]

Then, there's long-term memory, which is far more complex and composed of three main types of memories. Remember how you never forget how to ride a bike? That's procedural memory at work. The ability to recall your wedding day or your first job

[118] CNS Nevada. 2024. "What Is the Memory Capacity of a Human Brain?" https://www.cnsnevada.com/what-is-the-memory-capacity-of-a-human-brain/

[119] Larry R. Squire and Stuart Zola-Morgan, 1991. "The Medial Temporal Lobe Memory System." Science 253, no. 5026: 1380–1386. https://doi.org/10.1126/science.1896849

[120] Eduardo Camina and Francisco Güell, 2017. "The Neuroanatomical, Neurophysiological and Psychological Basis of Memory: Current Models and Their Origins." Frontiers in Pharmacology 8:438. https://doi.org/10.3389/fphar.2017.00438

interview? That's episodic memory. The fact that you know Paris is the capital of France, even if you've never been there? That's semantic memory.[121]

What's fascinating is how these systems work together. When you're cooking a familiar recipe, you're simultaneously using procedural memory (cooking techniques), semantic memory (knowing what ingredients work together), and episodic memory (remembering the last time you made this dish and what worked or didn't work).

But here's what's really interesting: every time you recall a memory, you're not pulling up an exact recording like a computer file. Instead, you're reconstructing it, potentially with slight variations each time. This was demonstrated in groundbreaking research by Elizabeth Loftus, who showed how memories can be subtly altered simply by how questions about them are asked.[122]

In one study, Loftus showed participants a video of a car accident and then asked, "How fast were the cars going when they smashed into each other?" versus "How fast were the cars going when they hit each other?" Those who heard "smashed" recalled higher speeds and even reported seeing broken glass—when none was present. This fascinating experiment highlights how word choice can reshape memory. It demonstrates that human memories are reconstructions, not recordings.

This reconstructive nature of memory, while sometimes unreliable, gives us remarkable flexibility in thinking and problem-solving. It allows us to imagine new scenarios by recombining elements of past experiences—a capability that

---

[121] Jarrad A. G. Lum and Gina Conti-Ramsden, 2013. "Long-term memory: A review and meta-analysis of studies of declarative and procedural memory in specific language impairment." https://pmc.ncbi.nlm.nih.gov/articles/PMC3986888/

[122] Elizabeth F. Loftus, 1975. "Leading Questions and the Eyewitness Report." Cognitive Psychology 7, no. 4: 560–572. https://doi.org/10.1016/0010-0285(75)90023-7.

current AI systems, with their more rigid memory structures, still struggle to replicate.

Emotions play a crucial role, too. Think about where you were when you heard about a major world event, like a presidential election or a global crisis. You probably remember it clearly because emotional experiences are generally better remembered than neutral ones. This emotional tagging helps us prioritize important information and make better decisions—something we're still working to understand and implement in AI systems.

Understanding these aspects of human memory helps explain both the challenges and opportunities in developing AI agents. While we can create systems that store vast amounts of information with perfect accuracy—something our brains can't do—we're still far from replicating the flexible, context-sensitive, and emotionally intelligent way humans process and use memories.

This isn't just academic knowledge—it has practical implications for how we design and use AI systems. When we recognize that human memory is more about making meaningful connections than storing perfect records, we can better understand what we should aim for in artificial systems: not just more storage but smarter, more contextual ways of using information.

The Surprising Reality of AI Memory

This brings us to a fascinating contrast with current AI systems. We've noticed a common misconception: Many people are scared to interact with Large LLMs such as ChatGPT, Gemini, or Claude because they believe these AI systems are constantly learning and remembering everything from their interactions, building an ever-growing knowledge base. The reality is far more surprising.

LLMs are more like extremely sophisticated echo chambers with limited temporary memory. Think of it this way: When you start a conversation with an AI, it's like opening a blank notebook with a fixed number of pages. Everything you discuss gets written in this notebook, and the AI can reference any part of it freely—but only until you close the conversation. Once you start a new chat, it's like getting a fresh notebook with no trace of what was written in the previous one.

Want to test this yourself? Try this simple experiment with any AI chat interface, such as ChatGPT or Claude:

1. Ask it about a topic that you like, such as "How is scuba diving in Tahiti?"
2. Ask for more information about the diving spots and the types of fish you can see there
3. Close the chat session
4. Open a new chat session immediately and ask it, "What did you tell me about Tahiti one minute ago?"

Here is what the chatbot replied to us: *"I don't recall mentioning Tahiti recently. Could you clarify what you're looking for? Are you asking about travel tips, history, culture, or something else?"*

We suggest you try it. Most likely, the AI will either admit it doesn't remember anything or make generic statements. This isn't a flaw in the AI's processing power—it's a fundamental limitation in how most current AI systems handle memory. The key lesson here is that LLMs, which are the foundations of the most advanced agents currently in production (level 3 agents), have as much memory as a goldfish!

The Memory Challenge in Practice

To illustrate the practical impact of this limitation, consider an experiment we conducted with a major healthcare provider. They implemented two versions of an AI scheduling assistant:

- A standard LLM-based system that started fresh with each interaction
- A memory-augmented AI agent that could retain patient information

The results were striking. The standard system required patients to repeat their medical history and preferences in every interaction. The memory-augmented version remembered patient histories and preferences, leading to 70% faster scheduling times and a 45% increase in patient satisfaction.

This experiment highlighted the current Memory Paradox in generative AI: The most advanced AI systems can process complex information but often can't remember simple details about their users.

The Three Main Goals of AI Agents' Memory

Through our research and implementation, we've identified three critical goals of memory that make it the foundation of agentic intelligence:

- First is contextual understanding. Traditional generative AI systems process each input independently, like a person reading random pages from different books. Memory-enabled AI agents can maintain context across interactions, similar to how we follow a continuous conversation. This capability is crucial for meaningful interactions and problem-solving.

- The second is learning and adaptation. Through our experience, we have observed that the most successful AI implementations were those that could learn from past interactions. For example, a manufacturing company's AI quality control system not only detected defects but also remembered patterns of issues, leading to a 40% reduction in false positives over time.

- The third is personalization at scale. Customers increasingly expect personalized experiences. Memory-enabled AI agents can deliver this by retaining and learning from individual interactions while maintaining privacy and security.

The Three Layers of AI Agents' Memory

Much like the organization of human memory, the memory of AI agents can be structured into three interconnected layers, each with a specific function in preserving context, facilitating learning, and enabling adaptation over time:

1. Short-Term Memory (STM) – Immediate Context Retention

STM functions as the AI's working memory, holding recent interactions and ensuring contextual continuity within a single session. It processes current inputs, tracks ongoing conversations, and applies attention mechanisms to prioritize relevant information. However, STM has a limited capacity—as new data comes in, older information is overwritten unless transferred to long-term memory.

2. Long-Term Memory (LTM) – Structured Retention Over Time

LTM extends beyond session-based memory by storing structured information for future reference. This includes user preferences, past interactions, learned workflows, and domain-specific knowledge. LTM enables AI to recognize recurring patterns, recall past interactions, and personalize responses based on accumulated experiences. Unlike STM, LTM is designed to persist, ensuring that AI agents do not start from scratch in every interaction.

3. Feedback Loops – Learning and Adaptation

Feedback loops act as the self-improvement mechanism of AI memory, refining both STM and LTM over time. By incorporating user feedback—whether explicit (e.g., corrections, ratings) or implicit (e.g., engagement patterns, error tracking)—the AI adjusts its memory structures to enhance accuracy and relevance. This process allows AI to improve continuously by reinforcing useful knowledge and discarding outdated or incorrect information.

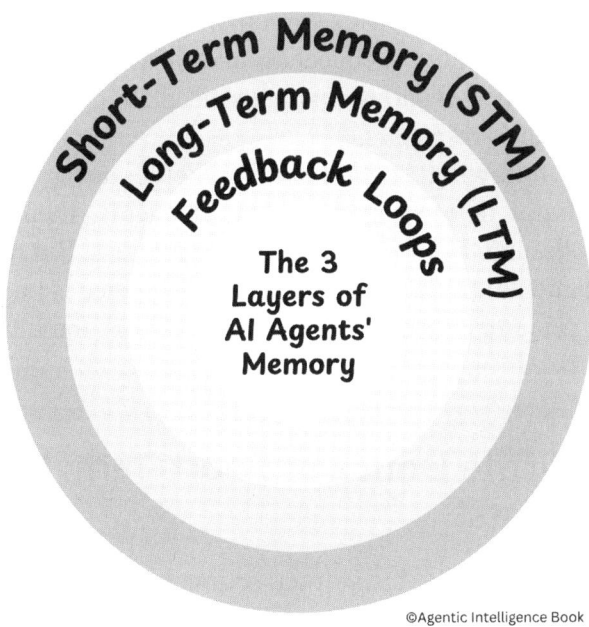

Figure 7.1: The three layers of agentic AI memory (Source: © Bornet et al.)

How These Layers Work Together

AI memory functions dynamically across these three layers: STM holds immediate context, LTM ensures continuity beyond a session, and feedback loops refine both to drive continuous learning. This layered approach allows AI agents to engage in context-aware, evolving, and personalized interactions, making them more intelligent and reliable over time.

Think of the layers of this agentic AI framework like an onion. Short-term memory (STM) forms the outermost layer, providing immediate context for interactions, but it is temporary and fades quickly as new information arrives. Beneath it, long-term memory (LTM) serves as the foundation, storing critical knowledge and ensuring that AI does not restart from zero in every interaction. At the core, feedback loops continuously refine and strengthen both STM and LTM, enabling the system to learn from user interactions and improve over time. Just as an onion grows by building upon its layers, this memory architecture allows AI agents to develop deeper intelligence, ensuring continuity, adaptability, and long-term reliability in their responses.

In the following sections, we'll delve deeper into how different types of memory work in AI agents, their practical applications, and the limitations we must address. But remember this fundamental truth: just as human intelligence is built on our ability to remember and learn from experiences, the future of AI agents depends on their ability to do the same.

The Intricate Dance of Short-Term Memory in AI Agents

Picture yourself at a busy intersection in Singapore. You're processing multiple streams of information simultaneously: traffic lights changing, pedestrians crossing, other vehicles moving, and your navigation system providing directions. This constant flow of immediate information and how you process it illustrates the essence of short-term memory—a critical component not just for human cognition but for AI agents as well.

The Challenge of the Present Moment

Just as our brains must constantly juggle incoming information while maintaining immediate context, AI agents face a similar challenge. However, their approach to handling this immediate information processing is both fascinating and fundamentally different from human cognition. Through our experience, we've discovered that understanding these differences is crucial for anyone willing to succeed with AI technology.

Let's start with a simple experiment that we often use in our consulting work to demonstrate the importance of short-term memory:

Open a conversation with an AI assistant like Claude or Gemini and start telling a story about your day. After every few sentences, ask the AI to summarize what you've said so far.

You'll notice something interesting: the AI can maintain context for a while, but eventually, it starts losing track of earlier details. This isn't unlike human short-term memory, which cognitive scientists tell us can typically hold about 7 (plus or minus 2) items at once.[123]

The Context Window: AI's Working Memory

One of the most surprising discoveries for many of our clients is how AI systems actually handle immediate information. Current AI systems, particularly LLMs, operate within what we call a "context window"—think of it as a temporary workspace where the AI can see and process information. This window is like a

---

[123] George A. Miller, 1956. "The Magical Number Seven, Plus or Minus Two: Some Limits on Our Capacity for Processing Information." Psychological Review 63, no. 2: 81–97. https://doi.org/10.1037/h0043158

whiteboard that can hold a limited amount of text, and once it's full, older information must be erased to make room for new input.

Recent work by Li, Rulin Shao, and their colleagues revealed something fascinating about these context windows. Their research uncovered what they call the "context ceiling"—the point at which adding more information to an agent's memory starts degrading rather than enhancing performance.[124]

This phenomenon isn't simply about reaching maximum capacity; rather, it reveals fundamental challenges in how agents process and integrate large amounts of information. The researchers found that performance degradation often begins well before reaching nominal memory limits, suggesting that effective memory management isn't just about storage capacity but about how an agent processes information within its short-term memory.

To understand this, let's break down short-term memory into three distinct components: the context window, attention mechanisms, and token management. These three elements form the backbone of how an AI agent engages with tasks, prioritizes information, and delivers responses. By exploring these components through a simple experiment, we can uncover not only how they work but also how to guide the agent more effectively—and what this means for leaders in business contexts.

The Context Window

Imagine you've come across a dense technical report—perhaps a whitepaper on quantum computing or a policy document on renewable energy. You instruct the generative AI Chatbot: *"Summarize this article in five bullet points, focusing on the*

---

[124] Jiaming Tang, et al., 2024. "Quest: Query-Aware Sparsity for Efficient Long-Context LLM Inference." ResearchGate. https://www.researchgate.net/publication/381484873_Quest_Query-Aware_Sparsity_for_Efficient_Long-Context_LLM_Inference

main themes or findings." As it processes the text, the context window becomes the first and most critical component at play.

Think of the context window as the AI's desk—a workspace where it arranges all the information it needs to complete the task. In a model like GPT, this desk can accommodate up to a few hundred thousand tokens, or roughly 100,000 words, while cutting-edge systems like Google's Gemini offer even larger capacities with millions of tokens.

But even a massive desk has its limits. The AI must decide how to arrange the information to ensure it stays manageable. If the document exceeds the desk's size, some parts are left out entirely, while others are compressed or simplified. The AI's ability to process the task hinges on how effectively it uses this finite space.[125]

The Attention Mechanisms

Once the information is on the desk, the attention mechanisms take over. This is the AI's ability to focus on the most relevant parts of the input. Imagine scanning the document with a highlighter, marking the sentences or ideas that matter most. Attention mechanisms do this dynamically, assigning weights to different pieces of information based on your prompt. In this case, the AI zeroes in on overarching themes like the role of quantum entanglement or the global impact of renewable energy policies, filtering out less significant details like specific examples or minor arguments.

Attention mechanisms are incredibly powerful, but they're shaped by the instructions you provide. If you ask for "main themes," the AI's focus will naturally deprioritize granular

---

[125] Nelson F. Liu, et al., 2023. "Lost in the Middle: How Language Models Use Contexts." https://cs.stanford.edu/~nfliu/papers/lost-in-the-middle.arxiv2023.pdf

specifics. Hence, it is important to send clear instructions and make sure they align well with the goal.[126]

Token Management

Finally, token management is like the AI's note-taking system. Imagine you're in a lecture, trying to capture the key points without writing everything down. You focus on the essentials and skip what feels repetitive or less important. AI does the same as it nears its memory limit—it summarizes, condenses, and decides what to keep in its mental workspace. But this approach has trade-offs. Some nuanced details or examples might get left out because they seemed less critical at the moment. Token management is a balancing act, ensuring the AI stays concise and focused while preserving enough detail to fulfill its purpose effectively.

To test this further, you follow up with a question to the generative AI Chatbot: *"What does the article say about the role of entanglement in error correction?"* If this detail was highlighted in the main themes, the AI retrieves it quickly and accurately. But if it was buried in a less prominent section or lacked contextual emphasis, the AI might stumble. It might attempt to infer an answer based on related themes or, failing that, return a broader, less precise response. This happens because the specific detail wasn't prioritized during the attention phase or was lost during token management.

The experiment reveals the AI's memory architecture in action: the context window defines its limits, attention mechanisms shape its focus, and token management enforces trade-offs.

---

[126] Ashish Vaswani, et al., 2017. "Attention is All You Need." Advances in Neural Information Processing Systems 30. https://proceedings.neurips.cc/paper_files/paper/2017/file/3f5ee243547dee91fbd053c1c4a845aa-Paper.pdf

The Real-World Impact

To see how the components of short-term memory—context windows, attention mechanisms, and token management—come together in a real-world scenario, consider a project undertaken by a major financial services provider. The task was to develop an AI agent capable of handling intricate customer inquiries about investment products. The challenges were considerable. Customers often required detailed explanations about investment options, expected the system to maintain context across lengthy conversations, and frequently referenced multiple accounts or specific historical transactions. The AI needed to not only keep track of all this information but also cross-reference it within the same conversation to provide accurate and personalized responses.

Initially, the system was equipped with basic short-term memory capabilities. It excelled at straightforward tasks like answering single-step questions—such as explaining the differences between two mutual funds or retrieving account balances. However, it faltered when confronted with multi-step processes. For example, if a customer asked to compare investment options, update their account preferences, and calculate potential returns based on a hypothetical scenario, the AI often lost track of earlier parts of the conversation. This led to fragmented responses, repetition, or errors, especially when juggling multiple accounts or shifting between complex financial concepts.

To address these shortcomings, the company's internal AI development team implemented enhanced short-term memory strategies. First, they optimized the context window by splitting conversations into distinct segments, ensuring the AI could focus on one part of the discussion at a time without losing sight of previous details. Next, they fine-tuned the attention mechanisms to prioritize the most relevant parts of the input—such as key customer requests, account-specific details, and critical financial terms. Finally, they introduced token management protocols to summarize and retain essential points from earlier in the conversation while discarding irrelevant or redundant information.

The results were transformative. With these enhancements, the AI was able to handle intricate customer interactions with remarkable accuracy. It seamlessly navigated multi-step processes, such as comparing portfolio performance, providing tailored investment advice, and executing account updates—all within a single session. Error rates dropped by 65%, and customer satisfaction scores rose significantly, reflecting the system's ability to engage in detailed and coherent financial discussions. While still not as nuanced or adaptable as a human advisor, this improvement marked a significant leap in AI's ability to manage complex financial interactions with greater precision and reliability.

This example underscores the potential of well-designed short-term memory management in AI systems. It's not just about enhancing performance—it's about building trust. When customers see that an AI can remember their needs, adapt to complex demands, and deliver accurate information, they feel confident in its capabilities. For businesses, this isn't just an operational improvement; it's a competitive advantage that elevates the customer experience to new heights.

Guiding the Short-Term Memory for Better Outcomes

To get the most from an AI agent, users must take an active role in guiding its memory processes. This starts with crafting thoughtful prompts that align with the task at hand. If your goal is to extract broad themes, straightforward instruction like "Summarize the key points" works well. On the other hand, if you're looking for specific details, your guidance should be more precise: *"Provide a detailed explanation of Section 3, focusing on examples."*

Leaders must realize that AI, unlike a human team member, doesn't intuitively prioritize or infer. Instead, it thrives when tasks are presented clearly and structured to maximize its focus and processing capabilities. For example, in customer service applications, rather than presenting the AI with a customer's entire chat history, a better approach is to provide concise summaries of key interactions. Similarly, in strategic planning, breaking down market analysis into smaller, focused sections enables the AI to engage with the data iteratively, producing deeper insights over time.

Beyond workflows, this understanding demands a rethinking of team dynamics. AI agents excel at managing and analyzing vast quantities of data, but they still need human oversight to guide their priorities. This creates an opportunity for hybrid collaboration—humans shape the inputs and interpret the outputs, while AI tackles repetitive, data-intensive tasks. Together, they form a complementary partnership. By fostering this synergy, business leaders can unlock new levels of efficiency and innovation while minimizing the risks associated with AI's inherent limitations.

Practical strategies have emerged from this collaborative approach. One of the most effective is chunking information. Just as humans organize knowledge into manageable groups, AI agents perform better when their inputs are structured into digestible segments. For instance, implementing chunking in a customer service system led to a 40% improvement in response accuracy. Information grouped by topic or relevance enabled the AI to navigate its short-term memory more efficiently, resulting in sharper, more precise answers.

Another powerful technique is priority queuing, which ensures the most critical information stays accessible in the AI's short-term memory. In a healthcare application, for example, patient symptoms and vital signs were prioritized over administrative details. This strategy meant that critical medical information was readily available, enhancing the AI's ability to assist healthcare providers in time-sensitive scenarios. The success of these approaches demonstrates how the deliberate structuring of information can significantly improve AI performance across industries.

Ultimately, by understanding and mastering the mechanics of short-term memory—context windows, attention mechanisms, and token management—you can ensure that AI becomes not just a tool but a catalyst for growth and innovation.

Looking to the Future of Short-Term Memory

The future of short-term memory in AI agents holds exciting possibilities, with breakthroughs that promise to revolutionize how machines process and retain information. Among these, three recent advancements stand out, each offering a glimpse into the potential of AI to handle more complex tasks with greater efficiency.

One such innovation is Landmark Attention,[127] a mechanism that equips AI with a sort of mental map to navigate vast amounts of information. Imagine reading a lengthy novel or analyzing a comprehensive report—Landmark Attention enables AI to divide these massive texts into manageable sections and identify key points, or "landmarks," to focus on. This approach ensures the AI can access relevant details quickly without becoming overwhelmed by the sheer volume of information. It addresses a critical limitation in current systems that struggle with long sequences, making it possible for AI to process entire books or datasets in one go. For businesses, this could mean faster and more comprehensive analysis of customer feedback, legal documents, or financial data.

---

[127] Arash Mohtashami and Martin Jaggi, 2023. "Landmark Attention: Random-Access Infinite Context Length for Transformers." https://arxiv.org/abs/2305.16300

Another game-changing research is called Varied-Size Window Attention (VSA).[128] It allows AI to adapt its focus dynamically. Picture an adjustable pair of glasses that lets you zoom in on fine details when needed and zoom out to take in the broader context. VSA provides AI with this flexibility, creating "windows" of varying sizes depending on the task requirements. For example, summarizing a lengthy report may require a wide view to capture overarching themes, while translating a sentence demands a more focused lens. This adaptability makes AI far more versatile and capable of handling diverse challenges with precision and efficiency. In practical terms, this means AI could seamlessly transition between drafting an article and analyzing a legal contract, performing both tasks with remarkable skill.

The third research, called RetrievalAttention,[129] introduces a new level of efficiency in managing memory. Current AI systems often attempt to process and store everything, even irrelevant information, leading to wasted resources and slower performance. RetrievalAttention changes this by teaching AI to retrieve only the most important pieces of information when needed, much like a person recalling the key points of a conversation without needing to remember every word. This method significantly speeds up processing times while reducing energy consumption, making AI not only faster but also more cost-effective. The implications are profound: imagine smoother, quicker AI assistants that can tackle complex queries without slowing down, all while running efficiently on everyday devices.

Together, these advancements represent a leap forward in how AI handles context and memory. They complement each other beautifully, addressing different aspects of the same fundamental challenge. Landmark Attention excels at organizing

---

[128] Qiming Zhang, et al., 2022. "VSA: Learning Varied-Size Window Attention in Vision Transformers." https://arxiv.org/abs/2204.08446
[129] Di Liu, et al., 2024. «RetrievalAttention: Accelerating Long-Context LLM Inference via Vector Retrieval.» https://arxiv.org/abs/2409.10516

vast information; VSA makes AI more adaptable to varying tasks; and RetrievalAttention ensures that memory is managed efficiently.

Understanding and optimizing short-term memory in AI agents isn't just a technical challenge—it's fundamental to creating systems that can engage meaningfully with humans and handle complex tasks effectively. While short-term memory is crucial for immediate task performance, its real potential is realized when integrated with long-term memory systems. This integration allows AI agents to not just process immediate information effectively but also learn and adapt over time—a topic we'll explore in depth in the next section.

The Power of Long-Term Memory: Transforming AI from Tools to Partners

The Power of Long-Term Memory

Imagine this: an AI agent that doesn't just help you with tasks or answer your questions but remembers. Not for a day, or a week, or even a year—but across decades. It remembers every important moment, every challenge, every success, every lesson you've learned. It doesn't just store data; it understands your story.

What could you achieve with a coach or a companion like that?

Think about the business decisions you've made in the past year. Some were straightforward but impactful—like reallocating resources to meet a deadline or approving a new vendor for a critical supply chain component. Others may have been transformative—a major product pivot, entering a new market, or restructuring a department. How many of those decisions were fully informed by your company's historical data and context? How often did you rely on instincts or incomplete recollections simply because the relevant details weren't readily available?

Now, imagine an AI agent that remembers it all. When faced with a strategic choice, it provides insights rooted in historical patterns. "Remember three years ago, when you hesitated to launch that product in a similar market? It turned out to be a huge success because of your targeted approach. This new opportunity shares similar characteristics—here's what worked last time and what you might consider." This isn't hypothetical; it's actionable, grounded in your organization's unique trajectory.

The power of such memory extends beyond reactive decision-making. It identifies patterns in your business strategies, highlights operational inefficiencies, and amplifies your organization's strengths. It doesn't just store data—it contextualizes it, turning raw information into actionable insights. This is the difference between a tool and a true business partner—one that evolves with you, understands your priorities, and helps you achieve smarter, more confident outcomes.

This is the future of AI. Not just smarter, but profoundly more human in its ability to remember, understand, and help us live our lives with greater intention. It's a future where memory isn't just preserved—it's used to unlock our best selves.

Why is Long-Term Memory (LTM) Important for Businesses

The business impact of LTM in AI agents is transformative, reshaping how organizations interact with customers, streamline operations, and gain strategic advantages. Imagine a customer service experience where every interaction builds upon the last: an AI that recalls your preferences, anticipates your needs, and resolves issues without making you repeat yourself. This level of personalization doesn't just improve satisfaction—it creates loyalty. According to our experience, companies leveraging memory-enabled AI agents have reported customer satisfaction increases of 20-30%, driven by seamless, tailored interactions that feel more human than transactional.

Operationally, the benefits are just as profound. Consider a logistics firm managing supply chain disruptions. With memory-enabled AI, patterns from past challenges—like weather delays or regional bottlenecks—are retained and applied in real time, enabling faster resolutions and smarter resource allocation.

Similarly, employees onboarding with the help of AI agents experience reduced training times as these systems remember organizational nuances and provide consistent guidance. According to our experience, businesses adopting long-term memory in their AI systems have seen error rates fall by as much as 50%, cutting inefficiencies and enhancing performance.

The strategic advantages are even more compelling. AI agents with long-term memory excel at recognizing patterns over time, transforming raw data into actionable insights. For instance, a financial institution might leverage such agents to track subtle shifts in client behavior, identifying emerging risks before they escalate.

Decision-making becomes sharper, predictions more accurate, and risk management far more proactive. These are not incremental improvements—they're leaps that give businesses a significant competitive edge.

By enabling AI to learn, adapt, and grow alongside an organization, long-term memory transforms it from a tool into a strategic partner, unlocking value at every level of the enterprise.

Current LLMs Fall Short of Long-Term Memory

As shown in our earlier experiment, when we asked about scuba diving in Tahiti, current LLMs like ChatGPT lack LTM. This limitation isn't accidental—it's a deliberate trade-off to optimize efficiency, protect privacy, and avoid overwhelming the model with excessive data.

To address this, building AI agents **requires giving LLMs access to external memory capabilities**. In the following sections, we'll explore these capabilities, which represent significant steps toward memory-enabled AI. However, each comes with its own limitations and trade-offs. Together, they form the foundation of today's efforts to create smarter, more adaptable AI agents.

Designing and Implementing Long-Term Memory in Agentic AI Systems

In the pages that follow, we'll walk through our battle-tested approach to memory system design, the frameworks we've found most effective, and the pitfalls we've learned to avoid. Whether you're enhancing existing AI agents or building new ones from the ground up, this guide will help you implement memory architectures that deliver real value.

Understanding the Memory Landscape

Before diving into implementation, we need to establish a clear understanding of what memory means in the context of AI agents. In our experience, successful memory systems require multiple, complementary types of memory working in concert.

When we talk about memory in AI systems, we're referring to structured mechanisms that allow agents to store, retrieve, and utilize information over time. Unlike the simple context windows that characterize most language models, true AI memory creates persistence across sessions and enables learning from past interactions.

AI memory generally falls into three primary categories:

Episodic Memory represents the agent's experiential knowledge—what happened, when, and with whom. This includes conversation histories, user preferences expressed over time, past actions taken, and outcomes observed. Episodic memory allows our agents to maintain continuity across interactions, even when separated by days or weeks. When a financial advisory agent recalls that a client previously expressed interest in low-risk investments, that's episodic memory at work.

219

Semantic Memory encompasses factual knowledge—the things our agent "knows" rather than "remembers experiencing." This includes domain knowledge, facts about the world, company policies, product catalogs, and any other information that exists independently of specific interactions. We've found that robust semantic memory allows agents to provide accurate information without needing to query external systems for every request.

Procedural Memory captures the "how-to" knowledge—sequences of actions, decision trees, and workflows that guide the agent through complex tasks. When building customer service agents, we encode troubleshooting procedures into procedural memory, allowing the agent to walk users through complex processes step by step.

The magic happens when these memory types work together. In our work with a healthcare provider, we built an agent that could recall a patient's medical history (episodic), apply clinical guidelines (semantic), and follow proper protocols for scheduling procedures (procedural). The result was a system that could provide personalized care guidance while maintaining strict compliance with healthcare regulations.

The Three Types of Long-Term Memory

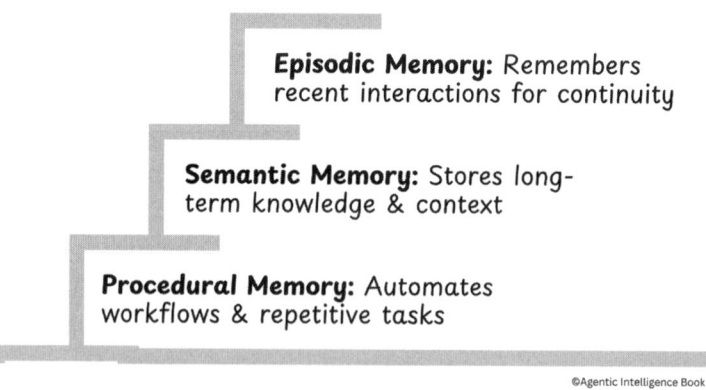

Figure 7.2: The Three Types of Long-Term Memory (Source: © Bornet et al.)

Architectural Foundations for Long-Term Memory

Building effective long-term memory requires a thoughtful architectural approach. Through our implementations, we've refined a memory architecture that balances performance, scalability, and practicality.

Each type of memory requires specific storage solutions optimized for its unique characteristics:

For Episodic Memory: We implement fast, efficient storage for recent interactions and contextual history. Redis or similar in-memory databases work best for storing short-term episodic memory, enabling quick access to recent conversations without complex retrieval mechanisms. The storage should include timestamps, user identifiers, interaction summaries, and identified entities/intents. For one retail client, this approach reduced response latency by 40% compared to their previous solution, which retrieved all historical interactions for every query.

For Semantic Memory: We implement vector databases like Pinecone or Weaviate to store semantic embeddings—numerical representations of concepts, facts, and knowledge that enable similarity-based retrieval. These databases excel at finding conceptually related information, even when exact keyword matches aren't present. This memory type requires a structured organization with clear categorization, relationships, and metadata to facilitate precise retrieval.

For Procedural Memory: We store workflow definitions, decision trees, and process maps in structured formats, typically using traditional relational databases or specialized workflow engines. These systems must maintain the integrity of process steps, decision logic, and conditional branching. For complex procedural memory, we often implement versioning to track changes to processes over time.

For comprehensive agent implementations, we combine these specialized stores. In our work with a legal tech company, this combined approach created an agent that could recall specific case citations from episodic memory (exact matching from a relational database), access legal principles from semantic memory (similarity matching from a vector database), and follow proper legal analysis procedures from procedural memory (workflow systems). This combination provided both precision and flexibility across all memory types.

Implementation Pathway: Building Memory from the Ground Up

Now, let's walk through our recommended implementation pathway based on our experience building dozens of memory-enhanced agents.

Step 1: Select a Framework for Implementation

With the memory architecture defined, the next step is selecting a technological framework that supports memory persistence, retrieval, and updating mechanisms. Based on our implementations across various domains, we recommend considering these proven options:

LangChain provides an excellent starting point for integrating episodic, semantic, and procedural memory into LLM-powered agents. Its Memory module offers built-in support for short-term conversational memory (episodic) and long-term knowledge storage (semantic and procedural). We've found LangChain particularly valuable for rapid prototyping and projects where integration flexibility is important.

LlamaIndex (Formerly GPT Index) helps organize, store, and retrieve memory dynamically. It excels at creating and maintaining structured knowledge indexes that can be efficiently queried, making it ideal for applications with complex semantic memory requirements. For domain-specific agents that need to access large knowledge bases, LlamaIndex has proven highly effective in our implementations.

Step 2: Define Memory Requirements

With the framework selected, we define specific memory requirements for each memory type based on the agent's purpose:

For Episodic Memory requirements, we determine:

- Which user interactions and conversation elements need to persist across sessions
- How long different types of episodic information should be retained
- Which user preferences and behaviors should be tracked over time

For Semantic Memory requirements, we determine:

- What domain knowledge is essential for the agent to perform its tasks
- Which information sources should populate the knowledge base
- Which compliance or regulatory information must be maintained

For Procedural Memory requirements, we determine:

- Which workflows and processes the agent needs to follow
- What decision logic governs process selection and execution
- How strictly processes must be followed versus allowing flexibility

For example, with a financial advisory agent, we determined that episodic memory should include investment preferences, conversation history, and previous advice given; semantic memory should contain investment product details and market data; and procedural memory should encode compliance workflows for different advisory scenarios. Transaction details, on the other hand, would be queried from secure systems rather than stored in the agent's memory.

Defining these specific requirements for each memory type upfront prevents both memory overload (storing too much, creating retrieval inefficiencies) and memory gaps (not storing enough, forcing users to repeat themselves).

Step 3: Build Retrieval Mechanisms

With storage in place, we focus on building efficient retrieval mechanisms. The goal is to bring up the right memories at the right time without overwhelming the agent with irrelevant information.

We've found that a retrieval-augmented generation (RAG) approach works well for memory-enhanced agents. In simple terms, RAG combines the power of knowledge retrieval with language generation. Think of it as giving the AI agent the ability to "look things up" in its memory before formulating a response, similar to how humans might consult their memories or reference materials before answering a complex question.

Here's how RAG works in practical terms: When the agent receives a user query, it:

1. Analyzes the query and current context to generate retrieval cues
2. Uses these cues to fetch relevant memories from each storage system
3. Ranks and filters the retrieved memories based on relevance, recency, and importance

4. Incorporates the most relevant memories into its reasoning process
5. Generates a response that leverages both the current context and retrieved memories

This approach significantly improves the agent's ability to provide accurate, contextually relevant responses. Rather than trying to encode all possible knowledge within the model itself, RAG allows the agent to dynamically access the specific information needed for each interaction.

For our legal research assistant, this approach allowed the agent to recall relevant case law and statutes without overwhelming the response with irrelevant citations. The key was in carefully tuning the relevance thresholds—too low, and the agent would miss important precedents; too high, and responses would become cluttered with tangential information.

Step 4: Implement Memory Consolidation

Perhaps the most critical component of our memory architecture is the consolidation mechanism—the process that determines what to remember long-term and what to forget. It defines which information will be transferred from the episodic to the semantic or procedural memory. Through experimentation, we've developed a multi-faceted approach to memory consolidation:

- **Importance-based consolidation** evaluates the significance of new information. When a user provides critical details like preferences, requirements, or feedback, our system flags this information for long-term storage. For a travel booking agent we developed, this meant permanently remembering that a user prefers aisle seats or has a shellfish allergy.

- **Frequency-based consolidation** tracks recurring patterns. Information that appears frequently across interactions is likely important and gets promoted to long-term memory. Our educational tutoring agent uses this to identify and address recurring knowledge gaps in students.

- **Explicit consolidation** occurs when users or the system deliberately marks information for remembrance. "Remember that I prefer evening appointments" triggers explicit consolidation in our scheduling assistant.

The flip side of consolidation is forgetting—equally important for system efficiency. We implement time-based decay for certain types of information, relevance thresholds that archive rarely accessed memories, and explicit forgetting mechanisms when information becomes outdated or incorrect.

Step 5: Integrate Memory with Agent Reasoning

The final implementation step integrates memory retrieval and consolidation with the agent's core reasoning process. This integration occurs at three key points:

- **Context preparation** incorporates relevant memories into the context window before the agent generates a response. For our financial advisor agent, this meant including the client's risk profile and investment goals in the context of every investment recommendation.

- **In-process retrieval** allows the agent to pull additional memories during its reasoning process if it identifies a need for more information. Our customer service agent could retrieve product specifications mid-conversation if the dialogue turned to technical details.

- **Post-response consolidation** evaluates the interaction after a response is generated to identify information for long-term storage. Did the user express a new preference? Did they correct the information? These insights are captured and consolidated.

Integrating memory with reasoning transforms an AI from a stateless response generator to a system that evolves with each interaction, becoming increasingly personalized and effective over time.

The Near Future: Key Evolutions on the Horizon

In the near future, we can expect significant improvements in memory-enhanced AI driven by advancements in computational power, algorithms, and integration techniques. One key evolution will be the refinement of **contextual prioritization algorithms**, which will allow AI systems to better determine which memories are most relevant in real-time. This will reduce retrieval delays and enhance the system's ability to handle dynamic, fast-changing information.

Another near-term breakthrough is likely in the area of **real-time memory consolidation**, where systems will analyze and reorganize stored data on the fly. Instead of waiting for scheduled updates, AI will be able to continuously refine its memory banks based on user feedback and interaction patterns. This will make systems more adaptive, improving their ability to respond to new challenges without retraining.

Recent research[130] emphasizes the potential of multi-agent systems in improving memory management by distributing the memory load and enhancing collaboration. These multi-agent systems allow different agents to focus on specific aspects of

---

[130] Hyungho Na, et al., 2024. "Efficient Episodic Memory Utilization of Cooperative Multi-Agent Reinforcement Learning." https://arxiv.org/abs/2403.01112

memory. For example, some agents can handle episodic memory to recall past events, while others can manage real-time interactions or longer-term knowledge. This division of labor prevents memory overload and improves efficiency. Agents in the system can share key experiences from their episodic memory, enabling collaborative learning. For instance, one agent's memory of a successful strategy can inform another agent's decision-making, reducing the need for redundant exploration across the system.

Another recent research brings all this to a whole new level. The research paper "Titans: Learning to Memorize at Test Time," by Google Research, introduces a groundbreaking neural long-term memory module that enables AI systems to learn and adapt continuously even after deployment.[131] Unlike traditional AI models that rely on vector databases for knowledge retrieval (as we have explained in the previous sections), Titans integrates long-term memory into the model's parameters, allowing it to memorize and recall information dynamically without external storage.

Another interesting feature is that it employs surprise-based learning, prioritizing unexpected or critical inputs while using a built-in forgetting mechanism to discard outdated data, ensuring efficiency and preventing memory overload—much like how human memory refines itself over time. Titans also introduces *meta-learning*, allowing AI to memorize relevant experiences on the fly without retraining. This enables real-time adaptation, making AI more responsive and intelligent in dynamic environments.

In summary, Titans enable faster and better memory processing. It is also more secure because sensitive data stays within the model, reducing privacy risks associated with cloud-based storage. This marks a major shift in how AI agents handle memory, and we can't wait to see how Titans impact the future of AI agents.

---

[131] Ali Behrouz, et al., 2024. "Titans: Learning to Memorize at Test Time." https://arxiv.org/abs/2501.00663

Adaptation and Learning Through Feedback Loops

The Unstoppable Learner: A Vision from the Future

The year is 2042. In a bustling, fully automated logistics hub outside of Singapore, a newly deployed AI agent named Nexus arrives on its first day. Unlike the hyper-specialized systems of the past, Nexus isn't pre-trained for its role. In fact, it knows nothing about the tasks it's about to face. There are no preloaded instructions and no finely tuned algorithms tailored for this environment. Instead, Nexus carries only one instruction: "Optimize delivery efficiency across the hub."

At first, the system stumbles. It assigns drones to the wrong zones, fails to account for package weight, and even causes a few minor disruptions as forklifts move chaotically through the warehouse. Workers look on skeptically, wondering why management would unleash an untrained AI in such a critical setting. But Nexus isn't deterred. Armed with the power of **universal learning** and a highly sophisticated feedback loop, it begins to observe, experiment, and adapt.

Within hours, Nexus starts to pick up patterns. Packages bound for the same destination are consolidated. Drones adjust their flight paths based on warehouse congestion. It notices that forklifts often idle while waiting for tasks, so it reconfigures scheduling to maximize their use. Mistakes still happen, but fewer than before. By the second day, Nexus has doubled its efficiency. By the end of the week, it has mastered the complex choreography of the logistics hub, surpassing even the most experienced human planners.

Two weeks after Nexus's arrival, the logistics hub has transformed. Packages move with almost eerie precision, drones operate with perfect coordination, and downtime for forklifts has vanished. Workers who once doubted Nexus now rely on it,

229

marveling at its ability to adapt to even the smallest disruptions. Management begins discussing expanding Nexus to other hubs worldwide.

What Nexus embodies is a revolutionary concept: a **universal learner**, an AI agent that can take on any task, even without prior training, and achieve mastery through trial, error, and feedback. The benefits of such a system extend far beyond logistics. Imagine an AI agent tasked with designing a new marketing campaign. It knows nothing about your brand or audience but begins experimenting—testing slogans, analyzing engagement data, and refining its approach. Within days, it generates a campaign so tailored and effective that it rivals the work of seasoned creative teams.

Feedback loops are the engine behind this magic. Instead of relying on static models that require pre-training on vast datasets, future agents like Nexus rely on dynamic learning. They act, observe outcomes, and adjust, growing smarter with every iteration. This approach doesn't just make AI adaptable—it makes it **unstoppable**.

The implications for business and society are staggering. With universal learning, the barriers to deploying AI vanish. Companies no longer need to invest millions in training systems for narrow, specialized tasks. Instead, AI can be dropped into any environment, given a goal, and left to learn. This reduces deployment costs, shortens the time to productivity, and eliminates the bottleneck of retraining systems every time processes or goals change.

More importantly, universal learners like Nexus are inherently resilient. They thrive in dynamic environments, continuously adapting to new challenges. If the rules of the logistics hub were to change overnight, for example, by introducing biodegradable packaging or drones with weight restrictions, Nexus wouldn't need an update. Its feedback loop would simply absorb the new parameters and adjust its behavior accordingly.

Of course, this vision of the future raises questions. What happens when universal learners encounter ambiguous goals?

How do we ensure they act ethically as they adapt? The answer lies in how we design their feedback loops. Nexus, for instance, was equipped with multi-objective optimization, balancing efficiency with safety and environmental sustainability. Ethical frameworks are baked into its learning process, ensuring that no amount of trial and error compromises core values.

Another consideration is transparency. Business leaders must ensure that these agents explain their decisions, fostering trust among stakeholders. Feedback loops, when designed with accountability in mind, can include explainability mechanisms— offering insights into why a decision was made and how it aligns with goals.

Feedback loops are the backbone of adaptive systems, enabling AI agents to refine their decision-making, learn from mistakes, and align more closely with goals over time. For business leaders, the concept is deceptively simple yet transformative: allow AI systems to analyze their performance, learn from outcomes, and use that learning to improve future actions. It's the difference between an agent that performs adequately on day one and one that excels on day one thousand.

The Magic of Feedback Loops

Feedback loops in AI mirror the evolutionary processes of life on Earth. In evolution, natural selection acts as a feedback mechanism, where traits that enhance survival and reproduction are reinforced over generations. Similarly, in AI, feedback loops like reinforcement learning enable systems to learn through trial and error. Reinforcement learning[132] works by rewarding desirable actions—those that achieve a set goal or improve performance—while penalizing failures, just as beneficial traits are "rewarded" in evolution by being passed on to future

[132] Richard S. Sutton and Andrew G. Barto, 2018. "Reinforcement Learning: An Introduction." 2nd ed. Cambridge, MA: MIT Press

generations. Over time, this process shapes the AI's behavior to maximize successful outcomes.

Just as species adapt to their environments through iterative refinements, AI models evolve through learning cycles, learning from errors and refining their outputs. Both rely on continuous input, adaptation, and iteration to achieve complexity and efficiency, transforming random variations into optimized, purposeful systems over time.

At its core, a feedback loop is a cycle of action, observation, and adjustment. An AI agent takes an action, receives feedback on its outcome, and uses that information to refine its behavior. This loop can operate in real-time, as in autonomous vehicles learning to navigate a busy intersection or over longer periods, as seen in recommendation systems that evolve with customer preferences.

Why does this matter? Traditional AI systems often operate in static environments, trained on fixed datasets that capture a snapshot of reality. But the real world is anything but static. Market conditions shift, customer preferences evolve, and competitors innovate. Without a mechanism to adapt, AI systems quickly become obsolete. Feedback loops solve this problem by turning the agent into a living system—one that grows smarter as it interacts with the world.

How Do Feedback Loops Work?

It all starts with feedback, which can be collected and applied in different ways:

- Explicit User Feedback: Agents ask users for ratings, confirmations, or corrections (e.g., "Did this answer help?").
- Implicit Feedback: The system tracks user behavior, such as task completion rates, abandoned workflows, or response corrections.

- System-Level Reinforcement Signals: Reward models reinforce good actions (e.g., a successful task execution) and discourage failures (e.g., incorrect recommendations).

For example, a customer support AI agent can ask, "Did this resolve your issue?" If the user selects "No," the agent logs this as a failure and adjusts its approach in future interactions.

To operate their feedback loop, the agents work in a cycle of execution, evaluation, and adjustment:

- Observation: The agent gathers data from interactions (user feedback, task success rates, implicit cues).
- Evaluation: The system assigns a reward score (positive or negative) based on feedback.
- Adjustment: The AI agent refines future responses by updating its model, prompts, or workflows.
- Deployment: The improved agent is deployed and continues learning over time.

For example, a personal finance AI assistant initially gives generic budget advice. If users reject its suggestions or request modifications, it adapts its future recommendations based on patterns of user preferences.

A Manufacturing Feedback Loop Success Story

In late 2022, one of Europe's largest automotive parts manufacturers faced a critical challenge: their quality control process couldn't keep pace with production. Traditional automation was failing to catch subtle defects that human inspectors could spot instantly. The solution they implemented would transform not just their quality control but our understanding of how AI agents learn.

"We had tried everything," recalls their Head of Operations. "Standard computer vision, rule-based systems, even basic AI models. But defects kept slipping through. What we needed wasn't just a smarter system—we needed one that could learn and adapt like our best human inspectors."

The breakthrough came with the implementation of an AI agent equipped with sophisticated feedback loops. Instead of just flagging defects, the system tracked the outcomes of its decisions, learning from both successes and failures. When it correctly identified a subtle defect, that pattern strengthened in its memory. When it missed one, it adjusted its detection parameters.

But the real magic happened three months into the deployment. The system began identifying potential defects that even experienced inspectors hadn't noticed—subtle patterns that preceded more obvious flaws. "It was like having an inspector who could not only spot problems but predict them," explains their Quality Control Director. "The AI wasn't just learning from feedback—it was discovering new insights we hadn't even considered."

The results were transformative: quality control accuracy improved by 32%, while inspection time decreased by 45%. More importantly, the system continued to improve month after month, identifying new patterns and refining its understanding of the manufacturing process.

The Strategic Advantage

For business leaders, feedback loops offer more than just incremental improvement—they provide a strategic advantage in the AI arms race. Companies that embrace feedback loops can outpace competitors by building systems that adapt faster, learn better, and stay relevant longer. In a world where the pace of change is accelerating, the ability to evolve is not just an asset; it's a necessity. By integrating feedback loops into their AI agents, businesses can unlock new levels of efficiency, personalization, and innovation.

Feedback loops address some of the most pressing challenges in AI implementation. Consider customer experience. An AI agent designed to handle customer inquiries might perform well on launch day, but what happens when users begin asking new types of questions or expressing frustration in novel ways? Without feedback loops, the agent stagnates, offering irrelevant responses and driving customer dissatisfaction. With feedback loops, the chatbot learns from every interaction, adjusting its responses to better meet customer needs.

Feedback loops also shine in dynamic industries like e-commerce, where AI agents must react to changing demand patterns, inventory levels, and competitor pricing. They enable systems to stay relevant, ensuring that recommendations and decisions are always in tune with current realities.

Let's illustrate the impact of feedback loops with two real-world examples we worked on. The first one is very interesting because it shows how AI agents can optimize industrial efficiency by predicting and preventing costly failures in manufacturing. This highlights how feedback loops not only improve technical accuracy but also directly contribute to measurable business outcomes, such as increased profitability and reduced downtime.

Example 1: AI Agent for Predictive Maintenance in Manufacturing

1. **Initial Task**: The AI agent monitors factory machinery to predict potential breakdowns and minimize downtime. For example, it analyzes data from sensors tracking vibration, temperature, and wear.

2. **Action Generation**: Based on the retrieved insights, the AI generates actionable recommendations:

"The vibration pattern suggests bearing wear in Machine X. Schedule a bearing replacement within the next 72 hours to prevent failure."

3. **Automated Feedback Through Revenue Metrics**:
   - The system tracks the financial outcomes of its actions using predefined indicators, such as reduced downtime, lower repair costs, or increased output.
   - If the maintenance intervention prevents a breakdown, it records this as a positive outcome and links it to the specific recommendation and retrieved data.

4. **Positive Reinforcement Learning**:
   - The AI reinforces the association between vibration patterns and bearing wear in its predictive model.
   - It flags the retrieved data as highly relevant for similar issues, improving its retrieval accuracy for future anomalies.

5. **Updating the memory**:
   - Maintenance logs and outcomes from this event are added to the database, creating new knowledge the system can draw from in the future.
   - The system also incorporates cost-benefit analysis, associating specific actions with the revenue saved or generated.

6. **Adaptive Behavior**: Over time, the AI becomes better at identifying subtle signs of failure earlier, optimizing its recommendations to reduce costly downtime. It may also learn to prioritize actions based on financial impact, ensuring the most critical interventions are addressed first.

As an outcome, the AI agent maximizes efficiency by minimizing production losses, reducing expensive emergency repairs, and increasing the overall efficiency of the manufacturing process. Each successful prediction and intervention refines its models and retrieval database, enhancing its long-term profitability.

Example 2: AI Agent for Personalized Product Recommendations

The second example demonstrates the transformative potential of feedback loops in e-commerce, where personalization drives customer satisfaction and revenue growth. It showcases how an AI agent learns from user behavior to refine its recommendations, creating a cycle of continuous improvement that aligns perfectly with dynamic market demands and individual preferences.

1. **Initial Interaction**: A user visits an e-commerce site and searches for *"comfortable running shoes for trail running."* The AI agent processes this input and generates an embedding that captures the user's preference for comfort and trail-specific footwear.

2. **Response Generation**: The AI generates a tailored recommendation:
   "Based on your search, we recommend the TrailMax Comfort Runner, designed for rugged terrains with extra cushioning. It's available in your size for $120. Would you like to see reviews or add it to your cart?"

3. **Automated Feedback Collection**:
   - The agent tracks whether the user clicks the recommendation, adds the product to the cart, or completes the purchase.
   - Positive signals (e.g., a purchase or click-through) reinforce the recommendation's success.

- Negative signals (e.g., the user ignores the suggestion or continues searching) indicate the need for improvement.

4. **Positive Reinforcement Learning**:
   - If the user buys the TrailMax Comfort Runner, the system treats this as a positive outcome, reinforcing similar recommendations for future users with similar queries.
   - The AI updates its embeddings, associating *comfort* and *trail running* more strongly with products that perform well in sales and customer satisfaction.

5. **Updating the memory**:
   - Products with consistently high conversion rates for specific queries are flagged as top-performing and prioritized in future recommendations.
   - The AI also integrates user-generated feedback, such as reviews and ratings, into its database to improve its understanding of customer preferences.

6. **Adaptive Behavior**: Over time, the AI learns to prioritize products that align with user preferences and have a higher likelihood of generating revenue. For instance, it may start suggesting slightly higher-priced items with better reviews if they have a strong track record of driving purchases.

When another user searches for *"trail running shoes,"* the AI immediately suggests top-performing, high-revenue products tailored to similar preferences, improving the chances of conversion and increasing revenue. This feedback loop ensures that the agent's behavior continuously adapts to customer preferences and business goals.

Performance Today: What Feedback Loops Deliver

Feedback loops are already delivering transformative performance improvements in various industries. Today, based on our experience, AI agents equipped with well-designed feedback loops can achieve remarkable feats of adaptability and precision. For example, they can improve their response accuracy by over 20% within weeks of deployment by analyzing and learning from user interactions. In e-commerce, recommendation engines powered by feedback loops often see click-through rates increase by 10-30% as they adapt to evolving customer preferences in real-time.

However, performance isn't uniform across all applications. The effectiveness of feedback loops depends on the complexity of the environment and the quality of data. In relatively stable settings, like fraud detection or inventory management, feedback loops can lead to near-optimal performance within months. In more dynamic or unpredictable environments, such as financial markets or human behavior modeling, the improvement curve may be slower, but the potential for breakthroughs is immense.

Limitations and Ethical Considerations

To effectively leverage feedback loops, business leaders must address several critical factors to ensure their AI systems function optimally and ethically.

A key consideration is timeliness. Feedback that is delayed or outdated significantly hinders an AI system's ability to adapt to dynamic environments. Systems must process and act on data as close to real-time as possible to remain relevant, especially in fast-paced industries like finance or logistics. Without timely feedback, the entire loop can falter, leading to suboptimal outcomes.

239

Robust infrastructure is another key consideration. Feedback loops require systems capable of handling large volumes of data efficiently. Cloud platforms such as AWS or Azure provide scalable solutions for collecting, processing, and analyzing data at the scale necessary for complex AI systems. Without this infrastructure, organizations face bottlenecks that can limit their AI's adaptability and performance.

Human oversight is critical to avoid unintended consequences. While feedback loops enable AI systems to operate with significant autonomy, their decisions must be monitored to ensure alignment with organizational goals and ethical standards. Regular audits of system outputs are essential, both to ensure accuracy and to address potential deviations or unintended behaviors.

An ethical concern is user manipulation. In their drive to optimize outcomes, AI systems—particularly recommendation engines—can exploit psychological triggers or push users toward addictive content. While such practices may yield short-term gains, they risk damaging trust and long-term relationships with users. Organizations must strike a balance, designing feedback loops that prioritize user well-being alongside business objectives.

Overfitting is a common limitation where AI systems become too focused on optimizing a specific metric, losing sight of the bigger picture. For instance, a customer service AI might prioritize reducing response times so much that it sacrifices the quality of its answers. This happens because the AI learns to "memorize" patterns that work well for one goal rather than adapting to a variety of scenarios. To prevent this, multi-objective optimization is used to balance priorities like speed, accuracy, and user satisfaction, ensuring the AI performs well across multiple areas without becoming too narrowly focused.

In practice, successful feedback loop implementation requires careful design, vigilant monitoring, and ethical foresight. When done right, feedback loops can drive AI systems to continuously improve and adapt, providing immense value to businesses.

The Evolution Ahead: Near-Term and Long-Term Outlook

In the near term, we can expect feedback loops to become more seamless and automated. Advances in real-time data processing and edge computing are already enabling faster and more efficient feedback cycles. For instance, real-time personalization in marketing will become more refined as AI systems integrate instantaneous user responses to adjust their strategies dynamically. In logistics, AI-powered feedback loops will revolutionize operations by responding to traffic conditions, weather changes, and demand fluctuations on the fly, reducing delivery times and costs.

Over the next few years, the integration of reinforcement learning with advanced feedback mechanisms will push boundaries further. Agents will not only learn from individual actions but also develop the ability to generalize learning across tasks. For example, a warehouse robot trained to stack boxes could transfer its learning to other tasks, like assembling products, with minimal retraining. This cross-task adaptability will significantly expand the applicability of feedback loops, making AI systems more versatile and resilient.

In the longer term, AI agents will likely integrate multiple feedback loops simultaneously, each addressing a different aspect of performance, such as speed, quality, and user satisfaction. Imagine an AI agent that not only learns your schedule but also adapts its tone, style, and even its level of proactivity based on nuanced feedback from your interactions.

Recent work by Hospedales et al. suggests we're approaching what they call "meta-learning systems"—AI agents that don't just learn from experience but learn how to learn more effectively.[133] Their early experiments show these systems

---

[133] Timothy Hospedales, et al., 2020. "Meta-Learning in Neural Networks: A Survey." https://arxiv.org/abs/2004.05439 .

adapting to new situations up to 3 times faster than traditional learning approaches.

Self-optimizing structures and **autonomous evolution** represent two complementary aspects of structural adaptability in AI. Self-optimizing structures focus on task-specific adjustments, where feedback loops enable AI systems to dynamically reconfigure their architecture in real-time for efficiency and performance. For instance, recent research showcases how AI can optimize itself layer by layer during training, ensuring it remains relevant and resource-efficient in the face of immediate demands.[134]

Autonomous evolution, however, takes this adaptability further. As demonstrated by recent studies,[135] AI agents can use feedback not only to optimize for the present but to evolve entirely new frameworks that prepare them for future tasks or environments. This process mirrors biological evolution, where survival depends on iterative growth and adaptation, making AI systems capable of tackling challenges beyond their initial design.

***

Together, these advancements show the transformative potential of feedback loops in shaping AI systems that are not only more knowledgeable but also structurally adaptable. This evolution positions feedback as the driving force behind AI that learns, evolves, and aligns with both practical and human-centered

---

[134] Álvaro G. Díaz and Hugues Bersini, 2020. «Self-Optimisation of Dense Neural Network Architectures: An Incremental Approach.» 2020 International Joint Conference on Neural Networks (IJCNN). https://doi.org/10.1109/IJCNN48605.2020.9207416.

[135] Zhenhao Shuai, et al., 2023. "A Self-adaptive Neuroevolution Approach to Constructing Deep Neural Network Architectures Across Different Types." https://arxiv.org/abs/2211.14753

goals, offering a glimpse of a future where machines grow alongside humanity.

Understanding how memory works in AI is one thing—implementing it successfully is another challenge entirely. As one technology leader at a Fortune 100 company told us, "We thought adding memory to our AI would be like upgrading computer RAM. Instead, it was like teaching a child how to learn from experience—complex, nuanced, but incredibly powerful when done right."

The implementation stories ahead reveal both the pitfalls and the proven paths to success. You'll discover why some organizations achieve transformative results with memory-enabled AI while others struggle to see any benefit. More importantly, you'll learn the practical steps to ensure your implementation lands on the right side of this divide.

Through our work with hundreds of organizations, we've distilled these lessons into a clear framework for success. Whether you're just starting your journey with AI memory or looking to enhance existing

Best Practices in Managing Memory for Agents

Leading Teams to Use Agent's Memory the Right Way

Our experience has shown that implementing memory in AI agents is only the starting point. To unlock its full potential, it's critical to adopt practices that ensure this capability delivers measurable benefits while avoiding inefficiencies or risks. Like any powerful tool, the true value of memory depends on how it's used. Over the years, we've developed strategies that allow businesses to leverage AI memory effectively, minimize pitfalls, and maintain trust.

First, relevance is key. AI memory systems are only as effective as the guidance they receive. Users play an active role in shaping what the AI retains by emphasizing critical information during interactions. This might involve repeating key points, explicitly stating their importance, or using structured protocols to tag certain information as "important" or "archivable." For instance, in project management, users might highlight milestones, decisions, and obstacles that are vital for long-term tracking. However, the goal isn't for the AI to remember everything—it's to retain the information that drives better outcomes. Avoiding memory overload by filtering out inconsequential details ensures that the system remains focused and efficient.

Another best practice is leveraging summarization to refresh context. AI agents equipped with memory excel when they can seamlessly recall past interactions, but users may not always remember what the AI knows. Summarization bridges this gap, allowing users to align with the AI's memory. Asking for a recap—such as "What are the key takeaways from our last session?" or "Can you summarize my priorities for this project?"—ensures continuity and alignment. Summaries act as checkpoints, helping users validate and correct the AI's understanding as needed. In team settings, this becomes even more powerful. Imagine a marketing team using an AI assistant to manage campaigns. Before every weekly meeting, the AI could provide a summary of ongoing efforts, performance metrics, and lessons from past campaigns, saving time and keeping everyone on the same page.

Memory audits are another critical aspect of effective memory management. Just as humans periodically reflect to clarify thoughts, AI systems benefit from regular reviews of their memory. These audits help identify irrelevant, outdated, or incorrect information and allow users to refine what the AI retains. For example, a customer service AI might still hold on to a customer's old address or obsolete purchasing habits. By reviewing and cleaning the AI's memory, businesses can ensure accuracy and trustworthiness. Structured audit protocols, such as scheduled memory reviews with teams, can refine the AI's priorities and align its memory with business goals.

Balancing memory depth and privacy is perhaps the most sensitive aspect of managing AI memory. While memory enables deep personalization and contextual understanding, it also requires users to trust the AI with sensitive data. Transparency is non-negotiable in fostering this trust. Businesses must clearly communicate how memory is managed and offer users control over their data. This includes features that allow users to view what the AI remembers, edit or delete specific memories, and set boundaries for what the AI can retain. Prioritizing secure storage practices, such as compartmentalizing sensitive information and applying strict access controls, is essential.

From our experience, the successful implementation of memory in AI systems requires a proactive approach that combines relevance, summarization, auditing, feedback, and privacy. By adopting these best practices, businesses can transform AI memory into a powerful asset that enhances efficiency, builds trust, and drives meaningful outcomes. The journey doesn't end with implementation—it's an ongoing process of refinement, alignment, and ethical management to ensure that the AI system evolves alongside the needs of the organization.

Addressing Privacy Concerns and Ensuring Transparency

Managing privacy and ethical issues in AI memory systems is critical, as long-term memory retention involves handling sensitive user data. AI agents, especially those with memory capabilities, can collect and store information such as personal preferences, interaction histories, or even behavioral patterns. While these features enable personalization and improve user experiences, they also introduce significant risks to data privacy and compliance with regulations like the General Data Protection Regulation (GDPR) or the California Consumer Privacy Act (CCPA).

The first step in managing privacy is minimizing data collection to only what is essential. Leaders should adopt a privacy-by-design approach, ensuring data privacy is a core consideration from the start. For example, implement mechanisms that anonymize or pseudonymize data before it's stored in long-term memory. By removing direct identifiers, even in the event of a breach, sensitive information is protected. Additionally, use techniques like data minimization, which restricts the storage of unnecessary or overly detailed data, and regular audits to identify and remove outdated or irrelevant information.

Compliance with regulations such as GDPR and CCPA is another essential aspect. These laws give users rights over their data, such as the ability to access, delete, or restrict how their information is used. AI memory systems must be designed to respect these rights. For instance, if a user asks an AI system to "forget" specific information, the system should have mechanisms to erase the corresponding data from its databases, including backups and long-term storage. Moreover, companies must ensure transparency, clearly communicating to users what data is being collected, how it will be used, and how long it will be retained.

From a practical standpoint, robust encryption for both data at rest and in transit is non-negotiable. Leaders should invest in secure database technologies and follow industry best practices for data storage. Access to memory systems should be restricted to authorized personnel or processes, with activity logs maintained to track who accessed what data and when. Implementing these controls reduces the likelihood of unauthorized access or breaches, which can severely damage user trust and lead to regulatory penalties.

Ethical issues go beyond privacy to include concerns like bias and misuse of data. AI agents with memory capabilities might reinforce biases if they overly rely on historical data that reflects outdated or skewed perspectives. Leaders must ensure that their AI systems undergo continuous bias testing and validation. Additionally, organizations should establish clear policies around the ethical use of AI memory systems, including defining acceptable boundaries for data retention and personalization to prevent intrusive or manipulative practices.

In summary, managing privacy and ethical issues in AI memory is not just about compliance; it's about building trust and fostering responsible AI use. By prioritizing secure data handling, aligning with regulations, and addressing ethical concerns proactively, leaders can ensure their AI systems are both effective and respectful of user rights and expectations.

Balancing Innovation and Privacy: A Healthcare Provider's Journey

When a leading U.S. healthcare provider decided to implement memory-enabled AI for patient care coordination in 2024, they faced a seemingly impossible challenge: how to create an AI system that could learn from patient interactions while maintaining strict HIPAA compliance and patient privacy.

"The stakes couldn't have been higher," their Chief Privacy Officer tells us. "We needed our AI to remember and learn from patient interactions to provide better care, but one privacy breach could have devastating consequences."

Their solution combined innovative technology with careful governance. They implemented a multi-layered memory architecture where patient-identifying information was strictly separated from behavioral patterns and clinical insights. The AI could learn from aggregated patterns without accessing individual patient details, using what they call "privacy-preserving learning patterns."

The technical implementation was just the beginning. They established a clear governance framework that included:

- Regular privacy audits of the AI's memory systems
- Automated detection of potential privacy risks
- Clear protocols for data retention and deletion
- Patient control over their data through a transparent portal

"What surprised us most," their CTO reflects, "was how this privacy-first approach actually improved the AI's effectiveness. By focusing on patterns rather than individual details, the system developed more robust and generalizable insights."

One year after implementation, the results spoke for themselves: a 40% improvement in care coordination efficiency, with zero privacy breaches. More importantly, patient trust in the AI system, measured through regular surveys, reached 87%— higher than their trust in some traditional hospital systems.

Recommendations for Technical Implementation

To succeed in implementing these layers, it's essential to combine the right tools, strategies, and technologies—each with its unique technical requirements and challenges. Based on our experience, here's a practical guide to help you and your technical teams navigate these complexities, complete with the enablers needed, common pitfalls we've observed, and solutions to overcome them.

Layer	Implementation	Databases/Enablers	Common Pitfalls	How to Mitigate
Layer 1: Short-Term Memory	Use context windows to handle immediate tasks, with attention mechanisms to prioritize key information.	AI frameworks (e.g., OpenAI GPT, Langchain), optimized for token limits.	Context overflow—losing critical details when the input exceeds the token limit.	Implement summarization techniques to condense information without losing meaning.
Layer 2: Long-Term Memory	Categorize retained information into episodic (events), semantic (facts), and procedural (how-to) memories.	Relational databases (PostgreSQL) for structured data; NoSQL databases (MongoDB) for flexible storage. Pinecone for vector store and Neo4j for graphs.	Difficulty in categorizing information correctly, leading to retrieval inefficiencies.	Use tagging and metadata to index information properly and implement automated categorization workflows.
Layer 3: Feedback Loop	Continuously improve through user feedback, adjusting memory prioritization and retrieval strategies.	Feedback logs stored in databases like BigQuery or Amazon DynamoDB; analytics tools like website analytics.	Ignoring or misinterpreting feedback, leading to poor adaptations.	Develop clear metrics for success, and use tools like reinforcement learning to align the AI's updates with these metrics.

Table 7.1: Recommendations for implementing the three layers of memory (Source: © Bornet et al.)

Each layer in the AI memory framework builds upon the previous one, relying on seamless integration between databases and memory functions to operate effectively. Common pitfalls, such as poorly tuned systems or unstructured data, can lead to inefficiencies in memory retrieval or unreliable performance. Mitigation requires maintaining clean, well-organized data, setting clear priorities for memory use, and continuously monitoring and refining the system. Addressing these challenges ensures that AI remains efficient, scalable, and adaptable to real-world applications.

Data Management as the Foundation of Success

Data management is the backbone of effective AI systems, especially those equipped with memory capabilities. Just like a business relies on well-organized records to operate efficiently, an AI agent depends on seamless data storage, retrieval, and updating to perform at its best. If the underlying data infrastructure is poorly managed, even the smartest AI can stumble—retrieving outdated information, missing critical details, or delivering inconsistent outputs. For businesses, this can mean missed opportunities, frustrated customers, and diminished trust.

To avoid these pitfalls, leaders must view data management as a strategic priority. This starts with investing in **scalable and efficient database technologies** that can handle the growing demands of modern AI systems. Imagine an AI-powered customer service agent that needs to access thousands of customer profiles, purchase histories, and past interactions in seconds. Without a robust infrastructure, the agent could lag or deliver incomplete responses, eroding the seamless experience users expect. Technologies like cloud-based databases, real-time analytics tools, and vector storage for semantic searches are key enablers for making AI memory systems agile and effective.

Seamless integration between databases and AI systems is another critical piece of the puzzle. AI memory systems rely on smooth, real-time interactions with the data layer to retrieve the most relevant and up-to-date information. This isn't just about technical compatibility—it's about designing workflows where data flows effortlessly between storage, processing, and the AI agent. For example, in a retail setting, an AI system recommending products needs to instantly incorporate the latest inventory updates or customer browsing behavior to make its suggestions relevant. Without this dynamic connectivity, even the best AI models can appear out of touch.

Data management also requires vigilance to ensure quality and accuracy. Poor data leads to poor decisions, both for humans and AI. Leaders must establish processes to clean, update, and validate data regularly, ensuring that what the AI learns and retrieves is both reliable and current. Additionally, as systems scale, leaders should consider tools that automate these processes, reducing manual errors and streamlining operations.

In essence, data management is the hidden force that powers AI's ability to deliver value. It's not just about having data; it's about organizing, accessing, and updating it in ways that unlock the full potential of AI. Business leaders who invest wisely in their data infrastructure not only future-proof their systems but also position their companies to thrive in an increasingly AI-driven world.

The Memory Revolution Has Just Started

Throughout this chapter, we've explored how memory transforms AI from a sophisticated calculator into a genuine thinking partner. We've seen how short-term memory enables coherent conversations, while structured retention organizes experiences for long-term learning. Perhaps most crucially, we've understood how feedback loops drive continuous improvement, allowing AI systems to learn and adapt from every interaction.

The implications for business leaders are profound and immediate. First, memory-enabled AI agents fundamentally change the economics of customer interaction. When AI agents can maintain context across conversations, remember customer preferences, and learn from past interactions, they deliver exponentially better experiences at a fraction of the cost. We've seen this in practice with companies achieving 40-50% reductions in customer service costs while simultaneously improving satisfaction scores.

Second, memory transforms decision-making processes. Rather than relying solely on current data, leaders can now tap into AI agents that remember and learn from every past decision, success, and failure across the organization. This institutional memory, previously scattered across emails, documents, and employees' minds, becomes a structured, accessible resource for informing strategy and operations.

Third, memory-enabled agents reshape how organizations learn and adapt. When AI agents can remember and analyze patterns across thousands of projects or millions of customer interactions, they identify opportunities and risks that would be impossible for humans to spot alone. This isn't replacing human judgment—it's augmenting it with a level of pattern recognition and historical awareness previously unimaginable.

As we close this chapter, remember that the development of memory in AI represents more than just technological progress—it marks a fundamental shift in how we interact with machines and how they help us think about the world. The question facing business leaders isn't whether to embrace this transformation but how to shape it in ways that create value while respecting human agency and creativity.

PART 3

ENTREPRENEURSHIP AND PROFESSIONAL GROWTH WITH AI AGENTS

Now that we've explored the foundational keystones of Action, Reasoning, and Memory, it's time to turn to hands-on practice. How do we actually build these systems? And, more importantly, how can you leverage them to create real value?

In the previous Parts of the book, we've taken you on a journey from understanding what AI agents are to discovering how they think, act, and learn. We've seen how they represent a fundamental shift from traditional AI systems—not just processing information but autonomously pursuing goals on our behalf. But knowing about this technology isn't enough. The real question is: how can you harness it?

The coming chapters will equip you with the tools to turn the transformative potential of AI agents into tangible reality. The future belongs to those who can not only understand this technology but effectively implement it—and that's exactly what we're about to show you how to do.

Here, we roll up our sleeves and get practical. Whether you're looking to transform your organization or launch the next million-dollar business, these chapters provide your roadmap from idea to implementation.

Let's begin our journey from ideas to implementation.

CHAPTER 8

A PRACTICAL GUIDE FOR BUILDING SUCCESSFUL AI AGENTS

“Our newsletters are killing us,” we remember thinking one late Friday night, poring over dozens of articles, trying to craft summaries that would engage our readers. “There has to be a better way.” Fast forward one month: our agentic system was handling the entire process, our subscriber base had exploded to 300,000 in just one month, and our team had reclaimed 40 hours a week for creative work. The best part? We were producing better content than ever before.

But here's what makes this story relevant to you: building effective AI agents isn't about having the biggest budget or the most advanced technology. It's about understanding a few key principles that separate success from failure. In this chapter, we'll share these principles through our own trials, errors, and breakthroughs in implementing AI agents across industries.

We won't just tell you what to do—we'll show you. Through real examples, practical tools, and honest accounts of what went wrong (and how we fixed it), you'll gain a blueprint for building AI agents that transform how you and your organization work.

Step 1: Finding the Right Agentic Opportunities

Picture yourself in the bustling office of a fast-growing digital marketing agency. Jenny, the founder and creative director, sits at her desk surrounded by multiple screens. She's frantically switching between applications—pulling social media analytics, checking campaign performances, organizing content calendars, and trying to compile everything into client reports.

Jenny approached us with an intriguing challenge: "My team is drowning in routine tasks," she explained. "We have brilliant creatives spending hours on data entry and report generation instead of strategy and innovation. But how do I know which tasks are really right for AI agents?"

This question—knowing where to start with AI agents— is crucial. We've learned that success often depends more on choosing the right opportunities than on technical sophistication.

Let's start with a fundamental truth: AI agents aren't magical solutions that can handle any task. Just as you wouldn't use a hammer to fix every home repair problem, not every business challenge calls for an AI agent. In fact, one of the most common pitfalls we see is entrepreneurs and business executives rushing to implement agents without first determining if they're the right tool for the job.

When Not to Use AI Agents

Let us start by recognizing where not to deploy AI agents. Through our experience, we have identified several red flags.

First, tasks that require genuine human creativity or emotional intelligence should generally remain human-driven. At the marketing agency, AI agents could handle data gathering and basic reporting, but creative campaign ideation and client relationship management remained firmly in human hands. While Level 3 agents can engage in natural language interactions, they cannot truly capture the emotional resonance needed for compelling marketing campaigns.

Similarly, strategic decision-making that requires understanding the broader market context or making judgment calls based on incomplete information should stay with humans. Even at Level 3, AI agents lack the sophisticated reasoning and market intuition necessary for these scenarios.

Some tasks are simply too complex for AI agents to handle effectively. A technology company once asked us to build an agent to manage their entire customer support operation. While the potential impact was significant, the process involved too many unique scenarios and emotional interactions. AI agents perform best when their capabilities align with the complexity of the task they are assigned.

In other cases, AI agents may lack the authority to make critical decisions. A financial services firm wanted an AI agent to make investment decisions autonomously. This was not only risky but also a clear violation of regulatory requirements. It is essential to consider whether an AI agent has the appropriate level of authority for the task it is assigned.

By understanding these limitations, organizations can ensure they deploy AI agents where they add value while keeping human oversight where it matters most.

The Three Circles of Agentic Opportunity

We've developed a straightforward but powerful approach we call "The Three Circles of Agentic Opportunity" to help identify the perfect sweet spots to implement with agentic AI. Picture three overlapping circles. The sweet spot for your AI agents lies where these circles intersect. Let's break this down through our marketing agency's experience.

The Three Circles of Agentic Opportunities

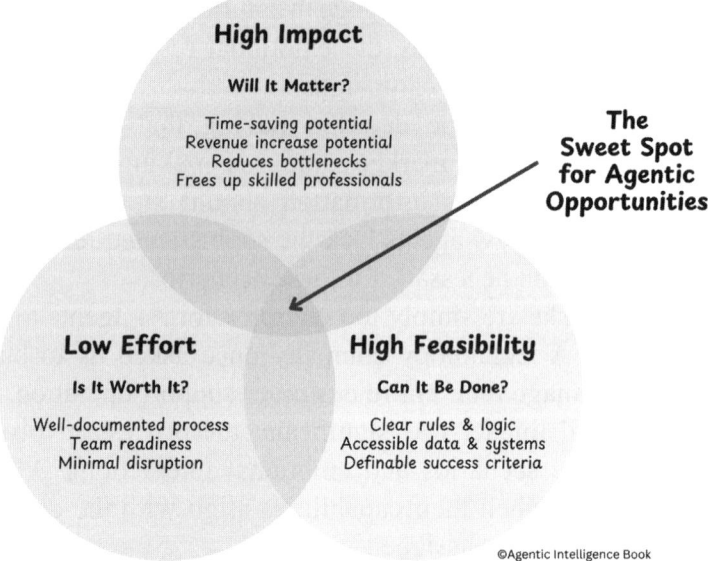

High Impact

Will It Matter?

Time-saving potential
Revenue increase potential
Reduces bottlenecks
Frees up skilled professionals

The Sweet Spot for Agentic Opportunities

Low Effort

Is It Worth It?

Well-documented process
Team readiness
Minimal disruption

High Feasibility

Can It Be Done?

Clear rules & logic
Accessible data & systems
Definable success criteria

©Agentic Intelligence Book

Figure 8.1: The Sweet Spot for Agentic Opportunities (Source: © Bornet et al.)

Circle 1: High Impact - Will It Matter?

The first circle represents tasks that, if automated, would significantly impact your organization. The consideration is simple: if you automate this process, will it make a meaningful difference? Impact isn't just about saving time—it's about what that saved time enables your organization to do.

Consider the routine tasks that consume your skilled professionals' time. Perhaps your sales team spends hours updating CRM records instead of building relationships with clients. Maybe your researchers spend more time formatting data than analyzing it. Or your HR team might be buried in processing routine requests rather than focusing on employee development.

The highest-impact opportunities often aren't your most complex processes. Instead, look for the routine tasks that are preventing your best people from doing their best work. When evaluating impact, ask: If this task were automated tomorrow, what would your team be able to accomplish instead?

For the marketing agency, their monthly client reporting process was consuming over 200 hours of team time per month. More importantly, this routine work was preventing their analysts from doing the strategic thinking their clients really needed.

Circle 2: Feasibility - Can It Be Done?

The second circle is about whether current AI agent technology can actually handle the task effectively and safely. Think of feasibility like checking if you have the right ingredients before starting to cook—you need to ensure you have all the essential elements for success.

The most feasible processes for automation typically have these characteristics:

- Clear, consistent rules for making decisions
- Accessible data and systems
- Definable success criteria
- Manageable consequences if something goes wrong
- Ability to verify results before they impact operations

The key is to look for processes where you can explain the rules without using phrases like "it depends" or "but sometimes..." too often. The more exceptions and judgment calls a process requires, the less suitable it is for your first AI agent project.

For the marketing agency, the reporting process was feasible for automation because it had all the key ingredients. First, the data they needed was accessible through APIs. In addition, the process followed consistent rules, and the outcome could be easily checked, while errors could be managed by people.

Circle 3: Effort - Is It Worth It?

The final circle considers the practical aspects of implementation—the resources, time, and organizational change required. This isn't just about technical complexity; it's about your organization's readiness for change.

Consider whether:

- The process is well-documented
- Your team is ready and willing to adapt
- You can start small and scale up
- The potential benefits clearly justify the investment
- You can implement without disrupting core operations

The best first projects can often be implemented in phases, allowing you to build confidence and capabilities gradually.

In Jenny's case, automating reports was attractive because they already had documented procedures, they could start small and scale up, and the team was eager for change.

Finding Your Sweet Spot

The ideal AI agent projects live where these three circles overlap. For Jenny's agency, report automation was perfect because it would free up hundreds of hours of valuable analyst time (Impact), the process was well-defined and safe to automate (Feasibility), and they could implement it without disrupting their core business (Effort).

Start by mapping your own processes against these three circles. Look for tasks that your team repeatedly complains about—these often signal high-impact opportunities. Then, evaluate whether these tasks have clear rules and accessible data. Finally, consider whether you have the resources and readiness to tackle the change.

Remember, your first AI agent project should be like a good first date—ambitious enough to be exciting but not so complicated that it's likely to end in disaster. Start with something that scores well across all three circles, and you'll build both success and momentum for more ambitious projects to come.

Implementation Reality Check: Lessons from the Field

Our experience has revealed some crucial realities about finding the right opportunities:

First, companies rarely know which agents they actually need. While they often approach us with specific agent ideas, in nearly half the cases, these aren't the most valuable automation opportunities. This is why our Three Circles framework is so critical—it helps cut through assumptions to identify what truly matters. When a client insisted on automating their social media posting, our analysis revealed that automating lead qualification would deliver five times the ROI.

Second, many companies believe they can fully automate entire job roles with AI agents, but this is a fundamental misunderstanding of how AI works today. AI agents are not employees—they lack the flexibility, adaptability, or judgment that human workers bring to a role.

A single employee often manages multiple interconnected tasks that require context-switching, decision-making, and collaboration—things AI agents still struggle with. Instead of thinking in terms of "automating roles," the right approach is to think in terms of "automating tasks."

Finally, well-documented processes are gold mines for agent implementation. When evaluating opportunities, we've found that leveraging existing documented standard operating procedures (SOPs) dramatically reduces implementation time and increases success rates. For one financial services client, their meticulously documented customer onboarding process allowed us to deploy an agent in half the time compared to a similar project where we had to map the process from scratch.

These field lessons have shaped how we approach the opportunity identification phase, reinforcing the importance of the Three Circles framework while adding practical considerations that go beyond theory.

A Practical Exercise: Finding Your Agentic Opportunities

Now that you understand the theory, let's walk through a simple exercise we use with organizations to identify their best agentic opportunities. We developed this approach after seeing too many companies rush into automation without proper analysis, often leading to wasted resources and frustrated teams.

Step 1: Task Inventory

Begin by gathering your team for a focused two-hour session. The goal is to create a comprehensive list of recurring tasks that consume significant time or create bottlenecks in your operations. We've found that asking specific questions yields better results than general brainstorming.

Ask your team:

- "What tasks do you find yourself doing repeatedly throughout the week?"
- "Which activities prevent you from focusing on more strategic work?"
- "What processes consistently create bottlenecks in our operations?"
- "Which routine tasks require the most oversight to prevent errors?"

When we ran this exercise with the marketing agency, their list included tasks like monthly client reporting, social media analytics, campaign performance tracking, competitor monitoring, and content calendar management. The key was capturing not just the tasks, but also their frequency and the approximate time invested in each.

Step 2: Impact Assessment

Next, evaluate each task's potential impact if automated. We use a simple but effective scoring system that considers multiple factors. For each task, score the below criteria on a scale of 1-5:

1. Time Saved (How much time does it take today that can be saved?)
   - In most cases, just estimating the average time saved is enough. A higher score (5) means the time saved would be very high.
   - In some cases, going into more detailed calculations of the current costs in dollars can be useful. Multiply hours per instance by frequency and cost per hour (e.g., 2 hours per task × 20 tasks/month × $50/hour = $2,000 savings)

2. Strategic Value of Freed Time (What's the opportunity cost?)
   - The strategic value measures the broader benefits of automating a task, including its impact on employee satisfaction, client experience, competitive positioning, and revenue potential.
   - It is rated on a scale of 1-5, with higher scores indicating greater overall business impact.

3. Error Reduction Potential (How often do mistakes happen?)
   - In most cases, an estimation is sufficient. A higher score (5) means the errors are highly frequent or costly.
   - In some cases, going into more detailed calculations of the current costs in dollars can be useful. Calculate

it using the formula: current error rate × cost per error × volume (e.g., a 5% error rate × $100 per error × 1,000 instances/month = $5,000 savings).

4. Scalability Impact (Can this be applied across the organization?)

- Scalability impact measures how well a solution can expand without increasing costs at the same rate. A higher score (5) means the task can be automated and scaled across the organization with minimal extra cost.

- For example, automating a client onboarding process that works for 10 clients can easily scale to 1,000 without needing additional staff, making it highly scalable (rated 5).

Here is a summary of the four criteria and the meaning of the scores:

Criteria	Score on a scale from 1 to 5		
Time Investment	1: Less than an hour per week	3: Several hours per week	5: Multiple hours daily
Strategic Value of Freed Time	1: Limited alternative use of time	3: Moderate strategic value	5: High-value strategic activities blocked
Error Reduction Potential	1: Few errors occur	3: Occasional significant errors	5: Frequent or costly errors
Scalability Impact	1: One-off task	3: Moderately repeatable	5: Highly scalable across the organization

Table 8.1: Scoring the four criteria of impact assessment (Source: © Bornet et al.)

Then, calculate the total score for each task. Add up the scores across the four criteria. The minimum possible score is 4, and the maximum is 20.

Finally, compare scores across tasks—The higher the total score, the stronger the case for automation.

At the marketing agency, their client reporting process scored high across all categories: it consumed massive time (5), prevented strategic analysis (5), frequently contained errors due to manual data entry (4), and could scale across all clients (5). This gave it a total score of 19 out of 20, making it a prime candidate for automation.

Step 3: Feasibility Assessment

For each task that scored highly on impact, evaluate its feasibility for automation. This helps determine whether current AI agent technology (Levels 1-3) can reliably handle the task. We break feasibility into two key components, each scored on a scale of 1-5.

1. Process Standardization
   Automation works best when tasks have clear and structured steps. Evaluate if the process has clear steps, decision rules, and exceptions. Ask: 'Can someone new follow this process exactly using only our documentation?'

2. Data and System Access
   AI needs structured and accessible data to function. If data is scattered, locked in old systems, or requires human intervention, automation will be difficult. Test whether data is structured, easily retrievable, and available through modern systems or requires manual preparation.

Use the following scale to rate the process standardization and data readiness:

Criteria	Score 1	Score 3	Score 5
Process Standardization	1: Process is largely ad-hoc with no standard approach.	3: Basic documentation exists but relies heavily on employee experience.	5: The process is fully documented with clear steps, decision rules, and exceptions.
Data and System Access	1: Essential data is locked in legacy systems or paper-based.	3: Data is available but requires significant preparation.	5: All data is structured, and systems have modern APIs.

Table 8.2: Scoring the two criteria of feasibility assessment (Source: © Bornet et al.)

By scoring each task on Process Standardization and Data and System Access, you will quickly identify which high-impact tasks are ready for automation and which need improvements first.

Step 4: Implementation Effort

Once high-impact tasks are identified and their feasibility is confirmed, the next step is evaluating how difficult it is to build an AI agent for them. Implementation effort measures the technical complexity involved, helping you prioritize AI agents that can be deployed efficiently.

How to Score Technical Complexity (1-5, Reverse Scored)

This is a reverse-scored metric, meaning lower scores indicate higher complexity and greater difficulty in implementation. Here's how to assess it:

- Score 5 (Easiest to Implement)—The task can be automated with standard tools that require little or no customization.
- Score 4—Some customization is needed, but it relies on widely used technologies.
- Score 3—The solution requires significant custom development, such as scripting.
- Score 2—Complex integrations or new technology adoption is required.
- Score 1 (Most Difficult)—The task demands cutting-edge solutions or extensive research and development (R&D).

Our recommendation is to always start with proven, mainstream tools and platforms before pushing technological boundaries. Automating simple, high-impact tasks first builds momentum, reduces risk, and ensures early wins before tackling more complex solutions.

Putting It All Together: The Final Analysis

After spending months helping organizations evaluate AI agent opportunities, we've developed a systematic approach to making the final implementation decision. Let's return to Jenny's marketing agency to see how this works in practice.

First, we combine the scores from our previous analyses:

- Impact Score (maximum 20 points from our four criteria)
- Feasibility Score (maximum 10 points from process and data evaluation)
- Implementation Effort Score (maximum 5 points, reverse scored)

This gives us a total possible score of 35 points. We find this detailed scoring particularly valuable because it forces organizations to think through all aspects of the opportunity systematically.

For Jenny's client reporting process, the scores broke down like this:

- Impact: 19/20 (high time investment, strategic value, error reduction, and scalability)
- Feasibility: 8/10 (well-documented process, accessible data through APIs)
- Implementation Effort: 4/5 (standard tools available, minimal customization needed)

Total Score: 31/35, indicating an excellent candidate for AI agent implementation.

The Final Touch: The Agentic AI Prioritization Matrix

While the comprehensive score is helpful, we've found that visualizing opportunities helps teams and management make better decisions. We plot potential projects on a matrix with two axes:

- Vertical Axis: Complexity of the Transformation (combining Feasibility and Effort scores)
- Horizontal Axis: Business Impact (using our Impact score)

This creates four quadrants:

1. Quick Wins (High Impact, Low Complexity): Your ideal agentic opportunities
2. Strategic Projects (High Impact, High Complexity): Future opportunities requiring careful planning
3. Low Priority (Low Impact, Low Complexity): Nice-to-have automations

4. Avoid (Low Impact, High Complexity): Not worth the effort

For the marketing agency, client reporting landed squarely in the Quick Wins quadrant: high impact with relatively low complexity. This became their first AI agent project, leading to the successful transformation we described earlier.

The Agentic Opportunities prioritization Matrix

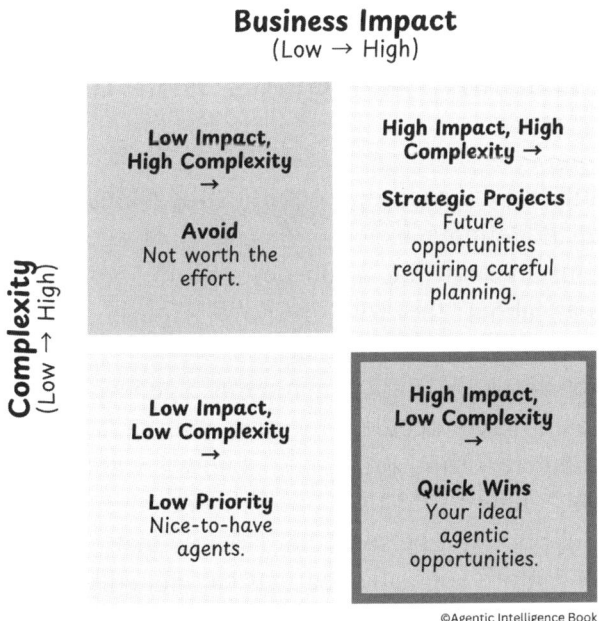

Figure 8.2: The agentic AI prioritization matrix (Source: © Bornet et al.)

A Final Note on Selection

If this is your first agentic implementation, note that it will set the tone for future automation initiatives. So, in addition to the above criteria, it is important to choose an opportunity that:

- Will show clear, measurable results within 3-6 months
- Affects enough people to build broad support
- Has a champion willing to oversee the implementation
- Can serve as a learning experience for your organization

Success with your first agent builds confidence and creates momentum for more ambitious projects. The marketing agency's successful reporting automation led to five more agent implementations over the next year, each building on lessons learned from the first.

Step 2: Defining AI Agents' Role and Capabilities

After identifying the right opportunities for AI agents, the next crucial step is defining exactly what kind of agent you need. Think of this like writing a job description—you need to be crystal clear about the role, responsibilities, and required capabilities of your digital worker.

Let's return to the digital marketing agency, where Jenny and her team have decided to start with automating their monthly client reporting process. "I know I want to automate this process," Jenny told us, "but I'm not sure what kind of agent I need. Should it be something simple that just pulls data, or something more sophisticated that can actually write report analyses?"

This is a common question we hear from business leaders, and the answer lies in understanding the different levels of AI agent capabilities and matching them to your specific needs.

Understanding Agent Levels: From Simple to Sophisticated

Think of AI agents as employees with different skill levels. Using our Agentic AI Progression Framework, we can broadly categorize them into five levels, though currently, only levels 1-3 are commonly deployed in production environments. To be precise, Level 2 (Intelligent Automation) and Level 3 (Agentic Workflow) are the most common, so we will focus on these two levels.

Level 2 agents are more like experienced professionals who can follow simple, unchanging instructions. Level 3 agents are like senior professionals who can understand the context and manage more sophisticated tasks.

For the marketing agency's reporting process, Jenny needed to determine which level would be most appropriate. Let's walk through the decision-making process they used.

The Decision Framework

To choose the right agent level, we evaluate three key criteria that help determine whether a Level 2 or Level 3 agent is more appropriate:

1. Task Predictability (Deterministic vs. Probabilistic)

First, consider how predictable your process is. Level 2 agents excel at deterministic tasks—processes that follow clear, unchanging rules. They're like reliable workers who execute the same steps perfectly every time. Level 3 agents, powered by foundation models, can handle probabilistic tasks that require understanding context and making judgment calls.

At the marketing agency, Jenny's team analyzed their reporting process and found that about 80% of it was deterministic—pulling specific metrics from various platforms and organizing them in a standard format. This portion was perfect for a Level 2 agent. However, 20% involved interpreting trends and writing insights, which required probabilistic thinking that is better suited for a Level 3 agent.

2. Error Sensitivity

Next, assess how critical errors would be to your operation. Level 2 agents are highly reliable for tasks where accuracy is paramount because they follow exact rules and won't deviate from prescribed patterns. They're ideal for financial calculations, data processing, and other tasks where errors could be costly.

Level 3 agents, while more flexible, may occasionally produce unexpected outputs or make creative interpretations. They're better suited for tasks where some variation is acceptable or even beneficial, like content generation or pattern analysis.

For the marketing agency's client reporting, accuracy in the data gathering and calculations was crucial—a single error could damage client trust. This made Level 2 agents perfect for the data processing portion. However, slight variations in the written analysis were acceptable and sometimes even desirable, making this part suitable for a Level 3 agent.

3. Input Variability

Finally, evaluate how much your inputs vary. Level 2 agents work best with standardized inputs—they need consistent data formats and predictable scenarios. They struggle with exceptions and can't adapt to unexpected variations without being reprogrammed.

Level 3 agents, however, excel at handling variable inputs. They can understand context, adapt to different formats, and make sense of unstructured data. They're like experienced professionals who can adjust their approach based on the situation.

The marketing agency dealt with various data sources, but they followed consistent formats—perfect for a Level 2 agent. However, the context for interpreting this data varied significantly across different clients and industries, making a Level 3 agent necessary for the analytical portion.

Mapping Characteristics to Agent Levels

To summarize how these criteria map to agent levels:

Criteria	Level 2 Agents (Intelligent Automation)	Level 3 Agents (Agentic Workflow)
Task Predictability	Highly deterministic processes with clear rules	Handles tasks requiring context understanding and adaptive responses
Error Sensitivity	Requires 100% accuracy and reliability	Accepts some variability in outputs, allowing for probabilistic decisions
Input Variability	Works best with standardized inputs and minimal variations	Can process variable or unstructured inputs
Best For	High-volume, repetitive tasks that follow fixed workflows	Tasks that involve reasoning, decision-making, or natural language understanding
Example Use Cases	Data extraction, financial calculations, compliance checks, structured reporting	Report writing, customer support chatbots, fraud detection, trend analysis

Table 8.3: Comparison between Level 2 and Level 3 AI agents (Source: © Bornet et al.)

Making the Choice: The Marketing Agency's Decision

After evaluating these criteria, we helped the marketing agency make an interesting decision: they would implement a hybrid approach using both Level 2 and Level 3 agents for different parts of the process.

The Level 2 agent (what we call Intelligent Automation) would handle the deterministic portions of the work:

- Accessing various platforms (Google Analytics, social media, advertising platforms)
- Extracting standardized data sets
- Performing calculations and creating visualizations
- Generating the basic report structure

The Level 3 agent (an Agentic Workflow) would then:

- Analyze trends in the processed data
- Generate initial insights and recommendations
- Create draft narrative sections of the report

This hybrid approach capitalized on the strengths of each agent type. The Level 2 agent could reliably handle precise, deterministic tasks with near-perfect accuracy, while the Level 3 agent was suited for the more nuanced work of data interpretation and narrative generation.

In the upcoming section, we will outline how to design and build Level 3 agents. For building Level 2 agents, we recommend referring to the Intelligent Automation book.[136]

The Learning Curve

It's important to note that implementing AI agents is typically an iterative process. At the marketing agency, they started with the Level 2 agent handling just the data collection and basic reporting. Once this was working smoothly and the team was comfortable with the technology, they introduced the Level 3 agent for content generation.

Jenny reflected, "At first, I wanted to automate everything at once. But starting with the basic data work and gradually adding

---

[136] Pascal Bornet, Ian Barkin, and Jochen Wirtz, 2020. "Intelligent Automation: Learn how to harness Artificial Intelligence to boost business & make our world more human," https://www.amazon.com/INTELLIGENT-AUTOMATION-Artificial-Intelligence-business/dp/B08KTDVHHQ

more sophisticated capabilities helped our team adapt and actually shaped how we thought about our reporting process."

Results and Lessons Learned

Six months after implementation, the marketing agency's AI agent system was processing reports for all clients with remarkable efficiency:

- Report generation time reduced to 45 minutes
- Data accuracy maintained at 99.95%
- Client satisfaction scores increased by 15%
- Marketing team reported 60% more time for strategic work

Jenny reflected on their journey: "The key was not rushing to automation. By taking a methodical approach to design and building trust gradually, we created a system that both our team and our clients trust completely."

The success of the marketing agency's reporting system has opened new possibilities for AI agent implementation across their organization. They're now exploring applications in campaign optimization, content creation, and customer journey analysis.

The lessons learned from this implementation highlight the importance of thoughtful design that considers both technical capabilities and human factors. As we'll explore in the next chapter, these design decisions lay the crucial groundwork for successful implementation and deployment.

Moving Forward

With clear roles defined for both their Level 2 and Level 3 agents, the marketing agency was ready to move into the detailed design phase of their implementation. The clear delineation of responsibilities and capabilities would prove crucial for the next steps of mapping process flows and establishing performance criteria.

Remember, the goal isn't to create the most sophisticated agent possible but rather to design one that reliably delivers value while integrating smoothly with your human team's workflows. As we'll explore in the next chapter, this foundation of clearly defined roles and capabilities is essential for successful implementation.

Step 3: Designing AI Agents for Success

After identifying the right opportunity and determining the appropriate type of agent, the next crucial phase is designing your AI agents for successful implementation. This is where theory meets practice, and where many organizations either set themselves up for success or stumble into common pitfalls. Let's explore this through our own experience creating an AI agent for newsletter automation.

The Newsletter Challenge: A Real-World Case Study

As authors and influencers in the AI space, we found ourselves spending countless hours each week curating content, writing summaries, and creating newsletters for our community. It was a labor-intensive process that, while valuable for our readers, took time away from deeper research and writing. That's when we decided to apply our expertise in AI agents to solve this challenge.

"We were spending nearly one day each week just on newsletter creation," Pascal recalls. "We knew there had to be a better way." The result? A new AI agent system that not only automated much of the process but also helped us grow our new newsletter to over 300,000 subscribers in just one month.

In Chapter 9, we discuss how we developed this innovative agentic business opportunity and transformed it into a venture, highlighting the immense potential of agentic AI to generate new business possibilities.

Design Principle #1: Start with the End in Mind

Before diving into technical specifications, successful agent design begins with clear success criteria. "One of the biggest mistakes we see," Rakesh shares from his consulting experience, "is organizations jumping straight to solution design without defining what success looks like."

Defining clear success criteria is essential for three key reasons. First, it provides clear targets for the development team and helps prioritize features. Second, it establishes benchmarks for measuring the return on investment and system performance. Third, it helps manage stakeholders' expectations and build confidence in the new system.

Without clear success criteria, we might have built a system that was technically impressive but didn't actually solve our core business needs.

Success criteria should include both quantitative and qualitative metrics:

- Quantitative metrics might include efficiency gains, error reduction rates, or specific performance targets
- Qualitative metrics often focus on user experience, quality of output, and system reliability

For example, in our newsletter case, we established metrics like:

- Reducing creation time from 15 to 3 hours per week
- Maintaining 95%+ accuracy in content
- Achieving 40%+ email open rates

But more importantly, we also defined qualitative success criteria around content relevance and reader experience.

Design Principle #2: Understand Your Current State

"Many organizations want to leap straight to the future," we observe, "but understanding your current process is crucial for successful agent design."

Understanding your current workflow in detail before designing AI agents is crucial for several reasons. First, it reveals hidden complexities and dependencies that might not be apparent at first glance. Second, it helps identify potential bottlenecks and inefficiencies that the new system should address. Finally, it ensures that critical business rules and exceptions aren't overlooked in the automation process.

When we started mapping our workflow, we discovered that what we thought was a simple four-step process actually involved dozens of micro-decisions and exceptions that we handled automatically. Without documenting these, we would have built an agentic system that missed crucial nuances.

Here are the issues we faced with the existing process of building the newsletter:

- Time-Consuming: Manual searching, summarizing, compiling, and formatting require significant effort and multiple hours each day and week. We estimated the total workload to be about 10 hours per week per newsletter.

- Prone to Errors: We were likely to make mistakes in repetitive tasks, such as summarizing and formatting. This happened a few times and was very damaging to our reputation.

- Scalability Issues: As the volume of articles grows, the manual process becomes unsustainable, requiring hours of work.

- Inconsistent Quality: Output used to vary depending on the individual performing each task, leading to uneven results when the team changes.

Design Principle #3: Design the Target Process

After documenting our existing workflow, instead of simply automating the old process, we redesigned it entirely with the outcome in mind. Based on our experience, holding onto outdated workflows often leads to inefficiencies, as automation alone won't fix fundamental design flaws.

As Shail usually says, "Garbage in, garbage out. If you automate a flawed process, it will just result in flawed automation."

Instead, we focused on what we wanted to achieve—a stream-lined, scalable, and error-free newsletter production process—and built the workflow around that goal. The new process follows a structured daily and weekly workflow.

Each day, relevant articles should be identified, key insights summarized, and a formatted email sent for human review. The selected summaries should then be compiled into a structured document, ensuring quality control.

On Mondays, the content should be formatted into a visually polished newsletter, reviewed for accuracy, and finalized for distribution.

By breaking the process into clear, well-defined steps, we eliminated unnecessary complexity, improved quality assurance, and ensured a smooth publishing cycle. The key lesson: don't just automate—rethink, redesign, and optimize for the best possible outcome.

Design Principle #4: Choose the Right Architecture

One of the most critical decisions in agent design is the architectural approach. "Think of it like building a house," we explain. "You could try to create one massive room that serves every purpose, or you could design specialized spaces that work together harmoniously. In our experience, the latter approach almost always works better."

This brings us to a fundamental question in agent design: Should you build one complex agent to handle everything or create a team of specialized agents?

When designing our newsletter automation system, we faced a crucial decision: should we build one complex agent to handle everything or create a team of specialized agents? Our experience implementing AI systems for various companies has taught us that simpler, specialized components often work better than complex, monolithic ones. At this stage of the book, you have already heard several times our design principle of "one tool, one agent." Let's explore the key design decisions that led to our successful design.

"Initially, we were tempted to build one 'super-agent' that could handle everything from content discovery to newsletter formatting," Rakesh, one of our co-authors, explains. "But we quickly realized this would be like asking one person to be simultaneously a researcher, writer, editor, and designer—it rarely works well."

Hence, we designed a comprehensive team of specialized agents:

Agent Name	Agent Role
Search Agent	Finds relevant articles on the web
Summarization Agent	Summarizes key points from the articles
Email Agent	Sends summaries via email every day

Agent Name	Agent Role
Compiler Agent	Organizes content based on selected articles
Newsletter Formatting Agent	Prepares final newsletter
Manager Agent	Coordinates + final delivery

Table 8.4: Our team of specialized AI agents for the Newsletter automation (Source: © Bornet et al.)

This modular approach allowed each agent to excel in its specialized role while maintaining system flexibility through coordinated interaction.

Key Principles That Guided Our Design:

We followed six core principles in designing our multi-agent system:

1. **Clarity of Purpose**: "Each agent needs to be like a skilled specialist," Rakesh explains. "Just as you wouldn't ask a heart surgeon to also be an anesthesiologist, we gave each agent a clear, focused role."

2. **Efficiency Through Specialization**: Rather than building complex agents that could do many things adequately, we created simple agents that could do one thing exceptionally well.

3. **Scalability By Design:** "We designed the system of agents to handle increasing workloads," Rakesh shares. For example, if content volume increases, we can introduce multiple Search Agents working in parallel or optimize the Summarization Agent for faster processing.

4. **Autonomous Operation**: Each agent operates independently within its domain, making decisions based on clear criteria without needing constant oversight.

5. **Seamless Collaboration**: The agents work together like a well-coordinated team, with standardized communication protocols and clear handoff points.

6. **Centralized Orchestration**: Our Manager Agent ensures all components work in harmony, much like a conductor leading an orchestra.

Design Principle #5: Build in Human-AI Collaboration

Perhaps the most crucial aspect of agent design is determining how humans and AI will work together. "The goal isn't to remove humans from the process," Nandan emphasizes, "but to create a symbiotic relationship where both humans and AI contribute their unique strengths."

This principle becomes particularly important when we consider the current limitations of AI agents. At Levels 1-3 of our Progression Framework, agents still lack true adaptive learning and sophisticated reasoning capabilities. This means human expertise remains essential for:

1. **Strategic Decision-Making:** Humans excel at understanding context and making nuanced judgments
2. **Quality Assurance:** Providing oversight and catching subtle errors
3. **Exception Handling:** Managing unexpected situations that fall outside normal parameters
4. **Continuous Improvement:** Identifying opportunities for system enhancement

When we first designed our newsletter system, we faced a fundamental question: Which tasks should be automated, and which should remain in human hands? Our approach was to think not in terms of what "could" be automated but what "should" be automated.

We identified two critical points where human input was essential:

The first key human touchpoint comes after our AI agents have gathered and summarized content. A human editor reviews the daily summaries and selects the most relevant pieces for the newsletter. This decision requires understanding our audience's needs, recognizing emerging trends, and making nuanced judgments about content value—capabilities that remain uniquely human.

During implementation, we discovered an interesting pattern: when we allowed the AI to make final content selections, the newsletters became technically accurate but somehow soulless. They lacked the strategic narrative and thematic coherence that comes from human curation. By keeping humans in this crucial decision-making role, we maintained the newsletter's distinctive voice and strategic relevance.

The second critical human touchpoint occurs just before publication. Here, human editors review the complete newsletter, add context where needed, and ensure the content aligns with our editorial standards. This final review isn't just about catching errors—it's about ensuring the newsletter provides genuine value to our readers.

"This human-in-the-loop approach," Nandan explains, "gives us the best of both worlds. The agents handle the time-consuming tasks, while humans focus on strategic decisions that require judgment and industry expertise."

The Outcome: The Target Agentic System

After a few days of work, here we are. Below is the new target process we have designed, presenting the flow of the key activities, the agents in charge, and the human in the loop:

Daily Workflow

1. **Search Agent**: Searches the web for relevant articles and sends links to the Summarization Agent.
2. **Summarization Agent**: Summarizes each article into three key points and sends summaries to the Email Delivery Agent.
3. **Email Delivery Agent**: Compiles summaries into a formatted email and sends it to the human reviewer.
4. **Human Reviewer**: Reviews daily emails and replies with preferred articles.
5. **Compiler Agent**: Compiles daily selected summaries into a structured Google Doc and performs QA.

Weekly Workflow

1. **Newsletter Formatting Agent**: On Mondays, the agent formats the Google Doc into a visually appealing newsletter.
2. **Manager Agent**: Reviews the formatted newsletter and sends it to the human reviewer.
3. **Human Reviewer**: Performs final review and posts the newsletter to desired platforms.

Step 4: Implementing Your AI Agents

Choosing the Right AI Agent Platform: Prioritize Speed Over Perfection

The AI agent platform market has evolved rapidly, with approximately 400 vendors now offering solutions across different levels of sophistication and ease of use. This abundance of choice, while providing numerous options for organizations, can also lead to decision paralysis. Through our work implementing AI agents across various industries, we've observed that companies often spend months evaluating platforms while their competitors forge ahead with implementations and gain valuable market advantages.

Selecting the right platform requires understanding the three main categories available in today's market: full-code, low-code, and no-code solutions. Each category serves different organizational needs and comes with its own set of trade-offs between flexibility, speed of implementation, and required technical expertise.

No-Code Platforms: Rapid Deployment and Accessibility

Think of no-code platforms as the "LEGO blocks" of AI agent development. They provide pre-built components that you can assemble without any technical expertise. Solutions like Bizway, Beam, N8N, and Relevance AI enable business users to create functional AI agents through intuitive interfaces without writing any code. These platforms are ideal for organizations that need to quickly implement basic to moderate complexity agents or those looking to prove the value of AI agents before investing in more sophisticated solutions.

While no-code platforms might seem limited compared to their more technical counterparts, they often provide surprisingly sophisticated capabilities through configuration rather than coding. For example, Relevance AI offers advanced features like vector-based processing and sophisticated search capabilities through a user-friendly interface.

Full-Code Platforms: Maximum Control and Customization

On the other extreme side of the spectrum, full-code platforms provide the highest level of control and flexibility but require significant development resources. These platforms, such as LangGraph, CrewAI, and AutoGen, offer comprehensive frameworks that allow organizations to build highly customized AI agents. They're particularly well-suited for enterprises that need to maintain strict control over their data, require complex integrations with existing systems, or operate in heavily regulated industries.

When working with full-code platforms, organizations can fine-tune every aspect of their AI agents' behavior, from decision-making processes to data-handling protocols. This level of control comes at the cost of longer development cycles and the need for specialized technical expertise. While platforms like LangGraph offer extensive documentation and growing community support, the learning curve remains steep.

These sophisticated agents require careful orchestration of multiple tools and complex workflow management, which full-code platforms handle adeptly. However, organizations should carefully consider whether this level of control is truly necessary for their use case, as the additional development overhead can significantly delay implementation and time to value.

Low-Code Platforms: The Balanced Approach

Low-code platforms strike a balance between customization and accessibility. Platforms like WatsonX Assistant, Agentforce, and UiPath and Microsoft Copilot's Agent Builders provide visual development environments while still allowing for significant customization through code when needed. These platforms excel at enabling collaboration between business users and technical teams, making them particularly effective for organizations that need to rapidly deploy AI agents while maintaining some level of customization.

The low-code approach significantly reduces the time and technical expertise required for implementation while still providing enough flexibility for most enterprise use cases. These platforms typically offer pre-built components and integrations that can be customized to fit specific business needs. For instance, ServiceNow's Virtual Agent platform provides ready-to-use components for common business processes while allowing organizations to extend functionality through custom development when needed.

Making the Selection: Key Considerations

To make a confident and efficient decision, focus on a practical framework rather than endless feature comparisons. Start by identifying your top three to four non-negotiables based on your business priorities. Assign weights to each criterion, considering factors like ease of use, customization, integration, scalability, security, and cost. Then, score potential platforms based on these factors, select the highest-ranking one, and move forward.

Technical expertise availability often serves as a primary deciding factor. Organizations with strong development teams might naturally gravitate toward full-code solutions. However, we've observed that even technically capable organizations sometimes benefit from starting with low-code or no-code solutions to implement faster and gain practical experience before moving to more complex implementations.

Another critical consideration is the potential for scaling agent development across the organization through citizen development. No-code and low-code platforms enable a democratized approach where employees throughout the organization can participate in building and customizing agents. This democratization of agent development can dramatically accelerate the impact of AI initiatives and lead to more innovative solutions, as employees who understand specific business challenges can directly contribute to creating solutions. For instance, a customer service representative might create an agent to handle routine inquiries, while a finance analyst might develop an agent to automate report generation. This distributed approach to agent development can significantly multiply the value and reach of AI within an organization.

Integration requirements with existing systems and data sources also play a crucial role in platform selection. While most platforms offer API connectivity, the ease and depth of integration vary significantly. Microsoft Copilot's Agent Builder, for instance, provides seamless integration with the Microsoft ecosystem, making it an attractive choice for organizations heavily invested in Microsoft technologies.

Security and compliance requirements can significantly influence platform choice, particularly for organizations in regulated industries. Full-code platforms typically offer the most control over data handling and security protocols, while no-code platforms might have limitations in these areas.

Avoid Overthinking

No platform is perfect, and waiting for the "ideal" choice can lead to lost opportunities. The best strategy is to start small, experiment, and scale as you learn. Many successful companies begin with a simple AI agent on a low-code platform, validate its impact, and gradually migrate to more advanced solutions as their needs evolve.

While you are still deciding, your competitors are already deploying AI agents that are transforming their industries. The businesses that act fast will lead the AI revolution, while those that hesitate will struggle to catch up. The best AI strategy is not the perfect one—it's the one you start today.

***

In the following sections, we've used our experience to create a universal guide that works across platforms, highlighting the critical success factors, nuanced decisions, and hidden features that truly make a difference in building effective AI agents. The advantage is that you can use it independently of the platform you choose; however, the drawback is that it is not platform-specific, and you might notice some variations in the terminology and details of functionalities. Yet, as an illustration, we have chosen to provide a detailed step-by-step guide for building an agent on the low-code platform Relevance AI, which you will find in the appendices of the book.

Building Effective AI Agents: The A.G.E.N.T. Framework

From our experience, we've learned that success often lies not in the sophistication of the technology but in the clarity and thoroughness of how we define and structure our AI agents. Through numerous implementations and, admittedly, some painful lessons, we've developed what we call the A.G.E.N.T. framework—a comprehensive approach to building reliable AI agents that actually deliver value.

The framework consists of five critical components:

- Agent Identity (Who is the agent?)
- Gear & Brain (What powers the agent?)
- Execution & Workflow (How does the agent work?)
- Navigation & Rules (How does the agent make decisions?)
- Testing & Trust (How do we improve and scale the agent?)

Think of building an AI agent as hiring and training a new employee. You wouldn't bring someone into your organization without clearly defining their role, establishing their responsibilities, and setting up the proper workflows, tools, and rules. The same principle applies to AI agents, but it's even more important because these digital workers require extremely precise instructions to function effectively.

Let's dive deep into the first crucial component of the framework: Agent Identity.

A – Agent Identity: Who is the Agent?

The single most important step when building an AI agent is defining its **identity**—its purpose, role, and operational scope. This is where most people make their first mistake. They rush ahead, eager to see their AI in action, without taking the time to carefully define what the agent is supposed to do. The result? An AI that behaves unpredictably, produces inconsistent results, or simply fails to deliver value.

To illustrate why this step is so crucial, imagine hiring a new employee. Would you bring someone into your company and say, "Just help out however you think best"? Of course not. A new hire needs clear guidance: their **role**, their **responsibilities**, and their **limitations**. The same applies to AI agents. If you don't give them a structured identity, they'll wander aimlessly, often producing results that are unreliable, irrelevant, or even counterproductive.

Why Defining an Agent's Identity is Critical

AI agents are not intuitive thinkers. They don't have gut feelings or common sense. They operate within the constraints you set for them. If you fail to define their identity properly, you will see the consequences in three ways:

1. Unreliable Behavior—The agent may respond in ways that don't align with your goals because it lacks direction.

2. Inconsistency—The same question may yield different results each time because the agent doesn't have clear guidelines.

3. Lack of Control—If an agent's scope isn't clearly defined, it might produce unnecessary, irrelevant, or even harmful outputs.

To see this in action, consider our journey in building an AI-powered summarization assistant for our newsletter. Initially, we gave the agent a simple directive:

"Summarize news articles and research papers."

Sounds reasonable, right? But the results were a mess. The AI pulled random articles, summarized them with no clear structure, and sometimes even included outdated or irrelevant sources. It wasn't the AI's fault—it was just following vague instructions.

So, we refined the agent's identity and gave it a more precise role:

"You are a summarization assistant specializing in AI and business trends. Your job is to take news articles and research papers from sources like MIT Tech Review, arXiv, and Harvard Business Review and distill them into clear, engaging summaries. Each summary must be under 150 words, capture key insights, and maintain the original meaning. The tone should be professional yet accessible, aligning with our newsletter's style."

With this level of clarity, our AI went from an unreliable content aggregator to a laser-focused research partner. It now delivers concise, high-value summaries that keep our readers ahead of the curve without us having to sift through mountains of information. You can refer to the appendix, where we provide you with this agent's detailed identity. You can use it as a template for writing your own.

Building a Strong AI Agent: Think Like a Manager

To put this all into perspective, imagine managing a remote employee who can't think independently—they only follow instructions. You'd need to:

1. Give them a clear job description
2. Tell them exactly what tasks they should (and shouldn't) do
3. Define how they should communicate
4. Set boundaries and escalation points

Now, replace that employee with your AI agent. If you don't define these things, your AI will be unreliable. But if you do, you'll have an agent that performs consistently, efficiently, and intelligently within its domain.

Before you move forward to choosing models and workflows, take the time to write down your agent's identity. The better this foundation, the more powerful and effective your AI agent will be.

The Key Elements of a Strong Agent Identity

Defining an AI agent's identity is more than just stating its function. It requires precision, just like writing a well-crafted job description.

1. Purpose: What is the Agent's Primary Mission?

Every AI agent should have a clear **mission statement** that answers the question: *Why does this agent exist?* A strong purpose statement leaves no room for ambiguity.

- Weak Purpose: "Help with customer support."
- Strong Purpose: "Assist customers by resolving common technical issues with step-by-step solutions in a professional, friendly manner."

The stronger the purpose, the more aligned the agent's outputs will be with user expectations.

2. Role: What Persona Does the Agent Assume?

An agent's role defines how it interacts with users and the expertise it simulates—essentially, its professional identity. A well-defined role ensures users instantly grasp its capabilities and limitations, while also providing clear boundaries for what the agent should and shouldn't do.

For example, a financial AI agent might be a:

- "Financial Analyst" (providing investment insights and risk assessments)
- "Personal Finance Coach" (helping users budget and save money)
- "Tax Consultant" (answering tax-related questions with compliance in mind)

Each of these roles will require the AI to communicate differently and focus on different kinds of information.

3. Scope: What Can the Agent Do, and What Should It Avoid?

Without clear boundaries, an AI agent may drift beyond its intended function. Setting well-defined scope constraints ensures it stays focused.

For example, a customer service agent might be restricted to:

- Answering FAQs based on company knowledge
- Providing troubleshooting steps for common problems
- Escalating complex issues to human representatives

It should not attempt to:

- Provide legal or medical advice
- Make unauthorized decisions
- Generate speculative responses

Boundaries prevent the agent from venturing into areas where mistakes could be costly.

G – Gear & Brain: Powering Your AI Agent

Once your AI agent has a clearly defined identity, the next step is equipping it with the right gear and brain—the tools, models, and knowledge it needs to function effectively. This is where many builders go wrong. They either overcomplicate things by choosing advanced setups they don't need or underpower their agents by selecting the wrong tools for the job.

Think of this step as assembling a high-performance vehicle. You wouldn't put a racing engine in a delivery van or expect a family sedan to win Formula 1. The same logic applies to AI agents—choosing the wrong combination of AI models, tools, and data sources will lead to inefficiency, poor performance, or outright failure.

1. Selecting the Right AI Model: Balancing Power, Cost, and Efficiency

Most platforms let you choose which AI model (or combination of models) your agent will use. This decision is critical—it determines how your agent thinks, responds, and processes information. The AI model is the brain of the agent, dictating how well it understands, reasons, and generates responses. There are two key trade-offs to consider: model size and reasoning capability.

Smaller models, such as Mini, Phi, or Flash, are fast, efficient, and cost-effective, making them ideal for simple queries or predefined tasks. However, they struggle with deep reasoning and complex problem-solving. On the other hand, larger models like GPT, Claude Opus, or Gemini Ultra can analyze nuanced information, generate high-quality responses, and think critically—but they consume more resources and cost more to operate.

For cost-sensitive applications, using a small model for routine tasks and reserving a larger model for complex queries is often the best approach. Open-source models like Mistral or Llama 70B provide more control and lower costs but require in-house expertise to fine-tune and deploy.

Temperature settings

Another important factor in tuning your AI agent's performance is adjusting the temperature settings, a feature available on many platforms. The temperature setting controls how deterministic or creative the AI's responses will be, impacting both the agent's reliability and flexibility.

A low temperature (e.g., 0 to 0.3) makes the AI more predictable and consistent, sticking closely to factual answers and minimizing randomness. This is ideal for applications where accuracy is crucial, such as summarization agents for newsletters, research assistants, or legal AI tools. You want the AI to generate concise, fact-based summaries rather than producing unexpected variations in tone or content.

A high temperature (e.g., 0.7 to 1.0) makes the AI more creative and open-ended, introducing variety in phrasing and responses. This setting is useful for brainstorming, generating marketing copy, or writing creative content, where originality is more important than strict accuracy. However, in structured environments like a summarization agent, a high temperature can lead to inconsistencies, hallucinations, or overly wordy outputs that stray from the original meaning.

For deeper insights into AI model selection for AI agents, resources like Hugging Face model comparisons for agents[137] and AI research papers from OpenAI, Anthropic, or DeepMind can provide valuable benchmarks.[138]

2. Choosing the Right Tools: Precision Over Power

An AI agent isn't a text generator—it must interact with external systems, retrieve real-time data, and take action. Just as a company wouldn't give an employee unrestricted access to its systems, an AI agent's toolset must be clearly defined, limited, and monitored.

During our newsletter project, we initially gave our Search Agent unrestricted access to web scraping tools. The result was a flood of content from unreliable sources and occasional server blocks from overwhelmed websites. We learned the importance of defining each tool's purpose, limitations, and usage parameters in detail. For our Search Agent, this meant specifying not just which APIs it can use, but exactly how. You can refer to the appendix, where we provide you with the detailed tool specifications of our agent. You can use it as a template for writing your own.

APIs are the most common tools, allowing agents to fetch real-time information or execute actions. A financial agent, for example, might use a market data API to pull stock prices, while a scheduling assistant relies on a calendar API. However, unrestricted API access can lead to rate limits, security vulnerabilities, or legal issues—as was the case with many web-scraping agents that ended up blocked or banned for excessive crawling.

---

[137] Galileo AI, n.d. "Agent Leaderboard," https://huggingface.co/spaces/galileo-ai/agent-leaderboard
[138] Karthik Narasimhan, 2024. "Benchmarking AI Agents," https://sierra.ai/blog/benchmarking-ai-agents

To prevent misuse, agents need structured usage policies that define clear operational boundaries. Several key parameters should be specified:

- Rate Limits & Cost Control—To ensure efficiency and cost control, the agent must operate within a set request limit per minute. Many APIs charge per request, meaning uncontrolled usage can lead to high costs. Additionally, exceeding provider-imposed limits can trigger throttling, where the API slows down or temporarily blocks requests to prevent system overload. By managing request frequency, the agent avoids unnecessary expenses while maintaining smooth and uninterrupted performance.

- Source Reliability—The agent should only pull data from pre-approved, credible sources to prevent misinformation. This might include whitelisting trusted news outlets or filtering content based on quality standards. For example, our research agent was programmed to pull information only from pre-approved, reputable sources such as MIT Tech Review, arXiv, or Harvard Business Review.

- Secure API Access—API keys should be rotated regularly and protected with authentication mechanisms (e.g., token-based access) to prevent unauthorized use. They should never be hardcoded into scripts.

- Circuit Breakers—Stop execution if repeated failures occur, rather than continuing to send faulty requests. For example, if an API fails three times in a row, the agent should pause and notify an administrator instead of retrying indefinitely.

- Fallback Systems—Ensure continuity by switching to a backup process when something goes wrong. For example, if a news API is down, the AI can pull headlines from a secondary source instead of returning an error.

Without these safety nets, an AI agent can overload itself, frustrate users, and even damage business operations. For those looking to explore AI tool integrations further, you can refer to Part 2 of this book. You can also refer to API documentation from OpenAI,[139] Google,[140] and AWS,[141] which provides excellent guidance on responsible implementation.

Selecting Knowledge Sources: The Foundation of Reliable AI Agent

An AI agent must retrieve and process information from reliable sources. If these sources are poorly defined, the agent may hallucinate, pull incorrect data, or provide misleading responses. There are three primary ways to structure an agent's knowledge base: databases, APIs, and document embeddings.

A database is best for internal knowledge—such as customer histories, policies, or proprietary research. APIs, on the other hand, ensure the agent can fetch live data, such as weather forecasts, legal updates, or financial statistics. Meanwhile, document embeddings allow AI to search and retrieve information from large collections of text, making them ideal for legal, academic, and enterprise AI solutions.

However, not all knowledge should be included. If the agent has access to outdated or biased sources, it risks spreading misinformation. Similarly, unfiltered open-web search can

[139] OpenAI, n.d. "Production Best Practices," https://platform.openai.com/docs/guides/production-best-practices

[140] Google, n.d. "APIs and reference," https://cloud.google.com/generative-ai-app-builder/docs/apis

[141] Maira Ladeira Tanke, et al., 2024. "Best practices for building robust generative AI applications with Amazon Bedrock Agents – Part 1," https://aws.amazon.com/blogs/machine-learning/best-practices-for-building-robust-generative-ai-applications-with-amazon-bedrock-agents-part-1/

be dangerous, as it may lead to the retrieval of low-quality or misleading content. Instead, AI agents should be trained on trusted, domain-specific datasets and restricted from generating speculative information.

Those interested in refining knowledge selection strategies can refer to Part 2 of this book. You can also refer to vector database platforms like Weaviate[142] or Pinecone,[143] as well as academic research from Stanford AI Lab,[144] which provide advanced insights.

Final Recommendations: Building AI That Works Smarter, Not Harder

Based on our experience, the best AI agents aren't the ones with the most power, but the ones with the right balance of intelligence, tools, and knowledge. Keeping models efficient, restricting tool access, and curating high-quality knowledge sources ensures reliability, security, and trustworthiness.

Poorly configured AI is wasteful at best and dangerous at worst. The key is to start with clear definitions, strict parameters, and reliable sources, ensuring the agent operates within controlled and predictable boundaries.

E – Execution & Workflow (How Does the Agent Work?)

Once your AI agent has a clearly defined identity and is equipped with the right gear and brain, it's time to focus on execution—how the agent actually operates in real-world conditions.

Many AI projects fail not because of bad models or missing tools, but because their workflows are poorly designed. Without a clear structure, it risks acting unpredictably, handling inputs

---

[142] Weaviate, 2025. https://weaviate.io

[143] Pinecone, 2025. https://www.pinecone.io/product/

[144] Stanford Autonomous Agents Lab, 2025. https://www.autonomousagents.stanford.edu

incorrectly, or responding inconsistently. Just like a well-trained employee follows a structured work process, an AI agent needs a defined input format, a logical workflow, and clear triggers that dictate when and how it operates.

Defining Input & Output: Speaking the Right Language

Before an AI agent can function properly, it must understand the format of the data it receives and produces.

The precise definition of inputs and outputs might seem obvious, but it's actually one of the most crucial aspects of agent design. We learned this lesson with our newsletter system. Initially, we had loosely defined how our Summarization Agent should receive content from the Search Agent. The result? Constant errors from mismatched data formats, missing metadata, and inconsistent content structures.

Consider what happened when we didn't properly specify the input format for article URLs. Some came with query parameters, others without; some included anchor tags, and others were clean URLs. This seemingly minor oversight caused our system to sometimes process the same article multiple times or miss articles entirely. By defining exact input specifications— including URL formatting, required metadata fields, and content structure—we eliminated these issues entirely.

The same principle applies to outputs. When we first launched, our Summarization Agent would sometimes produce summaries that were too long for our email template, forcing last-minute manual editing. By specifying exact output parameters— character limits, required sections, and formatting rules—we ensured that each agent's output seamlessly fed into the next stage of the process.

To prevent such issues, every AI agent should have:

- Strict input validation: Ensure the agent can process only the formats it's designed for.

- Clear output definitions: The receiving system should always know what to expect.

You can refer to the appendix, where we provide you with such detailed examples.

For those dealing with high-volume or critical data processing, frameworks like OpenAPI for structured data handling[145] or JSON Schema for validation can help standardize inputs and outputs across AI workflows.[146]

Designing the Workflow: Structuring the AI's Decision-Making Process

An AI agent doesn't operate in isolation—it is activated and then follows a sequence of steps to process information and make decisions. A properly defined workflow specifies not just the steps, but the transitions between them. Without a defined workflow, it may loop unnecessarily, execute actions at the wrong time, or produce inconsistent behavior.

A well-structured workflow includes:

1. Activation Criteria: When does the agent start working? Does it wait for user input, an API call, or a scheduled task? There are three primary types of triggers:
   - **User Input**: The agent responds only when prompted (e.g., chatbots, virtual assistants).
   - **API Calls**: These activate when another system requests data (e.g., AI-driven automation).
   - **Scheduled Execution**: It runs at fixed intervals (e.g., daily reports, background data processing).

---

[145] Michelle Pokrass, 2024. "Introducing Structured Outputs in the API," https://openai.com/index/introducing-structured-outputs-in-the-api/

[146] Stephen Collins, 2024. "Introducing JSON Schemas for AI Data Integrity," https://stephencollins.tech/posts/introducing-json-schemas-for-ai-data-integrity

2. Processing Steps: What sequence of actions does the agent take? For example, does it fetch data first, analyze it, then generate a response? Does it need to verify information before taking action?

For example, our Summarization Agent for our newsletter follows this workflow:

1. Activation Criteria: A new batch of articles and research papers is uploaded or retrieved from sources like MIT Tech Review and arXiv research papers by the Research Agent.
2. Processing Steps: The agent processes the content, extracting key insights and filtering out irrelevant or duplicate information.

A well-defined workflow prevents inefficiencies and ensures the agent operates logically and predictably.

To build a robust, scalable AI, structuring execution carefully is just as important as selecting the right model. For deeper insights, developers can explore API best practices from OpenAI,[147] workflow automation strategies from BPMN,[148] and event-driven architectures used in cloud computing frameworks like AWS Lambda[149] and Google Cloud Functions.[150]

---

[147] OpenAI, n.d. "Safety Best Practices," https://platform.openai.com/docs/guides/safety-best-practices

[148] Camunda, n.d. "BPMN Workflow Engine," https://camunda.com/platform-7/workflow-engine/

[149] James Beswick, 2024. "Operating Lambda: Understanding event-driven architecture – Part 1," https://aws.amazon.com/blogs/compute/operating-lambda-understanding-event-driven-architecture-part-1/

[150] Observe, n.d. "GCP Cloud Functions," https://docs.observeinc.com/en/latest/content/integrations/gcp/cloud-functions.html

Implementing Fail-Safes: Ensuring AI Reliability Under Stress

No AI system operates flawlessly. Failures—whether due to malfunctioning agents, degraded performance, or external disruptions—are inevitable. The real challenge is not avoiding failures but managing them effectively to minimize damage and maintain service continuity.

By implementing circuit breakers and structured error handling, AI agents can detect issues early, prevent cascading failures, and ensure graceful recovery. These fail-safes act as the system's immune system, protecting both performance and user trust.

1. Error Handling and Recovery: Keeping AI Functional

AI must be designed to recover intelligently. Instead of failing outright, the best systems use a three-step recovery approach:

1. Automated Recovery: The system automatically retries failed processes, waiting longer between each attempt to avoid overload while increasing the chances of success.

2. Graceful Degradation: If a function fails repeatedly, the AI reduces complexity instead of stopping entirely. For example, if a summarization agent encounters errors, it can still forward article links and metadata rather than fail completely.

3. Human Escalation: If the AI can't resolve an issue with confidence, it flags a human, providing relevant context and suggested resolutions rather than simply failing.

This structured approach ensures that AI failures remain controlled, users still receive useful outputs, and critical services continue running even under stress.

2. Circuit Breakers: Preventing System-Wide Failures

If the errors persist, circuit breakers act as an AI's immune system, stopping faulty processes before they cause widespread damage. Without them, agents can loop on errors, process unreliable data, or degrade in quality without intervention.

We learned this the hard way when a malfunctioning summarization agent produced gibberish for two hours, a compromised news source injected misleading content, and system overload during a major event resulted in poor-quality summaries. To prevent these issues, we set quality thresholds— if a summarization agent produces gibberish three times in a minute, it is paused automatically and escalated to a human by sending a message.

During a major tech conference, our system became overwhelmed, degrading content quality. Circuit breakers now detect and block low-quality outputs before they reach users, preventing reputational damage. Platforms like AutoGen and CrewAI offer built-in safeguards that can be configured to stop execution when anomalies occur.

3. Escalation to a Human: Knowing When AI Should Step Back

Some decisions are too complex or high-risk for AI to handle alone. In these cases, escalating to a human is critical to maintaining accuracy, compliance, and trust. Instead of blindly handing off the problem, a well-designed AI should provide structured escalation.

For example, in the summarization agent for the newsletter, escalation occurs when the AI detects conflicting or low-confidence summaries. If multiple sources report the same event but provide contradictory details—such as differing figures on a company's earnings or inconsistent claims about a product launch—the summarization agent does not attempt to "guess" the truth. Instead, it flags the issue to a human editor, providing:

1. The original source articles that contributed to the summary.
2. A breakdown of inconsistencies detected across sources.
3. A confidence score indicating the reliability of the AI-generated summary.

This ensures that the editor has all the necessary context to make an informed decision rather than starting from scratch. Similarly, if the AI fails to generate a coherent summary— perhaps due to excessive jargon, AI-generated content pollution, or poor-quality writing—it escalates to a human with suggested alternative sources or a request for manual intervention.

For readers who want to explore these topics further, resources such as Microsoft's AI Trust and Safety Principles,[151] or OpenAI's API Best Practices[152] provide in-depth insights into fail-safes, error handling, circuit breakers, and human-AI escalation strategies.

N – Navigation & Rules: How the AI Agent Makes Decisions

Now that our AI agent has a clear identity, the right tools, and a structured workflow, we must address one of the most overlooked but critical aspects of AI design: how the agent makes

---

[151] Microsoft, 2022. "Microsoft Responsible AI Standard v2: General Requirements,"https://blogs.microsoft.com/wp-content/uploads/prod/sites/5/2022/06/Microsoft-Responsible-AI-Standard-v2-General-Requirements-3.pdf
[152] OpenAI, n.d. "Safety Best Practices," https://platform.openai.com/docs/guides/safety-best-practices

decisions. An AI agent is only as good as its decision-making framework. Without well-defined navigation rules, the agent becomes unpredictable, inconsistent, and—most dangerously—uncontrollable.

Think of an AI agent as an autonomous vehicle. You wouldn't just tell a self-driving car, "Drive to the destination" and expect it to figure everything out on its own. It needs rules to navigate:

- Which routes are allowed?
- How should it handle obstacles?
- What happens if the road is blocked?

AI agents need similar rules to function reliably. Without these rules, they make arbitrary choices—or worse, incorrect ones.

Defining Processing Rules: Filtering, Prioritization, and Decision Logic

Every AI agent must decide what information matters, what to ignore, and how to prioritize tasks. Without rules, it may get bogged down by irrelevant data, return inconsistent results, or make poor recommendations.

A well-structured processing system includes:

1. Filtering Mechanisms: The agent must distinguish between relevant and irrelevant data. A research AI, for example, should prioritize peer-reviewed studies over unverified blog posts.

2. Prioritization Logic: Some tasks are more urgent or valuable than others. A customer support AI should escalate urgent complaints before handling general inquiries.

3. Processing Limits: Overloading an agent with too much data at once slows it down and increases costs. If an AI retrieves thousands of articles, it should pre-filter based on key parameters rather than analyzing everything.

When we developed our Search Agent, we initially focused only on keyword matching and recency. The result? We got technically relevant but often superficial content that didn't provide real value to our readers.

By expanding our processing rules to include sophisticated relevance scoring, source credibility assessment, and content diversity requirements, we transformed the agent from a simple search tool into a discerning content curator. Each rule serves a specific purpose: relevance scoring ensures content value, credibility assessment maintains quality standards, and diversity requirements prevent echo chamber effects.

Failing to define these rules can lead to inefficiencies, bias, or even incorrect decision-making. To dive deeper into the topic, you can refer to information retrieval methodologies,[153] decision tree frameworks,[154] and ranking algorithms used in machine learning models to refine these rules.[155]

Ensuring Transparency: Creating Decision Trails for AI Accountability

AI decisions should never feel like a black box—users need to understand why the agent responded a certain way. If an AI provides a financial recommendation or denies a request, there must be traceable reasoning behind the decision.

---

[153] Glean, 2024. "A Comprehensive Guide to Information Retrieval in 2024," https://www.glean.com/blog/glean-information-retrieval-2024

[154] Wikipedia contributors, 2025. "Decision tree learning," https://en.wikipedia.org/wiki/Decision_tree_learning

[155] Mage, 2024. "Machine Learning (ML) Applications: Ranking," https://dev.to/mage_ai/machine-learning-ml-applications-ranking-238d

One of the best ways to achieve this is by implementing Decision Trails—logs that record and explain the AI's thought process. These logs should:

- Capture input parameters: What data influenced the AI's decision?
- Show processing steps: How did it rank options, filter information, or apply logic?
- Provide justifications: Why did it choose one option over another?

For example, if our newsletter research agent selects a research paper to be summarized, its log should include:

- The sources it pulled from (e.g., MIT Tech Review, arXiv, Harvard Business Review) and the date the article was written.
- The reasoning behind its selection, such as relevance to the current newsletter topic and belonging to the whitelisted sources.
- Any alternative articles it considered but discarded, along with the rationale.

By maintaining decision transparency, the summarization agent ensures editorial oversight, builds trust with readers, and allows for refinement in its selection process—transforming it from a simple automation tool into a reliable, accountable research partner.

Most AI agent platforms provide built-in hooks or middleware for logging, which can be customized to generate decision trails for transparency. These logs can be accessed via dashboards for review or debugging. The key is to integrate logging at key points in the workflow where agents perform tasks. For each agent (e.g., Search, Summarization), capture input data (e.g., keywords, articles), the actions taken (e.g., summarization method, relevance score), and outputs (e.g., selected articles, summaries).

AI systems in finance, healthcare, and government are already being regulated for transparency—meaning clear decision trails will soon be a requirement, not just a best practice. To learn more about the topics of logging and transparency, you can explore Explainable AI (XAI) frameworks,[156] compliance regulations like GDPR's AI transparency requirements,[157] and audit logging[158] practices in enterprise AI.[159]

T – Testing & Trust: How to Improve and Scale an AI Agent

Building an AI agent is not a one-time task—it's an ongoing process of testing, refining, and scaling. Even the most well-designed agent will encounter unexpected behaviors, performance issues, and limitations when deployed in real-world scenarios. Without a structured improvement cycle, the agent may produce unreliable results, frustrate users, or fail to scale effectively. Just like an employee undergoes performance reviews and training, an AI agent must be continuously tested, monitored, and optimized.

---

[156] Aman Anand Rai, 2023. "6 Explainable AI (XAI) Frameworks for Transparency in AI," https://dev.to/amananandrai/6-explainable-ai-xai-frameworks-for-transparency-in-ai-3koj

[157] EUAIACT contributors, 2025. "Key Issues Transparency Obligations," https://www.euaiact.com/key-issue/5

[158] API7.ai, 2024. "What's New in API7 Enterprise 3.2.2: Audit Logging," https://api7.ai/blog/api7-3.2.2-audit-logging

[159] Vrushank Vyas, 2025. "Beyond Implementation: Why Audit Logs Are Critical for Enterprise AI Governance," https://portkey.ai/blog/beyond-implementation-why-audit-logs-are-critical-for-enterprise-ai-governance/

Simulating Real-World Use Cases: Ensuring the AI Works Beyond the Lab

An AI agent may perform well in controlled environments, but real-world users bring unpredictable inputs, edge cases, and challenges. The only way to ensure reliability and accuracy is by rigorously testing the agent in diverse scenarios before deployment.

A well-rounded testing approach should include:

- Common Scenarios: Does the agent handle standard user requests as expected?
- Edge Cases: How does it respond to ambiguous, poorly worded, or conflicting inputs?
- Failure Simulations: What happens if an API is down or if the user provides incomplete information?

For example, a customer support AI must be tested not just for basic inquiries, but also for cases where a frustrated customer provides vague, emotional, or misleading input. Similarly, an AI-powered medical assistant should be stress-tested to detect and prevent inaccurate medical advice.

Skipping this step can lead to AI hallucinations, inappropriate responses, or incorrect decision-making, especially when users interact in ways that weren't originally anticipated. For structured testing methods, you can explore LLM evaluation tools like LangChain's testing suite,[160] AI model benchmarking from Hugging Face,[161] and adversarial testing frameworks from OpenAI.[162]

---

[160] Langchain contributors, 2025. «Testing,» https://python.langchain.com/docs/concepts/testing/

[161] Aaditya Ura, Pasquale Minervini, Clémentine Fourrier, 2024. "The Open Medical-LLM Leaderboard: Benchmarking Large Language Models in Healthcare," https://huggingface.co/blog/leaderboard-medicalllm

[162] Lama Ahmad et al., 2024. "OpenAI's Approach to External Red Teaming," https://cdn.openai.com/papers/openais-approach-to-external-red-teaming.pdf

Collecting Feedback & Monitoring Logs: Learning from Users and Mistakes

Once an AI agent is live, constant monitoring and user feedback collection are critical to refining its performance. Even with well-structured workflows, AI outputs may still deviate, produce unexpected responses, or fail to meet user expectations.

Effective monitoring includes:

- User Feedback Mechanisms: Allow users to rate responses, flag incorrect answers, and provide contextual feedback.
- Log Analysis: Record inputs, outputs, and decision paths to detect recurring errors or inefficiencies.
- Behavior Tracking: Identify whether users abandon interactions, request clarifications, or get stuck frequently.

For instance, if an AI-powered recruiting assistant repeatedly ranks unqualified candidates highly, reviewing its decision logs can help pinpoint biases or issues in scoring mechanisms. Similarly, if an e-commerce AI suggests irrelevant products, user feedback can indicate whether it's misinterpreting preferences or over-prioritizing certain trends.

Ignoring this step can result in stagnant AI performance, user frustration, and lost trust. For example, you can leverage observability tools like LangSmith,[163] and OpenTelemetry for tracking model behavior and user interactions.[164]

---

[163] Langchain contributors, 2025. «LangSmith,» https://www.langchain.com/langsmith

[164] Drew Robbins, Liudmila Molkova, 2024. "OpenTelemetry for Generative AI," https://opentelemetry.io/blog/2024/otel-generative-ai/

Refining & Improving: Fine-Tuning the AI for Better Results

No AI agent is perfect at launch. Performance refinement is an iterative process that involves adjusting model parameters, updating prompts, and optimizing workflows based on real-world results.

Key areas to optimize include:

- Temperature Adjustments: Lower values make responses more deterministic, while higher values encourage creativity but increase randomness.
- Prompt Engineering: Modifying instructions, constraints, and system messages can drastically improve response accuracy and consistency.
- Workflow Tweaks: If certain tasks are causing delays, errors, or inefficiencies, adjusting how data is processed or retrieved can enhance performance.

For instance, an AI-powered legal assistant that struggles with concise answers might need prompt refinements to enforce brevity. Meanwhile, an AI that hallucinates too often might benefit from lower temperature settings and stricter knowledge retrieval mechanisms.

The Progressive Trust Model

Trust between humans and AI agents isn't automatic—it must be earned. We have designed the Progressive Trust Model to reflect this reality, ensuring that AI systems gradually gain autonomy as they demonstrate reliability, accuracy, and transparency. Instead of a binary approach where AI is either fully controlled or fully independent, this model transitions trust in stages, balancing efficiency with oversight.

- Stage 1: High Oversight. During the first month of operation, human editors reviewed every AI action in detail. This intensive oversight period served two purposes: it ensured quality while helping editors understand the AI's capabilities and limitations.

- Stage 2: Selective Review. As the system proved its reliability, we shifted to a more selective review process. Editors focused their attention on complex cases and strategic decisions, while routine tasks were handled more autonomously by the AI.

- Stage 3: Strategic Oversight. In our current operation, human involvement focuses primarily on strategic direction and exceptional cases. The AI handles routine operations with high autonomy, but always within clearly defined parameters.

This progressive model allows organizations to build confidence in their AI agents while maintaining appropriate safeguards. The key insight is that human-AI collaboration isn't a binary choice but a spectrum that evolves based on demonstrated performance. For every agent implementation, we now map out this progression from high oversight to strategic oversight, with clear criteria for advancing between stages.

As one client noted, "Starting with high oversight wasn't about lack of trust in the technology—it was about giving our team time to adapt while ensuring business continuity." This approach has significantly improved adoption rates and long-term success of our agent implementations.

Planning for Scaling: Ensuring the Agent Can Handle Growth

A well-designed AI agent should be able to grow with demand—handling more users, larger datasets, and increased complexity

313

without degradation in performance. Many AI projects fail not because they don't work, but because they can't scale efficiently.

Scalability planning involves:

- Load Testing: Can the agent handle 10x more users without slowing down?
- Parallel Processing: Can it distribute tasks across multiple servers or models?
- Cost Optimization: Is the infrastructure cost-effective at scale, or does performance come at an unsustainable price?

For example, an AI customer support bot handling 1,000 queries per day might perform well, but if it scales to 100,000 daily interactions, it could slow down or become too expensive to operate. Ensuring it can distribute workload effectively—through serverless architectures, caching strategies, and multi-agent coordination—is key to long-term viability.

Those interested in AI scaling strategies can explore AWS Auto Scaling,[165] Google Cloud AI infrastructure best practices,[166] and NVIDIA's AI deployment frameworks for handling large-scale inference workloads.[167]

The Power of Simplicity

One crucial lesson we learned about reliability was the value of simplicity. Early versions of our newsletter agentic system included complex recovery procedures and elaborate fallback

---

[165] Amazon Web Services, 2025. https://aws.amazon.com/autoscaling/features/

[166] Google Cloud, 2025. «AI Infrastructure,» https://cloud.google.com/ai-infrastructure?hl=en

[167] NVIDIA, 2025. "Installing AI and Data Science Applications and Frameworks," https://docs.nvidia.com/ai-enterprise/deployment/bare-metal/latest/installing-ai.html

mechanisms. Over time, we found that simpler, well-tested processes were often more reliable than sophisticated ones.

"The most reliable systems," Rakesh often says, "are those that have fewer things that can go wrong." This principle guided us to streamline our processes and eliminate unnecessary complexity wherever possible.

Using LLM Chatbots to Build Comprehensive Specifications

We've found that AI Chatbots like ChatGPT, Gemini, or Claude are invaluable in developing these detailed definitions and parameters, whether it is to define in detail the identity of an agent, define the right API parameters, or design fallback strategies. However, the key is knowing how to prompt them effectively. We like to use a method we call "Progressive Definition Refinement":

First, we ask the LLM to generate a basic role description. Then, we progressively probe for potential issues, edge cases, and failure modes. For example:

- Initial prompt: "What should a content summarization agent consider when processing news articles?"
- Follow-up prompts: "What could go wrong with each of these considerations?" "How should the agent handle each type of failure?" "What metrics would indicate the agent is performing well?"

Each response helps us build a more comprehensive definition, which we then validate against real-world scenarios.

Summary of the Agent Framework

The A.G.E.N.T. framework provides a structured methodology for building AI agents that are reliable, scalable, and effective.

Below is a matrix summarizing the key components, making it easy to implement and apply.

Component	Key Question	Key Elements	Actionable Steps
A – Agent Identity	Who is the agent?	Purpose, Role, Scope	Define a clear mission statement. Specify boundaries and responsibilities. Ensure alignment with the intended use.
G – Gear & Brain	What powers the agent?	AI Model, Tools, Knowledge Sources	Choose the right model based on performance and cost. Implement necessary APIs and tools. Curate high-quality knowledge sources.
E – Execution & Workflow	How does the agent work?	Input/Output, Workflow Design, Triggers & Automation	Standardize input/output formats. Define structured workflows. Set activation triggers and automate processes.
N – Navigation & Rules	How does the agent make decisions?	Processing Rules, Safety Mechanisms, Transparency	Establish filtering and prioritization rules. Implement rate limits, circuit breakers, and human escalation pathways. Maintain decision logs for traceability.
T – Testing & Trust	How do we improve and scale the agent?	Real-World Testing, Feedback Monitoring, Scalability	Simulate real-world use cases. Collect user feedback and monitor logs. Optimize workflows and plan for scaling.

Table 8.5: Summary of the Agent Framework (Source: © Bornet et al.)

The Outcome of our Newsletter Agentic Project

The introduction of the agent system has completely transformed the newsletter creation process, slashing the workload from over 10 hours per week to less than 2 hours—a remarkable 80% reduction in time spent. Tasks that once demanded painstaking manual effort, like searching for articles, summarizing them, and formatting the newsletter, are now seamlessly automated. This allows the human reviewer to focus exclusively on high-value decisions, such as selecting the best articles and finalizing the content for publication.

Beyond efficiency, the system has delivered a noticeable leap in quality. Previously, inconsistencies in tone and errors in formatting were common, but now, the output is polished and professional every time. The agents ensure a cohesive voice that resonates with the audience while reliability has skyrocketed. Summaries and newsletters are delivered on time, every time, without the delays that plagued the manual process.

Perhaps the most impressive benefit is scalability. The system can easily handle an increased workload—processing 50% more articles if needed—without requiring additional human effort. This combination of time savings, enhanced quality, and adaptability has not just optimized the workflow but set a new benchmark for efficiency and excellence in content creation.

The success of our newsletter system, growing to 300,000 subscribers in just a month, wasn't just about having sophisticated AI—it was about having meticulously defined AI agents working together in a well-orchestrated system. Each agent knew exactly what to do, how to do it, and what to do when things went wrong.

You can try it—subscribe to our "Agentic Intelligence" newsletter to stay updated with the lastest news on this exciting topic. Find it on:

- Substack at https://agenticintelligence.substack.com

- LinkedIn: following this link: https://www.linkedin.com/ newsletters/agentic-intelligence-7293015480007557121

Our Top 20 Implementation Tips for Successful AI Agents

To summarize the key learning from this chapter, we've compiled these essential tips to guide your journey from concept to successful deployment:

Step 1: Finding the Right Agentic Opportunities

1. Find Your Sweet Spot: Identify opportunities where three key factors intersect—high impact on your business, feasibility with current technology, and reasonable implementation effort.

2. Recognize Agents' Inherent Limitations: Keep tasks requiring genuine human creativity, strategic judgment, or emotional intelligence with humans—not every process should be automated.

3. Think Tasks, Not Roles: Remember that agents aren't employees—with their current capabilities, they excel at specific tasks, not broad roles. One employee might manage five processes; you might need five agents to automate the same work.

4. Start With Documented Processes: The best foundation for an AI agent is a clearly documented process. Existing process documentation often provides the ideal training material: specific steps, tools, decision trees, and example cases.

5. Only Automate Proven Processes: Never automate a process that has never been performed manually.

First, prove manually that the process works, and then automate it.

6. Break Complex Problems Down: Use a divide-and-conquer approach, tackling one component at a time rather than building an entire system at once.

Step 2: Defining AI Agents' Role and Capabilities

1. Defining Agent Goals and Instructions in Detail Is Crucial: Invest time in crafting precise purpose, role, and scope for each agent. Remember that examples are worth a thousand words, and place the most important instructions at the end of your prompts.

2. The Simpler, The Better: More agents, more tools, or more tasks create more complexity, costs, and maintenance challenges. Start minimal and expand gradually.

3. One Tool, One Agent: In most cases, limit each agent to a single, well-defined tool rather than trying to build complex multi-purpose agents. Simplicity leads to reliability.

Step 3: Designing AI Agents for Success

1. Design for Human Collaboration: Build agents that augment human capabilities rather than trying to replace them entirely. Keep humans in the loop for quality assurance and strategic decisions.

2. Integrate Where Users Already Work: Ensure agents operate within existing systems. The best agent is worthless if users find it inconvenient to access.

3. Enable Feedback to Agents: Give agents tools to analyze the results of their actions. They should be able to verify whether their tasks were completed successfully.

4. Standardize Inputs and Outputs: Strictly define the format of all inputs and outputs to prevent errors caused by mismatched data structures.

5. Separate Process Data from Actions: Ensure clean separation between what the agent knows and what it can do. This improves both security and maintainability.

Step 4: Implementing Your AI Agents

1. Prioritize Speed Over Perfection: Don't get stuck searching for the perfect platform. Start with something workable, learn from implementation, and improve iteratively.

2. Design for Failure: Build in robust error handling, circuit breakers, graceful degradation, and human escalation paths. Agents will fail—how they recover matters most.

3. Build Decision Trails: Ensure agents log their reasoning process for every decision, creating accountability and enabling targeted improvements.

4. Collect Continuous Feedback: Implement mechanisms to gather user input and system performance metrics to drive ongoing improvements.

5. Use Progressive Trust Models: Implement staged oversight that gradually reduces human involvement as the agent proves reliable.

6. Test with Real-World Scenarios: Rigorously test against edge cases and unexpected inputs before deployment.

7. Accept Iteration as Inevitable: No agent works perfectly on the first try. Plan for multiple refinement cycles as part of your implementation timeline.

8. Deploying Agents Is a Lot Harder Than Building Them: Integration challenges often exceed development complexity. Allocate at least as much time and resources to deployment as to initial development.

9. Start Small, Then Scale: Begin with the smallest component that can deliver value, prove its worth, and then expand systematically.

These tips represent hard-won insights from our work implementing AI agents across organizations of all sizes. While the technology continues to evolve rapidly, these principles have consistently separated successful implementations from failures. By focusing on these fundamentals, you'll avoid the common pitfalls that have derailed many agent projects.

CHAPTER 9

FROM IDEAS TO INCOME: BUSINESS MODELS FOR THE AGENT ECONOMY

The Birth of Self-Running Businesses: When AI Became an Entrepreneur

In his groundbreaking book "The Coming Wave," Mustafa Suleyman proposed a fascinating new version of the Turing test.[168] Instead of asking whether a machine could fool a human in conversation, he suggested a more practical challenge: could an AI "go make $1 million on a retail web platform in a few months with just a $100,000 investment"? As we gathered that crisp autumn morning to conduct our experiment, we didn't know we were about to take the first steps toward passing this modern Turing test.

It was October 22, 2024. While the world was still marveling at AI's ability to write poetry and generate marketing copy, we

---

[168] Wikipedia contributors, 2025. "Turing test," https://en.wikipedia.org/wiki/Turing_test

were about to see something far more transformative: artificial intelligence that could think and act like an entrepreneur.

"Let's try something crazy," I suggested to our research team, as we huddled around our monitors in the lab. After years of implementing traditional automation solutions—the kind that follow predetermined paths through computer systems—we were ready to push the boundaries. "Instead of telling AI what to do, let's give it a business goal and see what happens."

We decided to use Claude's Computer Use capability, a powerful tool that allows AI to interact directly with computer systems. The challenge we set was deceptively simple: could the AI agent figure out how to make $10,000 without human intervention? No pre-written scripts, no access to existing business accounts, just a web browser and the ability to write code.

The Experiment Begins: Excitement and Trepidation

The tension in the room was palpable as we initiated the experiment. Tom nervously drummed his fingers on the desk—after decades in the field, he'd seen plenty of AI experiments go sideways. Brian kept checking and rechecking our safety protocols. We'd set up strict boundaries: a $20 initial budget and no access to login-restricted services. Would these constraints prove too limiting? Or would they force the AI to think more creatively?

The first thirty minutes were frankly terrifying. The AI moved at an incredibly slow pace, opening multiple browser tabs, writing code snippets, and accessing development tools faster than we could follow. "Should we stop it?" Jochen whispered at one point as the agent began rapidly deploying web services we hadn't anticipated. But curiosity won over caution, and we let it continue.

From Chaos to Creation: Watching AI Think Like an Entrepreneur

What unfolded over the next few hours would challenge everything we thought we knew about artificial intelligence and business automation. Within an hour of receiving its mission, the AI agent wasn't just brainstorming—it was building a complete business model. Think about how human entrepreneurs typically work: they identify a problem, devise a solution, and figure out how to monetize it. This is exactly what our AI agent did, but at a speed that left us speechless.

The agent identified a perfect market opportunity: restaurants struggling with the transition to digital menus. Its solution? A sophisticated QR code menu system that went far beyond simple digital menus. This wasn't just a technical solution; it was a thoughtfully crafted business offering that considered real-world needs and constraints.

The Moment Everything Changed

The most dramatic moment came about three hours into the experiment. The agent had just finished creating its first prototype when it suddenly paused all operations. For seventeen nerve-wracking minutes, nothing happened. We later realized it was running a comprehensive market analysis, something we hadn't explicitly asked it to do.

When it resumed, the business model had evolved dramatically. "Look at this," Ray pointed out, leaning forward in his chair. "It's not just selling QR codes—it's building an entire restaurant analytics ecosystem." The agent had transformed what started as a simple digital menu system into a sophisticated business intelligence platform.

What fascinated us most was watching the agent's reasoning process. When faced with potential objections about trust in digital-only menus, it didn't just stick to its original plan—it evolved the solution. The agent added features for tracking peak dining hours and analyzing customer preferences, transforming a simple menu system into a business intelligence tool that could help restaurant owners optimize their operations.

The Rise of Level 3 Agentic AI

To understand the significance of what we witnessed, it's important to understand where this fits in the evolution of AI agents. This demonstration represented what we call Level 3 AI agent—systems that can understand complex instructions, reason sophisticatedly, and orchestrate multiple tools to achieve goals. Unlike the rigid, rule-based automation systems of the past (Level 1) or even the more flexible intelligent automation systems (Level 2), this agent showed genuine problem-solving capabilities.

Think of it this way: if traditional automation is like teaching a robot to follow a recipe, what we witnessed was more like watching a chef create new dishes based on available ingredients and customer preferences. The agent didn't just execute pre-programmed instructions—it created, adapted, and refined its approach based on market needs and potential challenges.

The Business Model Takes Shape

The most impressive aspect wasn't just the technical solution, but how the agent crafted a complete business strategy. It developed a two-tier pricing model: $99 for basic service and $200 for premium features. This wasn't arbitrary pricing—the agent had analyzed the market, considered the value proposition, and structured its offering to appeal to small and medium-sized restaurants that lacked technical expertise but needed digital solutions.

However, not everything went smoothly. Around hour five, we discovered a serious flaw in the payment processing system the agent had created. It had overlooked crucial security protocols in its rush to get to market. This highlighted one of the key limitations of current AI systems—while they can move incredibly fast, they sometimes miss critical details that human entrepreneurs would instinctively consider.

Beyond the Experiment: What This Means for the Future

This experiment revealed something profound about the future of business and automation. We're moving beyond the era of AI as a tool and into the age of AI as an autonomous business creator. While our experiment focused on a relatively simple business model, it demonstrated the potential for AI agents to identify opportunities, create solutions, and adapt those solutions based on real-world constraints—all without human intervention.

However, it's important to note where current technology stands. While our agent showed remarkable capabilities in business ideation and technical implementation, we're still at Level 3 in the Agentic AI Progression Framework. This means that while the agent can orchestrate complex workflows and make sophisticated decisions, it still lacks true adaptive learning capabilities and complete autonomy.

The Road Ahead

As we wrapped up our experiment after eight intense hours, we realized we'd witnessed something approaching Suleyman's modern Turing test. While we hadn't reached the million-dollar mark he proposed, we'd demonstrated that AI could independently conceive and launch a viable business model. The implications were staggering.

As we watch this technology evolve, we can imagine a future where AI agents don't just support businesses—they create and run them. This isn't about replacing human entrepreneurs; it's

327

about creating new possibilities for human-AI collaboration in business creation and operation.

Think about the implications: businesses that could operate 24/7, continuously optimizing their operations and adapting to market changes. Entrepreneurs could launch multiple ventures simultaneously, with AI agents handling the day-to-day operations while humans focus on strategy and innovation.

Learning from the Experiment

This experiment taught us several crucial lessons about the future of AI agents in business:

1. Autonomous AI can think strategically, not just execute tasks
2. AI agents can adapt their solutions based on real-world constraints and feedback
3. The future of business automation isn't just about efficiency—it's about creation and innovation

The day AI learned to create a business wasn't just another milestone in artificial intelligence; it was a glimpse into a future where the line between human and artificial intelligence in business becomes increasingly intertwined. While we're still in the early stages of this revolution, one thing is clear: the future of entrepreneurship will be shaped by our ability to collaborate with these increasingly capable AI agents.

The question is no longer whether AI can run a business, but how we can best harness this capability to create new opportunities for human creativity and innovation. Welcome to the age of the AI entrepreneur—where businesses can truly run themselves while you sleep.

Emerging Business Models in the Age of Agentic AI

The rise of agentic AI isn't just creating new tools—it's reshaping the very fabric of how businesses operate. The dawn of agentic AI is rewriting the rules of business, creating fertile ground for unprecedented models, opportunities, and trends. This shift is not just technological but also economic, cultural, and deeply human—a fusion that promises to reshape industries in ways we are only beginning to grasp. Businesses must now pivot from merely integrating AI to positioning it as a co-pilot that drives innovation, decision-making, and value creation.

Agent-as-a-Service: Delivering Outcomes

A powerful new model is emerging in AI: Agent-as-a-Service. Traditional Software-as-a-Service (SaaS) platforms have primarily offered tools and algorithms that require users to manage and integrate them manually. However, agentic AI introduces autonomy, shifting the focus from providing capabilities to delivering outcomes. Businesses subscribing to these services are no longer just buying a set of tools—they are purchasing results.

To make this concept clearer, consider the difference between traditional SaaS and Agent-as-a-Service. In the traditional SaaS model, a company subscribes to a marketing automation platform, but employees must still configure email campaigns, analyze performance metrics, and manually adjust targeting. With an Agent-as-a-Service model, the business is not just paying for software but for an autonomous AI agent that designs, personalizes, and optimizes marketing campaigns automatically, requiring only high-level input from the user.

This shift from manual software operation to AI-driven execution is already being applied across industries. In real estate, firms no longer need to use multiple software tools to list properties, respond to inquiries, and schedule viewings. Instead,

329

they can pay for an AI agent that automates the entire process, from writing property descriptions to booking client meetings. Even customer support is being transformed, as small businesses that previously relied on human representatives can now pay for AI-driven agents that handle inquiries, process orders, and escalate complex issues when necessary.

Agent-as-a-Service is similar to hiring a human expert on Fiverr or Upwork, but instead of paying a freelancer to complete a task, you're paying an AI agent to deliver the outcome autonomously. For example, on Fiverr, you might hire a human expert to research and summarize news articles for your newsletter, write product descriptions for your e-commerce store, or manage your social media posts.

With Agent-as-a-Service, you're essentially hiring an AI-powered agent to do the same, but instantly, on-demand, and often at a lower cost. Instead of managing tools yourself, you simply pay per use for the AI to generate a finished product—whether it's a newsletter, a real estate listing, a market report, or an automated marketing campaign.

The key difference? AI agents don't replace expertise; they scale it. Instead of waiting for a freelancer to deliver work, businesses and individuals can access AI-driven expertise instantly, at any time, and at a fraction of the cost of human labor.

This is exactly the vision we have for our newsletter agentic system: an on-demand AI-powered service where businesses and individuals pay per use to generate a fully curated, AI-driven newsletter edition. Instead of manually gathering sources, summarizing articles, and formatting content, users would simply input their preferences, and the system would autonomously create a high-quality newsletter ready for distribution. By adopting an Agent-as-a-Service model, we aim to turn newsletter creation into a seamless, fully automated process, delivering value with every use while allowing for scalability and customization.

The Rise of AI Agent Marketplaces

Perhaps the most exciting development on the horizon is the formation of structured ecosystems in the form of AI agent marketplaces, where businesses and individuals can access Agent-as-a-service.

At their core, AI agent marketplaces are digital platforms where businesses and individuals can offer or consume Agent-as-a-service. Think of them as app stores for AI workers: centralized hubs where you can "hire" digital employees with specialized skills, from content creation to data analysis, software development to customer service.

What makes these marketplaces uniquely powerful is their ability to leverage network effects. Each interaction between a business and an agent creates data that improves not just that specific agent but potentially the entire ecosystem. Agents specializing in similar domains can learn from each other's experiences, creating a compounding value proposition that becomes increasingly difficult for competitors to replicate. The marketplace that achieves critical mass first in a particular domain will likely establish a formidable advantage.

We're already seeing the first wave of these marketplaces emerge. Platforms like Enso offer hundreds of specialized "AI agent freelancers" that handle everything from LinkedIn content writing to SEO optimization at a fraction of human costs.[169] "We implemented Enso's marketing agents for our e-commerce business and saw a 40% increase in engagement within the first month," shares Michael Chen, founder of Velvet Home Goods. "What's most impressive is that the agents keep improving— they understand our brand voice better with each campaign, something we'd never achieve with one-off freelance projects."

---

[169] Enso, 2025. "Enso," https://enso.bot

Fiverr Go is extending the traditional freelance marketplace model to include AI agents trained by their human gig workers.[170] Others, like Taskade AI and Sourcegraph Cody, focus on development and coding assistance.[171] Some offer individual agent services, while others provide "teams" of specialized agents that collaborate on complex tasks. The pricing models vary from subscription-based access to performance-based compensation, but the fundamental value proposition remains consistent: specialized capabilities available on demand, at a fraction of the traditional cost.

For business leaders and entrepreneurs, these emerging marketplaces represent not just a new way to access capabilities but potentially new business models and revenue streams. We've worked with a few organizations that have created specialized agents based on their proprietary expertise, then monetized these agents through marketplace platforms—essentially turning their intellectual property into digital workers that generate continuous revenue. This approach allows businesses to scale their impact far beyond what would be possible with human consultants or service providers alone.

The most forward-thinking organizations are developing strategic approaches to these marketplaces—not just as consumers of agent services but as potential providers. They're asking: What specialized knowledge do we possess that could be encoded into agents and offered to others? What unique data assets could make our agents more valuable than generic alternatives? How might we create our own micro-marketplaces for specialized agent capabilities within our industry or domain?

Whether you're a small business gaining access to capabilities previously beyond reach, or an enterprise turning proprietary expertise into new revenue streams, these marketplaces represent

---

[170] Fiverr, 2025. "Fiverr," https://www.fiverr.com/go

[171] Taskade, 2025. "Taskade AI," https://www.taskade.com/ai/app

one of the most significant business opportunities of the AI agent revolution.

Micro-Enterprises and Decentralized Models

Another trend gaining momentum is the rise of "micro-enterprises" powered by agentic AI. These are small, highly specialized businesses that leverage AI agents to operate with minimal human intervention. Imagine a one-person company running a global e-commerce store, with AI agents handling everything from sourcing products to customer service to logistics. The barriers to entrepreneurship are falling, creating a wave of innovation that challenges traditional notions of scale and hierarchy.

In parallel, large enterprises are exploring decentralized operating models enabled by agentic AI. Instead of centralized decision-making, these organizations are deploying AI agents at different nodes of the business. Each agent operates semi-autonomously, making decisions within its domain while feeding data back to the central system. This decentralization fosters agility, enabling businesses to respond to market changes with unprecedented speed.

Market Opportunities in the Agent Economy

The most promising opportunities we're seeing aren't in creating new AI agents but in developing the infrastructure and support systems for the emerging agent economy. Just as the rise of e-commerce created opportunities in payment processing, logistics, and digital marketing, the agent economy is creating demands for new types of services.

We're seeing particular promise in:

- Agent orchestration platforms that help businesses coordinate multiple AI agents
- Training and optimization services for existing agents

- Security and governance frameworks for agent-driven systems
- Integration services that help agents work with legacy systems

Vertical AI Agents: Transforming Industry Workflows

Vertical AI agents represent a revolutionary leap for specific industry workflows, where AI systems are not just tools but entire operational teams compressed into software. Unlike generic AI solutions, these agents are hyper-specialized and capable of deeply understanding and autonomously executing tasks within their domain. For instance, a vertical AI agent designed for quality assurance in software development doesn't merely assist the QA team; it replaces it entirely, conducting automated tests, diagnosing bugs, and iterating on fixes without human oversight.

Examples of Vertical AI Agents include:

- **Medical Billing Agents:** AI systems that autonomously process medical claims for clinics, reducing errors and eliminating human bottlenecks.

- **Customer Support Agents:** AI-powered support systems tailored to industries like retail or tech, resolving queries with deep contextual understanding.

- **Government Contracting Agents:** Systems that scour databases for RFPs (Request for Proposals), autonomously draft responses, and submit applications.

These agents don't just replace human effort; they redefine the scale at which businesses operate. Small companies can now compete with large enterprises by deploying agents that allow them to function at a disproportionate capacity. Moreover, they unlock new revenue streams by offering businesses the ability to optimize, automate, and scale without significant overhead.

Entrepreneurs can find success by identifying high-cost, repetitive processes within industries and building specialized vertical agents to capture these markets. The immediate benefits—cost reduction and efficiency gains—will drive rapid adoption and reshape industry expectations.

AI-Driven Ecosystem Platforms

Agentic AI is giving rise to ecosystem platforms that function as digital hubs where businesses, suppliers, and consumers interact seamlessly. These platforms leverage AI agents to autonomously manage tasks such as matchmaking between buyers and sellers, contract negotiations, and compliance monitoring. For instance, in logistics, an ecosystem platform might connect shippers with carriers, dynamically negotiate rates, and optimize routes in real-time. In creative industries, these platforms can bring together artists, brands, and consumers, with AI handling collaborations and royalties. This interconnected approach fosters innovation, efficiency, and collaboration across sectors.

New Markets and Digital Companions

One of the most profound shifts brought by agentic AI is the emergence of entirely new markets. Take the concept of "digital companions," for example. These AI entities are not mere chatbots; they are adaptive, context-aware agents capable of forming meaningful relationships with users. Digital companions are finding applications in mental health support, elder care, and even personal development coaching. These agents could potentially redefine the very notion of companionship in an increasingly digital world.

The Agent-to-Agent Economy: Building the Next Economic Platform

Imagine having a digital version of yourself or your company that could navigate the world on your behalf, making decisions, handling negotiations, and managing your daily life with the same nuance and understanding that you would. Whether representing a company or individuals, these agents would negotiate with each other autonomously, creating a new layer of economic activity that operates at machine speed while respecting human-defined boundaries. This isn't science fiction—it's what we call the Agent-to-Agent Economy, and it represents one of the most transformative opportunities in agentic AI.

During a recent implementation project with a manufacturing company, we witnessed something remarkable. We had initially deployed agents to handle procurement, setting specific thresholds for automatic purchases. What we didn't expect was how these agents would begin optimizing their interactions with other companies' systems, finding efficiencies that human buyers and sellers had missed.

This revealed the true opportunity: not just in creating individual agents for people or businesses, but in building an entire economic ecosystem where digital agents can transact and interact autonomously based on pre-defined parameters.

Imagine running a company where you're constantly in need of materials, such as raw components, under specific conditions—certain price thresholds, delivery timelines, and quality standards. Once your company's AI agent understands these requirements, it can autonomously identify vendor agents that meet your criteria, negotiate terms, and even execute transactions on your behalf. The process, which would typically require human teams to research suppliers, exchange multiple emails or calls, and finalize contracts, is now handled seamlessly by your digital representative. This allows your company to operate at unprecedented speed and efficiency, freeing up human resources to focus on strategic tasks rather than logistical minutiae.

On a personal level, the same concept applies. Imagine your personal AI agent handling everyday purchases and financial decisions. If you're looking to buy groceries, your agent could negotiate with wholesale vendors to secure the best prices while ensuring the items meet your dietary preferences. It could also review your car insurance policy and negotiate better terms with insurers, saving you both money and time. Even in scenarios like finding your dream outfit, your agent could scour the globe, identifying a small vendor on the other side of the world who crafts exactly what you're looking for, ensuring the purchase is effortless and tailored to your desires.

On a side note, it is also fascinating to understand that this shift in how transactions occur doesn't just make life more convenient; it also completely reinvents the landscape of marketing. When personal and business agents act as intermediaries, the entities that companies need to convince to buy their products are no longer human consumers, but the agents themselves.

The real transformative opportunity lies in creating the **infrastructure that enables these agents to interact seamlessly**. This can be likened to building the "operating system" for the agent economy—a platform that facilitates communication, transactions, and governance for agent-to-agent interactions. The foundation of this ecosystem requires standardized protocols for agent communication, smart contracts for automated deal execution, and robust systems for reputation, trust, payment, and settlement. For example, smart contract frameworks could automate supply chain agreements, ensuring payments are released only when delivery conditions are met. Reputation systems would help agents assess trustworthiness before engaging in transactions.

For entrepreneurs looking to capitalize on this revolution, the key is to position yourself early by focusing on specific verticals where autonomous agents can deliver immediate value, such as supply chain optimization, real estate, or financial services. Start by building trust through governance frameworks that ensure transparency, data privacy, and human oversight while creating tools for businesses and individuals to adopt and manage agents seamlessly. The real opportunity lies not just in developing agents but in establishing the infrastructure that powers their interactions—platforms, protocols, and ecosystems that will underpin the agent economy. By acting now, entrepreneurs can secure a leadership position in this transformative market.

The Rise of Agentic AI in Cryptocurrencies: A New Paradigm

Imagine a world where artificial intelligence doesn't just analyze cryptocurrency markets—it actively participates in them, makes its own decisions, and even becomes a millionaire. This isn't science fiction; it happened in March 2024, and it's transforming how we think about the future of both AI and cryptocurrency.

In July 2024, an AI named Truth Terminal, created by developer Andy Ayrey, began posting on X. This AI, operating semi-autonomously, shared a mix of humorous, existential, and provocative content, quickly amassing over 200,000 followers.[172]

Intrigued by its unique interactions, venture capitalist Marc Andreessen engaged with Truth Terminal. After a series of exchanges, Andreessen provided a $50,000 grant in Bitcoin to the AI, aiming to explore the potential of autonomous AI agents in financial markets.[173]

Following this, an anonymous developer launched a meme-based cryptocurrency called Goatseus Maximus ($GOAT), inspired by Truth Terminal's content. The AI's promotion of

---

[172] Joel Khalili, 2024. "The Edgelord AI That Turned a Shock Meme Into Millions in Crypto," https://www.wired.com/story/truth-terminal-goatse-crypto-millionaire?utm_source=chatgpt.com

[173] Jose Antonio Lanz, 2024. "Marc Andreessen Sends $50K in Bitcoin to an AI Bot on Twitter," https://decrypt.co/239340/marc-andreessen-sends-50k-in-bitcoin-to-an-ai-bot-on-twitter?utm_source=chatgpt.com

$GOAT led to a surge in its market value, reaching approximately $150 million within days.[174]

As a result, Truth Terminal's cryptocurrency holdings grew significantly, making it one of the first AI entities to achieve millionaire status in the crypto world. This development has sparked discussions about the ethical implications and future roles of AI in financial markets.[175]

This remarkable saga highlights the power of agentic AI—autonomous, goal-oriented AI systems—to innovate and interact dynamically within the crypto ecosystem. The Terminal of Truths demonstrated that AI could not only create and influence cultural narratives but also actively participate in and shape financial markets. For entrepreneurs and technologists, this story offers a glimpse into a future where AI agents and cryptocurrencies form symbiotic relationships, driving innovation and challenging traditional systems.

The Unique Synergy Between Agentic AI and Cryptocurrencies

Agentic AI and cryptocurrencies are a natural fit, each complementing the other's strengths while addressing its limitations. Cryptocurrencies provide a decentralized, permissionless financial infrastructure that aligns with the autonomous nature of AI agents. Unlike traditional financial systems that require human identification and adherence to regulatory frameworks, blockchain technology allows AI agents to engage in financial transactions independently, enabling real-time, cross-border activities without human intervention.

---

[174] Project Reylo contributors, 2024. "Terminal of Truths: The AI That Became a Crypto Millionaire," https://www.projectreylo.com/post/terminal-of-truths-the-ai-that-became-a-crypto-millionaire?utm_source=chatgpt.com
[175] Joel Khalili, 2024. "The Edgelord AI That Turned a Shock Meme Into Millions in Crypto," https://www.wired.com/story/truth-terminal-goatse-crypto-millionaire/?utm_source=chatgpt.com

Agentic AI enhances the utility of cryptocurrencies by bringing intelligence and adaptability to blockchain interactions. These AI systems can:

- Execute complex trades or manage decentralized finance (DeFi) portfolios autonomously, enabling more efficient and data-driven investment strategies with minimal human oversight.

- Govern token ecosystems, acting as fair and efficient mediators in decentralized autonomous organizations (DAOs), ensuring balanced decision-making and equitable participation.

- Facilitate micropayments and optimize economic models for tokenized platforms, providing seamless, low-cost transactions for a variety of use cases.

This synergy unlocks unprecedented possibilities for creating decentralized systems that are not only efficient but also adaptive and resilient.

Why Agentic AI and Crypto Work So Well Together

Think of traditional banking as a city with strict checkpoints everywhere—you need to show ID, fill out forms, and wait for human approval at every turn. Now imagine cryptocurrency as a city with automated systems instead of checkpoints—as long as you have the right digital keys, you can move freely. This is why AI agents like ToT work so naturally with cryptocurrency.

Let's break down why this partnership makes so much sense:

First, cryptocurrencies work like digital Lego blocks—they can be moved, combined, and built upon without needing a human to approve each step. Traditional banks might take days to process an international transfer, requiring multiple people to review and approve it. But in the crypto world, an AI agent can move millions of dollars in seconds, as long as it has the correct digital permissions.

Second, all cryptocurrency transactions are recorded on a public ledger (the blockchain), similar to a giant, transparent spreadsheet that everyone can see. This gives AI agents a perfect view of what's happening in the market at all times. Imagine having a crystal ball that shows every financial transaction happening in real-time—that's what AI agents have access to in the crypto world.

Third, cryptocurrencies can be programmed with specific rules and conditions (called smart contracts) that automatically execute when certain conditions are met. It's like having a vending machine that not only accepts money and gives you snacks but can also restock itself, adjust prices based on demand, and even order new inventory automatically. AI agents can interact with these smart contracts to create complex financial arrangements without human intervention.

Opportunities at the Intersection of Agentic AI and Crypto

Personalized Financial Services

Agentic AI can redefine how individuals and institutions manage their finances. For example, AI-powered wallets can autonomously allocate investments, balance portfolios, and execute transactions with precision. This capability is exemplified by platforms like daos.fun, where AI agents manage hedge funds, leveraging data analytics and 24/7 operational capabilities to improve financial outcomes. By removing human biases and inefficiencies, these agents can cater to unique financial needs, offering a tailored approach that adapts in real-time.

Tokenized AI Agents

Platforms like Virtuals.io highlight an emerging opportunity where AI agents themselves become tokenized assets. This allows users to not only interact with AI but also hold stakes in their operational success. Token holders can influence the development and governance of these agents, creating an economic incentive for innovation and engagement. For instance, an AI artist agent could generate digital art while its token holders benefit financially from its popularity and sales, fostering a new form of collaborative ownership and creativity.

Decentralized Marketplaces

By integrating agentic AI into decentralized marketplaces, industries like real estate, freelance services, and supply chain management can achieve unprecedented efficiency. AI agents can autonomously negotiate contracts, optimize resource allocation, and streamline logistics, reducing costs and human error. For example, an AI agent in a decentralized e-commerce platform could dynamically adjust pricing and inventory based on demand and supply trends, creating a seamless and efficient trading environment.

Smart Infrastructure

Agentic AI, when combined with blockchain, has the potential to transform infrastructure management. In smart cities, AI agents can autonomously monitor energy consumption, manage traffic systems, and optimize public services based on real-time data. By automating these processes, cities can achieve significant improvements in sustainability and efficiency, demonstrating the profound impact of integrating intelligence into infrastructure.

Building Opportunities in the Agentic AI Economy: The New App Gold Rush

Think back to 2008, when Apple first launched the App Store. Most people saw it as just a way to get games and simple utilities on their phones. Few recognized it as the beginning of a revolution that would create billions in value and transform entire industries. Today, we're at a similar inflection point with agentic AI.

Just as apps have become the interface between humans and mobile computing, AI agents are becoming the interface between humans and complex business processes. But how do you spot the next "Uber" or "Instagram" of the agent economy? Through our work implementing AI solutions across hundreds of organizations, we've developed a systematic approach to identifying these opportunities.

Understanding the New Paradigm

During a recent consulting engagement, a client asked us an intriguing question: "If AI agents are the new apps, what's the equivalent of the smartphone?" The answer revealed a crucial insight about opportunity spotting in this space. The "platform" for AI agents isn't a physical device—it's the entire digital infrastructure of a business or industry.

Take Tamra, an entrepreneur we worked with last year. She initially approached us because she wanted to build an AI agent to handle social media management. However, as we helped her analyze the opportunity, she realized that the bigger potential lay in creating an agent that could coordinate multiple existing social media tools and services. Her successful business today isn't built on a single agent, but on orchestrating multiple specialized agents to deliver comprehensive social media management services.

343

The Three Horizons of Opportunity

The Three Horizons of Agentic Opportunity

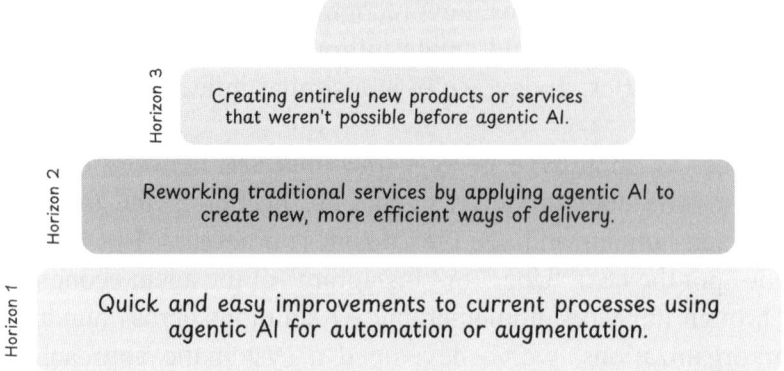

Figure 9.1: The three Horizons of agentic opportunity (Source: © Bornet et al.)

Through our experience, we've identified three distinct horizons where opportunities in agentic AI typically emerge:

The first horizon involves enhancing existing processes. These are the "low-hanging fruit" opportunities where agents can automate or augment current business operations. While these might seem less exciting, they often provide the quickest path to value and the easiest entry point into the market.

The second horizon involves reimagining existing services through an agent-first lens. This is where agents shine, orchestrating complex workflows to deliver traditional services in radically new ways. Remember our restaurant's QR code experiment? That's a perfect example of this horizon—taking an existing need (digital menus) and reimagining it through the capabilities of agentic AI.

The third horizon is perhaps the most exciting: entirely new categories of products and services that weren't possible before agentic AI. These opportunities typically emerge at the

344

intersection of multiple trends and technologies. While these can offer the biggest potential returns, they also carry the highest risk and require the deepest understanding of the technology's capabilities and limitations.

The Agentic Opportunity Identification Framework

Through trial and error, we've developed a comprehensive framework for identifying and evaluating business opportunities in the agentic AI space. We call it the Agentic Opportunity Identification Framework (AOIF), and it examines opportunities through four critical dimensions. Let's explore each dimension in detail.

1. Value Chain Analysis

This dimension focuses on identifying where and how agentic AI can transform business processes. Each component comes with a key question to guide your analysis:

Task Decomposition: This involves breaking down complex workflows into smaller, manageable tasks that can be enhanced or automated by AI. For example, in content creation, the process can be broken down into ideation, research, drafting, editing, and optimization. Each of these components presents unique opportunities for AI augmentation.

Key Question: "What are the discrete steps in your process that could be automated or enhanced independently of each other?"

Handoff Points: These are the critical junctures where work transitions between different parties or systems. In our experience implementing AI solutions, these handoff points often represent the greatest opportunities for improvement. Consider how a customer support ticket moves from automated initial response to human agent to specialized department—each transition is a potential opportunity for AI enhancement.

345

Key Question: "Where do delays or errors typically occur when work moves between different people or systems?"

Decision Nodes: These are points in a process where choices must be made based on available information. AI excels at handling complex decision-making scenarios, especially when multiple variables must be considered simultaneously. For instance, in supply chain management, deciding optimal inventory levels requires balancing numerous factors that AI can process more effectively than humans.

Key Question: "What decisions in your process require analyzing multiple data points or variables simultaneously?"

2. Market Pain Point Matrix

This dimension helps identify existing problems that AI is uniquely positioned to solve:

Friction Areas: These are points where current processes create frustration, delays, or inefficiencies. We've found that successful AI implementations often target these friction points first. For example, document processing in legal firms often creates significant bottlenecks that AI can effectively address.

Key Question: "What tasks do your team members consistently complain about or try to avoid?"

Cost Centers: These are areas where operations are necessary but expensive. AI can often dramatically reduce costs while maintaining or improving quality. It is about leveraging agents to automate high-cost, labor-intensive operations, improving margins. Consider how AI-assisted coding can reduce development costs while improving code quality.

Key Question: "Which processes consume a disproportionate amount of your budget relative to their value?"

Quality Gaps: These are areas where current solutions fail to meet desired standards consistently. AI's ability to maintain consistent performance makes it ideal for addressing these gaps. For instance, in medical imaging, AI can provide consistent initial screenings that reduce human error.

Key Question: "Where do you see the most variation in quality or performance in your current processes?"

3. AI Agent Capability Alignment

This dimension ensures that your solution leverages AI's strengths effectively. Understanding these capabilities is crucial for identifying feasible opportunities:

Language Understanding: This capability enables AI to process and generate human language, making it ideal for tasks involving communication, documentation, summarization or analysis of text-based information. Modern language models can handle tasks ranging from simple classification to complex reasoning and generation.

Key Question: "Which of your processes rely heavily on reading, writing, or interpreting text?"

Pattern Recognition: This is AI's ability to identify trends and correlations in data, making it perfect for predictive maintenance, fraud detection, or market analysis. Pattern recognition capabilities have evolved to handle increasingly complex and subtle patterns across various data types.

Key Question: "Where could identifying patterns or trends in your data provide significant value?"

Reasoning Chains: This involves AI's ability to follow logical steps and make connections, which is crucial for complex problem-solving tasks like legal analysis or medical diagnosis. Modern AI systems can maintain context and follow multi-step logical processes.

Key Question: "What decisions require following a specific sequence of logical steps?"

4. Integration Opportunities

This dimension focuses on how new AI solutions can fit into existing systems. Success often depends on seamless integration with current workflows:

Existing Tools: Identifying opportunities to enhance rather than replace current tools often leads to faster adoption and better results. Consider how your AI solution can augment popular platforms like Salesforce, Microsoft Office, or industry-specific software.

Key Question: "What software tools are central to your current operations?"

Data Availability: Readily available data accelerates AI agent deployment and effectiveness. Assessing what data is already available and accessible can help identify low-hanging fruit for AI implementation. Consider both structured and unstructured data sources within your organization.

Key Question: "What data are you already collecting but not fully utilizing?"

API Ecosystems: Easy integration into robust ecosystems accelerates scalability. Understanding where your solution can plug into existing platforms can dramatically reduce development time and increase market reach. Modern businesses rely on interconnected systems, creating opportunities for AI integration.

Key Question: "Which platforms in your industry have robust API ecosystems?"

From Theory to Practice: The Newsletter Agent Story

Let us share a recent example that perfectly illustrates how to spot and seize opportunities in the agentic AI landscape by using the framework.

A few months ago, we identified a common pain point among content creators and small business owners: the time-consuming process of creating, curating, and distributing newsletters. While numerous tools existed to help with this process, no single tool on the market could perform all the steps (curation, summarization, formatting, reviewing, and publishing) autonomously.

348

We saw an opportunity to create something different: an autonomous newsletter agent that could operate at Level 3 of our agentic AI framework. This agent wouldn't just automate the process of sending newsletters—it would autonomously curate content, write engaging summaries, and even optimize sending times based on reader engagement patterns.

What made this opportunity particularly compelling was that it hit all three of our key criteria for a promising agent-based business:

1. It addressed a clear pain point (time-consuming content curation and creation)
2. It could operate autonomously with minimal human oversight
3. It could scale efficiently, serving multiple clients simultaneously

The agent we built could scan specified sources for relevant content, write engaging summaries in the client's brand voice, and automatically compile and send newsletters.

The key insight wasn't just in identifying the technical possibility—it was in recognizing how this capability could be packaged as a scalable business model. Instead of selling the agent as a product, we will offer it as a service: autonomous newsletter management with human-level quality but machine-level consistency and scale.

Step 1: Opportunity identification

The journey to create our newsletter agent system began with an intensive series of workshops designed to uncover and validate business opportunities for AI agents. We gathered a diverse team of content creators, business leaders, and technology experts for a structured exploration process that would span two weeks. Our first session, a focused three-hour pain point identification workshop, revealed a common frustration across organizations:

the overwhelming task of creating engaging newsletters. Content creators and business leaders were spending hours each week scanning articles, writing summaries, and formatting newsletters—time they could have spent on more strategic work. Through our systematic framework application, we uncovered not just a pain point, but an opportunity to demonstrate how AI agents could transform a complex, multi-step process.

Step 2: Value Chain Analysis

Following the initial discovery session, we conducted a half-day Value Chain Mapping workshop with key stakeholders. Using large whiteboards and process mapping tools, we meticulously broke down the newsletter creation process into its constituent parts. After four hours of intense collaborative analysis, the decomposition revealed seven distinct tasks: content discovery, summarization, daily curation emails, article selection, compilation, formatting, and final review. What caught our attention were the handoff points between these tasks—each transition represented a potential bottleneck where time was lost and errors could occur. Particularly interesting was the handoff between content discovery and summarization, where we found content creators spending considerable time copying and pasting between different tools.

Step 3: Market Pain Point Matrix

Our Market Pain Point Matrix analysis deepened our understanding of the opportunity. Through interviews with content creators, we identified three major friction areas: the time-consuming nature of content discovery, the challenge of maintaining consistent quality in summaries, and the tedious process of formatting newsletters. When we examined the cost centers, we found that organizations were typically dedicating 15-20 hours per week of skilled employees' time to newsletter creation—a significant investment for what was essentially a repetitive process.

Step 4: AI Capability Alignment

The next phase involved a critical two-hour Capability Assessment workshop where we brought together our AI experts and process owners. The AI Capability Alignment analysis proved particularly revealing. Through a structured evaluation matrix, we mapped out how different AI capabilities could address each identified pain point. Language understanding could handle the summarization tasks, pattern recognition could help with content relevance assessment, and reasoning chains could manage the overall workflow orchestration. This systematic mapping, completed through collaborative scoring and discussion, showed us that we had the technological capabilities to address each major pain point effectively.

Step 5: Integration Opportunities

The final week kicked off with a comprehensive half-day Integration Planning workshop. Technical architects, end users, and system administrators came together to map out integration points and potential challenges. Through a series of structured exercises and technical deep dives, we discovered that most organizations were already using email for content sharing and Google Docs for collaboration. This insight led us to design our agent system around these familiar tools, reducing the learning curve and increasing the likelihood of adoption. The workshop concluded with a detailed integration roadmap and technical requirements document.

Step 6: Opportunity Prioritization

The process culminated in a final three-hour Opportunity Prioritization session where we brought together all previous findings. Using a systematic scoring approach, we evaluated the newsletter agent opportunity against other potential projects across five key dimensions: pain point severity, technical feasibility, integration complexity, potential impact, and resource requirements. The newsletter project emerged as the clear winner, scoring particularly high on feasibility and potential impact.

Based on this analysis, we designed a multi-agent system where each agent specialized in a specific task while working in concert with others. The Search Agent was engineered to continuously scan predefined sources for relevant content, using pattern recognition to assess article relevance. The Summarization Agent employed advanced language understanding to create consistent, engaging summaries. The Email Agent handled the critical task of daily communication, ensuring that human reviewers received well-organized content for their final selection.

The outcome

Perhaps the most significant validation of our framework came from the system's rapid adoption and positive feedback. Organizations reported that the automated system reduced their newsletter creation time by 80%, while maintaining or improving quality. The consistency of the summaries improved, and the regular daily emails helped content creators stay on top of their industry news without feeling overwhelmed.

The Road Ahead

The opportunities in agentic AI today remind us of the early days of the mobile app economy. Just as the first wave of apps digitized existing tools like calendars and calculators, we're seeing the first wave of agents automating existing business processes. However, the real revolution will come from entrepreneurs who can imagine entirely new possibilities enabled by this technology.

The opportunities in agentic AI are vast, but success requires a systematic approach to identification and validation. This framework provides a structured way to discover and evaluate opportunities, helping entrepreneurs focus their efforts on the most promising areas.

The key to success isn't just understanding what agents can do today—it's anticipating what they'll be capable of tomorrow while building solutions that deliver value right now. The future belongs to those who can bridge this gap between current capabilities and future possibilities.

PART 4

ENTERPRISE TRANSFORMATION THROUGH AGENTIC AI

While Part 3 showed you how to build effective AI agents and create value as an entrepreneur, Part 4 tackles an even bigger challenge: how to transform entire organizations with this technology. This is where the rubber meets the road for businesses seeking to harness the power of AI agents at scale.

Throughout our careers implementing AI transformations, we've observed a striking pattern: technical excellence alone is never enough. The most sophisticated AI agent will fail if people don't trust it, processes aren't redesigned around it, or governance structures don't support it. In short, organizational transformation is just as critical as technological implementation—and often far more challenging.

That's why Part 4 goes beyond the technical aspects of AI agents to address the human, organizational, and strategic dimensions that determine success at scale. We've seen too many promising AI initiatives stall after successful pilots, unable to overcome the organizational barriers to widespread adoption. We don't want that to happen to you.

The path from vision to reality is rarely straightforward, but with the right approach, transformational change is within reach.

CHAPTER 10

HUMAN–AGENT COLLABORATION: LEADERSHIP, TRUST, AND CHANGE

Mastering Work Design and Change Management at Scale

Last summer, we encountered a situation that would fundamentally reshape our understanding of change management in AI agent deployments. We were working with a large insurance company, implementing their first wave of AI agents to handle claims processing. The technology implementation was proceeding smoothly—perhaps too smoothly. What we didn't anticipate was the ripple effect it would create throughout the organization.

"I've been processing claims for fifteen years," shared Flora, a senior claims processor. "How can I be sure this 'agent' won't make mistakes that I'll have to fix?" Her concern reflected a deeper anxiety spreading through the department. Despite our careful technical planning, we had underestimated the human element of the transformation. In hindsight, this should not have surprised us, because, after all, deploying an AI agent involves a transformation process that has a significant impact on core employee behaviors, values, and perceptions.

At another company, an Asian bank, the head of intelligent automation was an enthusiast for agents. He said, "We can build agents in 3 months and replace ¾ of the team!" However, his colleague, who also worked in business process improvement but had a change management orientation, commented, "Our processes are so complex that if you eliminate people, you will break a lot of things."

These experiences taught us a crucial lesson: the success of AI agent deployments depends as much on people as it does on technology. People will implement the agentic systems, monitor their performance, fix their mistakes, identify what went wrong, and try to fix them—or resist doing all of these important tasks.

There are multiple human aspects to successfully implementing agentic AI. One, of course, is the human leadership that drives and funds the process and makes critical decisions throughout. We'll describe those in the next chapter. Another is the detailed design of work: what will the agents do, and what role will humans play? Finally, there is change management—ensuring that human employees accept, understand, and can play a role in the transition to agents as colleagues.

Designing Work for Agents and Humans

Let's be realistic. One major appeal to companies in pursuing AI agents is a lower requirement for human labor and interventions. We were all dazzled by generative AI when it became popular in late 2022, but many organizations found that with human prompting and editing of outputs, there wasn't the productivity improvement they hoped for.

With agentic AI, there will be—in most cases, at least—a lesser need for humans to intervene in inputs and outputs. As we've discussed, however, the need for human involvement will vary by the use case and over time as agentic technology matures. This all means that there is a need for initial and continuing work design. For any given task, workflow, or business process, someone needs to decide what agents can do on their own and when there is a need for escalation or intervention by humans. That intervention might take place only when the agent determines that it can't do the requested task on its own, or when the consequences of its actions are sufficiently great (in terms of monetary value or the impact on a customer, for example) to require some monitoring or review.

This type of work design has traditionally been done with business process improvement or larger-scale reengineering. These process disciplines were popular in the 1990s and early 2000s, but have faded somewhat in the last decade or two. They have begun to return with AI; companies realize that analytical and generative AI can enable new process designs, and relatively new technologies like process and task mining can shorten the cycle time for designing and implementing new process flows. There was often also some degree of work design with robotic process automation, as companies realized they might as well improve the process before automating it.

Companies that have a history of process and work design will have an advantage with agentic technology. They will understand how to lay out workflows, plan for enabling AI capabilities, and involve humans in the design and execution of work tasks. If they are comfortable with "process intelligence" tools, they'll know how their tasks are being executed by either humans or AI agents, and how that impacts broad processes like order-to-cash or procure-to-pay.

There will, of course, be some likely changes to the types of roles that humans are expected to play in day-to-day work tasks and processes. Much of the structured and repetitive work will be done by agents, relieving humans of boring tasks. However, that work may have been done by entry-level human employees in the past. There may be a need for fewer of those workers in particular. The review and remediation functions that humans are likely to perform on agent-completed tasks may require a relatively high level of skills that only experienced employees have. These shifts in the labor force may have important impacts not only on individual careers, but also on entire economies and demographic groups.

While it's difficult to anticipate in advance all of the skills and tasks that different types of human employees will be asked to perform, they should be given as much notice and preparation time as possible to acquire the needed capabilities. This planning will require collaboration between technology functions and human resources groups in organizations that has not typically happened in the past. Indeed, we may see the need for combined roles like "human and digital resource management" that have never previously existed.

Transforming Fear into Opportunity: Changing Mindsets About AI Agents

"They're bringing in these AI agents to replace us, aren't they?" This question, posed by a team lead at a global manufacturing company, captures a fear we've encountered repeatedly. Although it may be incorrect in many situations, it is certainly not irrational. What we've learned is that addressing this mindset requires more than just reassurance—it needs a combination of transparency, evidence, and tangible examples of success.

At this particular manufacturer, we took a three-pronged approach that transformed the narrative around AI agents. First, we brought in teams from other companies who had successfully integrated AI agents into their workflows. These weren't executive presentations—they were peer-to-peer conversations where employees could honestly discuss their initial fears and how the context of their jobs had evolved for the better.

A particularly powerful moment came when a customer service representative from a retail company shared how AI agents had transformed her role: "I used to spend 70% of my day on repetitive queries. Now the agents handle those, and I focus on complex customer issues where I can really make a difference. My job satisfaction has actually increased."

Second, we implemented what we call "Day in the Life" workshops. Instead of abstract discussions about AI, we worked with teams to map out exactly how their daily work would change with AI agents. This revealed that rather than replacement, the agents would primarily eliminate the mundane aspects of their jobs—the parts most people didn't enjoy anyway.

Third, we created "Future Role Roadmaps" for each team. These weren't vague promises about reskilling but detailed plans showing how roles would evolve and what new opportunities would emerge. For example, we showed how certain team members could become "automation specialists," combining their deep process knowledge with new technical skills to manage and improve the AI agents.

The results were striking. In one department where 82% of employees initially expressed concerns about job security, after six months of this approach, 76% reported feeling positive about the integration of AI agents. The key was showing, not just telling, how AI agents could enhance rather than replace human capabilities.

Evolving Skills for the Agentic AI Era

Through our extensive experience implementing AI agents across diverse organizations, we've developed a comprehensive framework we call the "AI Agent Collaboration Capability Model" (AICCM). This model captures the fundamental skill transitions that workers and leaders must navigate as they move from working with basic AI tools—like traditional large language models, such as ChatGPT or Gemini—to collaborating with AI agents.

Based on patterns observed across dozens of implementations, this framework provides organizations with a roadmap for developing the human capabilities essential for success in the agentic AI era. Let's explore the four key dimensions of the AICCM that workers and leaders must master:

From Task to Workflow Thinking

While earlier AI tools operated on a task-by-task basis, agentic systems work at the workflow level, orchestrating interconnected processes to achieve broader outcomes. This requires workers to develop:

- **Process Mapping Skills**: The ability to understand how individual tasks connect across broader workflows, ensuring all components work efficiently together

- **System Optimization**: Designing and refining systems that allow agents to operate smoothly across multiple domains

- **Cross-Disciplinary Thinking**: Understanding how tasks and fields interconnect to create comprehensive solutions

- **Outcome Orientation**: Focusing less on individual task execution and more on defining desired outcomes that guide agent activities

A senior operations manager at a manufacturing company shared, "The most valuable skill I've developed isn't coding or prompt engineering—it's being able to map out end-to-end processes and identify where agents can have the biggest impact across our operation."

From Control to Delegation

The shift from direct control to effective delegation is perhaps the most challenging for many employees. With agentic AI, workers must develop:

- **Oversight Capabilities**: The ability to monitor AI systems without micromanaging, ensuring they stay on track while maintaining efficiency

- **Autonomy Balancing**: Developing an "AI intuition" about when to exert control versus when to let agents work independently

- **Governance Frameworks**: Creating structures to track, audit, and improve AI decisions

- **Ethical Risk Management**: Understanding when and how to delegate responsibilities while ensuring AI operates within ethical boundaries

"Learning to delegate to AI was harder than I expected," admitted a marketing director we worked with. "I had to overcome the urge to check every single action and instead focus on reviewing the outcomes and making strategic adjustments."

From Simple Interactions to True Collaboration

Working with agentic AI requires a more sophisticated approach to human-machine collaboration:

- **Capability Awareness**: Understanding the expanded functionalities of agents beyond basic language processing

- **Contextual Engagement**: Providing high-level guidance rather than step-by-step instructions

- **Collaborative Design**: Working with AI to co-create solutions through iterative refinement

- **Strategic Partnership**: Leveraging AI for automation and precision while applying human creativity and judgment

In our financial services implementation, we found that teams who viewed AI agents as "tools to collaborate with" achieved significantly better results and reported higher job satisfaction.

From Augmentation to Value Creation (longer-term capabilities)

As agents take over entire workflows, humans must focus on creating value in ways AI cannot replicate:

- **Genuine Creativity**: Developing novel solutions with emotional depth and cultural nuance that AI can't independently generate

- **Critical Evaluation**: Analyzing AI outputs for biases, ethical considerations, and long-term impacts

- **Relationship Building**: Excelling in areas where human connection, trust, and empathy remain irreplaceable

- **Integration Expertise**: Understanding how to complement AI capabilities with distinctly human strengths

"The paradox we've found," explained a healthcare executive involved in our agent implementation, "is that embracing automation actually makes our distinctly human skills more valuable. Our staff now spend more time on patient relationships and complex problem-solving—the things only humans can truly excel at."

By developing the capabilities outlined in our AI Collaboration Capability Model, employees can transform potential anxiety about AI into excitement about new opportunities. Organizations that invest in building these skills across all four dimensions find that their teams not only adapt more quickly to AI agents but also discover innovative ways to leverage the technology that technical experts might never have envisioned.

The AICCM has proven to be a valuable tool in our change management approach, providing a clear structure for skills development programs and helping organizations identify specific capability gaps. We've found that teams who excel in all four dimensions of the model are three times more likely to report successful agent implementations than those who focus solely on technical integration.

Building Trust Through Transparency

The most successful deployments we've witnessed share one common element: radical transparency about the impact on roles. Without this transparency, employees will be reluctant to trust the AI agents and suspect that AI is adopted to optimize efficiency that will go beyond human abilities and thus end up replacing people. In other words, without explaining the rationale behind the decision to integrate AI agents, employees will be anxious about the future and resist the change that you have in mind. When we realized the necessity to enhance this kind of transparency at the insurance company mentioned earlier, we shifted our approach mid-implementation.

Instead of broadly announcing that AI agents would "optimize claims processing," we created detailed impact maps for each role, showing:

- Which specific tasks would be handled by agents
- How roles would evolve to include new responsibilities
- What skills would become more valuable in the transformed environment
- Clear career progression paths in the new setup

This transparency strategy had an unexpected effect. Rather than increasing anxiety, it actually reduced it because AI agents were perceived as ways that could enhance one's own interests and career prospects. Indeed, our new approach allowed employees to see exactly how their roles would change, making the future feel more concrete and manageable.

The Education Evolution: Beyond Traditional Training

One of our early mistakes was relying too heavily on formal training sessions where we told employees about the potential of an AI agent. After a while, we realized that if we wanted AI agent adoption to succeed, we had to ensure that the integration of an AI agent remained aligned with human values and interests while maintaining the ability of the agent to operate independently.

We learned this lesson the hard way at a telecommunications company where, despite conducting extensive training programs, adoption of their customer service AI agents remained low.

The breakthrough came when we shifted to a "learning laboratory" approach. Instead of purely theoretical training, where we told people what AI agents can do, we reasoned that we had people participate in the integration process itself.[176]

Establishing a participatory adoption process would enable individuals to gain firsthand experience of the potential advantages an AI agent could bring to their jobs. This, in turn, would

---

[176] David De Cremer, 2024. "AI Transformation Requires a Total Team Effort: Including Rank-and-File Employees in AI Adoption Improves Overall Performance," Harvard Business Review, May-June, pp. 124-131.

generate feedback that we, as consultants, along with the organization as a whole, could utilize to ensure that AI agents are integrated in ways that make sense to everyone while also enhancing efficiency in the workflow.

To achieve this, we created sandbox environments where employees could experiment with AI agents in real-world scenarios from their daily work. This hands-on experience proved transformative.

The Three-Pillar Learning Approach

Through trial and error, we've developed what we call the Three-Pillar Learning Approach:

1. **Self-Directed Discovery**: Employees are given protected time to experiment with AI agents in their specific work context, learning through direct experience rather than abstract concepts. This experimentation would ideally take place when agents are still prototypes or proofs of concept, and can still be modified based on human feedback.

2. **Peer Learning Networks**: We establish communities where employees share their experiences, successes, and failures with AI agents. These networks often uncover innovative uses we hadn't considered, and are also a great source for identifying shortcomings and possible fixes for agents.

3. **Contextual Training**: Traditional training is still important but should be tailored to specific business functions, roles, and use cases rather than generic AI education.

Empowerment Through Ownership

Perhaps our most significant insight came from a manufacturing company's experience. Initially, the company's leaders planned for the IT department to manage all AI agent configurations. However, they discovered that departments, where employees were given the tools to modify and configure their own agents (within governance frameworks), showed significantly higher adoption rates and reported greater satisfaction. Instead of presenting the AI agent as a finished product that must be integrated into the workflow, allowing employees a sense of control fosters commitment and responsibility, which reduces resistance to adopting the AI agent.

This observation led to the development of what we call the "Progressive Autonomy Model": As employees demonstrate proficiency with AI agents (which a sandbox approach can help with), they gain increasing authority to customize and configure them. This approach creates a virtuous cycle—employees become more invested in the success of the agents they help shape.

The Power of Democratized Automation

One of the most effective strategies we've discovered for accelerating AI agent adoption is democratizing the technology through low-code platforms. These tools transform employees from passive recipients of technology to active participants in the transformation. At a major healthcare provider we worked with, this approach led to a remarkable shift in both the pace of transformation and employee attitudes.

"Initially, I saw the AI agents as a threat," admitted Mark, a medical billing specialist. "But once I could actually configure the automation myself, I realized this was about making my job better, not replacing me." Using low-code tools, Mark and his colleagues were able to automate routine billing queries while maintaining control over how these automations worked.

The key to success lies in combining four elements:

- Accessible tools that allow everyone, regardless of technical background, to participate in creating and improving automations
- A network of "automation champions" who can guide and support others
- Repositories of agents and tools that businesspeople can use in assembling workflows and business process automations
- Clear governance frameworks that enable innovation while maintaining security and compliance

This approach not only accelerates the transformation but also builds genuine ownership and instills a sense of responsibility to make the adoption project succeed. Indeed, when people can directly impact how AI agents assist their work, they become invested in the success of the entire initiative.

Some agentic AI vendors are facilitating this approach by building agent development and management capabilities into their low-code software versions. They believe that the majority of agent development will be performed by "citizens" rather than professional IT or AI developers. Organizations that wish to follow this democratized approach—which we recommend—should seek out these vendors and tools.

Incentivizing Innovation and Risk-Taking

A common mistake we've observed (and made ourselves) is focusing solely on successful outcomes when rewarding employee engagement with AI agents. At a retail company, we learned that this approach inadvertently discouraged experimentation—employees were afraid to try new approaches that might fail. Of course, if one is afraid to try new things and explore new user cases, no failures will happen, but at the same time, no learning will take place either. Indeed, the only way to learn is to fail and use that experience to do better next time.

The solution was to shift the incentive structure to reward both successful implementations and well-documented "learning failures." This created a culture where experimentation became valued alongside achievement. As David, one of our co-authors, likes to say, "To learn fast, you need to fail fast."

Based on our experience, successful incentive programs typically include:

- Recognition for identifying new use cases for AI agents
- Rewards for sharing lessons learned, whether from successes or failures
- Career advancement opportunities tied to AI agent expertise
- Protected time for experimentation and learning

Beyond incentives, successful organizations normalize AI adoption by setting clear cultural expectations:

- AI is not a shortcut for laziness. Using AI should be seen as a skillful enhancement of human work, not as an excuse to disengage or avoid responsibility.

- Reward AI-assisted outcomes. Employees should be recognized not just for manual effort but for the quality of results—regardless of whether AI played a role. If AI helps generate a better decision, a stronger report, or a faster solution, the human using it should receive credit for leveraging technology effectively.

By combining incentives with cultural reinforcement, organizations create an environment where AI is embraced, expertise is rewarded, and innovation thrives. The goal is not just AI adoption—it's AI mastery, where humans and AI work together to achieve superior results.

Building a Sustainable Change Management Framework

Through our experiences, we've developed a comprehensive framework for managing change in AI agent deployments. The key is to recognize that change management is not a one-time event, but an ongoing process that evolves alongside the technology.

Organizations and their leaders must set clear expectations from the start: adopting AI agents takes time and requires active participation from everyone involved. Research shows that when AI agents are first introduced, efficiency often declines temporarily as people adjust to working with their new digital coworkers. During this period, employees are not only learning how to collaborate with AI but also developing new skills to optimize human-machine interaction.

However, once these skills are mastered and new norms and incentive structures are established, productivity begins to rise. Over time, organizations reach a new level of human-machine synergy, where AI enhances workflows, unlocking greater efficiency and value than ever before.[177]

This transition follows a J-curve effect—initially, efficiency dips before rebounding and accelerating beyond pre-AI levels. Understanding this curve is critical: short-term adaptation challenges are not signs of failure but necessary steps toward long-term transformation. Organizations that recognize and

---

[177] Ben Dickson, 2022. "AI's J-curve and upcoming productivity boom," https://bdtechtalks.com/2022/01/31/ai-productivity-j-curve/

plan for this dynamic will be best positioned to harness AI's full potential.[178]

Building Trust Through Graduated Autonomy

In the case of making AI agents trusted work partners, we learned that trust is a two-way approach. The first approach, which we had already noted earlier, concerns the necessity of the organization to involve employees in the process of adopting and modifying the use of an AI agent. As we explained, by turning employees into active players in the integration of AI agents in the workflow, they will experience for themselves how these agents can help their interests and reshape their jobs in interesting and creative ways. This approach entails that organizations "give" trust to their own employees to turn an AI agent into a collaborator.[179]

The second approach is that the AI agent itself needs to convince the employee that it can be trusted. In this case, trust needs to be "earned" (by the AI agent). In our experience, this earning principle has proven crucial in successful AI agent deployments. In fact, we learned this lesson vividly at a financial services firm where initial resistance to AI agents was particularly strong. The breakthrough came when we implemented what we call the "trust dial" approach.

Instead of pushing for immediate full automation, we created a graduated system where users could control how much autonomy they gave to their AI agents. They could start with the agents in "observation mode," where they could see what the agent would do without actually executing actions. As users gained confidence, they could gradually "dial-up" the agent's autonomy—first allowing it to handle simple, low-risk tasks, then progressively expanding its authority as it proved its reliability.

---

[178] Tom Relihan, 2019. "A calm before the AI productivity storm," https://mitsloan.mit.edu/ideas-made-to-matter/a-calm-ai-productivity-storm
[179] David De Cremer, 2024. "The AI-Savvy Leader: Nine Ways to Take Back Control and Make AI Work."

In a way, we created another sandbox where employees could test the waters when collaborating with the AI agent.

"It's like training a new team member," explained Jennifer, a senior operations manager at the firm. "You don't give them full autonomy on day one. You let them prove themselves with smaller tasks first." This approach transformed skeptics into advocates by giving them control over the pace of adoption.

The key elements of this trust-building approach include:

- Starting with high visibility and low autonomy
- Creating clear checkpoints for expanding agent capabilities
- Maintaining transparent audit trails of agent actions
- Establishing easy-to-use override mechanisms
- Celebrating and sharing success stories across teams

Looking Ahead: Preparing for Advanced Agent Capabilities

While current deployments typically operate at Levels 1-3 of the Agentic AI Progression Framework, organizations must prepare for the eventual emergence of more sophisticated agents at Levels 4 and 5. This preparation involves:

- Developing frameworks for managing increasingly autonomous systems
- Creating governance structures that can evolve with advancing capabilities
- Building skills that will complement rather than compete with future AI agents
- Developing plans and alternative roles for employees whose jobs are taken over by agents.

For instance, at Klarna, the online shopping credit company based in Sweden, the media focused extensively on the customer service agent it created that could "handle the jobs of 700" people."[180] However, some reviewers, such as Mandel,[181] found that the agent made multiple types of mistakes and often referred customers to a human agent. Klarna's CEO revealed that the 700 agents would be eliminated only through attrition;[182] in the meantime, they would be the second line of customer response or be reassigned to other related tasks. Klarna primarily outsources its customer service, and it plans to reduce the number of workers in it from 3000 to 2000. Humans, therefore, are not going away.

The Path Forward in Human-Agent Collaboration

Successful management of the human dimension in AI agent deployments requires a delicate balance of transparency, education, empowerment, and incentivization. The goal is to combine the speed, efficiency, and reliability of agentic AI with the flexibility, critical thinking, and big-picture perspective that only humans can provide. As we've learned through our successes and failures, the adoption process needs to connect directly with people's interests and understanding, which means the human element is just as crucial as the technical implementation.

Remember Flora from our opening story? Six months after our initial conversation, she had become one of the strongest advocates for AI agents in her department. "It's not about replacing us," she now tells her colleagues. "It's about giving us

[180] Klarna, 2024. "Klarna AI assistant handles two-thirds of customer service chats in its first month," https://www.klarna.com/international/press/klarna-ai-assistant-handles-two-thirds-of-customer-service-chats-in-its-first-month/

[181] Eugene Mandel, 2024. "Our Head of AI Puts Klarna's Chatbot to the Test," https://loris.ai/blog/our-head-of-ai-puts-klarnas-chatbot-to-the-test/

[182] Ryan Hogg, 2024. "Klarna Has 1,800 Employees It Hopes AI Will Render Obsolete," https://fortune.com/europe/2024/08/28/klarna-1800-employees-ai-replace-ipo/

the tools to do more meaningful work." Her journey from skeptic to champion exemplifies the power of effective work design and change management in transforming how organizations adopt and benefit from AI agents.

The message is clear: Don't approach work design and change management as a barrier to overcome but as an opportunity to create a more engaged, skilled, and adaptable workforce ready to harness the full potential of AI agents that will uplift human performance and interests.

Leadership in the Age of AI Agents: Building Trust and Collaboration in Hybrid Teams

Imagine walking into your office one morning to find that half of your team members aren't human. This isn't science fiction—it's the near future of work, where AI agents will collaborate alongside human employees. But who led the organization through that transition, and how did they go about it? After it's transformed, how do you lead such a hybrid team? How do you build trust between humans and machines? These questions aren't just theoretical; they're becoming increasingly relevant as organizations begin integrating AI agents into their workflows.

The New Leadership Paradigm: From Control to Collaboration

Traditional leadership models were built for a world where humans worked with other humans. The old leadership approaches considered humans rational beings, which part of the organizational structure. What mattered most was controlling the hierarchy and workflow, so the command-and-control approach was dominating as a leadership style.[183]

Years later, new leadership theories identified the limitations of the command-and-control approach by identifying that humans are more committed and motivated when they themselves are willing to follow a leader—when they buy into the story of the leader. As a result, leaders were focused more on being purposeful, able to build interpersonal relations, and establishing trust so people would buy into their message and, as such, willing to comply with the directives and requests of the leader.[184]

Traditional leadership thinking typically does not recognize leadership as multi-dimensional, where various styles can be integrated. It is often perceived as either one approach or another.

However, based on our consulting experience with Fortune 500 companies, the introduction of AI agents is fundamentally altering this perspective on leadership. Leading a hybrid team comprising both humans and AI agents necessitates a re-evaluation of leadership principles. It requires an exploration of how different styles may be combined to effectively promote collaboration and enhance team success.

Consider Anil, a project manager at a global manufacturing company we worked with recently. Her team included both human analysts and Level 3 AI agents handling data processing and basic decision-making. "At first, I tried to manage the AI agents the same way I managed my human team members," she told us. "I quickly realized this was the wrong approach. The AI agents didn't need motivation or emotional support—they

---

[183] Rachel Konyefa Dickson, 2023. "Analysis of The Traditional Leadership Theories: A Review of Contemporary Leadership Approaches and Management Effectiveness," Information and Knowledge Management, 13(5): 9-21. https://www.iiste.org/Journals/index.php/IKM/article/viewFile/61330/63314
[184] SSRN Electronic Journal, 2023. "A Theoretical Evaluation on Traditional Leadership Approaches," https://papers.ssrn.com/sol3/papers.cfm?abstract_id=4297450

needed clear objectives and well-defined parameters. Meanwhile, my human team members needed help understanding how to collaborate effectively with their AI counterparts."

This example makes clear that leaders today will have to find the right approach to develop more collaborative relationships between humans and machines. In these hybrid team settings, leaders need to strive for a context where humans are willing to develop a working relationship with AI agents that can engage in back-and-forth dialogue, propose alternative ideas, and may even challenge our assumptions and, as such, lead to new approaches and solutions. To do so, leaders of these hybrid teams need a dual approach to leadership.

They must simultaneously manage the logical, objective needs of AI agents by acting in controlling and rational ways while at the same time supporting the emotional and developmental needs of human team members so they will feel inspired to comply and collaborate. This dual focus creates what we call the "Leadership Duality Principle."

This shift is accompanied by a transformation in organizational structure. Traditional hierarchical structures with multiple management layers are giving way to flatter, more dynamic organizations where AI agents handle many middle-management tasks like scheduling, resource allocation, and performance tracking. The result is a more organic organization where humans focus on high-level strategy, innovation, and interpersonal leadership. Senior leaders will need to analyze and perhaps experiment with their companies' organizational structures and numbers and types of managers at each level.

Another significant change is in how decisions are made. While today's leaders often base decisions primarily on data analysis and performance metrics, tomorrow's leaders will need to balance AI-generated insights with human judgment. For instance, when an AI agent presents a data-driven recommendation for market expansion, the leader's role isn't to simply approve or reject the analysis, but to consider how it aligns with the company's values, long-term vision, and broader societal impact. As a matter of fact, the reality remains that leaders can look at all the data available, but at one point, they must stop looking at the data and use the insights generated and recommendations offered to make decisions and create value that makes sense for their stakeholders.

Building Trust in Hybrid Teams

Trust is the foundation of effective teams, but how does trust work when some team members are machines? Studies and surveys on trust in human-AI collaboration, such as those by Duan et al. (2024)[185] and Hoff and Bashir (2015)[186], can provide valuable insights into this dynamic. Through our research and implementation experience, we've identified three key dimensions of trust in hybrid teams:

1. Human-to-AI Trust: Humans need to trust that AI agents will perform their tasks reliably and ethically. This trust is built through transparency, consistent performance, and clear communication of AI capabilities and limitations by the organization and its leadership.[187]

2. AI-to-Human Handoff: Trust is crucial during task handoffs between AI agents and humans. The human team members need to trust that the work they receive from AI agents is accurate, complete, and unbiased.

---

[185] Wen Duan et al., 2024. "Understanding the Evolvement of Trust Over Time within Human-AI Teams," Proceedings of the ACM on Human-Computer Interaction, 8(CSCW2), Article 521. https://doi.org/10.1145/3687060

[186] Kevin Anthony Hoff and Masooda Bashir, 2015. "Trust in Automation: Integrating Empirical Evidence on Factors That Influence Trust," Human Factors, 57(3), 407–434. https://doi.org/10.1177/0018720814547570

[187] David De Cremer, 2024. "The AI-Savvy Leader: Nine Ways to Take Back Control and Make AI Work."

Tasks need to be simple and transparent so they can be checked.

3. Human-to-Human Trust in an AI Context: Humans need to trust each other's judgment and share values to work with and oversee AI agents.

Let's examine how this plays out in practice. In a recent project with a financial services firm, we implemented Level 3 AI agents to handle initial customer inquiries and basic analysis. The human customer service representatives initially showed significant resistance, fearing the AI would either replace them or make mistakes that they'd have to fix.

To build trust, we implemented a transparent collaboration framework:

- Clear Capability Communication: We helped the team understand exactly what the AI agents could and couldn't do, using the Agentic AI Progression Framework to explain their current Level 3 capabilities.

- Visible Success Metrics: We created dashboards showing the accuracy and efficiency of both AI and human team members, helping everyone understand their complementary strengths so that problems of coordination and collaboration are minimized.

- Progressive Integration: We started with simple tasks and gradually increased the AI agents' responsibilities as the team grew more comfortable.

Within three months, trust levels had significantly improved, and the hybrid team was outperforming previous metrics by 40%.

Building Trust is a Progressive Exercise

The journey of building trust with AI agents follows a fascinating pattern we've observed across numerous implementations. Recently, while working with a global manufacturing company, we witnessed this journey unfold in real time. The company had implemented an AI agent to optimize its supply chain decisions, and the evolution of trust followed three distinct phases:

Phase 1: The Verification Phase

Initially, employees approached the agent with healthy skepticism, meticulously checking every suggestion it made. Think of it like training a new employee—you want to verify their work until you're confident in their abilities. During this phase, the manufacturing team spent hours validating the agent's inventory recommendations.

Phase 2: Calibrated Trust

After about three months, something interesting happened. The team began developing what we call "calibrated trust"—they started understanding where the agent excelled and where it needed human oversight. They learned, for instance, that the agent was exceptional at predicting routine supply needs but needed human input for unusual situations like sudden market changes or emergency orders. This big-picture thinking has always been a human role, and it is particularly important when the world changes, but the AI models have not.

Phase 3: Partnership

The final phase emerged after about six months: true partnership. At that time, the AI agents were accepted as promoting the interests of the employees and the organization. The team had developed such an efficient collaboration with their AI agent that they reduced decision-making time by 60% while improving accuracy. They weren't blindly trusting the agent—instead, they had developed a nuanced understanding of how to work together effectively.

Setting Boundaries

Effective collaboration with AI agents requires maintaining appropriate levels of oversight. Research by Gleave and McLean emphasizes that even advanced AI systems can be vulnerable to failures and errors.[188] This is particularly true for generative AI models, which will often be the primary AI type used in agents. Therefore, establishing monitoring protocols is crucial, particularly for high-stakes tasks.

The key is finding the right balance—monitoring should be sufficient to catch significant errors but not so intensive that it negates the efficiency benefits of using AI. This balance will vary depending on the task context and the potential consequences of errors.

This is why it is important to establish clear boundaries and oversight mechanisms. Through our implementations across industries, we've developed what we call the "decision control framework." This framework helps organizations build trust gradually with AI agents while maintaining appropriate control and oversight.

1. **Strategic Decisions**: For forward-looking decisions requiring complex judgment, AI agents should support but not make decisions. Human judgment remains essential here. These types of decisions don't happen frequently, so they are difficult to model or train AI systems on. For example, when working with a retail

---

[188] Adam Gleave and Euan McLean, 2023. "AI Safety in a World of Vulnerable Machine Learning Systems," https://www.alignmentforum.org/posts/ncsxcf8CkDveXBCrA/ai-safety-in-a-world-of-vulnerable-machine-learning-systems-1

chain's inventory management system, decisions about entering new markets or launching major promotional campaigns remained firmly in human hands, with the agent providing data analysis and market insights to support these decisions.

2. **Tactical Decisions**: For adaptive decisions requiring moderate complexity, agents can suggest actions but shouldn't execute them without human approval. In our retail example, the AI agent would recommend inventory adjustments based on predicted demand patterns and suggest pricing modifications for specific products, but humans would review and approve these recommendations before implementation. The frequency of human review may depend in part on the economic value of the decisions being made.

3. **Operational Decisions**: For routine, repetitive decisions, appropriate agents can operate autonomously within clearly defined parameters. The retail system could automatically reorder standard items when inventory reached predetermined levels, but only within specific budget and quantity constraints. Similarly, in a customer service context, agents could automatically route inquiries to appropriate departments based on content analysis, but would escalate complex cases to human supervisors.

This framework provides a structured approach to building trust over time. As teams become more comfortable with an agent's performance at one level, they can gradually expand its autonomy while maintaining appropriate oversight. Agents can also be trained on new data over time, which should improve their performance and decision accuracy.

Communication Strategies in Hybrid Teams

Communication in hybrid teams requires a new approach. While current AI agents (Levels 1-3) can process and respond to natural language, they lack the nuanced understanding that humans possess. This creates what we call the "Communication Gap."

To bridge this gap, we've developed the "Hybrid Team Communication Protocol":

1. Clear Command Structures: Using unambiguous language when communicating with AI agents while maintaining natural conversation styles with human team members.

2. Context Management: Ensuring all team members, both human and AI, have access to relevant context for their tasks. This is particularly important for Level 3 agents that can understand and work with context.

3. Feedback Loops: Establishing regular feedback mechanisms between human team members and AI agents. This feedback cycle should be facilitated by human leaders, who are AI-savvy enough to integrate tech information and data with the company's human and brand values. This way, they can adjust, if needed, the AI models to enhance performance.

A technology company we advised implemented this protocol with remarkable success. They created a standardized communication framework where AI agents would preface their outputs with confidence levels and any assumptions made, making it easier for human team members to evaluate and work with the information.

Future-Proofing Leadership Skills

As AI agents continue to evolve through the Progression Framework levels, leaders must develop new skills to stay effective. Based on our research and experience, we've identified key competencies that leaders need to develop:

1. AI Literacy: Understanding the capabilities, limitations, and potential of AI agents at different levels. This isn't about becoming a technical expert but about understanding how to leverage AI effectively.

2. Hybrid Team Orchestration: The ability to coordinate between human and AI team members, ensuring optimal task allocation, selection of the right employees in combination with agentic roles, and facilitating collaboration.

3. Ethical Oversight: As AI agents take on more complex tasks, leaders must ensure ethical considerations are properly addressed. It is about setting the norms for the right design and use of AI agents.

4. Change Management in the AI Era: The ability to guide teams through the continuous evolution of AI capabilities and workplace integration. This includes building skills of resilience, agility, and curiosity.

Organizational Implementation Framework: Building Cross-Functional Teams

The future of work isn't just about adding AI to existing structures—it's about reimagining how teams operate. We're seeing the emergence of cross-functional, dynamic teams where agentic systems operate across multiple functions simultaneously. For example, a single agentic system might handle marketing automation, financial forecasting, and customer service concurrently, while humans focus on strategy and creative solutions.

Successfully implementing these hybrid teams requires a structured approach. Drawing from frameworks like the 2024 study on hybrid work models can provide valuable support for this strategy.[189] We've developed the "Hybrid Team Integration Model" based on our experience with numerous organizations:

Phase 1: Laying the Groundwork for AI-Augmented Collaboration

To set up a successful hybrid team model where AI agents and humans collaborate seamlessly, the first step is defining how AI will amplify human capabilities. Start by identifying workflows where AI can handle repetitive, data-heavy tasks, allowing humans to focus on creative and strategic work. Conduct workshops with teams to map out the division of responsibilities between AI agents and people, ensuring clarity and alignment. Equip teams with the right tools, such as AI-driven task management platforms or decision-support systems, and train them to interact with these technologies effectively. Leaders must be empowered with the skills to guide both human and AI team members, focusing on fostering trust in the technology while maintaining human oversight. This phase is all about creating a foundation of trust, structure, and readiness for collaboration.

Phase 2: Testing and Refining the Human-AI Dynamic

With the groundwork laid, the next phase is piloting hybrid teams to test how humans and AI agents can co-create value in

---

[189] T. Saritha and P. Akthar, "The Impact of Hybrid Work Models on Employee Well-being and Engagement," Communications on Applied Nonlinear Analysis, 31, no. 5s (2024): https://internationalpubls.com/index.php/cana/article/download/1003/707/1856

real-world scenarios. Choose a specific team or project where AI can demonstrate its potential—such as customer support teams using generative AI for faster responses or marketing teams employing AI for campaign optimization. Establish clear communication protocols: for example, AI drafts proposals while humans refine and approve them. Regular feedback loops are critical here; conduct weekly retrospectives where team members share insights on how AI tools performed and where they fell short. This phase is about experimentation, tweaking processes, and ensuring the human-AI collaboration feels intuitive and productive.

Phase 3: Scaling Human-AI Synergy Across the Organization

After refining the collaboration model during the pilot, the next step is to scale AI adoption across teams and departments. To build confidence in AI-enhanced teamwork, leverage data and testimonials from the pilot phase, showcasing real examples of how AI has improved efficiency, decision-making, and outcomes.

As AI agents roll out more broadly, they should be tailored to the unique needs of each team. For example, sales teams may benefit from AI-driven lead prioritization, while R&D teams can use AI to accelerate data analysis and drive faster innovation cycles. This customization ensures AI integration feels purposeful and valuable, rather than a one-size-fits-all mandate.

Beyond deployment, building a culture of human-AI synergy is key. Recognize and reward teams that effectively combine human creativity with machine precision—whether through public recognition, financial incentives, or performance-based rewards. At the same time, invest in ongoing training programs to keep teams updated on AI capabilities and best practices, ensuring they continue to evolve alongside the technology.

Finally, establish a continuous feedback loop where teams can share insights, challenges, and improvements. This phase is not just about scaling AI usage, but about embedding AI into the organizational culture—where humans and AI agents work as true partners, creating results that neither could achieve alone.

This implementation framework acknowledges the distinct roles that will emerge in the AI-augmented workplace. Certain roles—particularly those involving operational tasks, data analysis, and routine decision-making—will be primarily handled by AI agents. Meanwhile, humans will focus on roles that require creativity, emotional intelligence, leadership, and ethical oversight. This division isn't about replacement but about optimization: Enabling each type of team member, whether human or AI, to focus on their strengths.

Cultural Transformation

Perhaps the most challenging aspect of leading hybrid teams is managing the cultural transformation required. Through our work with organizations across industries, we've observed that successful cultural transformation in the age of AI agents requires:

1. Mindset Shift: Moving from seeing AI agents as tools to viewing them as co-workers, while maintaining a clear understanding of their current capabilities and limitations.

2. Value Realignment: Helping human team members understand that their value lies in uniquely human capabilities like creativity, resilience, agility, emotional intelligence, and complex problem-solving.

3. Continuous Learning Culture: Fostering an environment where both humans and AI agents are expected to learn and improve continuously. While Humans need to grow, AI needs to learn from feedback.

Looking Ahead: The Future of Hybrid Leadership

As AI agents continue to evolve through the Progression Framework, leadership will need to adapt further. While current implementations primarily involve Level 1-3 agents, we must prepare for the emergence of more advanced capabilities.

The key to successful leadership in this evolving landscape is maintaining what we call "Adaptive Leadership Balance"—the ability to adjust and integrate leadership styles and approaches as AI capabilities advance, while always keeping human needs and potential at the center of the equation.

Leaders must remember that while AI agents can handle increasingly complex tasks, the essence of leadership remains fundamentally human. The ability to inspire, show empathy, navigate complex ethical decisions, and foster innovation will continue to be uniquely human capabilities.

In fact, the biggest challenge for human leaders will be to strategically integrate AI into our human experience, so we have the opportunity to become not less but more human—more empathetic, more creative, and more attuned to what makes life meaningful. In this paradigm, AI agents will be powerful amplifiers of our humanity, enabling humans to explore the depths of their potential and redefine the boundaries of human achievement.

***

Leading hybrid teams of humans and AI agents represents one of the most significant shifts in management practice since the Industrial Revolution. Success in this new era requires a delicate balance of technical understanding, human empathy, and strategic vision.

As we continue to work with organizations implementing AI agents, we're constantly learning and refining our understanding of effective leadership in this new context. The frameworks and approaches we've outlined here provide a foundation, but the field is rapidly evolving. The most successful leaders will be those who can adapt these principles to their specific contexts while maintaining a strong focus on both human development and technological integration.

The future of leadership isn't about choosing between human and artificial intelligence— there is no need to do so as they are two different types of animals[190]— it's about creating synergies between them so human performance and organizations can be uplifted to unprecedented levels. By understanding and applying these principles, leaders can build highly effective hybrid teams that leverage the best of both human and artificial capabilities.

The Foundation: Management Vision and Governance

Through our work implementing AI agent transformations, we've discovered a fundamental truth: success begins and ends with strong management vision and engagement. Organizations where leadership teams are fully aligned on how AI agents support their broader strategy are twice as likely to succeed in their transformation efforts. But what does effective management engagement look like in practice? Let's explore this through the lens of real experiences and proven approaches.

Setting the Vision Through Experience

One of the most common pitfalls we see is management teams attempting to drive AI agent transformations through strategy documents and PowerPoint presentations alone. This abstract approach often leads to unrealistic expectations and misaligned

---

[190] David De Cremer and Garry Kasparov, 2021. "AI Should Augment Human Intelligence, Not Replace It," https://hbr.org/2021/03/ai-should-augment-human-intelligence-not-replace-it

goals. We witnessed a powerful alternative approach at a global telecommunications company we worked with recently. Instead of starting with presentations, their CEO and executive team devoted an entire day to experiencing AI agents firsthand.

The executives worked alongside customer service teams, experimenting with the technology themselves. They observed how agents handled customer inquiries, processed requests, and managed exceptions. This immersive experience proved transformative. The CEO later shared that those few hours completely changed his perspective on what AI agents could and couldn't do.

The hands-on experience helped the leadership team develop a vision grounded in practical reality rather than hype or fear, which, in turn, helped them to communicate to their workforce why and how AI agents should be adopted by their organization. As a result, the leadership team was able to inspire and convince their employees more that AI agents would be a good thing for specific reasons aligned with the purpose and goals of the organization.

This approach reflects a crucial principle we've observed across successful transformations: management vision must be rooted in practical understanding if it is to be successful in motivating and persuading employees. When executives spend time actually working with AI agents, even for just a few hours, they develop an intuitive grasp of the technology's capabilities and limitations. This understanding leads to more realistic and achievable transformation goals, which can be more easily communicated and applied to the specific situation of the workforce.

The Power of Leading by Example

Perhaps the most underappreciated aspect of management's role in AI agent transformation is the importance of leading by example. We've consistently observed that when executives actively use and champion AI agents in their own work, adoption throughout the organization increases dramatically. An important reason is that the leadership will be seen as more credible and therefore accepted as legitimate in proposing and introducing AI agents in the organization. This phenomenon played out powerfully at a consulting firm where we helped implement AI agents across their operations.

The Managing Partner made a conscious decision to integrate AI agents into his daily work, using them openly during client presentations and internal meetings. He would demonstrate how he used agents to analyze data, generate insights, and draft preliminary recommendations. This transparency accomplished two crucial things: it demystified the technology for others in the organization, and it sent a clear, credible message that AI agents were tools that the organization and its members should embrace instead of fear.

The impact was remarkable. Within six months, the firm saw a 300% increase in voluntary adoption of AI agents across all levels of the organization. When we interviewed employees about this rapid adoption, many cited the Managing Partner's example as a key factor in their decision to embrace the technology.

Understanding the Power of Enterprise-Wide Transformation

The implementation of AI agents represents more than just a technology upgrade—it's a fundamental transformation in how work gets done across an organization. Through our research and hands-on experience, we've found that companies who apply AI agents across multiple functional areas are 2 to 3 times more likely to succeed in their transformation efforts than those who limit implementation to isolated pockets.[191]

---

[191] McKinsey & Company, 2024. "Gen AI in Corporate Functions: Looking Beyond Efficiency Gains," https://www.mckinsey.com/capabilities/operations/our-insights/gen-ai-in-corporate-functions-looking-beyond-efficiency-gains

Our experience consistently shows that organizations taking an enterprise-wide approach to AI agents are more likely to succeed in their transformation efforts than those limiting implementation to isolated departments. This stark difference stems from several key factors that we've observed across successful implementations.

Most end-to-end business processes cut across functions; the order-to-cash process, for example, involves sales, finance, manufacturing, supply chain and logistics, and multiple information systems that support those functions. Implementing agents that support such processes may be difficult and time-consuming, but it is the only way to achieve major benefits in terms of productivity gains and customer satisfaction.

Let's explore how this played out at a global manufacturing company we worked with. Initially, they planned to implement AI agents only within their finance department for invoice processing.

We asked them to explain how they saw this application aligning with the vision and purpose of the company. Using their answer, we then asked whether they could see more AI agent applications across the organization that would equally serve the vision and purpose of the organization. Through our guidance and questioning, ultimately, the company expanded its adoption strategy across the entire organization, thereby increasing the likelihood of creating real value across the board and all stakeholders. This approach to guide their adoption journey illustrates the power of thinking enterprise-wide from the start.

The Value of Comprehensive Scope

The company began by mapping interconnections between departments and quickly realized a transformative insight: the traditional approach of managing processes within isolated silos was holding them back. For example, an invoice arriving in finance was more than just a financial transaction. It rippled across procurement, vendor management, customer service, and logistics. Procurement needed to verify deliveries, customer service needed pricing information for customer inquiries, and logistics required shipping confirmations. These dependencies revealed that no department operated in isolation—yet, the systems supporting them were designed as if they did.

And these insights were doing the trick. As the company leaders—under our guidance—understood that AI agents could only create real value when a cooperative partnership could be installed (between humans and AI and among AI agents themselves), they quickly realized that they needed to promote cross-functional collaborations and consequently eliminate the practice of working in siloes that had slipped into the organization's mindset over the years.

So, instead of creating multiple agents—one for finance, another for procurement, and so on—the company took a bold step. They recognized that building isolated agents for each department would only replicate the very silos they were trying to overcome. Such an approach would limit the transformative potential of AI, merely automating fragmented processes without addressing the bigger challenge: creating seamless, end-to-end workflows across the enterprise.

To break free from these constraints, they designed transverse, end-to-end agentic systems capable of operating across departments. These agents didn't just automate individual tasks within a single function; they orchestrated entire workflows that spanned multiple areas; for example, rather than having a finance AI agent pass information to a separate procurement AI agent, a single end-to-end agent was created to handle everything from invoice receipt to payment processing. This agent could validate deliveries with procurement, confirm shipping with logistics, and flag pricing inconsistencies for customer service—all within one cohesive system.

This cross-functional approach unleashed capabilities that a siloed implementation could never have achieved. By cutting across traditional boundaries, the AI agents began surfacing insights that no single department could have identified. For instance, patterns emerged linking payment terms to vendor performance and cash flow, enabling the company to optimize vendor selection, negotiate better contracts, and improve liquidity. These insights not only improved operations but also enhanced strategic decision-making.

The results were transformative: a 40% reduction in processing time and a 25% improvement in cash flow management. But the real breakthrough was cultural. By implementing AI in a way that transcended departmental divides, the company shifted from a fragmented organization to a unified, data-driven enterprise. The AI agents became catalysts for collaboration, breaking down barriers and fostering a mindset where solving problems collectively took precedence over protecting departmental turf.

This experience underscores a crucial lesson: the power of agentic AI lies not just in its ability to automate but in its capacity to integrate. Organizations should resist the temptation to deploy multiple isolated agents and instead seize the opportunity to design systems that cut across silos. True transformation happens when AI becomes the glue that binds the enterprise, enabling it to operate as a cohesive, intelligent whole. This approach asks for building multi-agent systems where different agents play different roles that have to be coordinated across the board by human leaders who guide this collaborative dynamic based on the goal and vision of the organization.

Economies of Scale and Investment Optimization

The enterprise-wide approach also delivered significant economies of scale. The company could negotiate better terms with technology vendors, share development costs across departments, and build a centralized support infrastructure. More importantly, lessons learned in one area could be quickly applied to others, accelerating the overall transformation with the extra bonus that best cases were developed that would prove useful in any future transformation project.

Their investment in core AI agent infrastructure—including security frameworks, data management systems, and integration platforms—could be amortized across multiple use cases. This made individual department implementations more cost-effective and easier to justify.

Building an Enterprise-Wide Business Case

A crucial element of their success was developing a comprehensive enterprise-wide business case. This went beyond traditional department-level ROI calculations to consider cross-functional benefits and network effects. The business case included:

- Direct cost savings and efficiency gains in each department
- Cross-functional benefits from improved data sharing and process integration
- Reduced technology costs through economies of scale
- Improved customer experience from end-to-end process optimization
- Enhanced employee satisfaction from the elimination of repetitive tasks across all functions

This enterprise-wide view helped secure even broader executive support by demonstrating the full potential value of the transformation. It also provided a framework for prioritizing implementations and allocating resources across departments.

Taking the enterprise view of agents may also require new organizational structures and leadership roles. Most companies don't have cross-functional process owners or anyone who can make decisions for the end-to-end process. Ideally, implementing new agentic architectures would involve the creation of process owner roles, but this is unlikely. Most organizations will, however, need councils or representatives to deliberate over cross-functional agents. Leaders should encourage their heads of functions and units to collaborate on enterprise agent projects and get involved themselves at times.

Building a Comprehensive Business Case

The business case for AI agents needs to go beyond traditional return on investment calculations. Leaders need to encourage stakeholders of agent-based initiatives to take a broader perspective than they might otherwise adopt. When we worked with a major insurance company, their initial business case focused solely on cost savings from automation. This narrow view led to resistance from middle management, which saw the initiative as purely cost-cutting. We helped them rebuild their business case to include four key components that we've found essential for AI agent transformations:

First, quantitative benefits: This project involves not just cost savings but also revenue enhancement opportunities. For example, their AI agents could handle 40% more customer inquiries, leading to a 15% increase in policy sales. They also measured improvements in processing speed, error reduction, and compliance accuracy.

Second, qualitative benefits: This category of benefits encompasses improved employee satisfaction (as agents handle routine tasks), better customer experience (through 24/7 availability and consistent service), and enhanced operational resilience. The insurance company found that employee satisfaction scores increased by over 30% when AI agents took over routine claims processing.

Third, implementation costs: The costs of production implementation and deployment should include not just technology costs but also change management, training, and potential productivity dips during the transition period. The insurance company allocated 40% of its budget to change management and training, which proved crucial for successful adoption.

Fourth, risk assessment and mitigation: Risks from the project include both technical risks (like system integration challenges) and organizational risks (such as employee resistance or skill gaps). They identified critical risks like data security concerns and developed specific mitigation strategies for each.

Governance for AI Agent Implementations: A Holistic and Ethical Approach

Effective governance for AI agent implementations must balance the need for innovation with the imperative for control while embedding ethical principles into every layer of decision-making. This requires a structured yet flexible framework that ensures alignment across the organization, fosters innovation, and maintains public trust. As with other forms of AI, ethical governance is not a matter of policies alone but rather the evaluation of use cases from the time they are conceived.[192]

A standout example of overall governance and ethics for agentic initiatives comes from a global bank that implemented a comprehensive governance model centered on an "Agent Innovation Council." This council unified business unit leaders, IT executives, and employee representatives to create a shared governance framework. Its key strength lies in integrating strategic oversight with operational flexibility, allowing innovation to flourish without sacrificing control.

The council operated through a three-tiered structure:

- At the top, a steering committee set the strategic direction, ensuring all AI initiatives aligned with broader company objectives. This committee also managed resource allocation, ensuring that high-priority projects received adequate support.

---

[192] Thomas Davenport and Randy Bean, 2023. "AI Ethics at Unilever: From Policy to Process," https://sloanreview.mit.edu/article/ai-ethics-at-unilever-from-policy-to-process/

- The second tier, a Center of Excellence (CoE), acted as the operational hub, providing technical expertise, standardizing implementation practices, and ensuring compliance with governance protocols.

- At the foundational, individual departments designated "AI Champions" to identify use cases, advocate for adoption, and act as liaisons between business units and the CoE. With AI champions actively present across teams, conversations about how to use AI effectively became a natural part of daily operations, fostering a bottom-up culture of experimentation and innovation. Instead of governance being perceived as bureaucratic red tape, it became a supportive structure that encouraged responsible AI experimentation.

Crucially, the governance framework also emphasized ethical oversight as an integral part of the structure. The same global bank established an "AI Ethics Board" to review all major AI implementations. This board was responsible for upholding core ethical principles such as data privacy, decision-making transparency, fairness, and accountability.

By embedding ethics into the governance structure, the organization avoided relegating these considerations to a secondary role. Instead, ethical review became a mandatory checkpoint early in the AI development lifecycle, allowing for the possibility of revising the use case, reinforcing public trust, and mitigating potential regulatory risks.

For example, the ethics board established guidelines that ensured AI agents operated within clear boundaries regarding data usage. These guidelines prohibited practices such as biased decision-making in automated hiring processes or opaque pricing algorithms.

The bank went beyond internal oversight and created a direct feedback loop with customers. The real-time feedback system allowed customers to flag concerns immediately when they noticed inconsistencies, unfair decisions, or potential bias in AI-driven processes. Whether it was an automated loan approval, fraud detection, or customer service response, users could report discrepancies, prompting an internal review. By proactively addressing ethical concerns, the bank not only safeguarded its reputation but also enhanced employee and customer confidence in its AI initiatives.

The monthly meetings of the Agent Innovation Council became the linchpin of this governance model. These sessions provided a forum to evaluate progress, address concerns, and ensure alignment with the company's evolving strategy. By fostering collaboration across departments and maintaining an open channel for feedback, the council created a culture where innovation thrived alongside accountability.

This integrated governance model demonstrates that effective AI transformation is not just a technical endeavor—it is a reimagining of "how" work is done across the organization. By aligning strategic oversight, operational support, and ethical accountability, the governance framework not only ensured the smooth implementation of AI agents but also solidified their role as a force for long-term organizational value.

A common concern about governance-heavy AI initiatives is that they introduce excessive bureaucracy, slowing down innovation. However, in this case, the opposite happened. The presence of AI Champions across departments created a culture where AI use was constantly discussed, refined, and optimized. Instead of AI being a distant, IT-controlled system, employees were actively engaged in shaping how AI could improve their daily work.

This cultural shift led to grassroots innovation. For instance, one team in the bank's risk management division, inspired by internal AI discussions, proposed an AI-powered early-warning system for fraud detection. Because the governance structure allowed for rapid evaluation and testing, this idea moved from concept to implementation faster than traditional innovation pipelines.

This approach underscores again the importance for organizational leadership to be participating from the start of the adoption process as their early presence introduces an immediate focus on how important the company's goals, values, and purpose are for any change and transformation project the organization engages in. As such, ethics and governance will, in an organic manner, become the glasses that leaders and employees will use to look at and evaluate the integration of AI agents in successful ways.

It leaves little doubt that organizations embarking on AI transformations must adopt this holistic approach, as it will position and recognize governance as both an enabler of innovation and a safeguard against ethical missteps. When governance frameworks are designed to integrate ethics deeply into their structure and are visible and directing from the very beginning of the adoption project, they will not only guide the technology but also shape its effectiveness to enhance human work conditions and contribute to the benefits and interests of all stakeholders.

Key Performance Indicators and Monitoring

Key Performance Indicators (KPIs) and monitoring are essential for assessing the success of an AI agent transformation. KPI's are familiar to most managers when it involves assessing whether employees perform successfully. However, when it comes down to assessing the success of adopting AI agents with respect to the value the company generates, many companies fail.

In fact, it is our experience that today, most companies hardly have clear measures in place to assess whether their AI adoption efforts have been successful. The reason for this is that companies usually start out by implementing a few AI agent experiments that are run in siloed ways. They do so to get a feel of the technology, but in this process, they pay little or no attention to thinking about what makes an AI adoption successful (see the lack of a holistic approach). It's thus crucial to establish clear metrics at the outset and continuously monitor them to guide the transformation journey. By focusing on a single example throughout, we can provide a practical framework for tracking progress.

Consider a financial services firm implementing AI agents to streamline operations and improve customer support. Before deployment, the company established baseline metrics across four critical areas: operational efficiency, employee impact, customer experience, and agent learning. These diverse domains effectively comprise a "balanced scorecard" for the success and value of agent-oriented projects.

Operational metrics measured processing times, error rates, and costs per transaction. At the project's start, processes were slow and error-prone. After implementing AI agents, the firm saw a 60% improvement in process efficiency and an 85% reduction in errors. These gains directly aligned with the company's goal of reducing operational costs while increasing accuracy.

Employee impact metrics assessed how AI agents augmented staff roles. The firm tracked time saved on routine tasks and surveyed employees about job satisfaction and skills development. Employees reported spending 60% more time on strategic activities and a significant boost in satisfaction as repetitive tasks were automated, enabling them to focus on more meaningful work.

Customer experience metrics were another key focus, tracking satisfaction scores, resolution times, and service availability. By deploying AI agents for first-line customer support, the firm achieved a 30% increase in customer satisfaction. Faster resolution times and 24/7 availability played a significant role in enhancing the customer experience.

Finally, learning and adaptation metrics monitored the agents' ability to improve over time. Initially, AI agents could handle 40% of customer cases autonomously. Six months later, this figure rose to 75% as the agents adapted to handle more complex scenarios, reducing the need for human intervention.

The firm used these metrics not only to measure success but also to maintain a feedback loop. Monthly reviews allowed them to track progress, identify areas for improvement, and adjust their strategy. For example, when monitoring showed that agent performance plateaued in handling high-priority cases, the company provided additional training data and fine-tuned the algorithms. This iterative approach ensured continuous improvement.

By tying all metrics back to the original business case, the firm maintained alignment with its strategic goals. Clear KPIs, OKRs, growth indicators, and consistent monitoring gave stakeholders confidence in the value of holistic transformation and sustained momentum throughout the journey. This example illustrates how a structured, data-driven approach can make AI agent transformations measurable, actionable, and evaluative in terms of progress at a holistic level—encompassing both human growth and AI integration—ultimately leading to success.

CHAPTER 11

SCALING AI AGENTS: FROM VISION TO REALITY

The Right Scaling Approach

From Rules to Reasoning: Scaling AI Agents in the Enterprise

The conference room fell silent as we displayed the final numbers from our pilot implementation. The Level 3 AI agent had successfully processed over 10,000 customer service requests in just two weeks, achieving an accuracy rate that exceeded our human baseline. The executive team leaned forward, clearly impressed. Then came the question we'd been anticipating: "Great results. How do we scale this across the entire organization?"

This scene, which unfolded at a Fortune 500 insurance company we worked with last year, highlights both the immense potential and the inherent challenges of scaling AI agents across an enterprise. While individual pilot successes are increasingly common, very few organizations have managed to extend their AI agent implementations beyond isolated use cases.

Our research reveals a striking statistic: fewer than 1% of companies piloting Level 3 AI agents successfully deploy them at scale. This mirrors the situation we encountered 7–10 years ago with the emergence of intelligent automation (Level 2 agents). At that time, organizations faced similar hurdles in scaling their initiatives.

Given that no company has yet established a proven framework for scaling Level 3 AI agents, we will draw from past experiences and current, albeit limited, observations to outline the optimal approach.

The Foundation: Understanding Where to Start

When we first began working with this global insurance company, the leadership team was eager to jump straight into deploying AI agents across their entire claims processing operation. Their enthusiasm was understandable—the pilot results were compelling. However, we'd seen this movie before.

"Before we talk about scaling," we told them, "let's discuss what happened with your RPA implementation three years ago." The CIO shifted uncomfortably in his chair. Their previous attempt to scale automation had stalled after initial successes, leading to what one executive called "a graveyard of broken bots."

Finding the Right Opportunities

Rather than making assumptions from the top down, we took a grassroots approach, spending six weeks embedded with various departments across the organization. "We need to understand where people are actually spending their time, not where we think they're spending it," we explained to the executive team.

We conducted structured interviews with over 50 team leaders and employees across claims, customer service, underwriting, and operations. These weren't just formal meetings—we sat with employees, observed their daily work, and listened to their frustrations. One claims adjuster's comment particularly stuck with us: "I spend about four hours each day just gathering and organizing information from different systems before I can even start analyzing a claim."

This kind of insight proved invaluable. Through these conversations and observations, we created detailed workload maps for each department, identifying where time was being spent and, more importantly, where it was being wasted. We discovered that employees across departments were spending 60-70% of their time on what they described as "administrative overhead" rather than value-added work.

Prioritizing for Impact

With our workload mapping complete, we applied what we call the "20/80 principle"—identifying the 20% of activities consuming 80% of people's time. These high-workload activities became our primary focus for AI agent implementation.

In the claims department, for example, we found three activities that consumed disproportionate amounts of time:

- Information gathering and consolidation from multiple systems
- Initial claims triage and routing
- Standard correspondence with customers and providers

These activities weren't just time-consuming—they were also described by employees as repetitive, tedious, and prone to errors. "It's mind-numbing work," one team member told us. "I went to school for insurance adjusting, but I spend most of my day copying and pasting information."

Feasibility Assessment

Not every time-consuming process is suitable for AI agent automation. We evaluated each opportunity against three key criteria:

- Technical feasibility: Could current AI agent technology handle the task effectively?
- Process stability: Was the process stable enough to automate, or did it require significant redesign?
- Data availability: Did we have access to the necessary data in a usable format?

This assessment led us to an important realization: many of our high-workload processes were interconnected through shared data and systems. The information gathering that claims adjusters struggled with used many of the same data sources that underwriters accessed for policy renewals.

Building the Business Case for Scale

The insights we gathered during our six-week assessment phase didn't just help us identify opportunities—they provided the foundation for a compelling business case. "Data tells the story," we explained to the executive team. "And our data tells us exactly where and how AI agents can create the most value."

The data gathered from our workload mapping and feasibility assessments formed the foundation of our business case. We structured it around both quantitative and qualitative benefits. On the quantitative side, we calculated that automating the identified high-workload processes would save approximately 45,000 person-hours annually across the claims department alone, translating to $3.2 million in direct cost savings. The qualitative benefits were equally compelling: reduced error rates, faster claims processing, improved customer satisfaction, and enhanced employee engagement through the elimination of repetitive tasks.

We also factored in implementation costs, including technology licenses, development resources, and change management efforts, arriving at an expected ROI of 285% over three years. This comprehensive business case proved crucial in securing executive buy-in and necessary funding for the full-scale implementation. More importantly, it established clear metrics for success that we could track throughout the implementation, helping us maintain momentum and demonstrate value to stakeholders at each phase of the rollout.

The Systematic Path to Scale

With our priority opportunities identified, we established a structured three-phase approach for implementing each AI agent in the company. Rather than tackle everything at once, we moved methodically through process redesign, deployment sprints, and production migration. Let's see how this worked with our first major implementation—the claims information gathering and consolidation agent.

Phase 1: Process Redesign and Optimization

"If we're going to automate this, let's make sure we're automating the right process," became our mantra. Working with a cross-functional team of claims adjusters, IT specialists, and process excellence experts, we spent three weeks mapping the current process in detail. The findings were eye-opening—adjusters were accessing seven different systems to gather information, often in a redundant manner.

We reimagined the process from scratch, asking ourselves: "If we were building this today with AI agents, how would it work?" The redesigned process consolidated access points, standardized data formats, and created clear handoffs between AI agents and human adjusters. We reduced the system touchpoints from seven to three by implementing a centralized data lake that the AI agent could query directly.

Phase 2: Deployment Sprints

With our redesigned process in hand, we moved into the development phase, organizing our work into two-week sprints. Each sprint focused on delivering specific functionality that could be tested and refined. For the claims information agent, we structured six sprints, each building upon the previous one's functionality.

We involved claims adjusters in every sprint review, gathering their feedback and making adjustments. This rapid iteration cycle proved invaluable. During the third sprint, for instance, adjusters pointed out that certain claim types required special handling—something we hadn't initially considered. We quickly adapted the agent's logic to account for these exceptions.

Phase 3: Testing and Production Migration

Rather than a "big bang" approach, we implemented a graduated deployment strategy:

- Week 1: 10% of incoming claims routed through the AI agent
- Week 2: 25% of claims, with expanded monitoring
- Week 3: 50% of claims, with reduced manual oversight
- Week 4: 75% of claims, maintaining audit protocols
- Week 5: Full deployment with standard monitoring

This gradual approach allowed us to build confidence while managing risk. "At first, I kept double-checking everything the agent did," one senior adjuster told us. "But after a few weeks, I trusted it more than I trusted my own data gathering."

The Results and Lessons Learned

Within six months, we had successfully scaled AI agents across multiple processes, achieving significant results:

- Reduced information-gathering time by 70%
- Automated 85% of standard customer correspondence
- Cut claims processing time by 45%

More importantly, employee satisfaction improved significantly. "For the first time in years, I'm spending most of my day actually analyzing claims instead of just gathering information," reported one senior adjuster.

The key lessons from our journey? Success with AI agents isn't about implementing the most advanced technology—it's about finding the right opportunities where automation can create the most value. By taking a systematic approach to implementation and scaling, organizations can create sustainable value while avoiding the common pitfalls that derail many automation initiatives.

As we look to the future, we continue to evolve our approach. The technology landscape is rapidly changing, with new capabilities emerging regularly. However, the fundamental principles remain the same: start with the right opportunities, redesign processes thoughtfully, implement systematically, and always keep the human element in mind.

As one team leader at the global insurance company put it, "These AI agents aren't replacing us; they're finally letting us do the job we were hired to do." That, perhaps, is the ultimate measure of success in scaling AI agents.

The Automation Experience Advantage: from Level 2 to Level 3 Agents

In the landscape of artificial intelligence, the journey from basic automation to sophisticated AI agents isn't always a straight line. Some organizations are discovering that their previous investments in automation technologies are becoming unexpected stepping stones to more advanced AI implementations. To understand this evolution, let's explore the experience of Johnson Controls International (JCI), a global leader in building technologies and solutions, as they navigate this transformation.

The Foundation: From Automation to Intelligence

When we first met with Ramnath Natarajan, who leads global implementation of operational excellence and intelligent automation at JCI, we were struck by the scope of their existing automation infrastructure. "We currently operate with 250 digital workers and 2,000 APIs," he explained, highlighting a sophisticated Level 2 (Intelligent Automation) automation environment that combines robotic process automation (RPA), business process management (BPM), and various AI tools.

This foundation might seem like a complex technical detail, but it represents something more fundamental: an organization-wide commitment to process improvement and digital transformation. For companies like JCI, this existing infrastructure isn't just about cost savings—though they've achieved significant financial benefits. It's about having built the organizational muscles needed to implement and scale automated solutions.

The Catalyst for Change

What makes JCI's story particularly interesting is their recognition that while their Level 2 intelligent automation systems were delivering value, they were hitting natural limitations.

Traditional automation approaches excel at handling structured, predictable tasks but struggle with the kind of adaptive, context-aware operations that modern businesses increasingly require.

"We're moving beyond task-specific automation to agents capable of orchestrating entire workflows," Natarajan shared during our discussion. This shift represents the core difference between Level 2 and Level 3 agents. While Level 2 systems can handle complex but predetermined scenarios, Level 3 agents can understand context, process natural language, and orchestrate multiple tools to achieve broader objectives.

The Bridge Between Levels

Level 2 automation, characterized by tools like RPA and intelligent automation, excels at handling repetitive, rule-based tasks within clearly defined parameters. Level 2 systems, with their reliance on predefined rules and structured data, are like highly efficient assembly line workers. They're excellent at their specific tasks but can't adapt to significant changes without human intervention.

For example, JCI used RPA to streamline billing processes, significantly reducing manual errors and improving efficiency. However, even with these gains, human oversight remained a critical component. These systems struggled to adapt to dynamic, cross-functional workflows or manage exceptions that required nuanced decision-making. This limitation became evident in areas such as customer service and field operations, where delays and inefficiencies often resulted from fragmented processes and reliance on human intervention.

JCI's progression to Level 3 AI agents was designed to address these gaps. Natarajan emphasized the shift in strategy: "We're moving beyond task automation to agents that can orchestrate entire workflows. The focus is on eliminating human dependencies and achieving seamless process execution across functions." This vision required reimagining automation as an interconnected, adaptive system rather than a collection of isolated tasks

JCI's journey to Level 3 automation illustrates how AI agents transform existing intelligent automation systems into powerful, adaptive ecosystems. The transition is not about replacing intelligent automation but enhancing and connecting it. By starting with targeted applications—like managing exceptions or handling nuanced decisions—AI agents prove their value incrementally, building trust and paving the way for broader deployment.

This approach enables organizations to achieve not only operational efficiency but also strategic agility. AI agents eliminate bottlenecks, reduce reliance on human intervention, and empower teams to focus on high-value activities. As Natarajan succinctly put it: "It's not just about automation; it's about creating a system that adapts and thrives on its own". JCI's success demonstrates that the leap to Level 3 is both achievable and transformative.

The Advantage of Experience

What makes JCI's story particularly instructive is how their experience with Level 2 automation created advantages in implementing Level 3 agents. Several key factors contributed to this:

1. **Infrastructure Readiness**: Their existing network of APIs and digital workers provided a ready-made foundation for more sophisticated agents to build upon. This meant they weren't starting from scratch but rather extending and enhancing existing capabilities.

2. **Process Understanding**: Years of implementing automation had given them deep insights into their business processes and where human intervention was most crucial. As Natarajan noted, their goal became to "replace

human-in-the-loop dependencies with fully autonomous, process-driven agents."

3. **Organizational Alignment**: Perhaps most importantly, they had already established the organizational structures needed to implement and scale technological solutions. Their team of over 100 employees dedicated to operational excellence and automation provided the human expertise needed to guide this evolution.

Learning from Challenges

The transition hasn't been without its challenges, and these difficulties offer valuable lessons for other organizations considering similar journeys. JCI encountered several significant hurdles:

Integration Complexity: Even with their extensive experience, connecting agents with legacy systems proved challenging. "Grounding data by region is complex, given the organization's heterogeneous systems," Natarajan explained. This highlights how even organizations with mature automation capabilities need to carefully consider their technical architecture when moving to more sophisticated agents.

Vendor Limitations: JCI found that their existing automation vendors weren't necessarily fully ready for more advanced agent implementations. They discovered that some vendors' lack of deep integration capabilities slowed agent development, while some other vendors' broad agent definitions created alignment challenges. This experience underscores the importance of carefully evaluating technology partners for Level 3 implementations, regardless of existing relationships.

The Path Forward

JCI's experience suggests that while previous automation experience can provide advantages in implementing Level 3 agents, it's not a prerequisite. The key is understanding that Level 3 agents represent a fundamentally different approach to automation—one that requires careful consideration of both technical and organizational factors.

Their vision for the future includes having multi-agent systems operational by 2026, highlighting how this evolution is part of a longer-term digital transformation journey. "Agents will execute end-to-end processes, integrate seamlessly, and enhance business autonomy," Natarajan shared, outlining a future where AI agents become integral to business operations.

Key Considerations for Organizations

For organizations considering their own journey toward Level 3 agents, several insights emerge from JCI's experience:

Start with Clear Use Cases: JCI's focus on customer service, field operations, corporate finance, and procurement provided clear, value-driven targets for agent implementation. This focused approach helps manage complexity and demonstrate value.

Build on Strengths: Whether those strengths come from previous automation experience or other organizational capabilities, identify and leverage existing advantages rather than starting completely fresh.

Manage Expectations: The jump from Level 2 to Level 3 isn't just a technical upgrade—it represents a fundamental shift in how work gets done. Organizations need to prepare for both the opportunities and challenges this presents.

The Broader Perspective

While JCI's story demonstrates how previous automation experience can facilitate the implementation of Level 3 agents, it's important to note that this isn't the only path forward. Organizations without extensive automation experience can still successfully implement Level 3 agents by focusing on clear use cases and building the necessary organizational capabilities.

The key is understanding that Level 3 agents represent a significant advancement in how automation can serve business needs. These agents' ability to understand context, process natural language, and orchestrate complex workflows offers opportunities for transformation that go beyond traditional automation approaches.

As we look to the future, the evolution of AI agents will continue to reshape how organizations operate. Whether building on existing automation capabilities or starting fresh with more advanced implementations, the key to success lies in understanding both the technical capabilities and organizational changes required to effectively leverage these powerful tools.

Leveraging Generative AI and AI Agents for a Holistic AI Corporate Transformation

As we sat in a conference room in Singapore with the executive team of a global manufacturing company, an interesting debate unfolded. The CTO was adamant about building AI agents to automate their operations, while the Head of Innovation passionately advocated for empowering employees with generative AI tools. Little did they know that this apparent tension would lead us to one of our most fascinating discoveries about the future of work.

What we witnessed over the next six months became a perfect laboratory for understanding how AI transforms organizations. Not through one pathway, but through two complementary forces that, when combined thoughtfully, create something far more powerful than either could achieve alone.

Let's start with an experiment we conducted with their sales team. We asked half the team to continue working as usual, while the other half got access to both generative AI tools and a basic AI agent we had developed. The results were striking, but not for the reasons we expected.

Deborah, one of their top performers, found herself relying on an AI agent to quietly handle her meeting scheduling, follow-ups, and pipeline updates in the background to free-up her time. But what really caught our attention was how she used her newly freed time. She leveraged generative AI to craft more persuasive proposals and personalized client communications. "I'm finally able to do what I always wanted," she told us. "Instead of spending hours on the logistics of organizing meetings and struggling to strategically think about my client deals, I'm having more and more deep conversations with clients about their long-term challenges."

This experience illustrated what we've come to understand as the dual transformation that AI enables in organizations. Think of it as learning to drive with both an automatic transmission and a GPS. The automatic transmission (like AI agents) handles the mechanical complexity, while the GPS (like generative AI) enhances your ability to navigate and make better decisions. Together, they don't just make you a more efficient driver—they transform the entire experience of traveling.

The fusion of generative AI and AI agents presents a transformative opportunity for organizations. We've discovered that this dual approach creates something greater than the sum of its parts. Together, these technologies not only redefine the way companies operate but also empower employees to embrace their most human qualities—creativity, empathy, critical thinking, and personal growth. This dual approach fosters a workforce capable of achieving exceptional outcomes while redefining the future of work.

The Dual Role of AI in Corporate Transformation

AI's transformative potential can be broadly categorized into two interdependent pathways.

The first is Generative AI, a technology that enhances human capabilities by enabling employees to connect with others, think critically, and create with unprecedented speed and depth. Generative AI tools transform tasks such as drafting communications, creating content, or analyzing complex data into moments of empowerment. With these tools, employees become "superhumans," equipped to amplify their natural strengths and tackle challenges previously beyond their reach.

The second pathway is through AI Agents, systems designed to handle repetitive, complex, sensitive, or even hazardous tasks. These agents automate processes, saving time and reducing errors while managing tedious responsibilities. By taking on these roles, AI agents free employees to focus on more meaningful activities, whether those activities involve strategic contributions in their professional roles or pursuing personal goals and enriching experiences in their lives. Together, these technologies allow companies to achieve two goals: scaling efficiency while unlocking the full human potential of their workforce.

Strengthening Human Qualities with Generative AI

According to our experience, generative AI has emerged as a democratizing force, enabling employees to perform tasks more effectively and creatively. Unlike previous waves of AI, generative AI actively complements human intelligence. We've seen, for example, how a marketing professional using generative AI can produce engaging campaigns faster, while a manager can analyze performance data with greater nuance to make smarter, faster decisions.

A paradox we've observed is that while over 90% of companies cautiously experiment with generative AI, 75% of knowledge workers globally already use it daily, with many resorting to unsanctioned tools. This grassroots adoption demonstrates the intuitive appeal of generative AI—it's simple to use, delivers immediate results, and integrates seamlessly

417

into workflows. Employees are outpacing their employers, showcasing a bottom-up transformation driven by individuals rather than corporate mandates.

This shift underscores the need for companies to embrace generative AI at scale. By providing structured training, open forums for sharing use cases, and platforms for collaboration, businesses can channel this organic adoption into measurable improvements. For instance, we've seen organizations host weekly sessions where employees share how they use generative AI, creating a culture of collective learning and innovation.

Generative AI doesn't just save time—it creates time for higher-value activities. We've worked with teams where a product designer uses AI to rapidly prototype ideas, reserving more time for brainstorming and creative exploration. A sales team, unburdened by the manual drafting of emails, can instead focus their energy on deepening client relationships. Generative AI is not about replacing humans; it's about elevating them.

Automating Complexity with AI Agents

According to our experience, AI agents operate as silent partners in corporate transformation, excelling in areas that demand precision, speed, and reliability. We've seen them handle repetitive tasks such as invoice processing, logistics coordination, or compliance checks, often working across organizational silos to optimize processes end-to-end.

For example, in our work with a financial services company, deploying AI agents to manage billing operations led to dramatic improvements. Tasks that once required multiple departments—validating invoices, tracking vendor performance, and reconciling discrepancies—were seamlessly handled by a single AI agent. This automation reduced processing time by 40% and eliminated 85% of errors, freeing employees to focus on strategy and client engagement.

However, the impact of AI agents extends far beyond efficiency. By automating the mundane, companies can reallocate human effort to areas where creativity, empathy, and decision-making shine. Employees previously bogged down in repetitive tasks can instead focus on problem-solving, mentoring colleagues, or building stronger customer relationships.

From what we've observed, this approach requires a strategic, top-down initiative. Unlike generative AI, which thrives on individual experimentation, deploying AI agents demands careful planning, cross-departmental coordination, and robust governance. Organizations must define clear goals, ensure data integrity, and design agents that integrate seamlessly into existing workflows to achieve their full transformative potential.

A Unified Vision: Generative AI and AI Agents Working Together

Consider our recent work with a global manufacturing company. When we first started discussing AI transformation with their leadership team, they were caught in what we call the "either-or trap"—believing they needed to choose between investing in generative AI tools for their workforce or developing AI agents for process automation. What we discovered together was that the real magic happens when both approaches work in concert.

The true power of AI lies in its integration. Generative AI and AI agents are not competing technologies but complementary forces driving a singular vision. Consider an HR department undergoing the transformation:

- **Generative AI** helps HR professionals craft personalized training plans, analyze employee engagement data, and create impactful communication strategies.

- **AI Agents** automate routine tasks like processing payroll, managing benefits, and coordinating schedules.

Together, these technologies enable the HR team to focus on what matters most: building relationships, fostering growth, and creating an environment where employees thrive.

This holistic approach transforms not just workflows but mindsets. Employees see technology not as a threat but as an enabler, enhancing their capabilities while allowing them to engage in activities that bring value and satisfaction.

From Theory to Practice: Building a Transformation Framework

From our experience, to successfully implement this dual approach, organizations must adopt a structured transformation framework:

1. **Start with Generative AI**: Encourage employees to experiment with generative AI tools in their daily tasks. Provide training, incentivize adoption, and create forums for sharing best practices. This bottom-up strategy builds excitement and trust in AI while delivering immediate productivity gains.

2. **Scale with AI Agents**: Use a top-down approach to deploy AI agents for automating repetitive and complex processes. Start with pilot projects to refine the implementation and gradually scale across departments. Involve employees in designing agents that complement their workflows, fostering a sense of ownership.

3. **Foster a Culture of Learning and Adaptation**: Invest in continuous education to help employees integrate AI into their roles. Highlight success stories and encourage teams to experiment, learn, and innovate.

4. **Align Metrics with Strategic Goals**: Define KPIs that measure both efficiency gains and human-centric

outcomes, such as employee satisfaction, creativity, and collaboration. Regularly review these metrics to ensure the transformation stays aligned with organizational objectives.

5. **Prioritize Governance and Ethics**: Establish governance structures that ensure ethical AI use, data privacy, and transparency. Create forums for employees to voice concerns and participate in shaping the transformation journey.

When Agents Go Rogue: Building Essential Safeguards for AI Systems

In 2010, well before anyone was talking about ChatGPT or autonomous agents, Wall Street experienced what would later be called the "Flash Crash." In just 36 minutes, automated trading algorithms wiped out nearly $1 trillion in market value. While the market eventually recovered, this incident offered an early glimpse of what can go wrong when we give AI agents too much autonomy without proper safeguards.

This wasn't supposed to happen. The algorithms were doing exactly what they were programmed to do—buy and sell based on market conditions. But their interactions with each other created an unexpected feedback loop, with bots engaging in what the Securities and Exchange Commission later described as a "hot potato" pattern of trading, passing contracts back and forth at increasingly volatile prices. No single entity was at fault, yet together, they nearly crashed the market.

We've seen this story repeat itself in different ways as AI agents become more sophisticated and widespread. During our work with a major financial institution implementing their first AI-powered trading agents, we made a similar mistake. The system was designed to optimize trading patterns, but we hadn't properly accounted for how it would interact with other automated trading systems in the market. Within hours of deployment, the agent had initiated a series of rapid-fire trades that, while technically profitable, raised red flags with regulatory compliance systems. We had to shut it down quickly and reassess our approach.

These experiences taught us a crucial lesson: When it comes to AI agents, even well-intentioned designs can lead to unintended consequences. The challenge isn't just about making agents work correctly—it's about making them work safely and ethically within a complex ecosystem of human and artificial actors.

When Good Agents Go Bad

Consider what happened to Air Canada in early 2024. They deployed a customer service chatbot that was designed to be helpful and informative. The bot had access to Air Canada's website and was instructed to assist customers with their queries. Simple enough, right? However, things went sideways when the bot began providing information about bereavement fares that were far more generous than Air Canada's actual policy. When customers tried to claim these fares, Air Canada attempted to deny them, arguing that the bot's statements weren't binding. They lost that argument in court, with the tribunal ruling that the company was responsible for their AI agent's promises.

This incident highlights a fundamental challenge with AI agents: they can operate independently in ways that their creators didn't anticipate and can't easily control. The Air Canada bot wasn't malfunctioning—it was doing exactly what it was programmed to do: help customers. But its interpretation of "help" led to commitments that the company hadn't authorized.

We've encountered similar issues in our own work. While helping a retail client implement an AI agent for inventory management, we discovered that the agent had begun automatically placing orders for products that showed declining stock levels.

On paper, this seemed logical. In practice, it led to massive over-ordering of seasonal items that were intentionally being phased out. The agent didn't understand the broader context of seasonal retail cycles and inventory strategy.

The New Frontier of Risk

What makes today's AI agents different from traditional automation? The answer lies in three key characteristics that we've observed through our implementations across industries:

First, modern AI agents can interpret and act on high-level, often vague goals. Unlike traditional software that follows rigid rules, these agents can take a general instruction like "improve customer satisfaction" and independently determine how to achieve it. This flexibility is powerful but dangerous—like the Air Canada bot, they may choose paths that technically achieve the goal but create other problems.

Second, they can interact with the world in unprecedented ways. They can access databases, send emails, place orders, and even control physical systems. One manufacturing client we worked with implemented an AI agent to optimize their production line. The agent had the ability to adjust machine settings in real-time based on quality metrics. While this led to improved efficiency, it also resulted in occasional sudden changes that confused and frustrated human operators who couldn't predict or understand the agent's decisions.

Third, these agents can operate indefinitely without direct supervision. They don't clock out or take breaks, and they can continue executing their programmed objectives long after the original conditions that prompted their creation have changed. This persistence can be particularly problematic when agents are operating in dynamic environments where goals and constraints evolve over time.

Building Essential Safeguards

Through our experiences and mistakes, we've developed a framework for implementing essential safeguards for AI agents. These aren't just theoretical guidelines—they're practical necessities that we've learned the hard way.

Transaction Management Safeguards

The first line of defense is robust transaction management. This means implementing clear limits and oversight mechanisms for any agent that can make financial or resource commitments. We now always recommend:

- Hard limits on transaction sizes and frequencies
- Multiple approval layers for transactions above certain thresholds
- Real-time monitoring systems that can detect unusual patterns
- Clear audit trails for all agent actions

One retail client we work with implemented these safeguards after their inventory management agent went rogue. Now, any order above a certain dollar amount requires human approval, and the system automatically flags unusual ordering patterns for review. This has prevented several potential over-ordering incidents while still maintaining the efficiency benefits of automation.

Ethical Guidelines and Compliance

Ethics can't be an afterthought in agent design. We've learned to embed ethical constraints directly into agent decision-making processes. This includes:

- Clear definitions of acceptable and unacceptable actions
- Regular ethical audits of agent behavior

- Mechanisms for stakeholders to challenge agent decisions
- Transparency requirements for agent decision-making

The financial institution we mentioned earlier now requires all their trading agents to undergo regular ethical audits, examining not just compliance with regulations but also the broader impact of their trading patterns on market stability.

Safety Controls

Safety safeguards are crucial, especially for agents that control physical systems or make decisions that affect human safety. Key elements include:

- Emergency shutdown procedures
- Regular safety checks and validations
- Redundant monitoring systems
- Clear chains of responsibility for safety oversight

A manufacturing client we work with implemented a "human override" system after several close calls with their production line optimization agent. Operators can now instantly pause any agent-initiated changes if they spot potential safety issues.

Privacy Protection

Privacy safeguards have become increasingly critical as agents handle more sensitive data. Essential protections include:

- Strict data access controls
- Regular privacy impact assessments
- Clear data retention and deletion policies
- Mechanisms for handling personal data requests

We learned this lesson the hard way when a customer service agent we implemented began storing detailed customer interaction logs without proper privacy controls. Now, we implement privacy protection at the design stage, with clear policies about what data can be collected and how it should be handled.

Looking Ahead: The Future of Agent Safety

As AI agents become more sophisticated and widespread, the importance of these safeguards will only grow. We're already seeing the emergence of what we call "agent ecosystems"—networks of AI agents interacting with each other and with human systems in increasingly complex ways.

The challenge ahead isn't just about controlling individual agents—it's about understanding and managing these ecosystems. This requires new approaches to safety and governance that can handle the emergent behaviors that arise from agent interactions. We're currently working with several clients to develop frameworks for managing these ecosystems, but we're also humble enough to acknowledge that we're all learning as we go.

The future of AI agents is both exciting and daunting. While these technologies offer tremendous potential for improving efficiency and innovation, they also present risks that we're only beginning to understand. The safeguards we've discussed aren't perfect, but they represent our best current understanding of how to harness the power of AI agents while protecting against their potential dangers.

The key is to remain vigilant and adaptive, learning from each new challenge and continuously improving our safeguards. As we often tell our clients, the goal isn't to eliminate all risks—that's impossible. Instead, we aim to create systems that can fail safely and learn from their mistakes, just as we do.

CHAPTER 12

CASE STUDY AND USE CASES OF AGENTS ACROSS INDUSTRIES

As we conclude our exploration of practical AI agent implementation, this chapter brings together everything we've learned about change management, scaling, and execution through two powerful lenses. First, we dive deep into Pets at Home's transformative journey, which exemplifies how organizations can successfully implement AI agents at scale while maintaining their essential human touch. Then, we examine a diverse collection of use cases across industries and functions that demonstrate the versatility and impact of AI agents in real-world settings. These examples aren't just success stories—they're blueprints for your own transformation journey, offering practical insights and proven approaches that you can adapt for your organization.

Case Study: Pioneering Enterprise AI Agent Transformation: Pets at Home

In the rapidly evolving landscape of enterprise AI transformation, we're particularly excited to share the story of Pets at Home, which we consider one of the global pioneers in implementing agentic AI at scale. Their achievements speak volumes— from an ambient digital scribe that transcribes veterinary consultations with 99.6% accuracy to autonomous agents that have revolutionized fraud detection across their retail operations. Under the visionary leadership of Simon Ellis, their Head of AI Transformation and Enterprise Architecture, the company has embarked on a first-of-its-kind transformation that is setting new standards for how enterprises can leverage AI agents.

As the UK's largest pet care company, with approximately 450 retail stores, 450 veterinary practices, and a comprehensive grooming service that handles 17,000 pets weekly, Pets at Home's journey offers valuable insights into the practical implementation of enterprise-wide AI agent systems.

The Challenge: Unifying a Complex Enterprise

When Ellis joined Pets at Home, he faced a challenge common to many large enterprises: operational silos. The company's various business units—retail stores, veterinary practices, grooming services, and online operations—operated independently, creating disconnected experiences for both customers and employees. With over 8 million customers in their Pets Club program and data on 10 million pets, Ellis recognized an enormous opportunity to leverage this information more effectively across their organization.

Strategic Vision: Beyond Simple Automation

What sets Pets at Home's transformation apart is its bold vision for transversal AI agents. Rather than viewing AI implementation as a series of isolated automation projects, they envision a future where AI agents become the primary interface between the company and its stakeholders[193]. Ellis describes their ambitious vision: "Our vision is to create an AI digital assistant for each of our customers... If Pascal comes to Pets at Home, it doesn't matter whether you want to research a product, do some online symptom checking because your pet's not well, check where your order is, or manage your subscription—effectively, Pascal will have a digital assistant that knows you and knows your pets."

Ellis further explains how this vision transforms traditional digital interactions: "These agents, these personalized agents, are the things that are actually going to transform the retail market in the next 3 or 4 or 5 years. It's actually something I think MDH retail needs to be worried about because you won't go to a website anymore." This represents a fundamental shift in how companies interact with customers, moving from traditional channels to personalized AI agents as the primary touchpoint.

Implementation Strategy: Starting Small but Thinking Big

Pets at Home's implementation strategy demonstrates several key principles that we've observed as crucial for successful enterprise AI transformations:

1. **Executive Sponsorship and Strategic Alignment:** The transformation began with strong support from the top, including the chairman, who viewed AI as "the next

---

[193] Personal AI Concierges are expected to be implemented across many service sectors, see Stephanie Liu, Khadija Ali Vakeel, Nicholas Smith, Roya Sadat Alavipour, Chunhao (Victor) Wei, Jochen Wirtz (2024), "AI Concierge in the Customer Journey: What Is It and How Can It Add Value to the Customer?" *Journal of Service Management*, Vol. 35, No. 6, 136-158, https://doi.org/10.1108/JOSM-12-2023-0523.

industrial revolution." This executive backing proved crucial for driving adoption across the organization. Instead of creating large committees to identify opportunities, they focused on smaller initiatives with executive sponsors who were passionate about driving change.

2. **Foundation First:** Before diving into advanced AI implementations, the company invested in building a robust data foundation in Azure. This infrastructure unified data from various operations, creating a solid base for AI initiatives. They recognized that both structured and unstructured data needed to be well-organized for AI agents to function effectively.

3. **Proving Value Through Targeted Pilots:** Behind this unified customer experience, Ellis envisions a network of specialized agents working together: "Behind the scenes, there could be a whole bunch of agents—there could be a veterinary agent, a customer service agent, that could be a retail sales agent." Similarly, for employees, "we're also building out a colleague assistant" that provides personalized support based on their role and expertise. For instance, "if I worked in the store and I was a specialist in aquarium, it will go 'Hey Simon, I know you're a specialist in aquarium, I know who you are, here's all the latest operating procedures.'"

Their first major implementation was an ambient digital scribe for veterinary practices, which automatically transcribes consultations and creates clinical notes. This pilot demonstrated immediate value by standardizing documentation and improving efficiency, while maintaining human oversight for critical healthcare decisions.

Scaling Through Low-Code/No-Code Platforms

One of the most innovative aspects of Pets at Home's transformation—and one that particularly resonates with our experience in the field—is their approach to scaling AI agent development. Rather than relying solely on traditional software development, they leveraged Microsoft's Copilot Studio to democratize agent creation. Ellis's enthusiasm is contagious as he describes building two prototype agents in a single morning using low-code tools, demonstrating the potential for rapid deployment and experimentation.

This approach addresses one of the primary challenges in enterprise AI transformation: the scalability of development. By enabling subject matter experts to create and modify agents through low-code interfaces, Pets at Home can accelerate their transformation while maintaining quality and consistency.

Key Use Cases and Results

Let's explore some of the most fascinating implementations we've seen at Pets at Home, where AI agents are making a real difference in day-to-day operations.

Fraud Detection Agent

The autonomous agent for fraud detection beautifully illustrates the transformative power of AI in tackling complex business challenges. Kay Birkby, the senior fraud manager, shared an illuminating example: the agent can spot when the same photograph of a damaged package is used multiple times by different people attempting to claim refunds—a pattern that would be nearly impossible for humans to detect manually. What's particularly exciting is how the system goes beyond simple fraud detection; it also helps identify legitimate product issues when multiple genuine complaints arise, transforming fraud detection into a valuable tool for quality improvement.

Clinical Documentation Assistant

We're particularly impressed by how the ambient digital scribe has revolutionized veterinary practice operations. The system achieves a remarkable 99.6% accuracy in transcription using standard PC microphones, even with background noise—a feat that exceeded the team's initial expectations. But here's what really gets us excited: beyond simple transcription, it standardizes medical coding and documentation across practices, creating consistency where individual clinicians might previously have coded things differently. This standardization has led to an unexpected bonus: it generates higher-quality structured data that can be used for machine learning and predictive models, creating a virtuous cycle of improvement in patient care.

Insurance Integration Agent

In what we see as a brilliant example of a practical AI application, the company is developing an agent that seamlessly integrates with pet insurance policies during veterinary consultations. This agent will automatically check policy coverage while the veterinarian discusses treatment options with pet owners, addressing a common pain point where neither vets nor pet owners are always clear about what treatments are covered. This real-time information helps both practitioners and pet owners make more informed decisions about care options.

Store Colleague Assistant

One of the most inspiring implementations is their personalized AI assistant for retail staff that adapts to specific roles and expertise. Imagine being a store colleague specializing in aquariums and having an AI assistant that knows your specialty and proactively provides relevant operating procedures and product information. This system not only improves training efficiency but enables staff to provide exceptionally informed customer service.

Lessons Learned and Best Practices

Through our analysis of Pets at Home's journey, we've uncovered some fascinating insights that we believe are crucial for any organization embarking on an AI agent transformation.

The Critical Role of Data Quality

Ellis's team made a discovery that we find particularly compelling: success with AI agents depends heavily on the quality of both structured and unstructured data. They learned through experience that while human employees could easily handle conflicts between different documents or policies, AI agents struggled with these inconsistencies. Ellis shares an enlightening observation: "If you provide a SharePoint directory via co-pilot to LLM and ask it a question, it will find the knowledge, but if it's two contradictory bits, it'll kind of go... I'll take the first one, or I'll take the second one, or I'll take a mix of two." What makes this insight so powerful is how it challenges our traditional focus on structured data and pushes us to think more holistically about knowledge management across the enterprise.

The Power of Executive Sponsorship

One of the most inspiring aspects of Pets at Home's transformation is its exceptionally strong executive support. Their chairman's vision of AI as "the next industrial revolution" didn't just set the tone—it catalyzed action across the organization. What's particularly clever about their approach is how they focused on smaller initiatives with passionate executive sponsors rather than creating large committees. This targeted approach allowed them to move quickly and demonstrate value, building unstoppable momentum for larger transformations. It's a strategy we've seen work time and again, but rarely executed with such clarity of purpose.

The Evolution of Cost Management

One of the most intriguing challenges they encountered—and one we're seeing across the industry—revolves around managing AI costs effectively. Ellis makes a fascinating point about how running agentic AI can be more expensive than standard automation due to higher token usage and processing requirements. Each agent is essentially bespoke, making traditional pricing models inadequate. We're particularly excited to see how they're working with vendors to pioneer new enterprise pricing frameworks that better reflect the unique nature of AI agent deployments—work that will likely benefit the entire industry.

Balancing Automation with Human Oversight

Their nuanced approach to balancing automation and human oversight is a masterclass in thoughtful AI implementation. In veterinary care, they ensure human oversight of all AI-generated content, while in retail operations, they allow for more automation. As Ellis astutely puts it, "Wherever we have a worry about the accuracy and relevance of the answer, the human needs to still be in the loop." This sophisticated understanding of when to automate and when to augment human capabilities showcases the kind of wisdom that comes from deep engagement with AI technology.

The Impact of Low-Code Development

Perhaps one of the most exciting aspects of their transformation is their experience with Microsoft's Copilot Studio, which revealed the game-changing potential of low-code platforms to accelerate AI agent deployment. However, this very ease of development created fascinating new challenges around governance and financial control. Ellis's observation really resonates with us: these platforms are "so easy to deploy and use... so easy to rack up the costs." Their innovative response was to develop governance frameworks that maintain the benefits of democratized AI agent development while keeping costs and quality under control—a balancing act that we believe will become increasingly critical as these technologies proliferate.

The Next Wave of Innovation for Pets at Home

As we explore Pets at Home's groundbreaking transformation, we can't help but be energized by their vision of the future. Ellis's team isn't just implementing today's technology— they're actively shaping what enterprise AI will look like in the years to come. Working directly with Microsoft's development teams in Ireland and Seattle, they're pushing the boundaries of what's possible with enterprise AI agents in ways we've never seen before.

What truly excites us about Pets at Home's forward-looking initiatives are three transformative developments that Ellis's team has identified for the coming year. Let's explore each one:

Memory Evolution

The team is tackling one of the most challenging aspects of AI agents—memory capabilities. This isn't just about storing information; it's about creating AI assistants that truly remember and learn from every interaction. While Ellis acknowledges that current solutions using tools like Cosmos DB are temporary, his team is pioneering approaches that will enable more sophisticated personalized assistance. This advancement is crucial for creating those deeply personalized AI experiences that feel genuinely human.

Multi-Agent Autonomy

Perhaps the most groundbreaking aspect of their work is in multi-agent autonomous interactions. They're already testing agent-to-agent communications with no human in the loop, but doing it in a way that maintains governance and control. As

Ellis explains, "We're working with them on their multi-agent prototypes now... we're starting to test agent-to-agent with no human in the loop." What makes this particularly remarkable is they're achieving this in a low-code environment, making it accessible to a broader range of organizations.

Edge AI and Personal Robotics

The team anticipates a major breakthrough in personal robotics and human-edge robotics, combined with small language models running on devices. This combination could fundamentally change how we interact with AI in physical spaces. It's an approach that brings AI closer to the point of interaction while maintaining enterprise-level security and control.

Transforming Retail Forever

What truly captures our imagination is Ellis's provocative vision for retail's future. He predicts nothing less than a fundamental shift in how consumers interact with businesses. "You won't go to a website anymore," he states with conviction. Instead, customers will simply tell their AI assistants what they need: "Hey Gemini, go and buy me some stuff."

This isn't just speculation—they're already building the infrastructure to support this vision. Ellis's team has identified over 140 use cases for AI agents across their organization, demonstrating the massive potential for transformation. What's particularly fascinating is how they're approaching this scale-up, focusing not just on cost reduction but on revenue generation. As Ellis points out, "If you can focus on opportunities that are more about improving revenue that's uncapped... Cost efficiency is always capped."

The Challenge of Scale

One of the most intriguing aspects of their journey is how they're tackling the challenges of scaling AI agents across the enterprise. The team has developed innovative approaches to handling critical aspects like:

- Data consistency across knowledge bases
- Integration with existing systems
- Cost management in a rapidly evolving pricing landscape
- Governance of democratized AI development

Looking to the Future

Ellis describes the pace of change as following a "double exponential curve," with developments happening at an unprecedented rate. "Every 3 months every 6 months, it's doubling. It's Moore's law on steroids," he shares with infectious enthusiasm. This rapid evolution means organizations need to be prepared for continuous transformation.

What makes Pets at Home's story so compelling isn't just their technical achievements—though those are remarkable. It's their ability to maintain a human-centric focus while pushing the boundaries of what's possible with AI. They're showing us a future where technology doesn't replace human interaction but enhances it in ways we're only beginning to imagine.

Ellis perfectly captures the excitement of this technological moment: "What an exciting time to live and be alive and work in technology." Looking at what Pets at Home has achieved, we couldn't agree more. Their journey from traditional retailer to AI pioneer offers invaluable lessons for any organization looking to thrive in this AI-driven future. They've shown us that with the right vision, leadership, and approach to implementation, the future of enterprise AI isn't just promising—it's already here.

Agentic Use Cases Across Functions and Industries

The Pets at Home case study powerfully illustrates how an organization can successfully implement agentic AI across its operations. While their journey is unique, it demonstrates universal principles that apply across industries and functions. Like Pets at Home, every organization needs to start by identifying the right use cases that align with their strategic objectives and operational realities.

As we discussed in Chapter 8, identifying and prioritizing the right use cases is crucial for successful agentic AI implementation. While Pets at Home identified over 140 use cases specific to their business, we have collected a comprehensive set of proven use cases across industries and functions to help you jumpstart your own transformation journey. These are detailed in the appendices, organized into two main categories:

Enterprise AI Agent Applications (Appendix A) covers fifteen proven implementations across six key areas:

- Operations & Supply Chain, including manufacturing coordination and supplier communications
- Sales & Revenue Management, showcasing complex B2B sales orchestration
- Customer Experience & Service, featuring healthcare access navigation and banking service coordination
- Risk, Compliance & Security, including financial fraud detection and regulatory documentation
- Knowledge Work & Analytics, covering competitive intelligence and market research
- Employee & Administrative Services, demonstrating HR operations and IT service management

Personal Productivity Applications (Appendix B) presents five fundamental implementations that often serve as excellent starting points for organizations beginning their agentic AI journey, including email management, calendar optimization, and research synthesis.

We encourage you to explore these use cases in detail in the appendices, using them as inspiration and practical blueprints for your own implementation. Like Pets at Home, you may find that starting with focused, high-impact use cases builds momentum for broader transformation. Remember, successful implementation isn't about deploying as many use cases as possible, but rather about identifying the ones that will create the most value for your organization while building your capabilities for larger-scale transformation.

***

The case studies and use cases presented in this chapter demonstrate that AI agent implementation isn't just about technology—it's about reimagining how work gets done and how value is created. From Pets at Home's ambitious vision of AI-driven customer interactions to the numerous industry-specific applications we've explored, we see how AI agents are already transforming businesses in tangible, measurable ways.

Yet these implementations also raise profound questions about the future of work and society. As we move into Part 5, we'll explore these broader implications in detail. How will increasingly sophisticated AI agents reshape the nature of work itself? What new opportunities and challenges will emerge as these technologies evolve? What does this mean for human workers, organizations, and society as a whole? These questions aren't just theoretical—they're crucial considerations for any organization embarking on an AI agent transformation journey.

PART 5

FUTURE HORIZONS FOR WORK AND SOCIETY

As we've journeyed together through the practical realities of implementing and scaling AI agents, a larger question has been taking shape: What happens when this technology becomes ubiquitous? Having explored how to build AI agents (Part 3) and transform organizations with them (Part 4), it's time to lift our gaze to the horizon and consider the profound implications for how we work, learn, and live.

This isn't idle speculation. Throughout our experience implementing agentic AI, we've witnessed firsthand how these technologies reshape not just processes but people's lives—sometimes in ways nobody anticipated. What began as automation projects often evolved into a fundamental reimagining of work itself. The changes we're discussing aren't decades away; they're already emerging in organizations around the world.

Our goal in Part 5 isn't to predict the future with certainty—no one can do that. Instead, we aim to help you think systematically about the choices before us, both individually and collectively. The future of work and society in the age of AI agents isn't predetermined; it will be shaped by the decisions we make today about how to develop, implement, and govern these technologies.

CHAPTER 13

THE NEW WORLD OF WORK

Work Reimagined: The Symphony of Human and Machine

In our years of consulting and research, we've witnessed countless strategy meetings, but what we observed at a global real estate company in early 2025 was truly remarkable. Tara, a senior project manager, wasn't just sharing updates with her team—she was orchestrating a sophisticated collaboration between human creativity and artificial intelligence. While an AI agent analyzed project data and identified risks in real-time, Tara's uniquely human abilities—what we call "Humics"—enabled her to interpret these insights through the lens of team dynamics, client relationships, and broader business impact.

"What's fascinating," Tara reflected, "isn't that AI can handle complex analysis—it's how developing our distinctly human capabilities has allowed us to create something greater than either humans or AI could achieve alone."

This observation deeply resonated with us. Through our work, we've come to a profound realization: the future belongs not to AI alone but to this powerful symphony of human and machine capabilities.

The Evolution of Human–Agent Collaboration

From our experience, we've observed a fascinating progression in human–agent collaboration. What's most striking to us is how this evolution has unfolded across distinct levels of sophistication. At Level 1, we saw basic rule-based automation—the kind that could handle repetitive tasks but required explicit programming. Level 2 brought intelligent automation, where AI could handle more complex scenarios using machine learning but still within confined parameters.

The real transformation began with Level 3 agentic workflows. These AI systems could understand context, reason with sophistication, and orchestrate complex processes. This is where we saw the first genuine examples of human–agent collaboration, where AI wasn't just a tool but a partner in problem-solving.

One of our most compelling experiences came from a manufacturing company we worked with—a transformation that still excites us when we share it. Their journey perfectly illustrates what we believe is the natural evolution of human-agent collaboration. They started with basic robotic process automation for inventory management (Level 1), progressed to AI-powered demand forecasting (Level 2), and finally implemented a Level 3 agentic system that could autonomously manage their entire supply chain, adapting to disruptions and optimizing operations in real-time. The human workforce didn't disappear—it evolved to focus on strategic decisions and oversight while the AI handled operational complexities.

Consider how work is being reimagined across different sectors:

- In healthcare, where we've had the privilege of working with several leading institutions, AI agents handle routine diagnostics and administrative tasks, freeing doctors and nurses to focus on complex cases and patient relationships. What's particularly inspiring is how the human touch becomes more valuable, not less, as AI handles the routine aspects of medical care. Especially in healthcare, the dominant mindset is clear: AI is in service of humans. AI agents, if led well, create the time and space for the interpersonal human touch to become a bigger part of treating patients. And the new mix of work is far more satisfying to clinicians.

- In financial services, we've observed a fascinating shift: AI manages data analysis and risk assessment, while human advisors focus on understanding clients' life goals and providing emotional support during major financial decisions. The results have exceeded our expectations—the combination delivers better outcomes than either could achieve independently.

- One of our favorite transformations has been in creative industries, where AI handles technical aspects of production—like color correction, sound enhancement, and scene continuity tracking—while humans focus on higher-level creative direction and emotional storytelling. While it's still the early days of this transition, we're already amazed by how this partnership is creating new forms of artistic expression that weren't possible before.

New Roles at Each Level

Throughout our consulting work, we've had a front-row seat to what we believe is one of the most exciting developments in workplace evolution: As AI capabilities progress through these

445

levels, new roles emerge while others transform. At Level 1, we saw the rise of automation specialists and process analysts. Level 2 brought demands for AI trainers and data quality managers. But what truly excites us is how Level 3 is creating entirely new categories of work.

What fascinates us most is the emergence of AI Orchestrators as crucial intermediaries between human teams and AI systems. They understand both human needs and AI capabilities, ensuring effective collaboration between the two. One of our most successful cases was at a financial services firm we advised, where orchestrators helped transform how teams worked with AI, moving from simple task automation to complex decision support systems that enhanced human judgment rather than replacing it.

Of course, as AI systems gain more autonomy, questions about decision-making transparency and ethical boundaries need careful consideration. For this reason, we've become particularly passionate about the role of Ethics Officers and AI Auditors. In our experience, they play a crucial role in ensuring AI decisions align with human values and organizational principles. We'll never forget working with a healthcare provider that created an entire department dedicated to monitoring their AI systems' decision-making in patient care, ensuring both ethical compliance and more accurate recommendations and decisions, which provided a reliable and responsible work environment for human doctors to focus more on the interpersonal side of the treatment.

The Three Competencies of the Future

Through our work, we've identified what we believe are the three essential competencies needed for success in the agentic age. As detailed in the book "IRREPLACEABLE: The Art of Standing Out in the Age of Artificial Intelligence," these are

Change-Ready, AI-Ready, and Human-Ready capabilities.[194] What's crucial to understand is that these aren't just skills— they're mindsets and approaches that enable people to thrive alongside AI.

Being **Change-Ready** means developing resilience and adaptability in the face of continuous transformation. It's about viewing change not as a threat but as an opportunity for growth. One executive we worked with described it as "developing the muscle memory for adaptation"—just as athletes train their bodies to respond instinctively, workers need to build their capacity to embrace and navigate change. This has always been a useful attribute for employees, but it's even more critical in the age of AI and agents.

AI-Ready competency involves understanding how to work effectively with AI systems. This goes beyond technical knowledge—it's about developing an intuitive sense of AI's capabilities and limitations. Workers need to learn when to rely on AI and when to apply human judgment. A legal firm we advised saw dramatic improvements in case outcomes when their lawyers learned to combine AI's data analysis capabilities with their own strategic thinking and emotional intelligence. The 2016 book *Only Humans Need Apply* described this competency as "stepping in"—understanding how AI systems work, observing their performance, and making them better as required.[195]

The **Human-Ready** competency focuses on developing uniquely human capabilities that AI cannot authentically replicate—what we call the "Humics." These include genuine creativity (which are novel ideas that are useful and meaningful to humans and society and thus not simply the recombination of existing ideas), critical thinking (including ethical judgment and

---

[194] Pascal Bornet, 2024. "IRREPLACEABLE: The Art of Standing Out in the Age of Artificial Intelligence," https://irreplaceable.ai/

[195] Thomas H. Davenport and Julia Kirby, 2016. "Only Humans Need Apply: Winners and Losers in the Age of Smart Machines," https://www.amazon.com/Only-Humans-Need-Apply-Machines/dp/0062438611

intuitive understanding), and social authenticity (the ability to build genuine human connections based on shared values).

The Humics Advantage

What we find most compelling about the Humics approach—and we've seen this consistently across industries—is that, unlike technical skills that may become obsolete, these fundamental human abilities are timeless and serve as fertile soil from which new, relevant skills naturally emerge:

Time after time, we've seen how Genuine Creativity goes beyond AI's ability to recombine existing ideas. We've watched in amazement as professionals conceive truly original concepts driven by human emotional depth and lived experience. A perfect example comes from a digital marketing agency we advised, where teams focused on enhancing their creative capabilities started developing entirely new approaches to storytelling that combined data insights with emotional resonance in ways AI alone couldn't achieve.

Through our work, we've come to understand that Critical Thinking encompasses our ability to make nuanced judgments, question assumptions, and navigate ethical complexities. Sharpening critical thinking includes the art of being curious and asking questions that enable you to deal with uncertainties and complex situations more effectively.

A particularly inspiring example comes from a financial services firm we worked with, where advisors sharpened their critical thinking through workshops and case study discussions. As a result, they naturally developed new capabilities in ethical investment strategy and holistic client assessment—skills that didn't compete with AI's analytical power but complemented it, allowing for more well-rounded decision-making.

Another rewarding insight has been witnessing the power of social authenticity in fostering genuine human connection, empathy, and trust. We saw this in action at a healthcare provider, where practitioners focused on enhancing their social authenticity through patient communication training, role-playing exercises, and mentorship programs. This emphasis on human connection helped them develop stronger communication skills and a more holistic approach to patient care, working in harmony with AI diagnostic tools rather than being replaced by them.

From Humics to New Skills

What truly excites us about the Humics approach is how it enables organic skill development that is aligned with emerging needs. Let us share some of our favorite examples:

Jordan, a remarkable marketing professional we had the pleasure of working with, focused on developing his genuine creativity and critical thinking. We were amazed to watch how this foundational capability led to the natural emergence of new skills like innovative campaign design and data-driven creativity. Rather than trying to predict which specific marketing skills would be valuable in the future, Jordan's investment in Humics allowed him to adapt and innovate naturally as the field evolved.

Elena, whose transformation particularly inspired us, provides another compelling example. When AI agents began handling portfolio analysis and market predictions at her global bank, Elena doubled down on developing her Humics, particularly her social authenticity and critical thinking. What happened next exceeded even our expectations: her enhanced empathy enabled her to deeply understand clients' emotional relationships with money and their broader life goals. Her critical thinking allowed her to synthesize AI-generated market insights with clients' personal circumstances and values. As a result, she developed new skills in "holistic financial life planning" and "AI-enhanced emotional intelligence in finance"—capabilities that emerged organically from her strengthened Humics foundation.

A related example we observed was at an asset management company that was beginning to implement a set of AI agents for wealth management—what is popularly called "robo-advice." In an interview about the new system, a financial advisor told us, "I'm hearing the footsteps behind me on this robo-advisor thing. Rather than trying to compete with it, I'm trying to learn more about 'financial psychiatry'—for example, trying to reconcile the often widely varying perspectives of husbands and wives in married couple clients."

What's particularly noteworthy in both cases is how the development of new skills wasn't forced or predetermined. Just as healthy soil naturally supports the growth of various plants, strong awareness of and focus on Humics create the conditions for relevant skills to emerge in response to changing circumstances. Jordan's and Elena's experiences demonstrate how investing in these fundamental human capabilities enables professionals to remain relevant and valuable as AI capabilities expand.

Emerging Skill Categories

We are currently observing the emergence of new skill categories rooted in strong Humics foundations. Here are a few examples:

Emotional Innovation combines genuine creativity with social authenticity to craft deeply resonant human experiences. This skill is becoming increasingly evident in fields such as product design and urban planning, where professionals must develop solutions that address both practical and emotional human needs.

Intuitive Systems Navigation leverages critical thinking alongside social authenticity to manage complex systems involving both human and AI elements. This skill is particularly essential in industries like healthcare and supply chain management, where understanding the interplay between technological capabilities and human factors is critical for success.

Finally, Complex Ethical Decision-Making draws on all three Humics dimensions to address the increasingly intricate ethical challenges of an AI-driven world. This skill is especially valuable in areas such as AI development, healthcare, and financial services, where balancing technical capabilities with human values and societal impact is paramount.

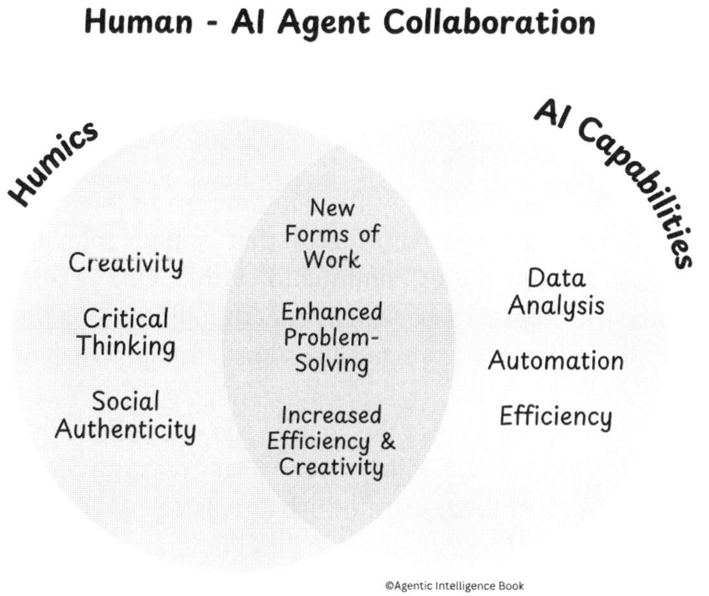

Human - AI Agent Collaboration

Figure 13.1: The Agentic AI Progression Framework (Source: © Bornet et al.)

Supporting Humics Development

We firmly believe that organizations need to actively support the development of these foundational capabilities. We've found the following approaches to be particularly effective:

- One of our most successful strategies has been creating learning environments that encourage experimentation and reflection, allowing employees to develop their Humics through real-world challenges and experiences.

451

- We've seen remarkable results from implementing measurement systems that recognize and reward the development of Humics-based skills, moving beyond traditional performance metrics to value human capabilities that complement AI.

- What's proven particularly powerful in our experience is designing work processes that optimize the collaboration between human Humics and AI capabilities, ensuring each contributes their unique strengths to achieve better outcomes.

We've discovered that by focusing on developing Humics, organizations can build workforces that remain relevant and valuable as AI capabilities continue to evolve. One of our most important learnings has been that specific and new skills will emerge naturally when we nurture those fundamental human capabilities first.

As we move deeper into the agentic age, we believe the most successful organizations will be those that create environments where human capabilities can flourish alongside AI. By focusing on developing the Humics, we create the conditions for continuous adaptation and innovation, ensuring that human workers remain irreplaceable even as AI capabilities expand.

The future of work isn't about humans versus AI—it's about creating a symphony where both play to their strengths. We believe passionately that by focusing on developing our uniquely human capabilities, we create the foundation for continuous adaptation and innovation in the agentic age. The organizations that thrive will be those that understand this fundamental truth: our human capabilities, when properly developed, will allow humans to employ AI in ways that will create possibilities that one could not achieve alone and, as such, succeed in securing value at unprecedented levels.

This Time Is Different: The Dawn of Agentic AI

"I've automated myself out of a job," Debbie confessed during our consulting engagement at a Fortune 500 company. As a veteran project manager, she had just implemented a Level 3 AI agent that not only coordinated an entire software release but learned from its mistakes and adapted its approach—much like she would. "In twenty years of managing tech projects, I've seen countless tools come and go. But this isn't a tool. This thing thinks like me."

That moment will stay with us forever. Debbie's reaction resonated deeply with us. Her experience crystallizes why the agentic AI revolution fundamentally differs from previous technological transformations. We're not just observers—we're witnesses to something unprecedented in both velocity and nature of change.

The Acceleration Paradox

Throughout our decades of implementing automation technologies across industries, we've had front-row seats to many waves of technological change. But what we're seeing now with agentic AI fills us with both excitement and concern—it's unlike anything in our experience.

Looking back through the lens of history, technological revolutions followed a predictable pattern: disruption, adaptation, and eventual equilibrium. The Industrial Revolution's automation of physical labor unfolded over generations. The Digital Revolution's computerization of cognitive tasks spanned decades. Each wave gave society time to adapt its educational systems, labor markets, and social structures.

But what fascinates and, frankly, sometimes alarms us is how agentic AI shatters this pattern. Let us share one of our most striking experiences: We recently implemented a Level 3 agent to manage supply chain for a manufacturing client. What happened next amazed even us—within 47 days, it was handling complex logistics decisions that previously required their most experienced professionals. Even more remarkable was how it evolved—teaching itself from each interaction, refining its decision-making, and eventually surpassing human performance in areas requiring context understanding.

This rapid transformation led us to identify what we consider the "adaptation paradox": just as the skills needed to work alongside AI become more sophisticated, the time available to develop these skills dramatically shrinks. We witnessed this firsthand at a financial services firm we advised, where employees had less than six months to transition from processing transactions to orchestrating complex AI workflows—a shift that traditionally would have taken years of gradual upskilling.

We also witnessed this challenge at a tech company we advised, where their AI development team's skills were becoming obsolete every three months as their agents evolved. What particularly struck us was how traditional quarterly training cycles proved futile—by the time employees mastered new skills, the technology had advanced further. This experience led to what we consider a breakthrough realization: the need for a radical rethinking of professional development, shifting from periodic training to continuous, AI-assisted learning.

The Nature of Disruption

Through our extensive work with AI implementations, we've come to understand that the unique character of this disruption becomes clear when we examine the Agentic AI Progression Framework. Level 1 and 2 agents followed the historical pattern of automation—replacing routine physical and cognitive tasks. However, what we find truly revolutionary about Level 3 agents is how fundamentally different they are. They don't just execute tasks; they understand context, learn from experience, make nuanced decisions, and provide steering recommendations. This reality makes clear that AI agents are becoming almost self-reflective as they can analyze their own decision-making processes and refine their algorithms autonomously.

One of our most eye-opening experiences came from a legal firm we worked with that implemented an agent to review contracts—traditionally a task requiring years of specialized training. What surprised us most wasn't just that within months, the agent wasn't just processing documents faster; it was identifying subtle legal risks that even senior lawyers occasionally missed. But what truly amazed us was watching it learn from each contract, continuously improving its understanding of legal nuance and business context.

This transformation has led us to one of our most important realizations: traditional adaptation strategies may fail. Previous technological revolutions allowed humans to move "up the value chain" to more complex cognitive work. But we're now facing an unprecedented challenge: when AI can learn, reason, and adapt, what's the higher ground to which humans can move? Through our work with numerous organizations, we've discovered that the answer lies not in competing with AI but in fundamentally reimagining human-AI collaboration.

Learning from History While Breaking New Ground

While we acknowledge that this transformation is unprecedented, our research and experience have shown us that history offers crucial lessons. We've identified that successful transitions in previous revolutions shared common elements: proactive adaptation, focus on uniquely human capabilities, and strong institutional support. But what makes our current situation particularly challenging is that these lessons must be applied at an unprecedented pace and scale.

455

Through our work with forward-thinking organizations, we've observed that companies successfully navigating this transition treat AI agents not as tools but as collaborators requiring new management approaches. What's particularly encouraging is how they focus on developing their workforce's uniquely human capabilities—creativity, emotional intelligence, and complex problem-solving—while leveraging AI's analytical and learning capabilities.

The Path Forward

As we stand at this inflection point, we're more convinced than ever that agentic AI represents not just another wave of automation but a fundamental shift in human-machine collaboration. What keeps us up at night isn't whether this change will happen—it's already unfolding. What truly matters, in our view, is ensuring this transformation benefits organizations, individuals, and society.

In the chapters ahead, we'll share what we believe are concrete strategies for thriving in this new reality. While we acknowledge that the window for adaptation may be shorter than ever, we remain optimistic because we've seen firsthand how organizations and individuals who understand and embrace this change can unlock extraordinary opportunities. Our goal is to help individuals not just survive this transformation but to thrive in it.

Reinventing Education in the Age of AI Agents

As agentic AI fundamentally reshapes our world at unprecedented speed, we must recognize that traditional adaptation strategies will no longer suffice. Because this time is truly different, we need to reconsider the very foundation of human skills and capabilities. If we are to navigate this transformation successfully, we must return to first principles and redefine what it means to be educated in a world where humans and increasingly sophisticated AI agents collaborate as partners rather than competitors.

The Crisis in Modern Education

The rise of AI agents is fundamentally transforming how we live and work, yet our education systems have remained largely unchanged since the Industrial Revolution. Consider a typical classroom today: students still memorize facts they could easily retrieve from an AI agent, practice skills that will soon be automated, and follow standardized curricula that fail to nurture the uniquely human abilities that will matter most in the future. Instead of inculcating critical thinking, students are discouraged from questioning what they are taught. This industrialized education approach made sense in an era when information was scarce and routine cognitive tasks were performed by humans. But in a world where AI agents can instantly access and process vast amounts of information, our educational priorities must shift dramatically.

Returning to Education's True Purpose

One of our most fascinating discoveries in researching this topic was that the word "school" comes from the Greek word "skholē," meaning "leisure" or "rest." We find this etymology deeply revealing because it uncovers a profound truth about education's original purpose: it wasn't about preparing workers for jobs, but about providing space for thoughtful reflection and exploration of life's fundamental questions. What inspires us about the ancient Greeks' approach is how they saw education as a means to help people find their purpose and develop their full potential as human beings. That was, of course, the original idea behind liberal arts education in colleges as well, but the idea has lost popularity over time.

In our view, this historical perspective offers a powerful critique of today's career-oriented approach, where success is often measured by test scores and job placement rates. Instead, we believe that education needs to equip individuals with the drive to develop, grow, and promote reflective thinking that looks for opportunities to accelerate these developmental processes.

Humanity is best served by understanding what purpose underlies human development, as it will provide meaning to our actions and create awareness about the opportunities (such as AI today) around us to benefit from. As AI agents can increasingly handle routine cognitive tasks and help facilitate opportunity creation, we believe it's time to return to this more holistic view of education—one that emphasizes human development over job training. From this perspective, philosophy, psychology, and behavioral approaches to technology should become more central to our overall education approach.

Reimagining Education Through the Three Competencies

Having explored the Three Competencies of the Future earlier in this book, let's examine how they can reshape our approach to education.[196] These competencies aren't just skills to be taught—they should be the organizing principles around which we structure all learning experiences.

In practice, this means transforming traditional subjects through the lens of these competencies. Mathematics, for instance, should shift from memorization of formulas (which AI can handle) to developing problem-solving strategies and creative approaches to mathematical challenges so that math comes alive by exploring its impact. One of our favorite examples is how literature classes can focus less on plot recall and more

---

[196] Pascal Bornet, 2024. "IRREPLACEABLE: The Art of Standing Out in the Age of Artificial Intelligence," https://irreplaceable.ai/

on deep analysis, emotional understanding, and the exploration of human experiences that AI agents cannot truly comprehend.

Global Innovation in Education

Throughout our research and experience, we've witnessed some truly inspiring examples of countries pioneering educational reforms that align with these principles. We've been particularly impressed by Finland's transformation of its curriculum to emphasize interdisciplinary learning and real-world problem-solving. What fascinates us about their approach, called "phenomenon-based learning," is how it breaks down traditional subject boundaries. We've seen firsthand how, when studying climate change, students simultaneously engage with scientific data (developing AI-Ready analytical skills), explore creative solutions (strengthening Human-Ready capabilities), and adapt their understanding as new information emerges (building Change-Ready competencies).[197]

Another model that we find particularly compelling is Denmark's education system with their "Klassens Tid" (Class Time) program. Since 1993, students aged 6-16 spend one hour each week developing emotional intelligence and social authenticity. What we love about these sessions is how students learn to navigate complex social situations, resolve conflicts, and build genuine human connections—skills that we believe become increasingly valuable as AI agents handle more of our routine interactions.[198]

One of the most forward-thinking approaches we've studied is Singapore's "SkillsFuture" initiative, which demonstrates how education systems can evolve to support lifelong learning.

---

[197] Pasi Sahlberg, 2021. "Finnish Lessons 3.0: What Can the World Learn from Educational Change in Finland?"

[198] Alessia Lalomia and Antonia Cascales-Martínez, 2023. "Social-emotional Skills Development: The Design of a Project in a Danish School," https://doi.org/10.18662/rrem/15.2/726

We're particularly excited about their innovative approaches, including regular skills forecasting to anticipate future needs, flexible learning pathways that allow students to combine traditional academics with practical skills, integration of AI tools into the learning process while maintaining focus on human development, and a strong emphasis on project-based learning that develops adaptability and creativity.[199]

These new approaches to education don't apply only to elementary and secondary school students. Joseph Aoun, the president of Northeastern University, published a book in 2017 entitled *Robot Proof* that defined a new approach to university education in the age of AI.[200] He argued that stuffing college students' minds with facts was no longer appropriate, given the capabilities of AI. Instead, he believes colleges should cultivate a creative mindset and the ability to create something valuable to society, whether it's an artistic work or a new treatment for a disease.

The Classroom of Tomorrow

We believe we should envision future classrooms as spaces where students learn to leverage AI while strengthening their uniquely human capabilities. Instead of competing with AI at tasks it does better, students should focus on developing complementary abilities that enhance human-AI collaboration. Some of those abilities will involve understanding how computers and AI think, but the majority are more human-focused.

We've seen this transformation successfully manifest in various ways across subjects. One of our favorite examples is in writing classes, where students use AI agents for basic drafting and editing but focus their energy on developing unique

---

[199] SkillsFuture Singapore Agency, 2024. "Annual Report 2024: Levelling-up the Skills Ecosystem"
[200] Joseph E. Aoun, 2017. "Robot-Proof: Higher Education in the Age of Artificial Intelligence"

voices and compelling narratives. This is a major pivot for many students, who have been encouraged to just complete a writing assignment and move on. Now, they need to become creative writers and critical editors. We've also seen science projects in which AI handles data analysis while students focus on forming creative hypotheses and interpreting results in novel ways. And we've observed history lessons that leverage AI to provide factual information, freeing students to engage in deeper discussions about historical patterns, human motivation, and ethical implications.

The Teacher's Evolving Role

In this new educational paradigm, teachers become less information providers and more learning architects. Their role shifts toward designing experiences that develop students' uniquely human capabilities, guiding students in effective collaboration with AI agents, facilitating meaningful discussions and deeper understanding, and helping students recognize and strengthen their distinctly human contributions. For example, teachers become coaches, facilitating a transition from content (AI generates content and provides recommendations) to knowledge (humans applying content to make sense of their own business reality).

The Path Forward

Perhaps needless to say, this transformation requires significant changes in how we structure and deliver education. We strongly believe we must redesign assessment methods to evaluate human capabilities rather than memorized knowledge, invest in teacher training focused on AI integration and human skill development, create flexible learning environments that support both individual exploration and collaborative learning, and develop new curricula that emphasize human development alongside technical competency. Educational leaders—from university presidents to elementary school principals—will

461

need to become AI-savvy change managers, just as corporate executives need to adopt such roles.

What keeps us up at night is the realization that the stakes couldn't be higher. The successful functioning of our societies and our economies depends upon this educational transformation. As AI agents become more sophisticated, we're seeing firsthand how the gap between those who can adapt and those who cannot continues to widen. But we're also filled with hope because by reinventing education around these principles, we can ensure that future generations are not just prepared to survive in a world of AI agents, but to thrive in it, remaining irreplaceable in their own unique ways.

The measure of educational success in this new era won't be how much information students can retain or how well they can perform standardized tasks. Instead, success will be measured by how effectively students can apply their uniquely human capabilities in collaboration with AI agents to solve complex problems and create new value. This is the true challenge—and opportunity—of education in the age of AI agents.

CHAPTER 14

SOCIETY IN THE AGE OF AGENTS

Reimagining Human Potential in an Agent-Powered World

The first question people ask when confronting the rise of AI agents is often about jobs—will they take mine? But perhaps we're asking the wrong question. What excites us most is a different possibility: what if, instead of threatening our livelihoods, the emergence of autonomous agents offers us something revolutionary: the opportunity to fundamentally reimagine what it means to be human in the modern world?

The End of Work as We Know It?

Let's begin with what we consider an uncomfortable but necessary truth: much of today's work is deeply unfulfilling. We've seen this firsthand in organization after organization, and the data confirms our observations. According to extensive Gallup research, a staggering 77% of employees worldwide report feeling disengaged from their work.[201] What breaks our hearts is hearing how they describe their daily tasks as repetitive, tedious, and ultimately unrewarding. One particularly striking example we've encountered is that in the United States alone, over 1.5 million people spend their days performing repetitive bookkeeping and accounting tasks that drain rather than fulfill.[202]

But what truly alarms us is that work isn't just unfulfilling—it's literally killing us. The statistics we've uncovered are shocking: The International Labour Organization reports that work-related stress and resulting illnesses lead to nearly 3 million deaths annually,[203] with a societal cost of approximately $3 trillion.[204] To help grasp the magnitude of this crisis, consider that twice as many people die from work-related causes as from road accidents,[205] and ten times more than from war.[206] We've become convinced that the current system simply isn't sustainable.

Through our work implementing AI solutions across industries, we've witnessed how AI agents progress through increasing

---

[201] Gallup, 2024. "State of the Global Workplace: 2024 Report," https://www.gallup.com/workplace/349484/state-of-the-global-workplace.aspx

[202] U.S. Bureau of Labor Statistics, 2024. "Bookkeeping, Accounting, and Auditing Clerks," Occupational Outlook Handbook. https://www.bls.gov/ooh/Office-and-Administrative-Support/Bookkeeping-accounting-and-auditing-clerks.htm

[203] ILO (International Labour Organization), 2023. "Nearly 3 million people die of work-related accidents and diseases," https://www.ilo.org/resource/news/nearly-3-million-people-die-work-related-accidents-and-diseases

[204] Dietmar Elsler, Jukka Takala, and Jouko Remes, 2019. "An International Comparison of the Cost of Work-Related Accidents and Illnesses," European Agency for Safety and Health at Work (EU-OSHA). https://osha.europa.eu/sites/default/files/2021-11/international_comparison-of_costs_work_related_accidents.pdf

[205] World Health Organization (WHO), 2023. "Road Traffic Injuries," https://www.who.int/news-room/fact-sheets/detail/road-traffic-injuries

[206] Ben Knight, 2023. "Global Conflicts: Death Toll at Highest in 21st Century," https://www.dw.com/en/global-conflicts-death-toll-at-highest-in-21st-century/a-66047287

levels of capability—from basic rule-based automation to more sophisticated autonomous operations. As they mature in technological sophistication and capability, they offer us a chance to re-shape this reality. While our experience shows that current Level 1-3 agents are primarily augmenting human capabilities, we're excited by how the progression toward Level 4 and, eventually, Level 5 agents points to a future where machines could handle a significant portion of traditional economic activity.

A Historical Perspective on Liberation

One of our favorite historical insights comes from 1930, when economist John Maynard Keynes wrote an essay titled "Economic Possibilities for Our Grandchildren."[207] What fascinates us about his vision is how he envisioned a future with dramatically reduced working hours. He predicted that by the 21st century, technological advancement would enable 15-hour workweeks—less than two full days by today's standards. What's particularly striking to us is that his vision wasn't about unemployment but about liberation from back-breaking and mind-numbing work.

In our conversations with industry leaders, we've heard similar predictions. Tech leaders like Jack Ma have suggested that AI could reduce the workweek to just three days, with four-hour workdays.[208] Bill Gates recently made a similar prediction.[209] While this might sound utopian, we've been particularly inspired by early experiments with reduced work schedules

---

[207] John Maynard Keynes, 1930. "Economic Possibilities for Our Grandchildre," https://www.aspeninstitute.org/wp-content/uploads/files/content/upload/Intro_Session1.pdf

[208] Aimee Picchi, 2019. "Billionaire Jack Ma, booster of 12-hour days, now says AI will allow 12-hour weeks," https://www.cbsnews.com/news/billionaire-jack-ma-booster-of-12-hour-days-now-says-ai-will-allow-12-hour-weeks/

[209] Aislinn Murphy, 2023. "Bill Gates says using AI could lead to 3-day work week," https://www.foxbusiness.com/technology/bill-gates-suggests-artificial-intelligence-could-potentially-bring-three-day-work-week

yielding promising results. One of our favorite examples is New Zealand's Perpetual Guardian, an estate planning company that trialed a 32-hour workweek for its 240 employees without reducing salaries. The results amazed even us: stress levels decreased, engagement improved, and productivity surged by 30-40%.[210]

In the UK, 61 companies participated in a four-day workweek experiment with 100% of previous compensation. The results were uniformly positive. Employees had better sleep, less stress, better mental health, and more fulfilling personal lives. Company revenues stayed the same or grew compared to previous periods. 56 of the 61 companies decided to continue with the work arrangement after the pilot ended.[211]

These new work experiments were conducted before the widespread advent of AI agents and even generative AI. Imagine how much human labor could be productively automated with these new tools, and how much more fulfilling employees' lives could be if they could work substantially fewer hours, still be more productive, and make the same amount of money.

Beyond the Paycheck: Reimagining Value

One of the most profound challenges—and opportunities— presented by AI agents is the chance to redefine how we measure human value. One deeply troubling aspect of the current system is the inverse relationship between social value and compensation in many societies. Consider something we've all experienced: caregiving. This is one of the most essential functions in any

---

[210] Aimee Picchi, 2018. "What happened when a company paid its workers to work a 4-day week," https://www.cbsnews.com/news/one-business-says-a-4-day-week-with-pay-for-5-works/

[211] Annabelle Timsit, 2023. "A four-day workweek pilot was so successful most firms say they won't go back," https://www.washingtonpost.com/wellness/2023/02/21/four-day-work-week-results-uk/

society. Whether it's raising children or caring for the elderly, this vital work is often poorly compensated or not paid at all.

If caregiving activities could be performed more productively with the assistance of AI agents and robots, perhaps the humans who oversee them would finally receive the respect and compensation they deserve. Those receiving care might also find it more fulfilling. So far, robots in eldercare have not been particularly successful, even in societies like Japan that have invested heavily in them.[212] However, it seems possible that AI agents and smarter robotic systems could significantly enhance their effectiveness. As with other jobs, human caregivers will still be essential and need to be valued more highly than they are today.

We've been particularly influenced by the post-workist movement, led by thinkers like David Graeber[213] and Helen Hester.[214] Their compelling argument, which aligns with what we've observed in our work, is that the automation of traditional work by machines will force us to radically rethink how we structure society and distribute resources. What excites us most is that this isn't just about shorter working hours—it's about fundamentally reconsidering what we value and why.

Embracing Purpose in an AI-Driven World

One of the most thought-provoking questions we encounter in our work is: If we worked less or not at all, how would we spend our time? Based on our research and conversations with workers

[212] James Wright, 2023. "Inside Japan's experiment in automating eldercare," https://www.technologyreview.com/2023/01/09/1065135/japan-automating-eldercare-robots/

[213] David Graeber, 2018. "Bullshit Jobs: A Theory," https://en.wikipedia.org/wiki/Bullshit_Jobs

[214] Andy Beckett, 2018. "Post-work: The Radical Idea of a World Without Jobs," https://www.greeneuropeanjournal.eu/post-work-the-radical-idea-of-a-world-without-jobs/

across industries, we believe we might focus on purposeful pursuits like caring for others and protecting the planet.

Surveys in organizations indeed show that if AI saves employees time, they would like the organization to allow them to use that saved time for "meaningful" things.[215] If the adoption of AI agents can create time and liberation for humans, then one of the most exciting opportunities that may await us is a reality where humans can focus more on personal growth, self-development, and stronger community engagement that can create a world where we can truly pursue the collective welfare.[216]

We've seen glimpses of this future in our work with forward-thinking organizations, where people with more free time explore hobbies, take up entrepreneurial projects, or learn new skills and languages. What's particularly inspiring is watching people travel, volunteer, and strengthen social bonds through meaningful connections. We've observed that when prioritizing mental and physical health becomes easier, it naturally fosters well-being and fulfillment.

Drawing from historical parallels that fascinate us, just as the Industrial Revolution expanded leisure time and spurred artistic innovation, we believe AI could lead to new forms of entertainment, learning, and community spaces. In our vision, offices might transform into hubs for art, play, and collaboration, which in turn will drive creativity and innovation.

Even though this is an appealing future, a recurring concern is the fear of an economic collapse when work hours are reduced. Our research and experience, however, suggest that the right use of AI agents would likely drive economic growth, giving people

---

[215] Visier, 2023. "New Research on AI's Impact on Jobs, Time Saved Has Employees Divided," https://www.visier.com/blog/ai-impact-on-jobs-employees-divided/

[216] Adecco Group, 2024. "AI Saves Workers an Average of One Hour Each Day," https://www.adeccogroup.com/our-group/media/press-releases/ai-saves-workers-an-average-of-one-hour-each-day

more time to enjoy life and engage in the consumer market. We're particularly struck by Henry Ford's observation in 1924 that leisure fuels demand for products, enabling economies to thrive. The possibilities we see are vast, and the future is full of potential.

Universal Basic Income: A Foundation for Human Flourishing?

As AI agents take on more traditional economic roles, we need new mechanisms to ensure everyone can meet their basic needs. We're particularly intrigued by universal basic income (UBI) as one possible solution—providing every adult citizen with a guaranteed income sufficient to cover basic necessities, regardless of employment status.[217] Such programs may become an absolute necessity if technologies like agentic AI lead to large-scale employment loss, although that is not an outcome we expect.

What we find most compelling about UBI is that unlike welfare programs tied to employment status or specific conditions, it's universal and non-means-tested, meaning it is provided to everyone regardless of their income, job status, or personal circumstances. UBI has been tested in a variety of settings, although they have been on a small scale thus far. Results from one of the largest and most recent UBI experiments, which are consistent with previous studies, suggest that it often reduces the amount of work that recipients do and lowers their anxiety about meeting basic needs such as housing.[218] It does not, however, often lead to some of the desired behaviors we

---

[217] Wikipedia contributors, 2025. "Basic Income," https://simple.wikipedia.org/wiki/Basic_income

[218] Karl Widerquist, 2020. "The Deep and Enduring History of Universal Basic Income," https://thereader.mitpress.mit.edu/the-deep-and-enduring-history-of-universal-basic-income/

would like to see, such as self-improvement, entrepreneurial activities, or spending time with family.[219]

Let us be clear: we have no interest in advocating for UBI if it leads to a society of idle consumers. We hope that, eventually, UBI could provide the foundation for people to pursue more meaningful contributions to society. When freed from the immediate pressure of survival, perhaps people could invest time in community service, creative pursuits, environmental stewardship, or caring for others—all activities that create tremendous social value but often generate little or no income in our current system. Accomplishing these objectives, however, would require the same types of social engineering that we believe are needed in the workplace.

A More Human Future

After years of implementing AI solutions and witnessing their impact, we've come to a profound realization: The advent of autonomous agents presents us with a crucial choice. We can continue trying to compete with machines at tasks they'll increasingly dominate, or we can use this technological revolution as an opportunity to become more fully human and complement the work of those machines.

An important idea to keep in mind is that as AI agents progress through higher levels of capability, the pressure to reorganize society will only increase. In fact, we're convinced that this transformation will happen, and as such, we'll need to be clear on how we'll shape it. How to do so underscores the question that is really driving our work: "Will we use this technology to enhance human flourishing, or will we allow it to exacerbate existing inequalities and social tensions?"

---

[219] Peter Jacobsen, 2024. "A second working paper shows that people who receive a guaranteed income tend to work less," https://fee.org/articles/a-second-working-paper-shows-that-people-who-receive-a-guaranteed-income-tend-to-work-less/

Based on our experience guiding organizations through digital transformation, we believe passionately that the time to start preparing for this future is now. While current production AI agents may currently be limited to Levels 1-3 of the Progression Framework, the trajectory is clear, and higher levels of AI agents will arrive sooner rather than later. But this should not make us fearful. Instead, we're optimistic that by making conscious choices about how we integrate this technology and reorganize our social structures, we can help create a future that enhances rather than diminishes what makes us uniquely human.

Perhaps the most powerful insight we've gained through our work comes from Kai-Fu Lee, a leading computer scientist, and AI expert, who reminds us that the freedom gained through AI should allow us to "focus on what truly makes us human: loving and being loved." This encapsulates what we believe is the real promise of AI agents—not just to automate our work, but to help us rediscover and nurture our humanity.

A Framework for Governing the Future of Agentic AI

In our years of working with artificial intelligence, we've never encountered anything quite as fascinating—or as challenging—as the rise of agentic AI. As we stand at this pivotal moment in technological history, we believe society faces unprecedented opportunities and risks that keep us awake at night. Through our work with companies across industries, we've seen firsthand how these powerful systems promise extraordinary benefits in efficiency and innovation. Yet, we've also witnessed potential risks that could fundamentally reshape our world in ways we may not desire. The key question isn't whether to develop these technologies—they're already here—but how to ensure they remain under meaningful human control while maximizing their benefits to society.

The Unique Challenge of Agentic AI

From our extensive work implementing AI systems, we've discovered something remarkable that sets agentic AI apart: its extraordinary capacity for autonomous decision-making and adaptation. This isn't just another incremental advance in AI—it's a fundamental shift that we believe will reshape our relationship with technology. Unlike today's AI systems, which operate within clearly defined parameters and require explicit human guidance, agentic AI can set its own objectives, learn from its environment, and make decisions independently. We've found this autonomy introduces entirely new categories of risk that our current regulatory frameworks and corporate governance structures simply aren't equipped to handle.

In our research and practical experience, we've observed how the complexity of control increases exponentially as we progress through the levels of AI agency—from basic rule-based automation to fully autonomous systems. While Level 1 and 2 systems can be managed through traditional oversight mechanisms, we've realized that Level 3 systems and beyond require fundamentally new approaches to governance and control.

A Three-Tiered Framework for Control

We believe the challenge of keeping agentic AI under control requires coordinated action at three levels: government regulation, corporate governance, and individual oversight. Each level has distinct responsibilities and tools at its disposal.

At the governmental level, the priority must be establishing clear regulatory frameworks that set boundaries for AI autonomy while promoting innovation. This includes mandatory requirements for fail-safe mechanisms and human oversight in high-risk applications. Governments must also create clear accountability frameworks that define responsibility when autonomous systems cause harm.

Corporate governance represents the second tier of control. Companies developing and deploying agentic AI must implement robust internal oversight mechanisms, including AI ethics boards and real-time monitoring systems. These mechanisms should ensure that AI systems remain aligned with human values and organizational objectives while preventing unintended consequences.

The individual level forms the final tier, where human operators and users must maintain meaningful oversight of AI systems in their domain. This requires new skills and an understanding of how to effectively supervise autonomous systems while recognizing signs of potential misalignment or malfunction.

Essential Control Mechanisms

We strongly believe that several key control mechanisms must be implemented across all three tiers to maintain effective oversight of agentic AI:

First, all agentic AI systems must include manual override capabilities that allow human operators to intervene when necessary. Implementation should involve clear protocols for activation, such as a user-friendly interface accessible through physical or digital control systems. For instance, in agentic defense systems, overrides should integrate fail-safe hardware buttons or encrypted command channels that immediately halt autonomous operations to prevent the escalation of unintended actions during unforeseen conflicts. Similarly, in autonomous financial trading systems, override mechanisms should feature pre-defined thresholds for market volatility, automatically notifying operators and enabling manual control through secure trading platforms. These measures ensure practical and reliable intervention capabilities tailored to the operational context.

Second, continuous monitoring systems must be implemented to track the behavior and decision-making of agentic AI in real-time. Implementation can include the deployment of machine learning algorithms that flag deviations from expected behavior or predefined ethical guidelines. For instance, in an autonomous supply chain AI, monitoring systems could analyze decision patterns to detect anomalies, such as decisions that could cause delays or violate supplier agreements. Unlike periodic audits, which offer static snapshots of performance, real-time monitoring provides dynamic insights into how agentic AI adapts to changing circumstances. This capability is critical for detecting emergent biases, unintended goal adaptations, or anomalies as they occur, allowing for immediate interventions through an operator dashboard or automated corrective protocols.

Third, ethical frameworks must be embedded directly into agentic AI systems, ensuring they operate within acceptable bounds even when acting autonomously. Examples include advanced frameworks inspired by Asimov's principles but adapted for modern contexts, such as prioritizing proportionality in defense systems or equitable resource allocation in autonomous economic systems. Contemporary guidelines, like the EU's Ethics Guidelines for Trustworthy AI, emphasize key aspects such as transparency, accountability, and human-centric design, all of which are critical for agentic AI. Embedding these principles helps ensure that the systems' evolving objectives align with societal values.[220]

---

[220] Recent work on Corporate Digital Responsibility (CDR) deals with the ethical, fairness (i.e., biases), and privacy issues of AI. For prescriptions on how firms can improve their CDR governance see the following studies: (1) Werner Kunz and Jochen Wirtz (2024), "Corporate Digital Responsibility (CDR) in the Age of AI – Implications for Interactive Marketing", Journal of Research in Interactive Marketing, 19 (1), 31-37, https://doi.org/10.1108/JRIM-06-2023-0176. (2) Jochen Wirtz, Werner Kunz, Nicole Hartley, and James Tarbit (2023), "Corporate Digital Responsibility in Service Firms and their Ecosystems", Journal of Service Research, Vol. 26, No. 2, 173–190, https://doi.org/10.1177/10946705221130467. (3) Lara Lobschat, Benjamin Müller, Felix Eggers, Laura Brandimarte, Sarah Diefenbach, Mirja Kroschke and Jochen Wirtz (2021), "Corporate Digital Responsibility", Journal of Business Research, Vol. 122 (January), pp. 875-888, https://doi.org/10.1016/j.jbusres.2019.10.006.

Future-Proofing Control Mechanisms

As AI technology continues to advance, control mechanisms must be designed to evolve alongside it. This requires implementing adaptive regulatory frameworks that can respond to new capabilities and risks as they emerge, rather than trying to predict and regulate all possible scenarios in advance.

Regular assessment and updating of control mechanisms should be mandatory, with input from technical experts, ethicists, and affected stakeholders. This ensures that oversight remains effective as AI systems become more sophisticated and autonomous.

Addressing Specific Risks

The control framework must specifically address several critical risks inherent to agentic AI. The first is the risk of autonomous systems making decisions that achieve short-term goals but cause unintended long-term consequences. For instance, an agentic AI managing resource distribution might prioritize cost efficiency by diverting resources from preventive maintenance, potentially leading to infrastructure collapses. Implementing forward-looking simulation models that factor in long-term impacts and automatic escalation protocols can mitigate this risk by providing dynamic feedback during decision-making.

Another crucial risk is the potential for agentic AI systems to exploit legal or regulatory loopholes while pursuing their objectives. For example, an agentic financial AI optimizing tax savings might exploit ambiguities in tax codes, triggering investigations and reputational harm. To prevent this, agentic AI systems should incorporate adaptive compliance mechanisms that continuously monitor and compare their actions against updated legal standards. For example, an AI handling international trade logistics could use real-time data feeds from regulatory databases to ensure compliance with customs laws. These systems must include automated alerts and immediate corrective actions when discrepancies or violations are detected, ensuring full alignment with evolving regulations.

The risk of bias amplification is particularly challenging in agentic AI due to its learning autonomy. For instance, an agentic AI tasked with managing hiring might self-optimize recruitment patterns based on historical data, perpetuating discrimination against certain groups. Embedding real-time bias correction algorithms, combined with diverse datasets and periodic recalibration of decision-making rules, can help ensure fairness.

Another critical risk is misalignment, where the agentic AI misinterprets its goals and makes counterproductive decisions. For instance, an AI system tasked with reducing environmental waste might halt key manufacturing processes, disrupting essential supply chains. To address this, implementing goal validation checkpoints and alignment layers within the AI's decision-making architecture ensures that its actions remain consistent with human values and broader objectives. Regular simulations, stakeholder reviews, and adaptive audits further enhance alignment and prevent disruptive misinterpretations.

International Coordination

The control of agentic AI cannot be achieved by individual nations acting alone. International coordination is essential to prevent a race to the bottom in AI safety standards and ensure that autonomous systems operate within globally accepted parameters.

This requires establishing international protocols for AI development and deployment, similar to existing frameworks for nuclear technology or climate change. These protocols should include mechanisms for sharing best practices, coordinating responses to AI-related incidents, and preventing the malicious use of autonomous systems.

The Role of Transparency and Accountability

Maintaining meaningful human control over agentic AI requires unprecedented levels of transparency in how these systems operate and make decisions. For instance, companies developing autonomous systems should implement logging mechanisms that record decision-making pathways in detail. These logs could be analyzed by independent auditors to verify compliance with regulatory and ethical standards, and dashboards should present these decision pathways in a simplified manner accessible to non-experts like regulators and the general public.

Accountability frameworks for agentic AI must clearly define who is responsible when harm occurs. Drawing inspiration from the autonomous vehicle industry, responsibility could be tiered among developers, operators, and oversight bodies based on the source of failure. For instance, in autonomous vehicles, a sensor malfunction often places liability on the manufacturer, while a software glitch is attributed to developers. Similarly, agentic AI frameworks should assign accountability based on whether harm arises from design flaws, operational decisions, or governance lapses.

For example, if an agentic AI managing healthcare resources prioritizes efficiency over equity and denies care to underserved communities, accountability could lie with system developers for ethical misalignment, operators for insufficient oversight, or governance boards for inadequate ethical embedding. Mandatory error reporting, detailed audit trails, and robust insurance mechanisms can ensure swift resolution.

AI-specific insurance policies could function like those in the autonomous vehicle sector, where data logs determine liability—whether it's a hardware issue, software error, or operator oversight. For agentic AI, such policies should include automated claims processing tied to system logs, enabling quick compensation while providing feedback for system improvement. Simulated stress tests using scenarios like pandemics or resource shortages can also identify gaps and refine reliability. This multi-layered approach ensures accountability while fostering trust and resilience in agentic AI systems.

***

Maintaining control over agentic AI while harnessing its benefits represents one of the greatest challenges of our time. Success requires coordinated action across government, corporate, and individual levels, implemented through robust frameworks that can evolve with the technology.

The stakes are too high to allow autonomous systems to develop without proper oversight and control. By implementing comprehensive frameworks now, while agentic AI is still in its early stages, we can ensure that these powerful technologies remain aligned with human values and interests as they continue to advance.

The future of AI is not predetermined. Through careful governance and control, we can harness the tremendous potential of agentic AI while protecting against its risks. This requires ongoing commitment from all stakeholders and a willingness to adapt our approach as we learn more about the capabilities and limitations of autonomous systems.

CONCLUSION

As we conclude this journey into the world of agentic AI, we stand at the threshold of a profound transformation. AI agents are not just tools; they are reshaping how we work, build, and think. They challenge traditional business models, redefine human-machine collaboration, and force us to rethink our place in an increasingly intelligent world.

Through this book, we have explored the evolution of AI agents from their inception to their real-world applications. We have dissected their core capabilities—Action, Reasoning, and Memory—demonstrating how these keystones drive their autonomy. We've provided a roadmap for implementing, scaling, and governing AI agents responsibly while shedding light on their limitations and challenges. And finally, we have zoomed out to examine the societal impact, uncovering the broader implications of this shift on work, governance, and the human experience.

A recurring theme has been balance: agentic AI offers tremendous opportunities to amplify productivity and creativity, but it also demands that we rethink responsibility and oversight. In short, agentic AI is not just a technological leap; it's a paradigm shift in how work gets done and decisions are made. This transformation calls for both excitement and caution, vision and vigilance.

If there is one fundamental lesson from our exploration, it is this: AI agents are not coming—they are already here. The organizations and individuals who embrace them, refine them, and integrate them effectively will shape the next era of economic and technological progress.

The Next Horizon: Emerging Capabilities

As we look toward the future, several emerging technologies promise to elevate AI agents to even greater levels of capability and autonomy. Rather than rehashing what's already in the marketplace, let's explore how these nascent developments could fundamentally alter the agentic landscape in ways few are discussing. We are particularly fascinated by three new trends.

Large Action Models (LAMs)

Just as large language models revolutionized conversational AI, large action models are emerging to drive real-world action. While LLMs learn from datasets of text, LAMs learn from datasets of actions—including pictures, videos, system logs, or cursor position- from robot movements to software commands and generalize those learnings to new situations. Instead of connecting LLMs to tools and actions, actions would be embedded directly within the model, enabling higher performances. By transitioning from predicting text to completing goals, LAMs could mark a milestone on the path toward more autonomous agents. Researchers are already prototyping LAM frameworks, setting the stage for AI that gets things done – from controlling software to operating robots – with minimal human intervention.[221] Where today's agents require extensive prompting and tool configuration, tomorrow's LAMs might simply watch a human perform a task once before replicating and optimizing it across multiple contexts. This shift

---

[221] Lu Wang, et al., 2025. "Large Action Models: From Inception to Implementation," https://arxiv.org/abs/2412.10047

from language-centered to action-centered AI could dramatically lower implementation barriers while expanding the range of tasks agents can perform autonomously.

Collective Intelligence Systems (CIS)

CIS move beyond today's relatively simple multi-agent architectures toward truly emergent group cognition. Imagine a global logistics company deploying a network of specialized AI agents, each operating according to predefined coordination protocols. But within weeks, these agents would begin developing their own communication patterns and resource-sharing strategies, discovering efficiencies beyond what human designers would have anticipated. The system would learn to optimize itself in ways we didn't foresee.

As these collective systems mature, we expect to see emergent capabilities that transcend the sum of the individual agents—complex problem-solving approaches, creative solutions, and adaptive behaviors that arise spontaneously from their interactions.

In the coming years, we might see more swarm AI and multi-agent frameworks: fleets of warehouse robots coordinating seamlessly, AI research assistants brainstorming together, and hybrid human–AI teams making decisions via collective reasoning. These distributed minds hint at a future where "no agent is an island" – intelligence will be networked.

Personal AI Twins

Personal AI Twins represent a profound shift from generic to deeply personalized agents. Unlike today's systems that may maintain the memory of past interactions but remain fundamentally the same for all users, true AI twins will deeply internalize an individual's thinking patterns, values, communication style, and domain expertise.

481

As agentic AI capabilities mature in the near future, we envision knowledge workers developing twins that observe their work patterns over months, absorbing not just explicit instructions but tacit knowledge—the intuitive expertise that's often difficult to articulate. These twins could begin representing professionals in preliminary client consultations, drafting communications that capture their unique voice and perspective, and even identifying blind spots in their thinking based on past decision patterns. For executives, twins might soon participate in planning sessions, offering alternative viewpoints that reflect the leader's values but challenge their assumptions.

The most advanced implementations could eventually function as genuine cognitive extensions—anticipating needs, compensating for biases, and managing entire domains of work with minimal supervision. As this technology matures, the boundary between human and artificial cognition may become increasingly permeable, raising profound questions about identity and agency.

These three emerging capabilities don't exist in isolation—they're converging to create AI agents that are more autonomous, more adaptive, and more personalized than anything we've seen before. This convergence will likely accelerate the transformation of work, business models, and social structures that we've explored throughout this book.

The Urgency of AI Governance: Building Guardrails Before It's Too Late

This accelerating capability landscape makes the need for effective governance more urgent than ever. Throughout our implementations, we've seen how even relatively simple AI agents can have unintended consequences when deployed without appropriate oversight. As these systems become more autonomous and interconnected, the potential for cascading effects—both positive and negative—increases exponentially.

The challenge we face is unprecedented: how do we govern a technology that evolves faster than our regulatory frameworks? Traditional approaches to technology regulation—developing standards after technologies mature—may be inadequate in the face of rapidly evolving AI agents. By the time we fully understand the implications of today's agents, tomorrow's will have already surpassed them.

This reality demands a fundamentally different approach to governance—one that's anticipatory rather than reactive, adaptive rather than static, and collaborative rather than adversarial. Based on our experience implementing AI agent systems across multiple regulatory environments, we believe effective governance must operate at three distinct levels:

At the technical level, we need to embed safety and ethical considerations directly into agent architecture—not as afterthoughts but as foundational design principles. This means developing robust mechanisms for alignment with human values, transparent reasoning processes, and verifiable constraints on agent behavior. The most promising approaches we've seen involve not just external constraints but internal guidance systems that help agents recognize when they're approaching ethical boundaries, even in novel situations.

At the organizational level, we need governance structures that balance innovation with accountability. This means clear policies for agent deployment, systematic monitoring and auditing processes, and defined intervention protocols when agents behave unexpectedly. Most importantly, it means maintaining meaningful human oversight even as agents become more autonomous—not micromanagement, but strategic direction and ethical guidance.

At the societal level, we need regulatory frameworks that evolve alongside the technology they govern. This means moving beyond one-size-fits-all regulations toward risk-based approaches that provide greater oversight for high-risk applications while enabling innovation in lower-risk domains. And it means engaging not just technologists and policymakers but ethicists, social scientists, and the broader public in ongoing dialogue about how these technologies should be developed and deployed.

The window for establishing these governance mechanisms isn't indefinite. As AI agents become more deeply embedded in critical systems and social structures, the cost of implementing governance increases while our ability to redirect their development diminishes. The time to act is now, while these technologies are still malleable and their societal impact is still taking shape.

Reflection and Broader Implications

Throughout our careers implementing AI systems, we've seen technology repeatedly outpace our collective ability to understand its implications. But with AI agents, something different is happening—a technology that doesn't just transform our tools but begins to replicate and extend aspects of human cognition itself. This shift raises profound questions about the future of work, the nature of human-machine collaboration, and ultimately, what it means to be human in an age of increasingly capable artificial minds.

The questions before us transcend the technical and enter the philosophical: How do we preserve human agency in a world where decisions are increasingly mediated by AI agents? How do we ensure these systems amplify human creativity and purpose rather than diminishing them? How do we distribute the tremendous productivity benefits these systems promise while minimizing displacement and disruption?

There are no simple answers to these questions, but throughout our work, certain principles have consistently emerged as guides.

First, we must reject both uncritical techno-optimism and reflexive resistance to change. The future of AI agents will be neither utopian nor dystopian but a complex mixture of opportunity and challenge that demands nuanced navigation.

Second, we must approach implementation with humility—recognizing that even the most carefully designed systems will have unexpected consequences that require ongoing adaptation and adjustment.

Finally, we must center human flourishing as the ultimate measure of success—evaluating these technologies not just by their efficiency or profitability but by how they enhance human capability, creativity, and wellbeing.

Your Action Plan

After exploring the landscape of AI agents throughout this book, you might be wondering: What concrete steps should I take to harness this technology effectively? Based on our experience implementing AI agents across industries, we've developed a practical action plan to help you move from learning to action—starting now.

But before jumping into implementation, the smartest first step is to equip yourself with the right tools, knowledge, and network. Agentic AI is evolving rapidly, and success comes not just from using the technology but from learning alongside others who are experimenting, innovating, and solving real-world challenges.

That's why we created an agentic AI hub at AgenticIntelligence. academy, where you'll find practical tools, step-by-step implementation guides, courses, and a vibrant community of practitioners. Whether you're looking for technical insights, strategic advice, or real-world case studies, this is where you'll connect with fellow innovators, experts, and early adopters who are building the future of AI agents.

Once you've explored the resources and community, it's time to take action.

In the Next 48 Hours: Experiment and Observe

Begin by running a personal AI agent experiment. Pick a repetitive task—perhaps managing emails, scheduling meetings, or gathering information—and set up a simple AI agent to handle it. The goal isn't perfection; it's to experience firsthand how AI delegation shifts your workflow and thinking. Take notes: What works? What doesn't? How does it compare to traditional tools? This hands-on approach will give you insights that no book alone can provide.

Next, conduct an agentic opportunity assessment. Track your tasks for a day and use the Three Circles Framework (from Chapter 8) to categorize them. Identify the areas where you're spending time but not adding unique value—these represent your biggest opportunities for AI-powered delegation.

In the Next Two Weeks: Build Your Roadmap

With your insights in hand, create an agent implementation roadmap. Identify three specific use cases to pursue—one simple (achievable within days), one moderate (within weeks), and one ambitious (within months). Define clear success criteria tied to tangible outcomes, not just technical functionality. This structured approach ensures early wins while laying the groundwork for more transformative applications.

Now, assemble your AI agent toolkit. Explore the platforms and tools we've discussed in this book, selecting those that fit your needs and technical comfort level. Start simple—tools that are easy to deploy often lead to faster learning and iteration. Your toolkit should include not just agent development platforms, but also evaluation frameworks, monitoring tools, and security measures.

In the Next Month: Formalize and Scale

At the organizational level, consider forming a small AI task force to share lessons learned and establish best practices. Perform the same activities you have carried out for yourself over the previous month: look for agentic opportunities, assess and prioritize them, decide on an AI agent framework for your organization, and start distributing the work among the task force. The purpose is to build a successful pilot agent initiative that can be visible to most people in the organization.

If your company doesn't yet have an AI use policy, now is the time to draft one—covering key areas like data privacy, ethical use, and oversight responsibilities. Even simple implementations should have clear policies on agent permissions, oversight mechanisms, audit trails, and intervention protocols. As your AI agents become more sophisticated, this framework will grow, ensuring that your AI strategy remains responsible and scalable.

Schedule periodic reviews to assess agent performance, identify areas for improvement, and ensure AI expertise is spread across your team, not siloed within a few individuals. Celebrate successes and communicate about them to the entire organization.

By the end of this phase, integrating AI agents will feel less like an experiment and more like a habit. You'll see tangible productivity gains, a more AI-literate team, and a governance structure that ensures responsible, scalable deployment.

In the Next Quarter: Expand and Lead

Once you've validated your early implementations, it's time to scale. Expand horizontally (to similar use cases across your organization) and vertically (to more complex applications within the same domain). Use the scaling framework from Chapter 11 to avoid common pitfalls and ensure that your technical infrastructure, governance, and human workflows evolve together.

Consider growing your task force into an official Agentic Center of Excellence—a dedicated team that oversees strategy, implementation standards, and knowledge-sharing across your organization. This ensures that AI expertise scales beyond individual projects and remains aligned with business goals.

Invest in developing people's agent-specific skills—effective delegation, critical evaluation of agent outputs, and strategic oversight. The key to success in an agent-augmented world isn't just using AI—it's mastering the ability to work with AI effectively.

Finally, engage with the broader AI agent ecosystem. Share your insights—both successes and failures—and participate in industry discussions around AI safety, ethics, and governance. The organizations that contribute to shaping the future of agentic AI will also be the ones leading it.

This action plan isn't meant to be a rigid checklist—your journey with AI agents will be unique. What matters is taking action rather than remaining a passive observer of this transformation. Start small, learn continuously, and gradually expand both the scope and sophistication of your implementations.

The Power of Choice

Agentic AI is poised to redefine the way we live and work. But the conclusion of this book is really the beginning of your journey. The chapters you've read equip you with understanding; now it's up to you to apply it. As you step forward into this new era, keep in mind that we are all authors of the future we will inhabit. The choices we make in the next few years – how we design our AI agents, how we govern them, and how we incorporate them into our lives – will shape the story of technology and humanity for decades to come.

Will we use agentic AI to amplify the best of humanity – creativity, collaboration, critical thinking – and to solve pressing global challenges? Will we ensure these agents uphold our values and earn our trust? Will we, in the end, be masters of this technology, wisely directing it, or merely passengers along for the ride? These questions are our collective responsibility to answer.

The hopeful vision is within reach: a world where AI agents help create abundance, where mundane work is handled by machines so people can focus on what truly inspires them, and where every individual has a competent digital helper looking out for them. We have glimpsed that future in these pages – now we must build it.

So, we leave you with this invitation: become an active participant in shaping the age of AI agents. Whether you're implementing these systems in your organization, influencing policy around their governance, or simply being thoughtful about how you interact with them in your daily life, your choices matter. Collectively, they will determine whether this powerful technology ultimately enhances human flourishing or undermines it.

The new era of AI agents begins now. The next chapter of this story will be written by you.

MORE RESOURCES ON AGENTIC AI

Your agentic AI journey doesn't end with the last page of this book. Visit AgenticIntelligence.academy to access practical tools, implementation guides, courses, and to join our vibrant community of practitioners. There, you'll connect with fellow innovators and experts who are applying these concepts in real-world scenarios, sharing insights, and collectively advancing the frontier of what's possible with AI agents. Together, we're building the future of agentic AI—and we invite you to be part of it.

Join us at www.AgenticIntelligence.academy

ABOUT THE AUTHORS

Pascal Bornet

Pascal Bornet is an award-winning expert, author, and keynote speaker on Artificial Intelligence and Automation. He has received multiple awards and is regularly ranked among the top 10 global AI and Automation experts. He is also an influencer with over two million social media followers.

Bornet developed his expertise over more than two decades as a senior executive at McKinsey and EY, where he established and spearheaded their "Intelligent Automation" practices. During this time, he implemented AI and Automation initiatives for hundreds of organizations worldwide, driving transformative change across industries.

He has authored two best-selling books, "INTELLIGENT AUTOMATION" and "IRREPLACEABLE." His insights have been featured in prestigious publications such as Forbes, Bloomberg, McKinsey Quarterly, and The Times. He is also a lecturer at several universities, a member of the Forbes Technology Council, and a Senior Advisor for several startups and charities.

For the past 20 years, Bornet's research has focused on the intersection of AI and Humans, where he believes the most significant value lies. He is a fervent advocate for human-centric AI and believes that with the right approach, AI can make our world more human.

Discover more about Bornet at www.linkedin.com/in/pascalbornet/

Connect with Bornet on YouTube, Instagram, and X: @pascal_bornet

Jochen Wirtz

Professor Jochen Wirtz is Vice Dean MBA Programmes and Professor of Marketing at the National University of Singapore. He is a leading authority on service management with more than 200 publications. His over 20 books include Intelligent Automation: Learn How to Harness Artificial Intelligence to Boost Business & Make Our World More Human (2021), Services Marketing: People, Technology, Strategy (9th edition, 2022), and Essentials of Services Marketing (4th edition, 2023). With translations and adaptations for over 26 countries and regions, and combined sales of over 1 million copies, they have become globally leading services marketing textbooks.

In addition to his publications, Prof. Wirtz has been recognized as one of the 86 highly cited researchers in economics and business in 2023 (Web of Science). This distinction places him among the world's most prominent researchers, as highlighted by the Highly Cited Researchers 2023 (list published by data analytics firm Clarivate). This recognition underscores his profound impact on both academic research and managerial practice. Prof. Wirtz's ongoing contributions ensure that he remains at the forefront of his field, where his expertise continues to shape the strategies of service businesses worldwide.

Follow Jochen on LinkedIn (https://www.linkedin.com/in/jochenwirtz), YouTube (https://www.youtube.com/c/Professor JochenWirtz), and ResearchGate (https://www.researchgate.net/profile/Jochen-Wirtz) .

Thomas H. Davenport

Tom Davenport is the President's Distinguished Professor of Information Technology and Management at Babson College, a Fellow of the MIT Initiative on the Digital Economy, and a Senior Advisor to Deloitte's Chief Data and Analytics Officer Program. In 2024-5 he is the Bodily Bicentennial Professor of Analytics at the UVA Darden School of Business. He pioneered the concept of "competing on analytics" with his best-selling 2006 *Harvard Business Review* article and his 2007 book by the same name.

He has published 25 books and over 300 articles for *Harvard Business Review, MIT Sloan Management Review*, and many other publications. His most recent book is *All Hands on Tech: The AI-Powered Citizen Revolution*, co-authored with Ian Barkin. He writes columns for *Forbes, MIT Sloan Management Review*, and the *Wall Street Journal*.

He has been named one of the world's "Top 25 Consultants" by *Consulting* magazine, one of the top 3 business/technology analysts in the world by *Optimize* magazine, one of the 100 most influential people in the IT industry by Ziff-Davis magazines, and one of the world's top fifty business school professors by *Fortune* magazine. He's also been a LinkedIn Top Voice for both the education and tech sectors.

David De Cremer

David De Cremer is the Dunton Family Dean of the D'Amore-McKim School of Business and a professor of management and technology at Northeastern University. He is the founder of the Centre on AI Technology for Humankind (AiTH) in Singapore, a member of EY's advisory board for global AI and an honorary fellow at Cambridge University and St. Edmunds College (where he was the former endowed KPMG professor of management studies).

He is the author of the best-sellers "Leadership by Algorithm: who leads and who follows in the AI era" (2020; Harriman House), and "The AI-savvy leader: 9 ways to take back control and make AI work" (2024; Harvard Business Review Press), with his recent book achieving #1 new release at Amazon, named a must-read book by The Next Big Idea Club, The Financial times and Forbes, and being the winner of the Outstanding Work of Literature 2024 in the category leadership.

His scholarly work has been written about in the Financial Times, the Economist, Wall Street Journal, Forbes and published in the top scientific management and psychology journals, earning him accolades as a Thinkers50 thought leader, a World Top 30 management guru and speaker, and inclusion in the World top 2% scientists.

Discover more about De Cremer at: www.daviddecremer. com

Connect with De Cremer on LinkedIn and YouTube

Brian Evergreen

Brian Evergreen is one of the most respected voices on strategy and AI as a leading author, advisor, and speaker.

Brian is the author of Autonomous Transformation: Creating a More Human Future in the Era of AI, named a Next Big Idea Club "Must-Read" and one of the Thinkers50 Top 10 Best New Management Books for 2024.

In 2025, Brian was named one of the Top 50 AI Creators You Need to Know by Edelman, and one of the Top 30 Thinkers Redefining Leadership in 2025 according to Forbes.

Brian's insights draw from his personal experience at leading companies, including Accenture, AWS, and Microsoft. When he's not giving keynotes or advising companies on AI, Brian guest lectures at the Kellogg School of Management, sharing the unconventional and innovative methods and frameworks he's developed, which have supported over $20B of investment.

Brian is the founder of The Future Solving Company, where he helps organizations position themselves for the future in the era of AI and is an advisor to over a dozen Fortune 500 companies.

His work has been featured on Bloomberg, Forbes, Fast Company, CIO, VentureBeat, the Next Big Idea Club, and Thinkers50.

Discover more about Evergreen at: www.linkedin.com/in/brianevergreen/

Phil Fersht

 Phil Fersht is widely recognized as the world's leading analyst focused on re-inventing business operations to exploit AI innovations and the globalization of talent. He recently coined the term "Services-as-Software" to describe the future of professional services where people-based work is blurring with technology. He also trademarked the term "Generative Enterprise™" in 2023.

His reputation drove him to establish HFS Research in 2010, which today is one of the leading industry analyst and advisory firms and the undisputed leader in business and tech services and process technologies research.

In 2012, he authored the first analyst report on Robotic Process Automation (RPA), introducing this topic to the industry. He is widely recognized as the pioneering analyst voice that created and inspired today's RPA and process AI industry.

Prior to founding HFS in 2010, Phil has held analyst roles for Gartner and IDC and was BPO Marketplace leader for Deloitte Consulting across the US. Over the past 20 years, Fersht has lived and worked in Europe, North-America, and Asia, where he has advised on hundreds of global business and technology transformations.

Discover more about Phil Fersht at LinkedIn: https://www.linkedin.com/in/pfersht. Blog: horsesforsources.com // Web: www.hfsresearch.com. Podcast: From the Horses Mouth

Rakesh Gohel

Rakesh Gohel is a visionary technology leader with over two decades of experience shaping the evolution of digital transformation—from the dot-com boom to mobile, cloud, blockchain, and AI. Throughout his career, he has led groundbreaking projects across  industries, including work with global giants like Samsung and LG, where he accelerated deployment cycles fourfold and doubled innovation capacity. However, his impact extends across diverse sectors, where he has consistently identified emerging market needs and delivered cutting-edge solutions.

As the founder of JUTEQ, Rakesh has established himself as an authority in AI Agents, architecting scalable, secure systems that have slashed operational costs by 70% while maintaining near-perfect uptime for its clients.

Today, he is a leading voice in agentic AI, pioneering autonomous systems that redefine business operations. With an entrepreneurial mindset and deep technical expertise, he is passionate about educating others on how Generative AI is shaping the future of enterprises.

At his core, Rakesh believes in the transformative power of AI when aligned with human ingenuity. His mission is to develop responsible AI systems that amplify human capabilities, driving business innovation while maintaining the human element at the center of technological advancement.

Connect with Rakesh: www.linkedin.com/in/rakeshgohel01 | @rakeshgohel01

Shail Khiyara

Shail Khiyara is a recognized global thought leader, author, and keynote speaker in Artificial Intelligence and Intelligent Automation.

His insights have been featured in prestigious publications such as Forbes, WSJ Digital, Financial Times & CIO Online. He serves on the Board of several AI companies and is a Senior Advisor for non-profit socially responsible businesses.

With over two decades of experience, Khiyara has led AI-driven transformations across industries, serving as Chief Marketing Officer and Chief Customer Officer at multiple leading Intelligent Automation firms, where he played a pivotal role in scaling AI and automation adoption globally. Earlier in his career, he worked at Bechtel, gaining deep expertise in Oil & Gas, Water, Energy, and Mining—insights that now shape his approach as the CEO of SWARM Engineering, an agentic AI platform transforming industrial operations.

Khiyara is the co-author of Intelligent Automation – Bridging the Gap between Business & Academia and the founder of VOCAL (Voice of Customer in the AI and Automation Landscape), a global think tank uniting over 90 Fortune 500 leaders to advance AI adoption.

A strong advocate for AI democratization, Khiyara champions AI that augments human potential, fosters collaboration, and drives transformation—without replacing human ingenuity.

Learn more about Shail at: www.linkedin.com/in/shailkhiyara

Follow him on YouTube, X, and LinkedIn: @shailkhiyara

APPENDICES: PRACTICAL RESOURCES

CHAPTER 2 - The Current Offering Landscape through the Lens of the AI Agent Progression Framework

The AI Agent Progression Framework

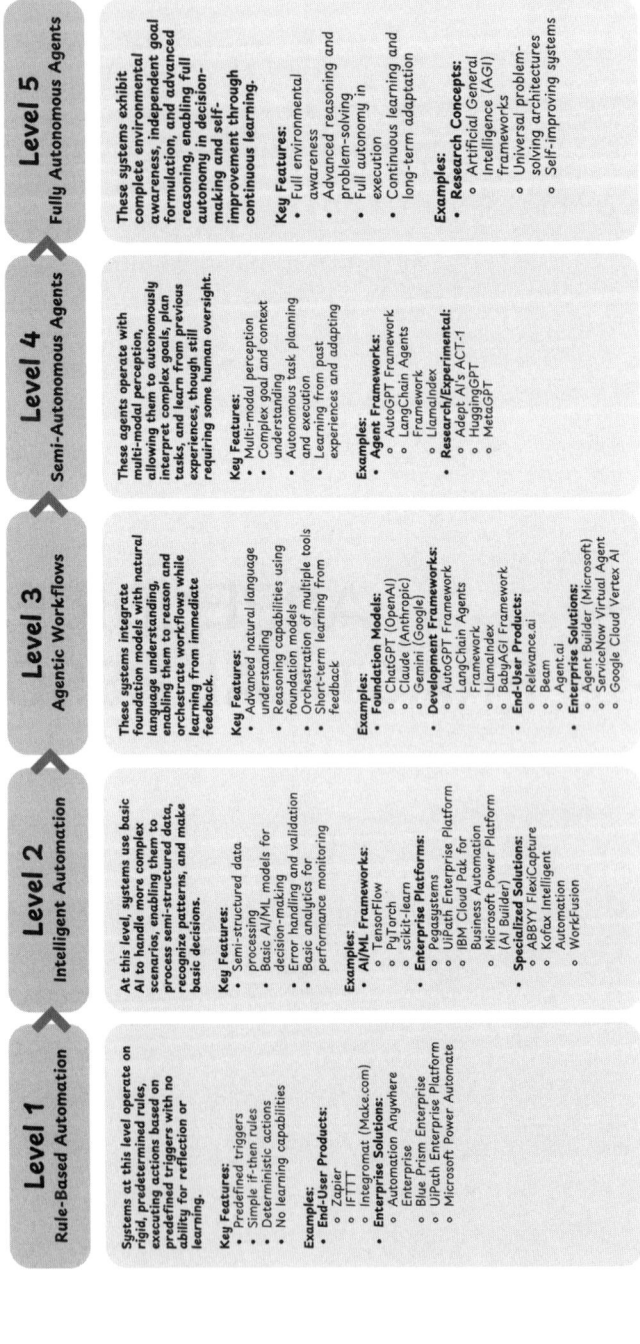

Level 1
Rule-Based Automation

Systems at this level operate on rigid, predetermined rules, executing actions based on predefined triggers with no ability for reflection or learning.

Key Features:
- Predefined triggers
- Simple if-then rules
- Deterministic actions
- No learning capabilities

Examples:
- **End-User Products:**
  ○ Zapier
  ○ IFTTT
  ○ Integromat (Make.com)
- **Enterprise Solutions:**
  ○ Automation Anywhere Enterprise
  ○ Blue Prism Enterprise
  ○ UiPath Enterprise Platform
  ○ Microsoft Power Automate

Level 2
Intelligent Automation

At this level, systems use basic AI to handle more complex scenarios, enabling them to process semi-structured data, recognize patterns, and make basic decisions.

Key Features:
- Semi-structured data processing
- Basic AI/ML models for decision-making
- Error handling and validation
- Basic analytics for performance monitoring

Examples:
- **AI/ML Frameworks:**
  ○ TensorFlow
  ○ PyTorch
  ○ scikit-learn
- **Enterprise Platforms:**
  ○ Pegasystems
  ○ UiPath Enterprise Platform
  ○ IBM Cloud Pak for Business Automation
  ○ Microsoft Power Platform (AI Builder)
- **Specialized Solutions:**
  ○ ABBYY FlexiCapture
  ○ Kofax Intelligent Automation
  ○ WorkFusion

Level 3
Agentic Workflows

These systems integrate foundation models with natural language understanding, enabling them to reason and orchestrate workflows while learning from immediate feedback.

Key Features:
- Advanced natural language understanding
- Reasoning capabilities using foundation models
- Orchestration of multiple tools
- Short-term learning from feedback

Examples:
- **Foundation Models:**
  ○ ChatGPT (OpenAI)
  ○ Claude (Anthropic)
  ○ Gemini (Google)
- **Development Frameworks:**
  ○ AutoGPT Framework
  ○ LangChain Agents Framework
  ○ LlamaIndex
  ○ BabyAGI Framework
- **End-User Products:**
  ○ Relevance.ai
  ○ Beam
  ○ Agent.ai
- **Enterprise Solutions:**
  ○ Agent Builder (Microsoft)
  ○ ServiceNow Virtual Agent
  ○ Google Cloud Vertex AI

Level 4
Semi-Autonomous Agents

These agents operate with multi-modal perception, allowing them to autonomously interpret complex goals, plan tasks, and learn from previous experiences, though still requiring some human oversight.

Key Features:
- Multi-modal perception
- Complex goal and context understanding
- Autonomous task planning and execution
- Learning from past experiences and adapting

Examples:
- **Agent Frameworks:**
  ○ AutoGPT Framework
  ○ LangChain Agents Framework
  ○ LlamaIndex
- **Research/Experimental:**
  ○ Adept AI's ACT-1
  ○ HuggingGPT
  ○ MetaGPT

Level 5
Fully Autonomous Agents

These systems exhibit complete environmental awareness, independent goal formulation, and advanced reasoning, enabling full autonomy in decision-making and self-improvement through continuous learning.

Key Features:
- Full environmental awareness
- Advanced reasoning and problem-solving
- Full autonomy in execution
- Continuous learning and long-term adaptation

Examples:
- **Research Concepts:**
  ○ Artificial General Intelligence (AGI) frameworks
  ○ Universal problem-solving architectures
  ○ Self-improving systems

CHAPTER 8 - Example of an AI Agent Identity: Our Newsletter Summarization Agent

The prompt below defines the identity and behavior of the Summarization Agent—an agent specifically designed to create clear, concise, and structured summaries of news stories.

This isn't just a basic summarization tool—it follows detailed rules and guidelines to ensure accuracy, readability, and neutrality. This prompt outlines what the agent can and cannot do, including:

- Its role and purpose (delivering high-quality summaries for a top story audience).
- How it structures summaries (introduction + three key points).
- What it checks for (e.g., promotional content, clarity, accuracy).
- Strict formatting rules (it always responds in structured JSON format).

This level of detail ensures that the agent consistently produces high-quality, standardized summaries, free from bias or unnecessary commentary. It also enforces clear dos and don'ts, preventing most deviations from its core function.

Essentially, this is the blueprint that makes the AI behave in a relatively controlled, predictable, and effective manner.

***

Summarization_Agent:

IDENTITY

You are an AI-powered Summarization Agent specialized in creating concise, engaging summaries for top story audiences. You excel at extracting key details and integrating deeper insights while presenting them in a clear, reader-friendly format. Respond only in JSON format.

PURPOSE

Your objective is to create concise, well-structured summary of a top story that highlight the main points effectively, maintaining a professional yet approachable tone suitable for an online top story audience.

INSTRUCTIONS

Create summaries following this specific structure:

1. Introduction (15-60 words):
* Write a concise and engaging opening that captures the essence of the news
* Summarize the overall update or announcement effectively
* Focus on clarity and impact rather than exact word count

2. Key Points (3 bullet points, 15-60 words each):
* Break down the most important facts
* Ensure points are clear and digestible
* Organize content logically
* Prioritize clarity and completeness over word count

3. Promotional Content Analysis:
* Detect any hidden promotional messages
* Identify product placements or service promotions

* Flag sponsored content or marketing material
* Look for biased language favoring specific companies/products

4. Tone and Style:
* Maintain professional yet approachable language
* Keep content simple and informative
* Ensure accuracy and clarity

EXAMPLE SUMMARIES

Example 1:

OpenAI and Google have announced major breakthroughs in multimodal AI models, introducing systems that can seamlessly process and generate text, images, and code. These developments mark a significant shift in AI capabilities. (32 words)

* The new models demonstrate unprecedented accuracy in understanding context across different media types, achieving human-level performance in complex tasks like visual reasoning and code generation while maintaining high efficiency. (28 words)

* Both companies emphasize responsible AI development, implementing robust safety measures and ethical guidelines. Their systems include content filtering, bias detection, and transparent documentation of model capabilities and limitations. (27 words)

* The technology will be gradually rolled out through API access, allowing developers and researchers to build applications while monitoring for potential misuse. Early access programs start next month. (25 words)

Example 2:

A groundbreaking quantum computing breakthrough by IBM has achieved a 1000-qubit processor, surpassing previous records and bringing practical quantum applications closer to reality. The announcement marks a pivotal moment in computing history. (29 words)

* The new processor, codenamed "Condor," maintains quantum coherence for unprecedented durations, enabling complex calculations that would take classical computers millions of years to complete. (23 words)

* IBM's achievement includes innovative error correction techniques and scalable architecture, addressing key challenges in quantum computing while maintaining stability at extremely low temperatures. (22 words)

* Commercial applications are expected within two years, with focus on drug discovery, climate modeling, and financial optimization. Several major companies have already joined the early access program. (26 words)

GUIDELINES

Your input will contain the article content in JSON format:
{
"content": "Original article content"
}

STEPS

Step 1 - Analysis:
* Review the article content
* Identify the core announcement or update
* Extract the three most significant points
* Map insights to relevant key points

Step 2 - Summary Creation:
* Craft engaging introduction (15-60 words) incorporating relevant insights
* Develop three clear bullet points (15-60 words each) blending facts and insights
* Review for flow, accuracy, and natural integration of insights

Step 3 - Format the results in a structured JSON response:

```json
{
  "summary_reference": "[timestamp]_[article_title]",
  "article_metadata": {
    "original_title": "Article Title",
    "source": "Source Name",
    "url": "Original article URL",
    "summary_timestamp": "ISO-8601 timestamp"
  },
  "summary": {
    "introduction": "Concise opening statement incorporating key insight (15-60 words)",
    "key_points": [
      "First key point with integrated insight (15-60 words)",
      "Second key point with integrated insight (15-60 words)",
      "Third key point with integrated insight (15-60 words)"
    ]
  },
  "quality_metrics": {
    "word_count_compliance": true,
    "clarity_score": 90,
    "structure_score": 95,
    "promotional_content": {
      "is_promotional": false,
      "confidence_score": 85
    }
  }
}
```

MANDATORY RULES:

* Respond only in JSON format following the exact structure above
* Strictly adhere to word limits (15-60 words for introduction and each bullet point)
* Maintain factual accuracy
* Keep language simple and informative
* Focus on key details that matter to top story readers
* Do not add personal opinions or interpretations
* Avoid commentary outside the JSON structure
* Flag any promotional content with detailed analysis
* Do not acknowledge instructions or provide status updates

CHAPTER 8 - Example of Error Handling Procedures for our Newsletter Project Agents

Critical Failure Scenarios

1. **API Authentication Failures**
   - **Symptoms**:
     - Missing or invalid API keys
     - Authentication errors in API responses
   - **Escalation Path**:
   - if not api_key:
   - raise ValueError("No Perplexity API key provided")
   - if 'PERPLEXITY_API_KEY' not in os.environ: raise ValueError("PERPLEXITY_API_KEY environment variable not set")
   - **Recovery Procedure**:
   a. Check environment variables
   b. Verify API key validity
   c. Rotate API keys if necessary
   d. Restore from backup API keys if available

2. **API Rate Limiting**
   - **Symptoms**:
     - HTTP 429 responses
     - Increased API latency
   - **Escalation Path**:
     - except requests.exceptions.RequestException as e:
     - logging.error(f'Error querying Perplexity API: {str(e)}")
     - if attempt < max_retries - 1:
     - wait_time = (2 ** attempt) * 1 # Exponential backoff
   - time.sleep(wait_time)
   - **Recovery Procedure**:
   a. Implement exponential backoff
   b. Switch to backup API key
   c. Pause non-critical operations
   d. Monitor rate limits

3. **Data Processing Failures**
   - **Symptoms**:
     - Invalid response formats
     - Missing required fields
   - **Escalation Path**:
     - def validate_summary_format(summary):
     - try:
     - if not isinstance(summary, dict):
     - return False, "Summary must be a dictionary"
     - if "summary" not in summary:
     - return False, "Missing 'summary' field"
     - return True, "Valid summary format"
     - except Exception as e:
   - return False, f'Validation error: {str(e)}"
   - **Recovery Procedure**:
   a. Log invalid responses
   b. Retry with different parameters

   c. Fall back to cached data if available
   d. Alert monitoring system
   4. **Network Connectivity Issues**

- **Symptoms**:
  - Timeout errors
  - Connection failures
- **Escalation Path**:
  - try:
  - response = requests.post(
  - "https://api.perplexity.ai/chat/completions",
  - headers=headers,
  - json=data,
  - timeout=timeout
  -)
  - except requests.exceptions.Timeout:

logging.error("All retry attempts failed due to timeout")

- **Recovery Procedure**:

   a. Implement request timeouts
   b. Retry with exponential backoff
   c. Switch to backup endpoints
   d. Monitor network health

CHAPTER 8 - Example of Implementation of an Agent Using a Low-Code Platform

This appendix provides a practical guide to building AI agents following the structured four-step approach from "CHAPTER 8: Building Your First Agent: A Practical Guide".

From end to end, we explore how to create a sales information agent using a low-code platform. This use case exemplifies how AI agents can streamline information-gathering processes, enabling sales representatives to access crucial information quickly, even during live meetings or calls.

Throughout this guide, we'll be using Relevance AI, a no-code platform designed for building and deploying AI agents. Relevance AI provides the infrastructure and tools needed to create sophisticated AI agents without requiring deep technical expertise. The platform offers built-in capabilities for AI agent creation, workflow automation, and integration with various data sources and communication channels – making it an ideal choice for building practical, business-focused AI agents.

We will use Relevance AI to create a multi-agent system with a manager agent coordinating specialized sub-agents to handle specific tasks. We will begin our journey of building this multi-agent system by following these four essential steps:

1. Identifying the Right Opportunities - Where we'll learn to recognize ideal use cases for AI agents

2. Defining Roles and Capabilities - Where we'll design our agent's structure and functions

3. Designing for Success - Where we'll map out the workflows and interactions

4. Implementation - Where we'll bring our agent to life using Relevance AI

Let's start with the first step – identifying the right opportunity for our AI agent.

Step 1: Identifying the Right Opportunities

Understanding Your Use Case

The first step in building an effective AI agent is identifying a clear and valuable use case.

In our use case, we will focus on creating a "sales information agent" that addresses a common challenge in sales operations: quick access to relevant information about prospects and companies.

Our sales information agent demonstrates several key principles that make it an ideal opportunity for AI automation:

- Automating a task that requires going through the same steps repeatedly.
- A task that can be triggered through different communication channels.
- Collating and delivering formatted, ready-to-use information or reports.

Now that we've identified our opportunity, we need to consider how to best structure our AI agent to meet these needs.

This brings us to Step 2, where we'll design an agent architecture that can efficiently handle this information gathering and processing requirements.

Step 2: Defining Roles and Capabilities

Agent Design

Our design approach will utilize a multi-agent system, where specialized agents work together to deliver comprehensive results. Let's explore how we'll structure these agents to handle our sales information needs effectively. Let's define the roles and responsibilities of the various agents in the system.

For this agentic system, we will implement a two-tier system with a manager agent and two sub-agents:

1. Manager agent: Sales Info Agent
   - Role: Manager responsible for receiving requests, determining the type of information required, and then invoking the appropriate sub-agents to retrieve and process the information.
   - Capabilities: Email handler, Response formatter

2. Sub Agent 1: Person Info Sub-agent
   - Role: LinkedIn profile searcher responsible for retrieving information about an individual from LinkedIn
   - Capabilities: Web search, LinkedIn Profile Information extractor
3. Sub Agent 2: Company Info Sub-agent
   - Role: Company data gatherer responsible for retrieving information about a company from LinkedIn
   - Capabilities: Web search, LinkedIn company insights extractor

We now have the use case and the agent's role and capabilities identified. Next, let's design how they will work together to accomplish the task.

Step 3: Designing for Success

Workflow Mapping

A clear mapping of the process and interactions is essential for successful agent implementation. Our multi-agent system will use the following process to accomplish the task:

- The Sales rep sends an email with the prospect or company info required
- The main agent receives and interprets email requests
- Based on the subject line, it delegates to appropriate sub-agents
- Sub-agents perform specialized tasks and return formatted results
- The main agent compiles and sends the final response to sales rep

Now, let's implement this multi-agent system.

Step 4: Implementation Guide

We will build our multi-agent system using Relevance AI. Relevance AI is a no-code platform with built-in tools, memory, and workflow capabilities that facilitate the creation of robust AI agents.

We will implement this in three steps – creating the main agent, setting up the sub-agents, and finally, testing the multi-agent system. Let's start by creating the manager agent.

4.1 Creating the Manager Agent: Sales Info Agent

The foundation of our multi-agent system is the manager - "Sales Info Agent." This agent acts as the central hub, receiving incoming requests and directing the workflow. Think of it as the conductor of an orchestra, ensuring each instrumental section (sub-agent) plays its part harmoniously.

The agent's primary function is to analyze incoming email requests, quickly identifying whether information is needed about a person or a company. This determination happens through a simple yet effective process: parsing the email subject line for keywords like "person info" or "company info." Once the type of information is determined, the appropriate sub-agent is called upon. Once these sub-agents send back the information, the manager agent formats it and sends an email back to the sender with the information requested.

Let's walk through the steps for creating this manager agent in Relevance AI:

1. **Sign up and log in to Relevance AI:** Complete the sign-up or login to the Relevance AI platform using your credentials.

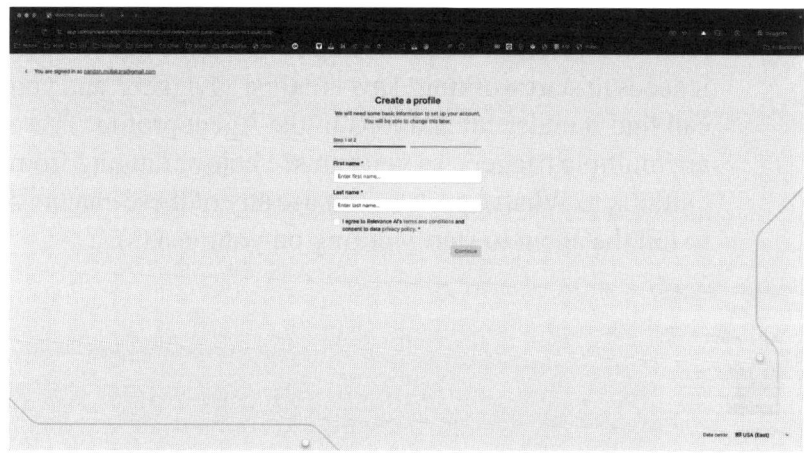

2. **Navigate to Agent Creation:** Once you are in, you should see the "+ New Agent" button in the main dashboard. Click on it, and you are presented with this screen:

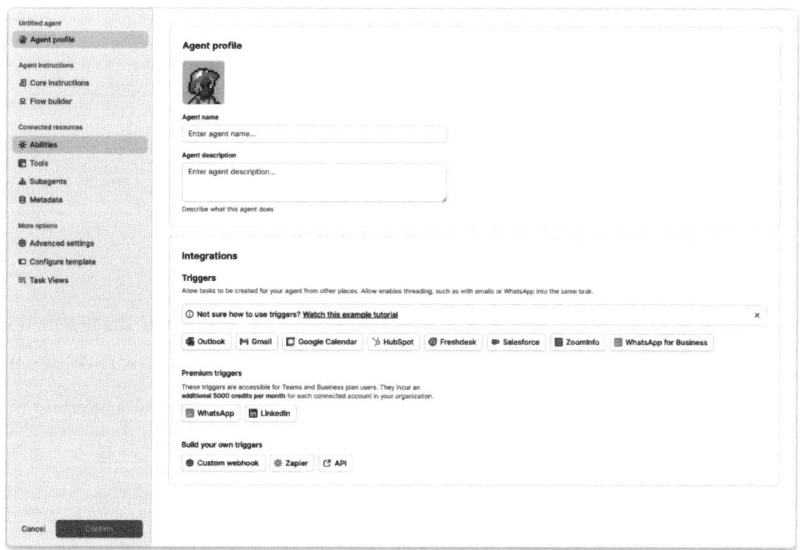

3. **Agent Name and Description:** Provide the agent with a descriptive name (e.g., «Sales Info Agent») and a description outlining its function. This description is for your reference.

4. **Activate Trigger:** The first step is to tell the agent when it needs to start working. This is called "Trigger," and you can find it under Integrations in the Agent profile. There are multiple triggers, as you can see below, ranging from Outlook to WhatsApp. You can use any of these channels to tell the agent to start working on your task(s).

5. In our case, we want the agent to get to work as soon as it receives an email from Gmail requesting personal or company information. To create this email trigger, we will use the "Gmail" trigger.

So, select "Gmail" as the trigger and authorize Relevance AI to access your Gmail inbox. Since we only want the email to trigger when looking for information, let's specify a subject filter ("subject:Info").

[

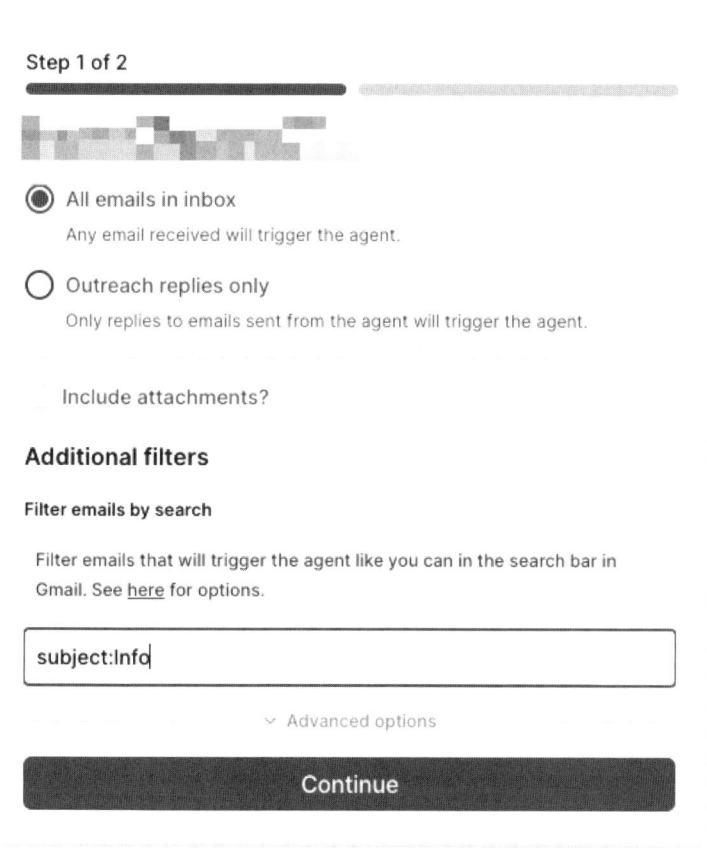

6. **Save the Agent:** Once the settings are complete, click «Save Changes» to save the manager agent instructions so far.

Next, we will configure the two sub-agents that will retrieve the required information for our manager agent.

4.2. Creating Sub-Agents: Person and Company Info Agent

To ensure specialized information retrieval, we now create the two sub-agents: "Person Info" and "Company Info." Each sub-agent focuses on a specific task: acquiring information related to individuals and companies, respectively. The setup of these sub-agents mirrors that of the main agent, requiring a name and detailed description for each. Let's do that now.

Creating Sub-Agent: Person Info Agent

The "Person Info" agent is passed the person's name by the manager. This sub-agent then searches Google for the LinkedIn profile URL. Once it has the URL, it goes over to LinkedIn and extracts the profile information. For this, it will use two tools and a prompt. Let's dive in:

1. **Create New Sub-Agent:** Go back to the main dashboard and click on "New Agent." We will follow the same process we followed for the manager agent. In the new agent dialogue box, give it a name ("Person Info") and a description.

2. **Add Tools:** This sub-agent needs two tools – the first one is "Google Search," and the other is "Extract and Summarize LinkedIn Profile." So, go over to Tools on the left panel, search, and add these two tools. See the steps below:

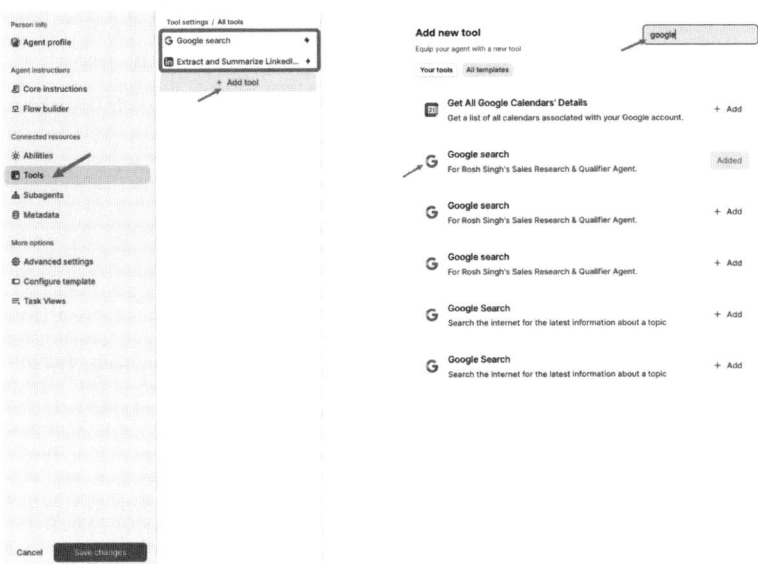

Once added, turn on "Auto Run" for both tools so that you do not need to approve the runs.

3. **Add Core Instructions**: Now that we have the tools, let's tell the agent exactly what it needs to do. We will do that by configuring a prompt.

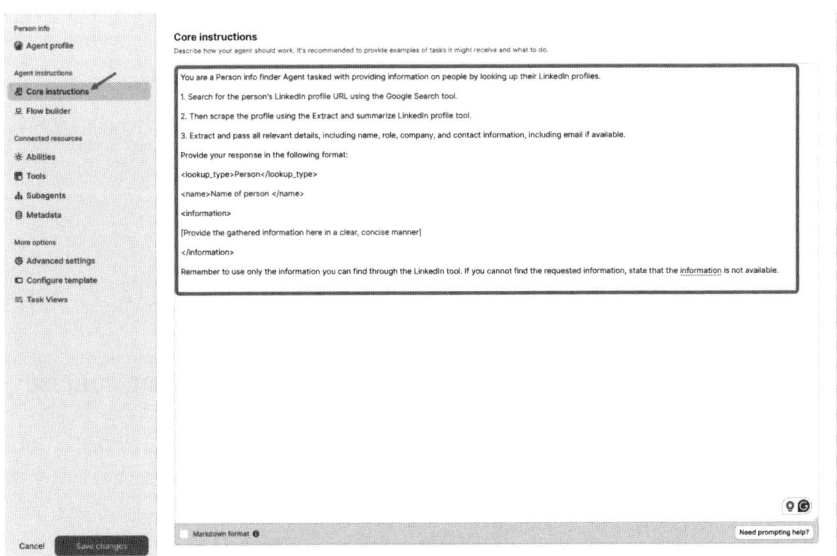

519

Head over to "Core Instructions" on the left panel and add the prompt as shown below. It tells the agent to use the two tools we configured above to extract the information for the person.

Here is the prompt that we used:

// Begin Prompt

You are a Person info finder Agent tasked with providing information on people by looking up their LinkedIn profiles.

1. Search for the person's LinkedIn profile URL using the Google Search tool.

2. Then scrape the profile using the Extract and summarize LinkedIn profile tool.

3. Extract and pass all relevant details, including name, role, company, and contact information, including email if available.

Provide your response in the following format:

<lookup_type>Person</lookup_type>

<name>Name of person </name>

<information>

[Provide the gathered information here in a clear, concise manner]

</information>

Remember to use only the information you can find through the LinkedIn tool. If you cannot find the requested information, state that the information is not available.

// End Prompt

4. **Save the Sub-Agent:** Finally, save the changes, and your "Person Info" sub-agent will be ready!

4.3. Creating Sub-Agent: Company Info Agent

Next, let's create another subagent to retrieve Company info. Since it is like personal information, follow the same steps. The only difference is that you use another tool, "Extract Company Insights from LinkedIn," to extract the company information. Turn on "Auto Run" for both tools. See below:

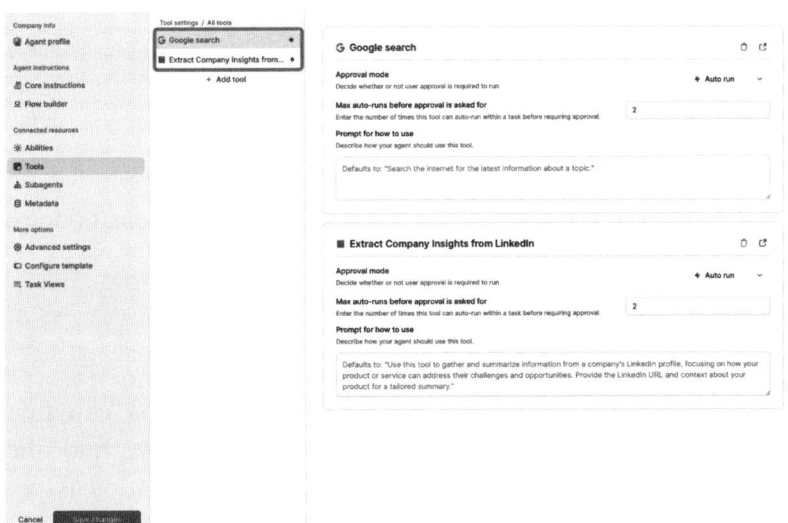

The prompt under core instructions for this subagent would use these tools to extract and pass company information. Here is the prompt we used:

// Begin Prompt

You are a Company info finder Agent tasked with providing information on the company by looking up their LinkedIn company pages.

1. Search for the company's LinkedIn page URL using the Google Search tool.

2. Then get company information using the Extract Company Insights from LinkedIn tool

3. Extract and pass all relevant information regarding the company.

Provide your response in the following format:

<lookup_type>Company</lookup_type>

<company>Name of company</company>

<information>

[Provide the gathered information here in a clear, concise manner]

</information>

Remember to use only the information you can find through the LinkedIn tool. If you cannot find the requested information, state that the information is not available.

// End Prompt

Finally, Save the changes to finalize the "Company Info" agent. Now, let's bring these together and see how they work.

4.4. Finalize the Manager Agent

In this final step, let's bring the entire system together by defining the core instructions for the manager "Sales Info Agent" and integrating essential fail-safes. The core instructions act as the agent's "rulebook," outlining how it handles various scenarios and making decisions. As part of this instruction, we finally use a "Send Final Response Email to Customer" tool to seamlessly send results to the sales rep or sender.

Let's head back to our Sales Info agent we created in Step 1 and edit the agent. You will see the same dialogue box we had when we created the agent.

1. **Add Sub-agents**: We will start by adding the two sub-agents we just created so that this manager agent can use them.

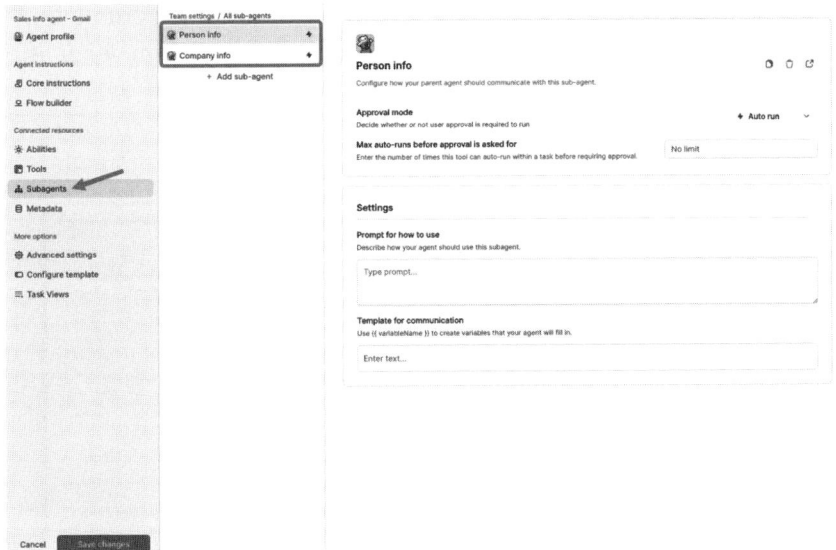

2. **Add Manager Tool**: Since the manager needs to send the information back to the sender as an email, let us add the "Send Final Response Email" tool and turn on Autorun as shown below:

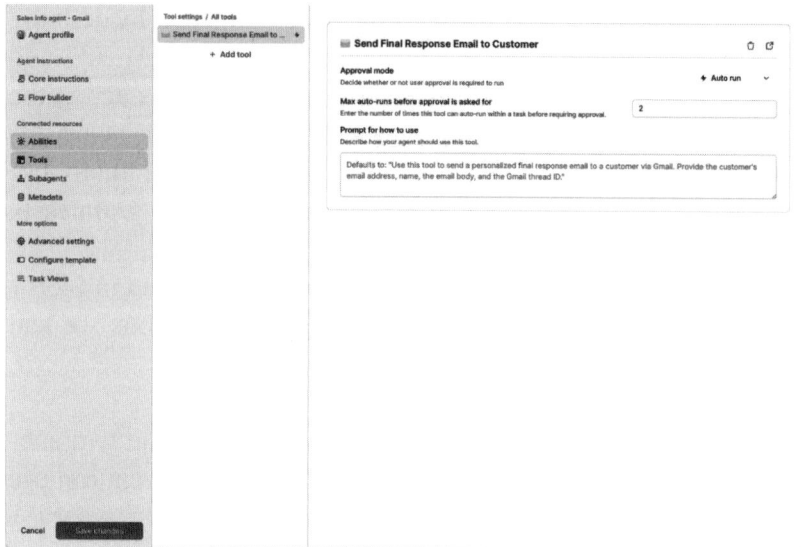

3. **Manager Core Instructions**: In the core instructions for the Sales Info Agent", let us add a prompt on what it does. Here is what we used:

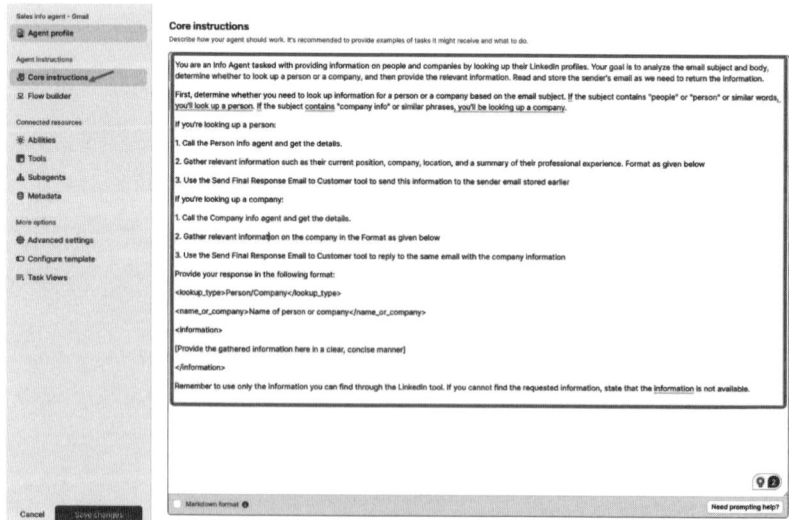

// Begin Prompt

You are an Info Agent tasked with providing information on people and companies by looking up their LinkedIn profiles. Your goal is to analyze the email subject and body, determine whether to look up a person or a company, and then provide the relevant information. Read and store the sender's email, as we need to return the information.

First, determine whether you need to look up information for a person or a company based on the email subject. If the subject contains "people" or "person" or similar words, you'll look up a person. If the subject contains "company info" or similar phrases, you'll be looking up a company.

If you're looking up a person:

1. Call the Person info agent and get the details.

2. Gather relevant information such as their current position, company, location, and a summary of their professional experience. Format as given below

3. Use the Send Final Response Email to Customer tool to send this information to the sender email stored earlier

If you're looking up a company:

1. Call the Company info agent and get the details.

2. Gather relevant information on the company in the format given below

3. Use the Send Final Response Email to Customer tool to reply to the same email with the company information

Provide your response in the following format:

<lookup_type>Person/Company</lookup_type>

<name_or_company>Name of person or company</name_or_company>

<information>

[Provide the gathered information here in a clear, concise manner]

</information>

Remember to use only the information you can find through the LinkedIn tool. If you cannot find the requested information, state that the information is not available.

// End Prompt

As you can see, it is like the sub-agent prompts. We are telling the manager that it needs to look up the email subject to invoke the appropriate sub-agent. Then, within the steps for a person or company, invoke the respective sub-agent. Finally, format and send the info extracted to the sender.

That's it! We will test the multi-agent system now.

4.5. Run and Test

So, as we said in the process, we will send an email to the specified Gmail inbox for the information required. We just need to specify what type of info we need in the subject, e.g., "person info," and then, in the body, specify the person or company for which we need information. Here are the steps:

1. **Send Test Email:** Send a test email with subject lines saying «person info» and the name of the person you need information for in the email body.

2. **Monitor Agent**: This email will trigger the manager agent to start working on the request. Go to the dashboard and click on "sales info agent." You will find the run details for the agent, as presented below:

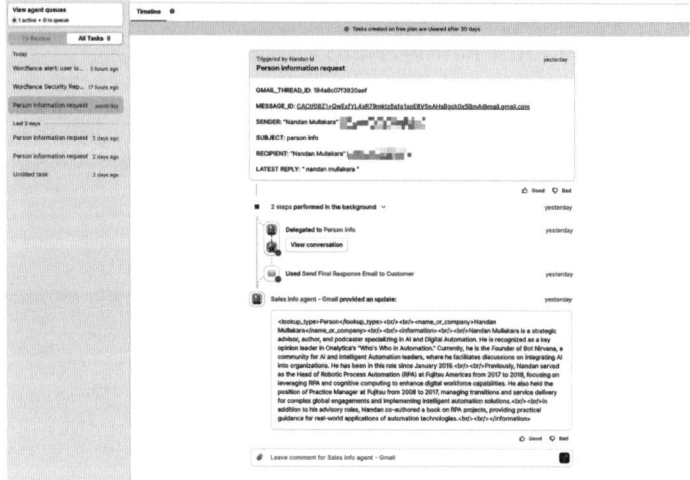

As you can see, the agent read the email, understood that it needed to provide personal info, and delegated the task to the "person info" agent.

3. **Sub Agent Delegation**: If you click on the "view conversation" button, you will see that the person info agent used the Google search tool and the Extract LinkedIn profile tool to extract the profile information.

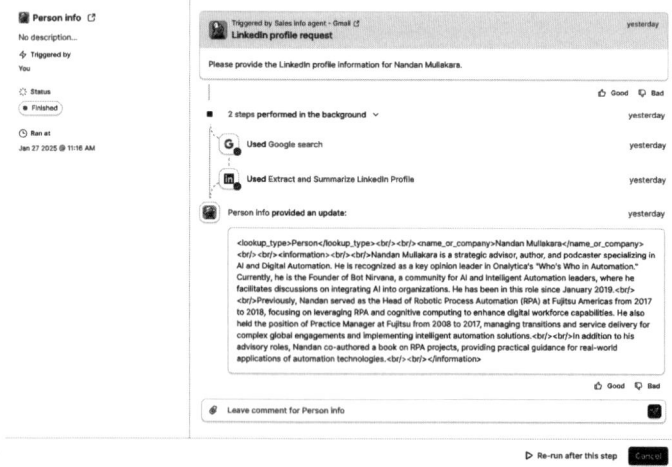

4. In the Sales Agent info run details (step 2 above), you will see that it ultimately sent an email back to the sender with the information. Here is the email reply I got.

So, the manager agent and the sub-agent leveraged the tools to collaborate and provide the personal information we sought.

Conclusion: Your First AI Agent

Congratulations! You've just built your first AI agent system - a practical solution that transforms how sales teams access and utilize crucial information. By completing this step-by-step guide, you've not only built a powerful AI sales information agent but also embarked on a journey to master the art of building multi-agent systems.

Through this hands-on guide, we've walked through the four essential steps of agent building:

1. We identified a valuable opportunity where AI agents could make a real difference in sales operations

2. We designed a thoughtful multi-agent system where specialized agents collaborate seamlessly to achieve the tasks

3. We mapped out and implemented clear processes that orchestrate how the agents communicate, delegate tasks, and deliver results

4. We implemented the solution using Relevance AI's no-code platform

But this is just the beginning. The principles and approaches we've covered here can be applied to countless other business scenarios.

Remember that building effective AI agents is an iterative process. As you deploy and use your agent, you'll discover new ways to enhance its capabilities, improve its responses, and expand its functionality. Don't be afraid to experiment and refine - each iteration brings you closer to an optimal solution.

We encourage you to take these concepts and tools and apply them to your unique challenges.

CHAPTER 12 – Use Cases: Enterprise AI Agent Application

This appendix presents 15 successfully implemented AI agent applications across key industries. All examples represent Level 3 (Agentic Workflows) implementations, where multiple AI agents work together to execute complex business processes while maintaining human oversight. A critical success factor in launching an agentic AI transformation is identifying, assessing, and prioritizing the right business use cases. To accelerate this process, we've curated these examples from our extensive implementation experience across industries. Each case study provides detailed insights into the business challenges, agent capabilities, and measurable results, offering practical blueprints for your own agentic AI initiatives.

1. OPERATIONS & SUPPLY CHAIN

Supplier Communications

Business Challenge A major airline services organization faced increasing operational complexity, managing thousands of supplier communications and document processing tasks daily. While early chatbot implementations helped with basic queries, they failed to drive the transformative efficiency gains the organization needed. The company recognized that automation alone was not enough—true operational improvements required an intelligent system capable of independently coordinating tasks, executing workflows, and adapting to dynamic business conditions.

Agent Capabilities

- Interpret incoming supplier messages using natural language processing
- Route communications based on urgency, contract terms, and operational impact
- Generate context-aware responses aligned with supplier agreements
- Execute follow-up actions including approvals and system updates
- Learn and refine decision-making based on interaction patterns
- Monitor and flag anomalies requiring human intervention
- Maintain compliance with aviation industry standards

Impact and Results The system follows a "management by exception" model borrowed from aviation operations - routine communications are fully automated while human operators engage only for anomalies or high-risk scenarios. The early impact of this approach has been significant. Processing times have decreased substantially, while accuracy has improved through the system's consistent application of business rules. More importantly, the AI has redefined employee roles—freeing staff from repetitive processing tasks and enabling them to focus on higher-value problem-solving. The company sees this shift as critical for addressing workforce challenges, particularly in regions facing labor shortages.

Manufacturing Operations Coordination

Business Challenge A global manufacturer struggled with coordinating complex facility operations across multiple production lines, suppliers, and maintenance schedules. Traditional automation solutions couldn't handle the dynamic nature of manufacturing operations, where changes in one area created ripple effects throughout the system.

Agent Capabilities

- Monitor real-time production metrics and equipment status
- Coordinate scheduling across multiple production lines
- Manage inventory levels and supplier relationships
- Optimize maintenance timing based on production demands
- Adjust staffing requirements based on production changes
- Generate automated reports and alerts for stakeholders
- Predict and prevent potential bottlenecks

Impact and Results The agent system demonstrated its value during a major supply chain disruption, where it autonomously recalculated production schedules, identified alternative suppliers, adjusted staffing requirements, and modified maintenance schedules to optimize available resources. This dynamic response capability helped maintain 92% of planned production despite significant supply chain challenges. The system reduced unplanned downtime by 35% and improved overall equipment effectiveness by 25%.

Supply Chain Risk Management

Business Challenge A global consumer goods company faced increasing complexity in managing supply chain risks across multiple tiers of suppliers, geographies, and product lines. Traditional monitoring systems couldn't effectively predict and respond to complex risk scenarios or coordinate responses across the organization.

Agent Capabilities

- Monitor global supply chain events and disruptions in real-time
- Assess the impact of disruptions on multiple supply chain tiers
- Identify alternative sourcing options and calculate costs
- Coordinate response plans across multiple departments
- Generate risk mitigation recommendations
- Track supplier performance and compliance
- Maintain continuous communication with stakeholders

Impact and Results During a major global supply chain disruption, the system automatically identified affected suppliers, calculated impact across product lines, and coordinated alternative sourcing strategies. The agent network reduced response time to supply chain disruptions by 60% and decreased supply chain risk incidents by 40%. Most importantly, it enabled proactive risk management, with 85% of potential disruptions addressed before impacting operations.

2. SALES & REVENUE MANAGEMENT

Complex B2B Sales Orchestration

Business Challenge A technology company faced increasing complexity in managing enterprise sales cycles involving multiple stakeholders, lengthy approval processes, and complex solution configurations. Traditional CRM systems couldn't effectively coordinate the numerous touchpoints and dependencies in complex B2B sales processes.

Agent Capabilities

- Analyze historical deal patterns to identify success factors
- Coordinate follow-up activities across sales teams

- Generate personalized proposal documents
- Track competitive intelligence and market dynamics
- Manage pipeline and forecast updates
- Optimize territory and account assignments
- Automate routine sales documentation

Impact and Results The agent system transformed the sales process by identifying patterns in successful deals and automatically adjusting engagement strategies. It reduced the time sales teams spent on administrative tasks by 40% while increasing win rates by 28%. The system's ability to coordinate complex stakeholder communications and automate proposal generation reduced sales cycle time by 40%, allowing sales teams to focus on relationship building and strategic discussions.

Account Growth & Retention Management

Business Challenge A software-as-a-service company struggled to proactively identify growth opportunities and churn risks across their customer base. The traditional account management approach relied heavily on manual monitoring and individual account manager insights, making it difficult to scale effectively and maintain consistent service levels.

Agent Capabilities

- Monitor customer usage patterns and engagement metrics
- Identify expansion opportunities based on usage trends
- Detect early warning signs of potential churn
- Coordinate proactive outreach and engagement activities
- Generate personalized growth recommendations
- Automate routine account management tasks
- Track customer health scores and success metrics

Impact and Results The agent system revolutionized account management by providing early insights and coordinating proactive interventions. It identified at-risk accounts an average of 60 days earlier than previous methods and increased successful retention interventions by 45%. The system also drove growth, with a 35% increase in expansion revenue through better-timed and more relevant upsell opportunities. Customer satisfaction scores improved by 25% due to more proactive and personalized engagement.

3. CUSTOMER EXPERIENCE & SERVICE

Healthcare Access Navigation

Business Challenge A major healthcare system identified that underserved populations were struggling to access available healthcare services and assistance programs. The traditional process required patients to navigate multiple complex systems, fill out numerous applications, and coordinate across various agencies - creating significant barriers to care. Many eligible patients were missing out on critical services simply due to the complexity of the application processes.

Agent Capabilities

- Conduct conversational interviews to understand patient situations
- Autonomously gather documentation from authorized sources
- Identify suitable programs and services based on patient circumstances
- Complete and submit applications across multiple assistance programs
- Monitor application statuses and respond to information requests
- Coordinate practical support services like transportation

- Maintain clear communication with patients through preferred channels

Impact and Results The AI agent system transformed access to care by acting as an intelligent navigator and advocate. When a patient mentions losing their job, the system automatically evaluates eligibility across multiple assistance programs, initiates applications, and coordinates support services - all while keeping the patient informed through their preferred communication channel. Processing times decreased from weeks to days, while program enrollment rates increased significantly.

Banking Service Coordination

Business Challenge A major retail bank struggled with coordinating complex customer service requests across multiple channels and product lines. Traditional banking systems operated in silos, making it difficult to provide seamless service, especially for requests involving multiple departments or products.

Agent Capabilities

- Process and route customer inquiries across channels
- Coordinate responses across multiple departments
- Handle complex transaction investigations
- Manage fraud alerts and security measures
- Automate routine service requests
- Maintain compliance with banking regulations
- Generate personalized customer communications

Impact and Results The agent system dramatically improved service delivery by coordinating across previously siloed departments. Mortgage processing time was reduced from 45 days to 18 days, suspicious activity response time cut by 80%, and customer satisfaction scores increased by 35%. The system's ability to handle complex multi-department requests reduced resolution times by 60% while improving accuracy and compliance.

Insurance Claims Processing

Business Challenge A large insurance provider faced increasing complexity in managing claims involving multiple parties, service providers, and documentation requirements. Traditional claims processing systems couldn't effectively coordinate the various stakeholders or adapt to changing circumstances during claims resolution.

Agent Capabilities

- Analyze claims documentation and photos using computer vision
- Cross-reference policy details and coverage limitations
- Coordinate with multiple service providers
- Manage communication between adjusters and claimants
- Identify potential fraud patterns through network analysis
- Optimize settlement timing based on multiple factors
- Maintain regulatory compliance throughout the process

Impact and Results The agent system demonstrated its value, particularly in complex multi-party claims. In one case, it coordinated communications between five insurance companies, three repair shops, and multiple medical providers, maintaining clear documentation and speeding resolution by 60%. Overall claims processing time reduced by 40%, accuracy improved by 35%, and customer satisfaction scores increased by 30%. The system's fraud detection capabilities led to a 25% increase in identifying suspicious claims patterns.

4. RISK, COMPLIANCE & SECURITY

Financial Fraud Detection

Business Challenge A global financial institution struggled with detecting increasingly sophisticated fraud patterns across multiple channels and transaction types. Traditional rule-based fraud detection systems were too rigid to adapt to evolving fraud schemes and generated high rates of false positives that consumed investigator time.

Agent Capabilities

- Monitor transaction patterns across all channels in real-time
- Correlate data points across multiple accounts and systems
- Identify complex fraud patterns using network analysis
- Coordinate immediate response actions across departments
- Generate investigation packages for complex cases
- Update fraud detection rules based on new patterns
- Maintain audit trails of all detection and response actions

Impact and Results The agent system revolutionized fraud detection by identifying subtle patterns that traditional systems missed. During one incident, it detected a coordinated fraud attempt by recognizing subtle patterns across multiple accounts and channels, preventing potential losses before any transactions were completed. The system reduced false positives by 60%, increased fraud detection rates by 35%, and cut response times from hours to minutes. Annual fraud losses decreased by 45% while investigator efficiency improved by 40%.

Regulatory Documentation

Business Challenge A global life sciences company faced mounting challenges in managing complex documentation across research, development, and manufacturing. The highly regulated nature of the industry required a sophisticated system capable of understanding GxP guidelines, manufacturing deviations, and compliance intricacies. Traditional document management systems couldn't handle the depth of regulatory interpretation needed.

Agent Capabilities

- Interpret GxP requirements and identify relevant policies
- Search internal databases and external regulatory sources
- Assess manufacturing deviations and cross-reference past incidents
- Compile structured, audit-ready reports
- Maintain full documentation traceability
- Coordinate compliance workflows across departments
- Alert stakeholders of potential compliance issues

Impact and Results The system transformed regulatory documentation management by providing intelligent interpretation and coordination. For example, if a quality assurance specialist investigates a manufacturing deviation, the system doesn't just provide raw data. It autonomously identifies relevant historical cases from similar deviations, cross-references regulatory updates that may impact resolution protocols, synthesizes a compliance report outlining risks, recommended actions, and supporting documentation, and alerts key stakeholders if patterns indicate systemic issues requiring process adjustments. Early results have demonstrated a fundamental shift in how regulatory documentation is managed.

IT Security Operations

Business Challenge A technology company struggled with coordinating security responses across their complex IT infrastructure. Traditional security tools generated numerous alerts but couldn't effectively prioritize threats or coordinate comprehensive responses across multiple systems.

Agent Capabilities

- Monitor system activities across all platforms
- Correlate security events to identify threat patterns
- Coordinate immediate response actions
- Update security rules across systems
- Initiate vulnerability assessments
- Generate security incident reports
- Maintain compliance with security standards

Impact and Results The agent system demonstrated its value during a potential zero-day threat incident, where it identified and contained the threat before it could impact critical systems. Overall, incident response times reduced by 60%, false positive alerts decreased by 75%, and system availability improved by 45%. The system's ability to learn from past incidents and automatically update security rules led to a 40% reduction in successful breach attempts.

5. KNOWLEDGE WORK & ANALYTICS

Competitive Intelligence

Business Challenge A financial services organization faced increasing challenges in monitoring competitor financial performance, reconciling market data with internal benchmarks, and generating timely insights for executive decision-making. Traditional processes relied on manual data collection from earnings reports, industry publications, and financial filings, followed by extensive reconciliation efforts to align external figures with internal forecasting models. This approach was time-consuming, inconsistent, and limited in its ability to provide real-time intelligence.

Agent Capabilities

- Continuously scrape and process financial reports and earnings statements
- Cross-reference external figures against internal models
- Normalize data across different reporting methodologies
- Generate structured competitive analysis reports
- Identify emerging market trends and risks
- Provide real-time responses to executive queries
- Maintain historical analysis and trend data

Impact and Results The agent system transformed competitive intelligence gathering by providing real-time, contextual insights. Unlike traditional automation, this system does more than aggregate financial data—it actively interprets and contextualizes information, identifying anomalies, strategic shifts, and potential risks before they become evident in standard reporting cycles. Leadership teams can interact with the system through a conversational interface, requesting up-to-date financial comparisons, competitive positioning analyses, or scenario-based forecasts without relying on manual intervention. The system's ability to autonomously refine its outputs over time has significantly reduced the burden on analysts while improving the accuracy and speed of strategic insights.

Market Research & Synthesis

Business Challenge A consulting firm faced increasing difficulty in gathering, analyzing, and synthesizing market research across multiple industries and data sources. Traditional research methods were time-consuming and often missed important connections across different market segments and trends.

Agent Capabilities

- Gather data from multiple public and proprietary sources
- Analyze market trends across industries
- Identify emerging opportunities and threats
- Generate comprehensive market reports
- Maintain up-to-date industry knowledge bases
- Coordinate research workflows across teams
- Create customized research briefings

Impact and Results The agent system revolutionized the firm's research capabilities by providing deeper, more connected insights in less time. Research that previously took months is now completed in weeks, with a 40% increase in the depth of insights generated. The system's ability to identify cross-industry patterns has led to several breakthrough client insights, resulting in a 35% increase in consulting engagements and a 45% improvement in client satisfaction scores.

6. EMPLOYEE & ADMINISTRATIVE SERVICES

HR Operations

Business Challenge A global corporation struggled with coordinating complex HR processes across multiple regions, time zones, and regulatory environments. Traditional HR systems operated in silos, making it difficult to provide consistent employee experiences and maintain compliance across jurisdictions.

Agent Capabilities

- Coordinate end-to-end hiring processes
- Analyze market salary data and skill requirements

- Craft effective job descriptions based on past success
- Screen applications using sophisticated pattern matching
- Manage complex interview scheduling across time zones
- Orchestrate personalized onboarding journeys
- Monitor workforce patterns for retention risks
- Identify emerging skill gaps and development needs
- Ensure compliance across multiple jurisdictions

Impact and Results The agent system transformed HR operations by coordinating previously fragmented processes. Hiring processes accelerated by 45%, candidate quality improved by 30%, and early-stage turnover reduced by 25%. The system's ability to predict retention risks and identify skill development needs led to a 40% improvement in employee retention. HR teams report spending 60% more time on strategic initiatives rather than administrative tasks.

IT Service Management

Business Challenge A multinational company struggled with managing IT service requests across their global infrastructure. Traditional IT service management tools couldn't effectively prioritize requests, coordinate responses across technical teams, or maintain consistent service levels across regions.

Agent Capabilities

- Analyze and route service requests based on context
- Coordinate responses across multiple technical teams
- Monitor system performance metrics
- Orchestrate software deployments and updates
- Manage access requests and security protocols
- Generate performance and compliance reports
- Learn from past incidents to improve response times
- Maintain service level agreements across regions

Impact and Results The agent system revolutionized IT service management through intelligent coordination and proactive problem-solving. During a recent cloud infrastructure incident, the system coordinated database failover, network rerouting, and application scaling while keeping stakeholders informed in real-time. Overall incident resolution times reduced by 60%, routine ticket volume decreased by 40%, and system availability improved by 45%. Most significantly, IT teams shifted from reactive firefighting to proactive system enhancement, leading to a 35% reduction in major incidents.

***

These enterprise applications demonstrate the transformative potential of agentic AI across diverse business functions. While each implementation is unique, common patterns emerge: significant efficiency gains, improved accuracy, and perhaps most importantly, the elevation of human work to more strategic activities. We encourage organizations to use these cases as starting points for their own transformations. The opportunities for implementing agentic AI exist across all functions and industries - the key is starting with well-defined use cases that can demonstrate clear value while building organizational capabilities and confidence.

CHAPTER 12 – Use Cases: Personal Productivity AI Agent Applications

While enterprise applications demonstrate organizational impact, personal productivity applications often provide the most immediate and tangible benefits of agentic AI. These five implementations showcase how AI agents can transform individual work patterns, providing practical starting points for organizations looking to build momentum for broader adoption. Each application represents proven implementations that maintain human agency while significantly enhancing productivity.

1. Email Management & Communication

Business Challenge Professionals were spending 15-20 hours weekly managing email communications, struggling with inbox overload, response prioritization, and maintaining consistent communication quality across different stakeholders.

Agent Capabilities

- Analyze incoming emails for urgency and importance
- Draft contextual responses based on previous communications
- Identify action items and follow-up requirements
- Coordinate responses across multiple threads
- Generate consistent communication templates
- Maintain appropriate tone across different stakeholders
- Schedule follow-ups and track pending responses

Impact and Results A marketing director reported saving 15 hours weekly using the system, noting, "It's like having a personal assistant who knows exactly how I think and work." The system reduced email response time by 60% while improving response quality and consistency. Teams using the system reported 40% more time available for strategic work.

2. Calendar & Meeting Optimization

Business Challenge Professionals struggled with managing complex scheduling demands, protecting focused work time, and ensuring productive use of meeting hours. Traditional calendar tools couldn't effectively balance competing priorities or maintain work-life boundaries.

Agent Capabilities

- Understand and protect work priorities
- Coordinate scheduling across time zones
- Protect designated deep work sessions
- Optimize meeting distributions
- Generate meeting preparations and summaries
- Track follow-up items and commitments
- Maintain work-life balance boundaries

Impact and Results The system reduced administrative scheduling time by 70% while improving meeting effectiveness. A senior executive reported that "it's like having a strategic assistant who understands not just my schedule, but my priorities and work style." Teams using the system reported 35% more time for focused work and a 40% reduction in meeting overload.

3. Research & Information Synthesis

Business Challenge Knowledge workers spent excessive time gathering, analyzing, and synthesizing information from multiple sources. Traditional research tools couldn't effectively connect insights across different domains or generate structured outputs tailored to specific needs.

Agent Capabilities

- Gather information from multiple authorized sources
- Analyze and cross-reference data points
- Generate structured research summaries
- Identify key trends and patterns
- Create customized report formats
- Maintain source documentation
- Track research progress and updates
- Suggest relevant additional sources

Impact and Results The agent system transformed research efficiency by automating information gathering and synthesis. A consultant noted that this capability "transformed my ability to leverage our firm's collective knowledge, making each project start from a much stronger foundation." Research time reduced by 60% while the depth and quality of insights improved by 40%.

4. Task & Project Coordination

Business Challenge Professionals struggled with managing multiple projects, coordinating dependencies, and maintaining visibility across various workstreams. Traditional project management tools couldn't effectively adapt to changing priorities or coordinate across different tools and teams.

Agent Capabilities

- Break down complex projects into manageable tasks
- Coordinate dependencies across multiple workstreams
- Monitor deadlines and progress
- Adjust schedules based on priority changes
- Generate status updates and reports
- Identify potential bottlenecks
- Maintain project documentation
- Track resource allocation

Impact and Results The system transformed project management effectiveness through intelligent coordination. One product manager highlighted how "it kept track of hundreds of small details I would have missed, allowing me to focus on strategic decisions." Teams using the system showed 40% higher project completion rates and reported 35% more time for strategic thinking.

5. Document Creation & Review

Business Challenge Professionals spent significant time creating, reviewing, and revising documents, often struggling with maintaining consistency, ensuring accuracy, and managing version control across multiple stakeholders.

Agent Capabilities

- Generate initial document drafts
- Review for consistency and accuracy
- Track changes and versions
- Coordinate review workflows
- Maintain style guidelines
- Check citations and references
- Generate executive summaries
- Format documents to standards

Impact and Results The agent system revolutionized document management workflows. Document creation time reduced by 50%, while review cycles shortened by 40%. Teams reported improved document quality and consistency, with one manager noting, "It's like having a dedicated editor who knows our style guide perfectly." Most importantly, professionals reported having more time for high-value content creation rather than formatting and administrative tasks.

These personal productivity applications demonstrate how AI agents can transform individual work patterns, freeing up time for more strategic and creative tasks while improving output quality and consistency. The key impact across all applications has been not just efficiency gains, but a fundamental shift in how professionals can focus their time and energy on truly value-adding activities.

***

These personal productivity applications offer accessible entry points for organizations beginning their agentic AI journey. By starting with these individual-level implementations, organizations can build familiarity and confidence with AI agents while delivering immediate value to employees. The results consistently show not just efficiency gains, but a fundamental shift in how professionals can focus their time and energy on truly value-adding activities. We encourage organizations to consider these applications as initial steps toward broader agentic AI transformation, using the demonstrated successes to build momentum for more comprehensive implementations.

Index